Gretchen Bitterlin
Dennis Johnson
Donna Price
Sylvia Ramirez
K. Lynn Savage, Series Editor

Ventures 4

TEACHER'S EDITION

with **Arlen Gargagliano**

CAMBRIDGE
UNIVERSITY PRESS

CAMBRIDGE UNIVERSITY PRESS
Cambridge, New York, Melbourne, Madrid, Cape Town, Singapore, São Paulo, Delhi

Cambridge University Press
32 Avenue of the Americas, New York, NY 10013-2473, USA

www.cambridge.org
Information on this title: www.cambridge.org/9780521721059

First published 2009

Printed in the United States of America

A catalog record for this publication is available from the British Library

ISBN 978-0-521-60098-9   pack consisting of Student's Book and Audio CD
ISBN 978-0-521-67961-9   Workbook
ISBN 978-0-521-72105-9   pack consisting of Teacher's Edition and Teacher's Toolkit Audio CD / CD-ROM
ISBN 978-0-521-67732-5   CDs (Audio)
ISBN 978-0-521-67733-2   Cassettes
ISBN 978-0-521-67586-4   Add Ventures

Cambridge University Press has no responsibility for the persistence or
accuracy of URLs for external or third-party Internet Web sites referred to in
this publication, and does not guarantee that any content on such Web sites is,
or will remain, accurate or appropriate.

Art direction, book design, and photo research: Adventure House, NYC
Layout services: Page Designs International
Audio production: Richard LePage and Associates

....

Contents

To the teacher

What is *Ventures*?

Ventures is a five-level, standards-based, integrated-skills series for adult students. The five levels, which are Basic through Level Four, are for low-beginning literacy to high-intermediate students.

The *Ventures* series is flexible enough to be used in open enrollment, managed enrollment, and traditional programs. Its multilevel features support teachers who work with multilevel classes.

What components does *Ventures* have?

Student's Book with Self-study Audio CD

Each **Student's Book** contains a Welcome Unit and ten topic-focused units, plus five review units, one after every two units. Each unit has six skill-focused lessons. Projects, self-assessments, and a reference section are included at the back of the Student's Book.

- **Lessons** are self-contained, allowing for completion within a one-hour class period.
- **Review lessons** recycle, reinforce, and consolidate the materials presented in the previous two units and include a pronunciation activity.
- **Projects** offer community-building opportunities for students to work together – using the Internet or completing a task, such as making a poster or a book.
- **Self-assessments** are an important part of students' learning and success. They give students an opportunity to evaluate and reflect on their learning as well as a tool to support learner persistence.
- The **Self-study Audio CD** is included at the back of the Student's Book. The material on the CD is indicated in the Student's Book by an icon SELF-STUDY AUDIO CD.

Teacher's Edition with Teacher's Toolkit Audio CD/CD-ROM

The interleaved **Teacher's Edition** walks instructors step-by-step through the stages of a lesson.

- Included are learner-persistence and community-building tasks as well as teaching tips, expansion activities, and ways to expand a lesson to two or three instructional hours.

- The Student's Book answer key is included on the interleaved pages in the Teacher's Edition.
- The Teacher's Toolkit Audio CD/CD-ROM contains additional reproducible material for teacher support. Included are picture dictionary cards and worksheets (Levels 1 and 2), extended reading worksheets (Levels 3 and 4), tests with audio, and student self-assessments for portfolio assessment. Reproducible sheets also include cooperative learning activities. These activities reinforce the materials presented in the Student's Book and develop social skills, including those identified by SCANS[1] as being highly valued by employers.
- The unit, midterm, and final tests are found on both the Teacher's Toolkit Audio CD/CD-ROM and in the Teacher's Edition. The tests include listening, grammar, reading, and writing sections.

Audio Program

The *Ventures* series includes a **Class Audio** and a **Student Self-study Audio** SELF-STUDY AUDIO CD. The Class Audio contains all the listening materials in the Student's Book and is available on CD or audiocassette. The Student Self-study Audio CD contains all the unit conversations and readings from the Student's Book.

Workbook

The **Workbook** has two pages of activities for each lesson in the Student's Book.

- The exercises are designed so learners can complete them in class or independently. Students can check their own answers with the answer key in the back of the Workbook. Workbook exercises can be assigned in class, for homework, or as student support when a class is missed.
- Grammar charts and explanations at the back of the Workbook allow students to use the Workbook for self-study.
- If used in class, the Workbook can extend classroom instructional time by 30 minutes per lesson.

Add Ventures

Add Ventures is a book of reproducible worksheets designed for use in multilevel classrooms. The worksheets give students 15–30 minutes of additional practice with each lesson and can be used with

---

[1] The Secretary's Commission on Achieving Necessary Skills, which produced a document that identifies skills for success in the workplace. For more information, see wdr.doleta.gov/SCANS.

homogeneous or heterogeneous groupings. These worksheets can also be used as targeted homework practice at the level of individual students, ensuring learner success.

There are three tiered worksheets for each lesson.

- **Tier 1 Worksheets** provide additional practice for those who are at a level slightly below the Student's Book or who require more controlled practice.
- **Tier 2 Worksheets** provide additional practice for those who are on the level of the Student's Book.
- **Tier 3 Worksheets** provide additional practice that gradually expands beyond the Student's Book.

  These multilevel worksheets are all keyed to the same answers for ease of classroom management.

Unit organization

Within each unit there are six lessons:

LESSON A Get ready The opening lesson focuses students on the topic of the unit. The initial exercise, *Talk about the pictures*, involves several pictures. The visuals create student interest in the topic and activate prior knowledge. They help the teacher assess what learners already know and serve as a prompt for the key vocabulary of each unit. Next is *Listening*, which is based on an extended conversation or several short conversations. The accompanying exercises give learners the opportunity to relate the spoken and written forms of new theme-related vocabulary. The lesson concludes with an opportunity for students to practice language related to the theme in a communicative activity.

LESSONS B and C focus on grammar. The sections move from a *Grammar focus* that presents the grammar point in chart form; to *Practice* exercises that check comprehension of the grammar point and provide guided practice; and, finally, to *Communicate* exercises that guide learners as they generate original answers and conversations. The sections on these pages are sometimes accompanied by a *Useful language* note, which provides explanations or expressions that can be used interchangeably to accomplish a specific language function.

LESSON D Reading develops reading skills and expands vocabulary. The lesson opens with a *Before you read* exercise, whose purpose is to activate prior knowledge and encourage learners to make predictions. A *Reading tip*, which focuses learners

on a specific reading skill, accompanies the *Read* exercise. The reading section of the lesson concludes with *After you read* exercises that check students' understanding. In the Basic Student's Book and Student's Books 1 and 2, the vocabulary expansion portion of the lesson is a *Picture dictionary*. It includes a *Word bank*, pictures to identify, and a conversation for practicing the new words. The words are intended to expand vocabulary related to the unit topic. In Student's Books 3 and 4, the vocabulary expansion portion of the lesson occurs in the *After you read* exercises. These exercises build awareness of word families, connotations, compound words, parts of speech, and other vocabulary expansion activities.

LESSON E Writing provides writing practice within the context of the unit. There are three kinds of exercises in the lesson: prewriting, writing, and postwriting. *Before you write* exercises provide warm-up activities to activate the language students will need for the writing and one or more exercises that provide a model for students to follow when they write. The *Write* exercise sets goals for the student writing. A *Writing tip*, which presents information about punctuation or organization directly related to the writing assignment, accompanies the *Write* exercise. In the *After you write* exercise, students share with a partner using guided questions and practice an important step in the writing process.

LESSON F Another view has three sections.

- **Life-skills reading** develops the scanning and skimming skills that are used with documents such as forms, charts, schedules, announcements, and ads. Multiple-choice questions that follow the document develop test-taking skills similar to CASAS[2] and BEST.[3] This section concludes with an exercise that encourages student communication by providing questions that focus on some aspect of information in the document.
- **Fun with language** provides exercises that review and sometimes expand the topic, vocabulary, or grammar of the unit. They are interactive activities for partner or group work.
- **Wrap up** refers students to the self-assessment page in the back of the book, where they can check their knowledge and evaluate their progress.

The Author Team

Gretchen Bitterlin	Sylvia Ramirez
Dennis Johnson	K. Lynn Savage
Donna Price	

---

[2] The Comprehensive Adult Student Assessment System. For more information, see www.casas.org.
[3] The Basic English Skills Test. For more information, see www.cal.org/BEST.

Scope and sequence

UNIT TITLE TOPIC	FUNCTIONS	LISTENING AND SPEAKING	VOCABULARY	GRAMMAR FOCUS
Welcome Unit pages 2–5	• Exchanging information • Making introductions • Discussing study habits and strategies for studying	• Asking about personality types • Asking about likes and dislikes • Introducing a classmate	• Personality traits • Activities • Study habits and strategies	• Verb tense review: present, present continuous, past, present perfect, present perfect continuous, past continuous, and future with *be going to*
Unit 1 **Personal information** pages 6–17 Topic: **Ways to be smart**	• Describing personal strengths • Expressing opinions • Expressing agreement and disagreement	• Asking about aptitudes • Discussing multiple intelligences • Giving opinions	• Adjectives and adverbs • Multiple intelligences • Prefixes and roots	• Noun clauses with *that* • Contrasting adjectives and adverbs
Unit 2 **At school** pages 18–29 Topic: **Planning for success**	• Inquiring about educational opportunities • Describing educational goals • Describing successful people	• Asking about courses and classes • Discussing how to continue one's education • Discussing obstacles and successes	• Education and careers • Educational requirements • Making vocabulary cards	• The present passive • Infinitives after passive verbs
Review: Units 1 and 2 pages 30–31		• Understanding a conversation		
Unit 3 **Friends and family** pages 32–43 Topic: **Parents and children**	• Discussing appropriate behaviors at home and school • Using polite forms of language • Expressing agreement and disagreement	• Asking about rules at home and at school • Asking questions indirectly • Talking about past events and experiences	• Rules and expectations • Word families	• Indirect *Wh-* questions • Indirect *Yes / No* questions
Unit 4 **Health** pages 44–55 Topic: **Stressful situations**	• Discussing stress • Expressing necessity and lack of necessity • Making suggestions • Expressing past regrets	• Asking about stress • Discussing ways to cope with stress • Giving advice about past actions	• Stress and how to cope • Suffixes	• *ought to, shouldn't, have to, don't have to* • *should have, shouldn't have*
Review: Units 3 and 4 pages 56–57		• Understanding a phone conversation		
Unit 5 **Around town** pages 58–69 Topic: **Community involvement**	• Describing volunteer responsibilities • Describing a sequence of events • Describing repeated actions in the past and present	• Asking about volunteer activities • Discussing personal experiences of volunteering or helping people • Discussing schedules	• Volunteerism • Positive and negative words	• Clauses with *until* and *as soon as* • Repeated actions in the present and past

READING	WRITING	LIFE SKILLS	PRONUNCIATION
• Reading a paragraph about an accident	• Writing sentences about your partner	• Discussing study habits and strategies for learning English	• Pronouncing key vocabulary
• Reading an article about multiple intelligences • Skimming to predict what a reading is about	• Writing a descriptive paragraph about a primary intelligence • Using a topic sentence and supporting details	• Using a dictionary • Reading and understanding a visual diagram	• Pronouncing key vocabulary
• Reading an article about an immigrant family • Scanning to find specific information	• Writing a descriptive paragraph about a successful person • Using specific details such as facts, examples, and reasons	• Using a dictionary • Reading and understanding a chart about the location of vocational classes	• Pronouncing key vocabulary
			• -ed verb endings
• Reading an article about barriers between generations • Paying attention to words that repeat to get an idea of what a reading is about	• Writing an expository paragraph about a difference between generations • Using transition words to show relationships	• Using a dictionary • Reading and understanding a bar graph • Interpreting a survey of student behaviors	• Pronouncing key vocabulary
• Reading an article about stress • Relating personal experience to the content of a reading	• Writing a descriptive paragraph about how to cope with stress • Using actions and results to organize a paragraph	• Reading and understanding a bar graph • Discussing stress in the workplace	• Pronouncing key vocabulary
			• Contrasting intonation of direct and indirect questions
• Reading an article about volunteers • Using context to guess if the meaning of a word is positive or negative	• Writing a descriptive paragraph about someone who made a difference • Making writing more interesting by including details that answer questions	• Reading and understanding ads for volunteer positions • Discussing volunteer activities	• Pronouncing key vocabulary

UNIT TITLE TOPIC	FUNCTIONS	LISTENING AND SPEAKING	VOCABULARY	GRAMMAR FOCUS
Unit 6 **Time** pages 70–81 Topic: **Time and technology**	• Expressing agreement and disagreement • Giving opinions and reasons	• Talking about time-saving devices • Discussing the advantages and disadvantages of technology	• Technology and time-saving devices • Words with multiple definitions	• *although*, *even though* • Contrasting *because* and *although*
Review: Units 5 and 6 pages 82–83		• Understanding a radio interview		
Unit 7 **Shopping** pages 84–95 Topic: **Buying and returning merchandise**	• Explaining problems with a purchase • Discussing preferences • Explaining mistakes • Asking for information about store policies	• Asking about returning merchandise • Asking about store policies • Talking about shopping mistakes • Identifying store personnel • Describing people, places, and things	• Buying and returning merchandise • Compound nouns	• *who* and *that* as the subject of a dependent clause • *that* as the object of a dependent clause
Unit 8 **Work** pages 96–107 Topic: **Success at work**	• Giving advice • Making suggestions • Explaining job responsibilities • Describing the duration of an activity	• Discussing work schedules • Talking about workplace problems and their solutions • Asking questions about work experiences	• Job responsibilities and skills • Prefixes and roots	• Contrasting present perfect and present perfect continuous • Adjectives ending in -ed and -ing
Review: Units 7 and 8 pages 108–109		• Understanding a class lecture		
Unit 9 **Daily living** pages 110–121 Topic: **Living green**	• Describing environmental issues and concerns • Giving advice • Making suggestions • Describing actions one can take	• Asking questions about "living green" • Discussing causes and effects of environmental problems • Discussing actions that could help the environment	• The environment • Synonyms	• Present unreal conditional • *since, due to, consequently, as a result*
Unit 10 **Leisure** pages 122–133 Topic: **Celebrations**	• Describing future possibility • Describing actions based on expectations • Expressing hopes and wishes • Comparing customs and celebrations	• Asking about and comparing wedding customs • Discussing possible and hypothetical holiday plans • Talking about hopes and wishes	• Celebrations • Words with multiple meanings	• Real future conditional and unreal conditional • *hope* and *wish*
Review: Units 9 and 10 pages 134–135		• Understanding a street interview		

Projects pages 136–140
Self-assessments pages 141–145
Reference pages 146–153
Irregular verbs page 154
Self-study audio script pages 155–161

READING	WRITING	LIFE SKILLS	PRONUNCIATION
• Reading a blog about videoconferencing • Recognizing the difference between facts and opinions	• Writing an expository paragraph about a time-saving device or activity • Using advantages and disadvantages to organize a paragraph	• Using a dictionary • Reading and understanding a table • Discussing Internet use • Discussing survey results	• Pronouncing key vocabulary
			• Stressed and unstressed words
• Reading a newspaper advice column about return policies • Recognizing synonyms	• Writing a persuasive paragraph about shopping online • Using transition words such as *first*, *second*, *next*, *furthermore*, *moreover*, and *finally* to signal a list of reasons in a paragraph	• Reading and understanding a returned-merchandise form • Talking about returning or exchanging merchandise	• Pronouncing key vocabulary
• Reading an article about hard and soft job skills • Reading a cover letter to apply for a job • Recognizing that quotations can explain or support a main idea	• Writing a cover letter to apply for a job • Including critical information in a cover letter	• Using a dictionary • Discussing a good work ethic • Reading and understanding a table about the fastest-growing service occupations • Discussing work skills	• Pronouncing key vocabulary
			• Stressing function words
• Reading a fable about how all things in life are connected • Asking questions to identify a cause-and-effect relationship	• Writing a paragraph about an environmental problem • Using cause and effect to organize a paragraph	• Using a dictionary or thesaurus • Reading and understanding a chart about reasons to "live green" • Discussing ways to help the environment	• Pronouncing key vocabulary
• Reading an article about special birthday celebrations around the world • Using punctuation as a clue to meaning	• Writing a descriptive paragraph about a favorite holiday or celebration • Concluding a paragraph by relating it to your personal life	• Using a dictionary • Reading and understanding a recipe • Discussing traditional meals and recipes	• Pronouncing key vocabulary
			• Identifying thought groups

Correlations

UNIT/PAGES	CASAS	EFF
Unit 1 **Personal information** pages 6–17	0.1.2, 0.1.4, 0.1.5, 0.1.6, 0.2.1, 0.2.4, 4.1.7, 4.1.8, 4.4.2, 4.5.2, 4.5.5, 4.6.1, 4.7.3, 4.8.1, 4.8.2, 7.1.1, 7.1.4, 7.2.3, 7.2.4, 7.4.1, 7.4.2, 7.4.5, 7.4.9, 7.5.1	Most EFF standards are met, with particular focus on: • Conveying ideas in writing • Cooperating with others • Listening actively • Reading with understanding • Speaking so others can understand • Taking responsibility for learning
Unit 2 **At school** pages 18–29	0.1.2, 0.1.5, 0.1.6, 0.2.1, 0.2.4, 2.3.1, 2.3.2, 2.5.5, 2.7.6, 4.1.4, 4.1.7, 4.1.9, 4.4.1, 4.6.1, 4.8.1, 4.8.2, 4.9.1, 6.0.1, 7.1.1, 7.1.4, 7.2.1, 7.2.2, 7.4.1, 7.4.2, 7.4.5, 7.5.1	Most EFF standards are met, with particular focus on: • Attending to oral information • Paying attention to the conventions of spoken English • Reflecting and evaluating • Selecting appropriate reading strategies • Speaking so others can understand • Understanding and working with pictures
Unit 3 **Friends and family** pages 32–43	0.1.2, 0.1.3, 0.1.4, 0.1.5, 0.2.2, 0.2.4, 4.4.3, 4.8.1, 4.8.2, 6.0.1, 6.6.5, 7.1.1, 7.1.4, 7.2.1, 7.2.3, 7.5.1, 7.5.5, 7.5.6, 8.3.1, 8.3.2	Most EFF standards are met, with particular focus on: • Conveying ideas in writing • Listening actively • Paying attention to the conventions of spoken English • Reading with understanding • Resolving conflict and negotiating • Taking responsibility for learning
Unit 4 **Health** pages 44–55	0.1.2, 0.1.3, 0.1.5, 0.2.4, 3.1.1, 3.5.2, 3.5.8, 3.5.9, 4.5.2, 4.5.5, 4.8.1, 6.0.1, 7.1.4, 7.2.1, 7.3.1, 7.3.2, 7.4.1, 7.4.2, 7.5.1, 7.5.5, 7.5.7, 8.3.1, 8.3.2	Most EFF standards are met, with particular focus on: • Advocating and influencing • Attending to oral information • Cooperating with others • Reading with understanding • Solving problems and making decisions • Speaking so others can understand
Unit 5 **Around town** pages 58–69	0.1.2, 0.1.5, 0.1.6, 0.2.4, 2.7.3, 3.1.3, 3.5.8, 3.5.9, 4.1.4, 4.8.1, 6.0.1, 7.1.1, 7.1.3, 7.1.4, 7.2.1, 7.2.2, 7.4.1, 7.4.2, 7.4.3, 7.5.1, 7.5.2, 7.5.5, 8.3.1, 8.3.2	Most EFF standards are met, with particular focus on: • Listening actively • Monitoring progress toward goals • Reading with understanding • Seeking feedback and revising accordingly • Speaking so others can understand • Understanding and working with pictures

SCANS	BEST Plus Form A	BEST Form B
Most SCANS standards are met, with particular focus on: • Demonstrating individual responsibility • Improving basic skills • Interpreting and communicating information • Knowing how to learn • Reasoning	Overall test preparation is supported, with particular impact on the following items: Locator: W5–6 Level 1: 4.2 Level 2: 4.2 Level 3: 4.1	Overall test preparation is supported, with particular impact on the following areas: • Employment • Oral interview • Personal information • Reading passages • Writing notes
Most SCANS standards are met, with particular focus on: • Acquiring and evaluating information • Participating as a member of a team • Serving clients and customers • Teaching others • Understanding systems	Overall test preparation is supported, with particular impact on the following items: Locator: W5 Level 3: 2.3	Overall test preparation is supported, with particular impact on the following areas: • Employment/Training • Oral interview • Personal information • Reading passages • Reading signs, ads, and notices • Time/Numbers • Writing notes
Most SCANS standards are met, with particular focus on: • Knowing how to learn • Negotiating • Organizing and maintaining information • Participating as a member of a team • Seeing things in the mind's eye	Overall test preparation is supported, with particular impact on the following items: Locator: W3 Level 2: 4.2 Level 3: 1.3, 2.3, 5.2	Overall test preparation is supported, with particular impact on the following areas: • Emergencies and safety • Housing • Oral interview • Personal information • Reading passages • Reading signs, ads, and notices • Time/Numbers • Writing notes
Most SCANS standards are met, with particular focus on: • Demonstrating individual responsibility and self-management • Improving basic skills • Making decisions • Reasoning • Solving problems	Overall test preparation is supported, with particular impact on the following items: Locator: W6 Level 3: 1, 1.2	Overall test preparation is supported, with particular impact on the following areas: • Health • Numbers • Oral interview • Personal information • Reading passages • Reading signs, ads, and notices • Shopping for food • Writing notes
Most SCANS standards are met, with particular focus on: • Demonstrating integrity • Interpreting and communicating information • Knowing how to learn • Organizing and maintaining information • Teaching others	Overall test preparation is supported, with particular impact on the following items: Locator: W5 Level 1: 4, 4.1, 4.2 Level 3: 2.2, 4, 4.1, 4.2	Overall test preparation is supported, with particular impact on the following areas: • Employment/Training • Oral interview • Personal information • Reading passages • Reading signs, ads, and notices • Time/Numbers • Writing notes

UNIT/PAGES	CASAS	EFF
Unit 6 **Time** pages 70–81	0.1.2, 0.1.5, 0.1.6, 0.2.4, 1.1.3, 1.3.1, 1.4.1, 1.7.4, 2.1.1, 2.2.3, 4.5.1, 4.5.2, 4.5.5, 4.8.1, 6.0.1, 7.1.1, 7.1.4, 7.2.1, 7.2.3, 7.2.4, 7.2.5, 7.4.1, 7.4.2, 7.4.8, 7.5.1	Most EFF standards are met, with particular focus on: • Conveying ideas in writing • Cooperating with others • Listening actively • Reading with understanding • Speaking so others can understand • Using information and communications technology
Unit 7 **Shopping** pages 84–95	0.1.2, 0.1.3, 0.1.5, 0.1.6, 1.2.2, 1.3.1, 1.3.3, 1.4.1, 1.6.3, 1.7.1, 4.8.1, 6.0.1, 7.1.1, 7.1.4, 7.2.1, 7.2.3, 7.2.5, 7.4.2, 7.4.3, 7.4.8, 7.5.1	Most EFF standards are met, with particular focus on: • Advocating and influencing • Attending to oral information • Reflecting and evaluating • Selecting appropriate reading strategies • Solving problems and making decisions • Taking responsibility for learning
Unit 8 **Work** pages 96–107	0.1.2, 0.1.3, 0.1.5, 0.2.4, 2.3.1, 2.3.2, 2.4.1, 4.1.2, 4.1.6, 4.1.7, 4.1.8, 4.4.1, 4.4.2, 4.4.3, 4.4.4, 4.5.2, 4.5.5, 4.6.2, 4.7.3, 4.8.1, 4.8.2, 6.0.1, 7.1.1, 7.1.4, 7.2.1, 7.2.3, 7.2.7, 7.3.1, 7.3.2, 7.4.1, 7.4.2, 7.4.5, 7.5.1, 7.5.2, 7.5.6	Most EFF standards are met, with particular focus on: • Attending to oral information • Monitoring comprehension and adjusting reading strategies • Paying attention to the conventions of spoken English • Seeking input from others • Taking stock of where one is • Understanding and working with pictures
Unit 9 **Daily living** pages 110–121	0.1.2, 0.1.5, 1.4.1, 2.2.3, 2.3.3, 2.7.3, 4.8.1, 5.6.1, 5.7.1, 7.1.1, 7.2.1, 7.2.2, 7.2.6, 7.3.1, 7.3.2, 7.3.4, 7.4.2, 7.4.3, 7.5.1, 7.5.4, 8.3.1	Most EFF standards are met, with particular focus on: • Conveying ideas in writing • Guiding others • Listening actively • Reading with understanding • Solving problems and making decisions • Speaking so others can understand
Unit 10 **Leisure** pages 122–133	0.1.1, 0.1.2, 0.1.5, 0.1.6, 0.2.4, 1.1.1, 1.1.5, 2.3.2, 2.5.7, 2.7.1, 2.7.2, 2.7.4, 4.5.2, 4.5.5, 4.8.1, 6.0.1, 7.1.1, 7.1.4, 7.2.1, 7.2.3, 7.2.4, 7.2.6, 7.4.1, 7.4.2, 7.4.4, 7.4.5, 7.5.1, 7.5.6	Most EFF standards are met, with particular focus on: • Attending to oral information • Attending to visual sources of information • Interacting with others in positive ways • Paying attention to the conventions of written English • Reading with understanding • Selecting appropriate reading strategies

SCANS	BEST Plus Form A	BEST Form B
Most SCANS standards are met, with particular focus on: • Applying technology to task • Improving basic skills • Interpreting and communicating information • Knowing how to learn • Selecting technology	Overall test preparation is supported, with particular impact on the following items: Locator: W5 Level 2: 2.3	Overall test preparation is supported, with particular impact on the following areas: • Oral interview • Personal information • Reading passages • Numbers • Writing notes
Most SCANS standards are met, with particular focus on: • Demonstrating individual responsibility and self-management • Organizing and maintaining information • Seeing things in the mind's eye • Solving problems • Understanding systems	Overall test preparation is supported, with particular impact on the following items: Level 1: 1.2, 1.3 Level 2: 3.1, 3.2, 3.3	Overall test preparation is supported, with particular impact on the following areas: • Numbers • Oral interview • Personal information • Reading passages • Reading signs, ads, and notices • Shopping
Most SCANS standards are met, with particular focus on: • Acquiring and evaluating information • Allocating human resources • Knowing how to learn • Participating as a member of a team • Reasoning	Overall test preparation is supported, with particular impact on the following items: Locator: W5 Level 3: 2.3	Overall test preparation is supported, with particular impact on the following areas: • Employment/Training • Envelopes • Oral interview • Personal information • Reading passages • Time/Numbers • Writing notes
Most SCANS standards are met, with particular focus on: • Improving basic skills • Knowing how to learn • Seeing things in the mind's eye • Teaching others • Understanding systems	Overall test preparation is supported, with particular impact on the following items: Level 1: 2.3, 3.2, 3.3 Level 2: 2.1, 2.2, 2.3 Level 3: 3.3	Overall test preparation is supported, with particular impact on the following areas: • Emergencies/Housing • Reading signs, ads, and notices • Safety • Oral interview • Personal information • Reading passages • Writing notes
Most SCANS standards are met, with particular focus on: • Applying technology to task • Improving basic skills • Organizing and maintaining information • Thinking creatively • Working with cultural diversity	Overall test preparation is supported, with particular impact on the following items: Locator: W1, W7 Level 1: 4.2 Level 3: 4.1	Overall test preparation is supported, with particular impact on the following areas: • Calendar • Food labels • Numbers • Oral interview • Personal information • Reading passages • Shopping • Writing notes

Features of the Student's Book

The **Ventures** Student's Book is based on high-interest topics that reinforce the vocabulary and language adult language learners need in their daily lives. Not only are skills integrated throughout a lesson, but **Ventures** also teaches listening, speaking, reading, and writing individually in every unit.

To encourage learner persistence, the **Ventures** series is designed so that the one-hour lessons in the Student's Book are self-contained; each lesson moves from presentation to guided practice to communicative activities.

The self-study audio CD at the back of the Student's Book provides a way for students to practice at home.

The core philosophy of **Ventures** is:
Hear it before you say it.
Say it before you read it.
Read it before you write it.

Before producing language, students need input that can be internalized and understood. This holistic approach is essential to successful language acquisition and is the foundation of the **Ventures** series.

The Student's Book, combined with the **Workbook**, **Teacher's Edition Toolkit Audio CD / CD-ROM**, and **Add Ventures**, offers maximum flexibility of use in multilevel classrooms, classes of various duration, and classes that encourage independent learning.

Unit Opener

- Introduces the unit topic
- Activates students' prior knowledge
- Previews unit grammar and vocabulary

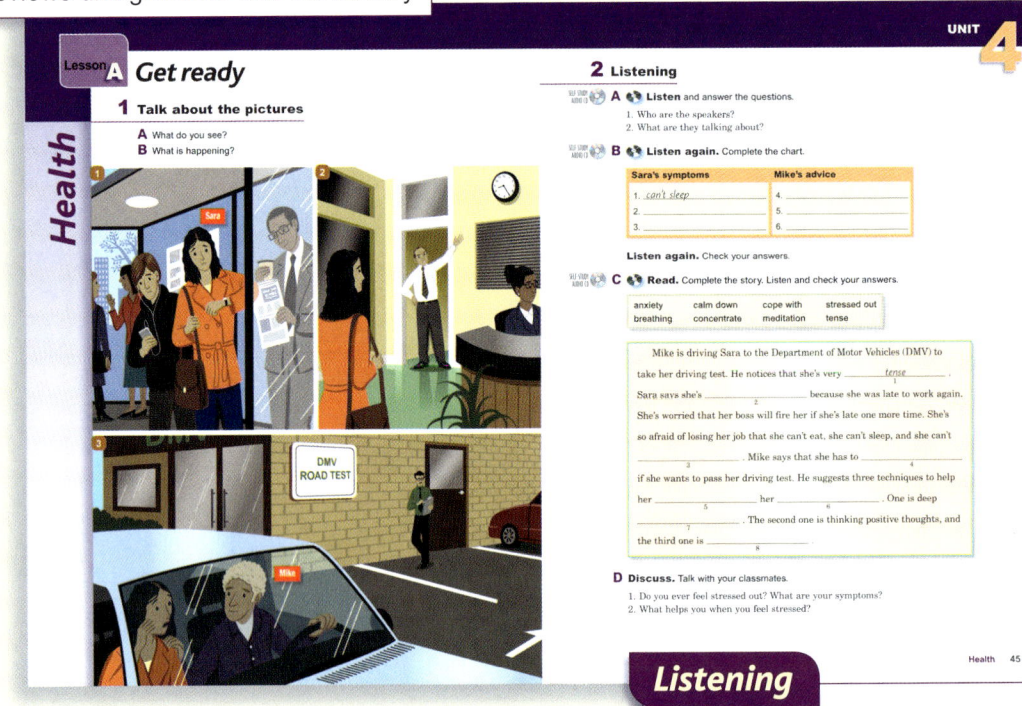

Listening

- Provides guided listening and speaking practice
- Expands topic vocabulary
- Encourages learner persistence and autonomy with self-study audio CD

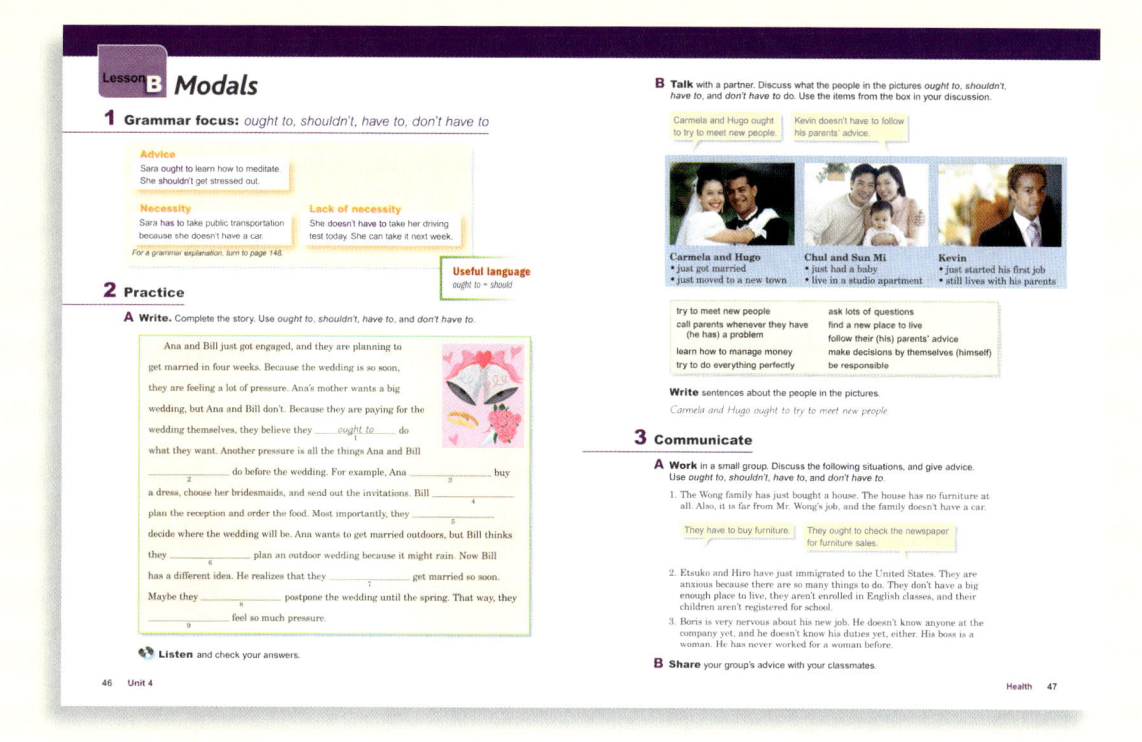

Lesson B Modals

1 Grammar focus: *ought to, shouldn't, have to, don't have to*

Advice
Sara ought to learn how to meditate.
She shouldn't get stressed out.

Necessity
Sara has to take public transportation because she doesn't have a car.

Lack of necessity
She doesn't have to take her driving test today. She can take it next week.

For a grammar explanation, turn to page 148.

Useful language
ought to = should

2 Practice

A Write. Complete the story. Use *ought to, shouldn't, have to,* and *don't have to.*

Ana and Bill just got engaged, and they are planning to get married in four weeks. Because the wedding is so soon, they are feeling a lot of pressure. Ana's mother wants a big wedding, but Ana and Bill don't. Because they are paying for the wedding themselves, they believe they ____ought to____ do what they want. Another pressure is all the things Ana and Bill ____2____ do before the wedding. For example, Ana ____3____ buy a dress, choose her bridesmaids, and send out the invitations. Bill ____4____ plan the reception and order the food. Most importantly, they ____5____ decide where the wedding will be. Ana wants to get married outdoors, but Bill thinks they ____6____ plan an outdoor wedding because it might rain. Now Bill has a different idea. He realizes that they ____7____ get married so soon. Maybe they ____8____ postpone the wedding until the spring. That way, they ____9____ feel so much pressure.

🔊 **Listen** and check your answers.

46   Unit 4

B Talk with a partner. Discuss what the people in the pictures *ought to, shouldn't, have to,* and *don't have to* do. Use the items from the box in your discussion.

Carmela and Hugo ought to try to meet new people.

Kevin doesn't have to follow his parents' advice.

Carmela and Hugo
• just got married
• just moved to a new town

Chul and Sun Mi
• just had a baby
• live in a studio apartment

Kevin
• just started his first job
• still lives with his parents

try to meet new people	ask lots of questions
call parents whenever they have (he has) a problem	find a new place to live
	follow their (his) parents' advice
learn how to manage money	make decisions by themselves (himself)
try to do everything perfectly	be responsible

Write sentences about the people in the pictures.
Carmela and Hugo ought to try to meet new people

3 Communicate

A Work in a small group. Discuss the following situations, and give advice. Use *ought to, shouldn't, have to,* and *don't have to.*

1. The Wong family has just bought a house. The house has no furniture at all. Also, it is far from Mr. Wong's job, and the family doesn't have a car.

They have to buy furniture.   They ought to check the newspaper for furniture sales.

2. Etsuko and Hiro have just immigrated to the United States. They are anxious because there are so many things to do. They don't have a big enough place to live, they aren't enrolled in English classes, and their children aren't registered for school.
3. Boris is very nervous about his new job. He doesn't know anyone at the company yet, and he doesn't know his duties yet, either. His boss is a woman. He has never worked for a woman before.

B Share your group's advice with your classmates.

Health   47

Grammar

- Builds fluency through two grammar lessons
- Moves from guided practice to communicative activities
- Includes *Useful language* notes
- Includes audio to check comprehension and practice pronunciation

---

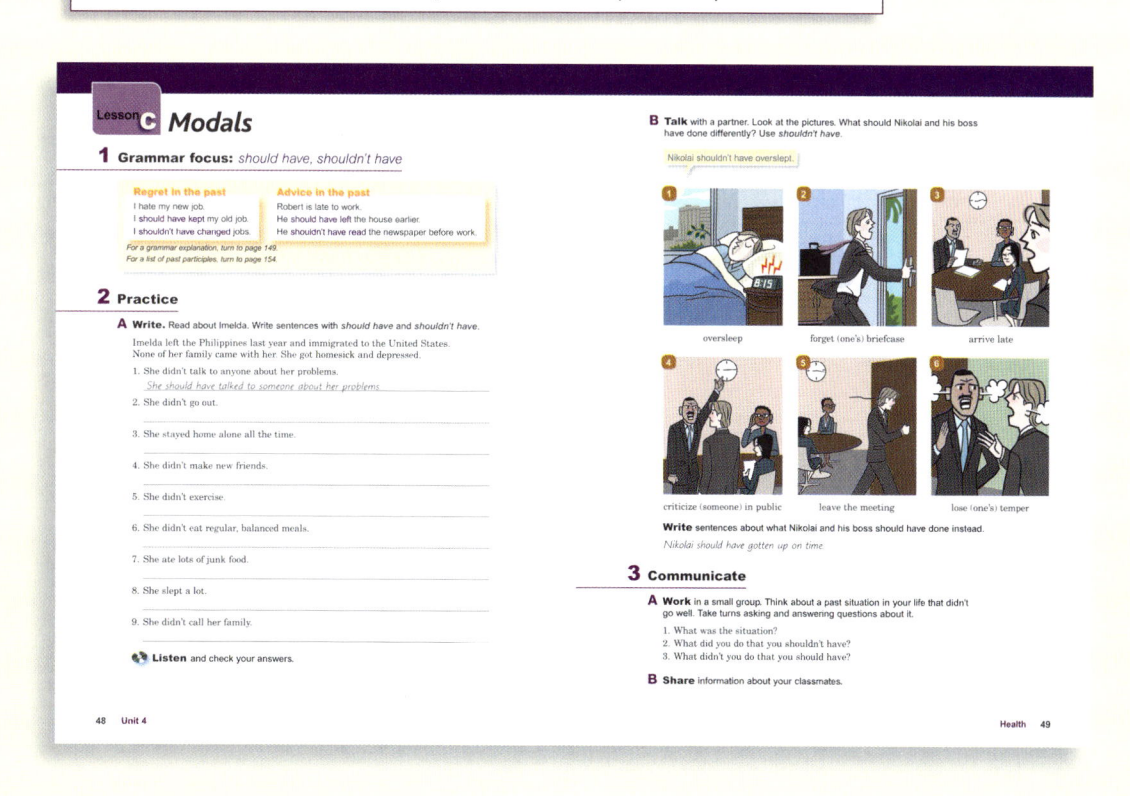

Lesson C Modals

1 Grammar focus: *should have, shouldn't have*

Regret in the past
I hate my new job.
I should have kept my old job.
I shouldn't have changed jobs.

Advice in the past
Robert is late to work.
He should have left the house earlier.
He shouldn't have read the newspaper before work.

For a grammar explanation, turn to page 149.
For a list of past participles, turn to page 154.

2 Practice

A Write. Read about Imelda. Write sentences with *should have* and *shouldn't have.*

Imelda left the Philippines last year and immigrated to the United States. None of her family came with her. She got homesick and depressed.

1. She didn't talk to anyone about her problems.
   She should have talked to someone about her problems.
2. She didn't go out.
3. She stayed home alone all the time.
4. She didn't make new friends.
5. She didn't exercise.
6. She didn't eat regular, balanced meals.
7. She ate lots of junk food.
8. She slept a lot.
9. She didn't call her family.

🔊 **Listen** and check your answers.

48   Unit 4

B Talk with a partner. Look at the pictures. What should Nikolai and his boss have done differently? Use *shouldn't have.*

Nikolai shouldn't have overslept.

oversleep	forget (one's) briefcase	arrive late
criticize (someone) in public	leave the meeting	lose (one's) temper

Write sentences about what Nikolai and his boss should have done instead.
Nikolai should have gotten up on time

3 Communicate

A Work in a small group. Think about a past situation in your life that didn't go well. Take turns asking and answering questions about it.

1. What was the situation?
2. What did you do that you shouldn't have?
3. What didn't you do that you should have?

B Share information about your classmates.

Health   49

Features of the Student's Book   xv

Reading

- Features three-step approach to reading: **Before you read**, **Read**, **After you read**
- Highlights reading strategies and skills
- Contextualizes unit vocabulary and grammar
- Integrates four skills: speaking, listening, reading, writing
- Presents a variety of reading texts on audio

Reading expansion

- Includes comprehension check and reading skills notes
- Builds vocabulary development skills
- Reinforces vocabulary through conversation

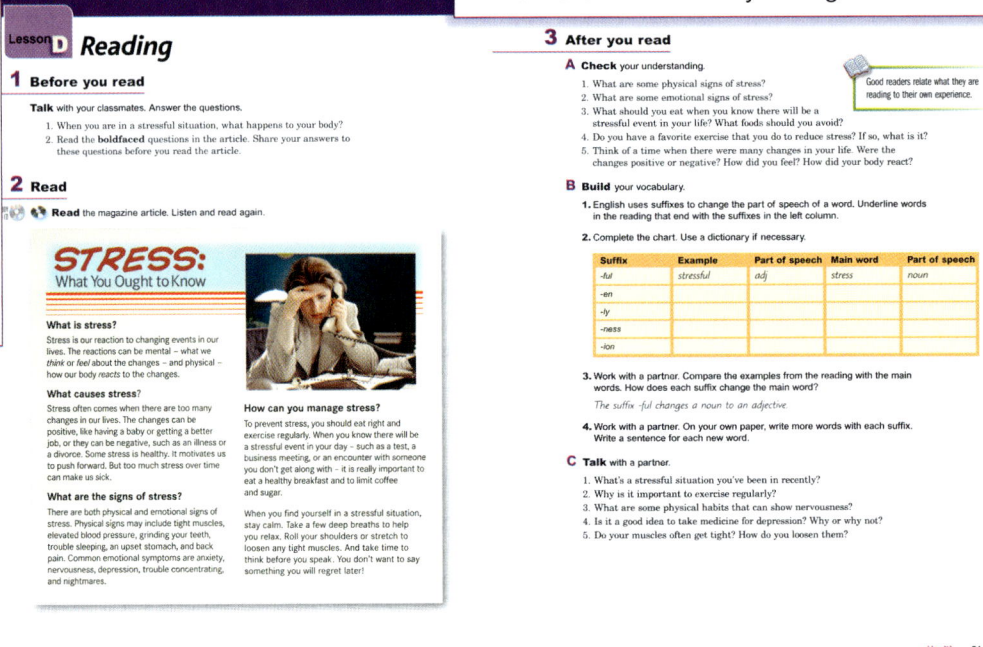

Writing

- Includes a process approach to writing: prewriting, writing, and self- and peer review
- Contextualizes unit vocabulary and grammar
- Features integrated skills: speaking, listening, reading, writing
- Moves from guided practice to personalized writing

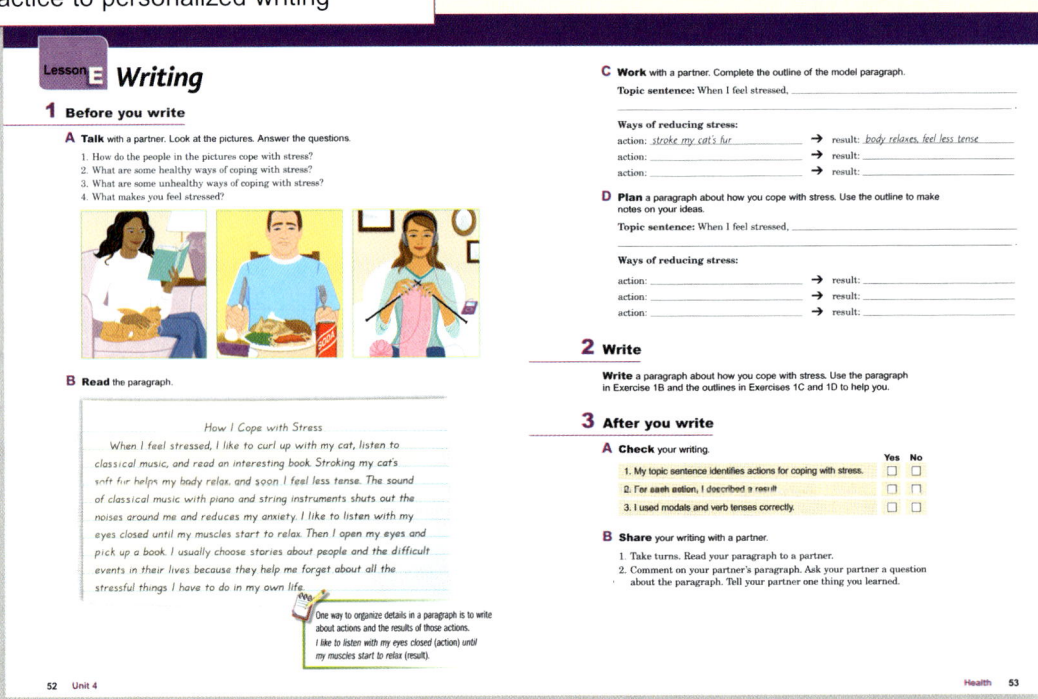

xvi   Features of the Student's Book

- Concludes unit with practical and playful practice
- Familiarizes students with real-life documents
- Reviews unit content
- Provides test-taking practice and self-assessment
- Motivates students as they see progress

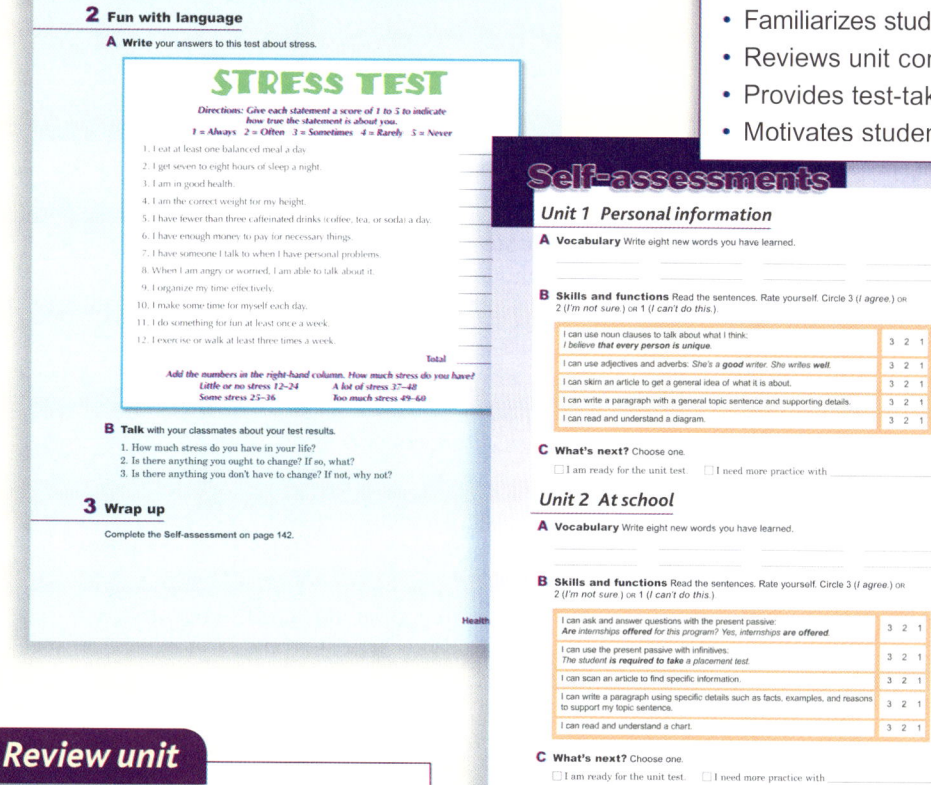

Review unit

- Reinforces language of previous two units
- Focuses on listening, grammar, and pronunciation

Project

- Builds community among students
- Enhances learner persistence
- Exposes students to simple Internet searches
- Reinforces the theme of the unit

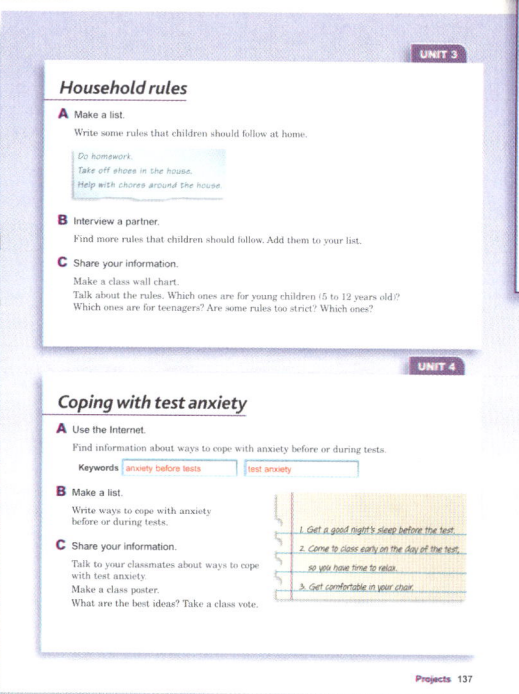

Features of the Student's Book   xvii

Features of the Teacher's Edition

Introduction

Ventures **Teacher's Edition** includes step-by-step teaching notes for each lesson. The teaching notes divide the lesson into six stages. Each lesson begins with a warm-up and review followed by a presentation stage. The practice, comprehension, application, and evaluation stages do not follow a strict sequence in the Teacher's Edition. They vary depending on the content of the lesson being presented.

Stages of a lesson

Warm-up and review Each lesson begins with a review of previous material and connects that material to the present lesson. Quick review activities prompt students' memory. Warm-up activities at the beginning of class introduce the new lesson. These activities may take many forms, but they are quick, focused, and connected to the new material to be introduced. A warm-up also helps teachers ascertain what students already know about the topic and what they are able to say.

Presentation During this stage of the lesson, the teacher presents new information, but it should not be a one-way delivery. Rather, it is a dynamic process of student input and interaction – a give-and-take between the teacher and students as well as students and students. The teacher may give examples rather than rules, model rather than tell, and relate the material to students' experiences.

Practice It is important that students have enough time to practice. A comfortable classroom environment needs to be created so that students are not afraid to take risks. The practice needs to be varied and interesting. There should be a progression from guided to independent practice. In the *Ventures* grammar lessons, for example, practice begins with mechanical aspects such as form, moves to a focus on meaning, and ends with communicative interactions.

Comprehension check Asking, "Do you understand?" is not enough to ascertain whether students are following the lesson. The teacher must ask concrete questions and have students demonstrate that they understand. In this stage, students are asked to repeat information in their own words. Students are also invited to come to the board or to interact with other students in some way.

Application A teacher must provide opportunities for students to practice newly acquired language in more realistic situations. These situations could be in class or out of class. The important point is that students use what they have learned in new ways. In the grammar lessons, for example, the *Communicate* section asks students to role-play, interview, share information, or ask questions.

Evaluation An ongoing part of the lesson is to determine whether students are meeting the lesson objectives. This can be done formally at the end of a unit by giving a unit test and having students complete the self-assessment, but it can also be done informally toward the end of the lesson. Each lesson in the Teacher's Edition ends with a review and verification of understanding of the lesson objectives. Any in-class assignment or task can serve as an evaluation tool as long as it assesses the objectives. Having students complete **Add Ventures** worksheets or **Workbook** pages can also serve as an informal evaluation to gauge where students may be having difficulty.

The following chart presents the most common order of each stage and suggests how long each stage could take within a one-hour class period.

Stages of the lesson	Approximate time range
Warm-up and review	5–10 minutes
Presentation	10–20 minutes
Practice	15–20 minutes
Comprehension check	5–10 minutes
Application	15–20 minutes
Evaluation	10–15 minutes

Lesson B Modals

Presentation

- Tell Ss that they are going to read and talk about different situations in which people need advice. Read the instructions aloud for Exercise **2B**.
- Books open. Direct Ss' attention to the pictures in Exercise **2B**.
- Call on three Ss to read the descriptions under the pictures.
- Ask individual Ss to read one piece of advice from the box. Explain the meaning of any phrases that are unclear to Ss.
- Model the task with a S. Read the two examples above the pictures.
- Ss complete the exercise in pairs. Walk around and help as needed.

Practice

- Direct Ss' attention to the second part of the instructions for Exercise **2B**. Read the instructions aloud.
- Ask a S to read the sample sentence to the class.
- Ss work individually to complete the exercise. Walk around and help as needed.
- Have Ss come to the board to write their sentences. Work with the class to make corrections on the board as needed.

Application

- Direct Ss' attention to Exercise **3A** and read the instructions aloud.
- Model the task. Ask a S to read the first situation aloud. Have another S read the sample advice.
- Ss work in small groups to complete the exercise. Walk around and help as needed.
- Direct Ss' attention to Exercise **3B** and read the instructions aloud.
- Have groups share with the class the advice they gave for each situation.

Expansion activity (small groups)

- Ask Ss if they have ever heard of "Dear Abby" or a similar advice column. If not, explain that "Dear Abby" is a newspaper column that advises people about how to handle personal problems or difficult situations.

- Have each group brainstorm ideas to create a list of personal problems that might make a person write for advice. Write a sample letter on the board. For example:
  Dear Abby,
  I have a friend whose boyfriend ignores her. Even though she is so nice, he doesn't return her calls. I think that he has another girlfriend. What should I do to help my friend?
  Sincerely,
  Worried Friend
- Explain that sometimes the letter writer will use a descriptive name to sign the letter rather than his or her real name. Ask Ss why the person might do this. (to hide his or her identity)
- Call on a S to use the grammatical structures they learned in this unit (*ought to, shouldn't, have to, don't have to*) to respond to *Worried Friend's* request for advice.
- Have Ss in each group work together to write a group letter of advice. Walk around and help as needed.
- When groups have finished, invite a member from each group to read the group letter to the class.
- Allow time for questions and answers so that Ss can discuss some of the advice that was given.

Evaluation

- Books closed. Direct Ss' attention to the lesson focus on the board.
- Write the following sentences on the board:
  1. You ought to go to the meeting tonight.
  2. You have to go to the meeting tonight.
- Ask a S what the difference is in the meaning of the two sentences. Elicit an appropriate response: *The first sentence gives advice. The second sentence shows necessity, or what you must do.* Ask a S for another way to say the first sentence. (*You* **should** *go to the meeting tonight.*)
- Check off the lesson focus as Ss demonstrate an understanding of what they have learned in the lesson.

> **More Ventures** *(whole group, pairs, individual)*
> Assign appropriate exercises from the *Teacher's Toolkit Audio CD / CD-ROM, Add Ventures,* or the *Workbook.*

T-47 Unit 4

B **Talk** with a partner. Discuss what the people in the pictures *ought to, shouldn't, have to,* and *don't have to* do. Use the items from the box in your discussion.

> Carmela and Hugo ought to try to meet new people.

> Kevin doesn't have to follow his parents' advice.

Carmela and Hugo
- just got married
- just moved to a new town

Chul and Sun Mi
- just had a baby
- live in a studio apartment

Kevin
- just started his first job
- still lives with his parents

try to meet new people	ask lots of questions
call parents whenever they have (he has) a problem	find a new place to live
learn how to manage money	follow their (his) parents' advice
try to do everything perfectly	make decisions by themselves (himself)
	be responsible

Write sentences about the people in the pictures.

Carmela and Hugo ought to try to meet new people.

3 Communicate

A **Work** in a small group. Discuss the following situations, and give advice. Use *ought to, shouldn't, have to,* and *don't have to.*

1. The Wong family has just bought a house. The house has no furniture at all. Also, it is far from Mr. Wong's job, and the family doesn't have a car.

> They have to buy furniture.

> They ought to check the newspaper for furniture sales.

2. Etsuko and Hiro have just immigrated to the United States. They are anxious because there are so many things to do. They don't have a big enough place to live, they aren't enrolled in English classes, and their children aren't registered for school.

3. Boris is very nervous about his new job. He doesn't know anyone at the company yet, and he doesn't know his duties yet, either. His boss is a woman. He has never worked for a woman before.

B **Share** your group's advice with your classmates.

Health 47

Class time guidelines

Class time varies in different educational settings. The flexibility of the *Ventures* series provides for the expansion of a one-hour class into a two- or three-hour class. For longer class periods, the expansion activities, teaching tips, culture notes, and community building and learner persistence activities in the Teacher's Edition offer ample material to expand the lesson. The Projects at the back of the Student's Book as well as the Games suggested in the Teacher's Edition offer further ways to enrich the two- or three-hour class. In addition, the materials on the **Teacher's Toolkit Audio CD / CD-ROM** as well as in the other components of the series can be used in class or as homework to satisfy the needs of the longer class period.

The chart below illustrates how the **Ventures** series might be used in a one-hour, two-hour, and three-hour class.

A one-hour class

Follow *Teacher's Edition* step-by-step lessons for the *Student's Book*.

Assign *Workbook* for homework.

Assign appropriate level *Add Ventures* worksheets for homework.

Optional: Projects and Games; Collaborative Activities on the *Teacher's Toolkit Audio CD / CD-ROM*

A two-hour class

Follow *Teacher's Edition* step-by-step lessons for the *Student's Book*.

Assign *Workbook* for homework.

Use appropriate level *Add Ventures* worksheets as an in-class activity.

Optional: Projects and Games; Collaborative Activities and Extended Reading Worksheets on the *Teacher's Toolkit Audio CD / CD-ROM*

A three-hour class

Follow *Teacher's Edition* step-by-step lessons for the *Student's Book*.

Use *Workbook* as an in-class activity.

Use appropriate level *Add Ventures* worksheets as an in-class activity.

Optional: Projects and Games; Collaborative Activities, Extended Reading Worksheets, and Tests on the *Teacher's Toolkit Audio CD / CD-ROM*

Meet the *Ventures* author team

Gretchen Bitterlin has been an ESL instructor and ESL department instructional leader with the Continuing Education Program, San Diego Community College District. She now coordinates that agency's large noncredit ESL program. She was also an ESL Teacher Institute Trainer and Chair of the TESOL Task Force on Adult Education Program Standards. She is a co-author of *English for Adult Competency*.

Dennis Johnson has been an ESL instructor at City College of San Francisco, teaching all levels of ESL, since 1977. As ESL Site Coordinator, he has provided guidance to faculty in selecting textbooks. He is the author of *Get Up and Go* and co-author of *The Immigrant Experience*.

Donna Price is Associate Professor of ESL and Vocational ESL/Technology Resource Instructor for the Continuing Education Program, San Diego Community College District. She has taught all levels of ESL for 20 years and is a former recipient of the TESOL Newbury House Award for Excellence in Teaching. She is also the author of *Skills for Success*.

Sylvia Ramirez is a professor at MiraCosta College, where she coordinates the large noncredit ESL program. She has more than 30 years of experience in adult ESL, including multilevel ESL, vocational ESL, family literacy, and distance learning. She has represented the California State Department of Education in providing technical assistance to local ESL programs.

K. Lynn Savage, Series Editor, is a retired ESL teacher and Vocational ESL Resource teacher from City College of San Francisco, who trains teachers for adult education programs around the country. She chaired the committee that developed *ESL Model Standards for Adult Education Programs* (California, 1992) and is the author, co-author, and editor of many ESL materials, including *Teacher Training through Video*, *Parenting for Academic Success: A Curriculum for Families Learning English*, *Crossroads Café*, *Building Life Skills*, *Picture Stories*, *May I Help You?*, and *English That Works*.

Welcome

1 Meet your classmates

A Look at the picture. What do you see?

B What are the people doing?

Lesson objectives

- Ask and answer questions about personal information
- Introduce a partner to the class

Warm-up and review

- Before class. Write today's lesson focus on the board.
  Welcome unit:
  Exchange information
  Introduce your partner to the class
  Ask about personality types and likes and dislikes

- Begin class. Books closed. Say: *Welcome to English class.*

- Introduce yourself to the class. Write your name on the board. Point to it. Tell Ss your name and ask them to repeat it. Tell Ss where you are from and anything else of interest that you would like to add, for example: *I am married. I have two children and a dog. I love dancing, cooking, and eating. My lucky number is seven.*

- Ask Ss to introduce themselves to the class. Encourage them to say their names, where they are from, and anything else they would like to add.

▼ **Teaching tip**

If any Ss feel uncomfortable or unable to add extra information to their introduction, don't force them. Ss can share more information later as they become more familiar with you and one another.

Presentation

- Books open. Set the scene. Hold up the Student's Book. Direct Ss' attention to the picture on page 2. Ask the question from Exercise **1A**: *What do you see?* Elicit and write on the board any vocabulary that Ss know, such as: *library, calendar, students, books, book stacks, computer, desk, table, librarian.*

- Direct Ss' attention to Exercise **1B**. Read the question aloud: *What are the people doing?* Hold up the Student's Book. Point to the librarian. Ask: *What is she doing?* Elicit an appropriate answer, for example: *She's talking to some students* or *She's answering questions.* Point to the Ss in front of the librarian. Ask: *What are they doing?* Elicit an appropriate response, for example: *They're listening.*

- Ss in pairs. Have Ss continue the exercise by pointing to people in the picture and asking questions about what they are doing. Walk around and help as needed.

- Ask several pairs to ask and answer the questions for the rest of the class.

Expansion activity (whole group)

- Point to people in the picture and ask more questions, or encourage Ss to think of more questions to ask about the picture.

- Call on Ss individually or put Ss in pairs to ask and answer additional questions, such as: *Who are they? Where are they? Take a guess: Where are they from? What will they do after class? What have they been studying?*

Comprehension check

- Hold up the Student's Book. Ask Ss *Yes / No* questions about the people's actions in the picture. Encourage Ss not to answer with single-word answers *Yes* or *No*, but to use the short form, such as: *Yes, she is. / No, she isn't. / Yes, they are. / No, they aren't.*
  Point to the S writing on paper at the desk. Ask: *Has he been studying?* (Yes, he has.)
  Point to the librarian. Ask: *Has she been studying?* (No, she hasn't.)
  Point to the two Ss walking to the door. Ask: *Are they going someplace else?* (Yes, they are.)
  Point to the Ss listening to the librarian. Ask: *Are they talking to one another?* (No, they aren't.)

Community building (small groups)

- Have small groups of classmates visit your school library or community public library. You can help Ss prepare for their library visit by inviting your school librarian or a librarian from your public library to visit your class to talk about the library's offerings. Work with Ss to prepare some questions for the librarian beforehand. Tell Ss that the purpose of their library visit is to become familiar with their library and also to compare it to the school library in the picture, comparing not only details of the library itself but also of the people in it.

- While they visit the library, have Ss collect any useful information about your community (e.g., a community calendar of cultural events, a newsletter, announcements).

- Invite each group to present its findings to the class at a later date. Follow up with a general discussion of the benefits of your school or community public library.

Welcome

Warm-up

- Books closed. Write the word *adjectives* on the board. Then write the words *strong* and *outgoing*. Ask Ss to brainstorm more examples of adjectives in English. Write these words on the board, or have Ss write them.
- Invite Ss to think of questions they can ask their classmates that can be answered with adjectives. Write Ss' questions on the board, for example: *What are you like?* (I'm nice.) *How would you describe your best friend?* (He's honest, fun-loving, and reliable.)
- Write *activities* on the board. Write the words *dancing* and *cooking*. Ask Ss to brainstorm more examples of activities, including those that they choose to do and those that they have to do.
- Tell Ss that they will practice using this kind of vocabulary in today's lesson.

Presentation

- Books open. Direct Ss' attention to Exercise **2A**. Read the instructions aloud. Ss can use adjectives on the board or think of their own adjectives to complete the exercise.
- Ss complete the exercise individually. Walk around and help as needed.
- When Ss have finished Exercise **2A**, direct their attention to Exercise **2B**. Read the instructions aloud. Ss can use activities written on the board or write their own activities to complete the exercise.
- Ss complete the exercise individually. Walk around and help as needed.

Practice

- Have Ss focus their attention on Exercise **2C**. Read the instructions aloud.
- Ss complete the task in pairs. Walk around and help as needed.
- Direct Ss' attention to Exercise **2D**, and read the instructions aloud.
- Tell Ss to write their partner's name in the blank and to complete the sentences with the information about their partner that they learned in Exercise **2C**.
- Ss work independently to write sentences about their partner. Then Ss check their sentences with their partner. Walk around and help as needed.

Application

- Direct Ss' attention to Exercise **2E**, and read the instructions aloud.
- Model the task. Choose a S to introduce. Say: *This is _____. She is _____. She enjoys _____. She dislikes _____.*
- Have volunteers introduce their partners to the class, using the sentences they wrote in Exercise **2D**.
- Ask each S to introduce his or her partner.

▼ **Teaching tip**
This exercise serves two purposes. It allows Ss to get to know each other, and it allows the teacher to find out on the first day of class how much English Ss already know.

Expansion activity (individual work)

- **Materials needed** Large sheets of drawing paper and colored markers.
- Write on the board: *What do you look like? What do you like to wear? What do you enjoy doing? What do you dislike doing?* Read each question aloud and have Ss repeat.
- Ask each S to draw a self-portrait. Encourage Ss to use the questions on the board as they think about and draw their picture.
- When they have finished drawing, ask individual Ss to show the class their drawings and to speak briefly about themselves.

Evaluation

- Direct Ss' attention to the lesson focus on the board. Ask individual Ss to ask other Ss questions similar to the ones in Exercise **2C**. For example: *What are some adjectives that describe you?* (friendly, intelligent, strong) *What are some activities that you enjoy doing?* (dancing, cooking, playing sports, helping people)
- Listen and make sure that Ss ask and answer questions correctly.
- Check off each part of the lesson focus as Ss demonstrate an understanding of what they have learned in the lesson.

2 Introductions: What kind of person are you?

A Read the list of adjectives. Add two more. Put a check (✓) next to the ones that describe you.

☐ active	☐ confident	☐ intelligent	☐ quiet
☐ artistic	☐ creative	☐ kind	☐ reliable
☐ busy	☐ enthusiastic	☐ nice	☐ shy
☐ careful	☐ friendly	☐ outgoing	☐ strong
☐ caring	☐ fun-loving	☐ patient	☐ _____
☐ clever	☐ honest	☐ punctual	☐ _____

B Read the list of activities. Add two more. Put a check (✓) next to the ones you enjoy doing.

☐ camping	☐ reading	☐ using the Internet
☐ cleaning the house	☐ shopping	☐ volunteering
☐ cooking	☐ singing	☐ washing dishes
☐ dancing	☐ socializing	☐ watching TV
☐ helping people	☐ staying home	☐ working out
☐ painting	☐ talking on the phone	☐ _____
☐ playing sports	☐ traveling	☐ _____

C Talk with a partner. Ask questions. Write your partner's answers.

1. What are some adjectives that describe you?

_____

2. What are some activities that you enjoy doing?

_____

3. What are some activities that you dislike?

_____

D Write sentences about your partner.

My partner's name: _____

1. My partner is _____ .
2. My partner enjoys _____ .
3. My partner dislikes _____ .

E Introduce your partner to the class.

3 Verb tense review

A **Listen** to each sentence. Circle the verb form you hear.

1. (cleans) cleaned
2. lived (has lived)
3. was talking (talked)
4. is looking (is going to look)

5. has been making (is making)
6. (has been working) is working
7. (was watching) is watching
8. were waiting (have been waiting)

Listen again. Check your answers.

B **Read.** Complete the story. Use the correct verb form.

> Last Monday evening, I _was driving_ home from work when
> 1. drive
> I ___had___ a car accident. It ___was___ dark,
> 2. have 3. be
> and it ___was raining___ . About five blocks from my house, I
> 4. rain
> ___stopped___ for a red light. While I ___was waiting___ for
> 5. stop 6. wait
> the light to change, another car ___hit___ my car. I guess
> 7. hit
> the driver ___didn't see___ me because of the rain. The accident
> 8. not / see
> ___damaged___ my car badly.
> 9. damage
>
> Since the accident, I _have been going_ to work by bus. It's
> 10. go
> really inconvenient because I ___work___ more than 20
> 11. work
> miles from my home. The bus is slow, and I ___have been___
> 12. be
> late several times already. It ___will take___ at least two more
> 13. take
> weeks to fix my car. Until then, I ___need___ to find a
> 14. need
> better way to get to work. I ___don't want___ to be late anymore.
> 15. not / want

Listen and check your answers.

C **Talk** in a small group. Ask and answer the questions.

1. Have you ever had or seen a car accident?
2. What were you doing before the accident happened?
3. Describe the accident. Explain what happened.

Lesson objectives

- Review these verb forms: simple present, present continuous, simple past, present perfect, present perfect continuous, past continuous, and future with *be going to*
- Read and talk about car accidents

Warm-up and review

- Before class. Write today's lesson focus on the board.
  Welcome unit:
  Review verb forms
  Read and talk about a car accident
- Begin class. Books closed. Write the following questions on the board:
  What do you do for a living? (simple present)
  What am I doing right now? (present continuous)
  What did you do on your last birthday? (simple past)
  What kind of work have you done in the past?
  (present perfect)
  How long have you been working at your present job?
  (present perfect continuous)
  What were you doing this time last year?
  (past continuous)
  What are you going to do this time next year? (future
  with *be going to*)
- Point to the first question. Ask a S to tell you what he or she does for a living, using the present tense. Elicit appropriate answers, such as: *I work in a restaurant. I work in a doctor's office. I drive a truck.* Continue with the remaining questions.
- Write several answers on the board. There should be at least one answer per question on the board.
- Call on individual Ss to come to the board, underline the verbs, and identify the verb form (simple present, present continuous, simple past, present perfect, present perfect continuous, past continuous, or future with *be going to*). Help Ss as needed.

Presentation

- Books open. Direct Ss' attention to Exercise **3A**, and read the instructions aloud.
- [Class Audio CD1 track 2] Model the task. Play or read the audio program for number 1 (see audio script, page T-155). Pause the audio program after the first sentence. Write *cleans* and *cleaned* on the board. Ask: *Which verb should I circle?* (cleans)
- Hold up the Student's Book. Point to the circled example answer *cleans* in number 1. Say: *Listen and circle the correct verb form for the rest of the sentences.*
- [Class Audio CD1 track 2] Play or read the rest of the audio program (see audio script, page T-155). Ss listen and complete the exercise individually.

- Focus Ss' attention on the second part of Exercise **3A**. Read the instructions aloud.
- [Class Audio CD1 track 3] Play or read the audio program again (see audio script, page T-155). Ss listen and check their answers.

Learner persistence *(individual work)*

- [Self-Study Audio CD tracks 2 and 3] Exercises **3A** and **3B** are recorded on the Ss' self-study CD at the back of the Student's Book. Ss can listen to the CD at home for reinforcement and review. They can also listen to the CD for self-directed learning when class attendance is not possible.

Practice

- Direct Ss' attention to Exercise **3B**, and read the instructions aloud.
- Model the task. Ask a S to read the first sentence aloud, including the example answer in number 1 and filling in the correct verb form in number 2. Ask Ss: *Is the answer for number 2 correct?* Have Ss correct if needed.
- Ss complete the exercise individually. Walk around and help as needed.
- Direct Ss' attention to the second part of the instructions for Exercise **3B**.
- [Class Audio CD1 track 4] Play or read the audio program again (see audio script, page T-155). Ss listen and check their answers.
- Write the numbers *1–15* on the board. Ask individual Ss to come to the board to write their answers. Ask other Ss if the answers are correct. Make corrections on the board as needed.

Application

- Direct Ss' attention to Exercise **3C**. Read the instructions aloud.
- Model the task. Ask for a volunteer to answer the first question.
- Ss work in small groups to complete the activity. Walk around and help as needed.
- Have several Ss ask and answer the questions for the rest of the class. Make sure that Ss use the correct verb form when responding to the questions.

Warm-up and review

- Write on the board: *study habits* and *strategies*. Point to the words. Ask: *What are study habits? What are strategies?* Elicit appropriate responses, such as: *Study habits are the ways that we usually study. Strategies are things you do to achieve a goal (such as learning English).*
- Tell Ss one of your study habits, for example: *I always like to study in the library.* Tell Ss one of your strategies. Say: *When I was studying Spanish, and I learned new words, I always made vocabulary cards.*

Presentation

- Direct Ss' attention to the chart in Exercise **4A**, and read the instructions aloud.
- Model the task. Ask a S: *Have you ever made vocabulary cards?* Tell Ss that they will be working with a partner to record their partner's answers by writing a check mark in the appropriate column in the chart.
- Ss complete the activity in pairs. Walk around and help as needed.
- After several minutes, have Ss change partners.
- Call on a S to read the second part of the instructions for Exercise **4A**.
- Ss complete the activity with a different partner. Walk around and help as needed.
- Ask individual Ss to tell the class about the study habits and strategies of the first partner they interviewed.

Practice

- Focus Ss' attention on Exercise **4B**, and read the instructions aloud.
- Model the task. Ask a S to read aloud the example question and answer.
- Remind Ss that they use the phrases in the book to form *Yes / No* questions in order to get the information they need to fill in the chart.

- Ss complete the exercise by talking to several Ss in order to get a positive answer to each of the eight questions. If a S answers *No* to one question, the interviewer should continue asking questions until he or she gets a *Yes* response. Ss should not write a classmate's name in the chart more than twice. Walk around and help as needed.

Application

- Direct Ss' attention to the second part of the instructions for Exercise **4B**. Call on individual Ss to say one thing they learned about another classmate's study habits or strategies.

  Option Draw a chart on the board with the eight different strategies from the chart in Exercise **4B** (*watches TV in English every day, asks questions when he or she doesn't understand, underlines important information in textbooks,* etc.). Call out each strategy, and ask Ss to raise their hands if they practice the strategy. Count how many Ss practice each strategy, and write the tally on the board. Discuss the results together.

Evaluation

- Direct Ss' attention to the lesson focus on the board.
- Write on the board: *simple present, present continuous, simple past, present perfect, present perfect continuous, past continuous,* and *future with "be going to."* Encourage Ss to give you examples of sentences in each of these verb forms.
- Ask several Ss in the class to tell you a study habit that is not on Student's Book page 5. Have them tell you one study strategy they plan to use in the future.
- Write on the board Ss' ideas for study habits and strategies.
- Check off each part of the lesson focus as Ss demonstrate an understanding of what they have learned in the lesson.

4 Study habits and strategies

A **Talk** with a partner about study habits and strategies for learning English. Ask questions. Check (✓) your partner's answers.

Partner's name: _____ Have you ever . . . ?	Yes, I have.	No, I haven't.
made vocabulary cards		
used a dictionary to learn new words		
asked a stranger a question in English		
studied English with a friend		
used a to-do list to organize your time		
tried to guess the meaning of new words		

Talk with a different partner. Tell about the classmate you interviewed.

> Carmen has made vocabulary cards. She hasn't used a to-do list.

B **Talk** with your classmates. Complete the chart.

> Song Mi, do you watch TV in English every day?

> Yes, I do.

Find a classmate who . . .	Name
1. watches TV in English every day	*Song Mi*
2. asks questions when he or she doesn't understand	
3. underlines important information in textbooks	
4. likes to sing songs in English	
5. speaks English at work	
6. sets goals for learning	
7. writes new English words in a notebook	
8. reads newspapers and magazines in English	

Share information about your classmates.

> Song Mi watches TV in English every day.

Get ready

1 Talk about the pictures

A What do you see?
B What is happening?

Emily

Nina

Lesson objectives
- Introduce students to the topic
- Find out what students know about the topic
- Preview the unit by talking about the pictures
- Practice key vocabulary
- Practice listening skills

Warm-up and review

- Before class. Write today's lesson focus on the board. *Lesson A:*
  Ask about aptitudes
  Discuss multiple intelligences
  Give opinions

- Begin class. Books closed. Point to *Ask about aptitudes* in the lesson focus. Say the words aloud. Ask: *What are some examples of aptitudes?* Since this language may be new to Ss, you should start them off with some examples, such as *artistic, athletic, mechanical, mathematical, musical.* Tell Ss that these are personal strengths. On the board, write these words and any other examples that Ss brainstorm.

- Point to each word on the board and say the words aloud. Make sure that all Ss understand the meaning of each word.

- Ask: *What are your personal strengths? Are you _____?* (Point to each word on the board in turn.) Ss can say *yes* or *no* in response.

Presentation

- Books open. Set the scene. Direct Ss' attention to Picture 1 on page 6. Ask the question from Exercise **1A**: *What do you see?* Elicit and write on the board as much vocabulary about the picture as possible: *kitchen, food, cooking, jogging clothes, apron.* Continue eliciting words to describe the remaining pictures.

- Direct Ss' attention to the question in Exercise **1B**. Read it aloud. Ask individual Ss to describe what is happening in each of the pictures. Elicit appropriate responses, such as: *Emily has just finished jogging. Emily and Nina are talking. Nina is cooking in the kitchen. The girl is doing her homework. The boy is playing the guitar. The other boy is fixing the car.*

▼ **Teaching tip**
Encourage Ss to be creative. At this point, there is no single correct answer.

Practice

- Direct Ss' attention to Emily in the first picture and again ask what she has just been doing.

- Ask Ss: *Does anyone like to jog?* If some Ss answer *yes,* find out where and how often they like to run. Ask Ss who say they jog if they are athletic.

- Direct Ss' attention to Nina in Picture 1. Ask Ss: *Do you like to cook?* Ask Ss who answer *yes* what they like to make and how often they cook. Write *gifted in cooking* on the board. Ask Ss what that means, and try to elicit the definition.

- Direct Ss' attention to the young woman in Picture 2. Ask Ss: *What is she doing?* (She's studying.) *Do you like to study English?* When your Ss say *yes,* tell them that if they like to study – or study frequently – then we would say they are studious. Write *studious* on the board.

- Direct Ss' attention to the boy playing the guitar. Say: *If someone is good at playing music, we say that he or she is musical.*

- Direct Ss' attention to the picture of the young man fixing a car. Ask Ss: *What is this young man doing?* (He's working on a car.) Tell Ss that when someone is talented at fixing things, we say that the person is *mechanical.*

Expansion activity *(student pairs)*

- Have Ss work in pairs. Direct Ss' attention to the four pictures on page 6. Tell Ss that they are going to think of and practice a conversation between any two of the people in the pictures. Ss should use information from the picture, and each person should speak at least five times. Encourage Ss to use the different verb forms they reviewed in the Welcome unit.

- Model the activity. Ask Ss to come up with the beginning of the conversation as a class. Write the beginning of the conversation on the board.

- Ss finish the conversation in pairs. Walk around and help as needed.

- If you have enough class time, ask several pairs to role-play the conversation for the rest of the class.

- As a follow-up (either in class or at home), have Ss choose one of the people in any of the pictures and write a description of his or her day, again recycling information from the verb review in the Welcome unit.

Presentation

- Books open. Direct Ss' attention to Exercise **2A**. Read the instructions aloud. Tell Ss that they are going to hear a conversation between Nina and Emily, the two women in Picture 1 on page 6. Have Ss listen for the main ideas.
- 💿 [Class Audio CD1 track 5] Play or read the audio program (see audio script, page T-155).
- Ask Ss if they understand everything in the listening exercise. Write any unfamiliar words on the board, and help Ss understand the meaning of each of the new words.
- Elicit answers to the questions.
- Focus Ss' attention on Exercise **2B**. Read the instructions aloud. Tell Ss to listen and complete the chart based on the information they hear.
- 💿 [Class Audio CD1 track 6] Play or read the audio program again. Tell Ss to listen for details about Emily, Nina, and Nina's children. Model the task. Pause the program after Nina says: *Yes, it's true! She's really good at math. She just loves it.* Call on a S to read the example answers in the chart (*math, got first place in a math contest*). Tell Ss to listen and complete the chart individually.
- Play or read the rest of the audio program.
- Read aloud the second part of the instructions for Exercise **2B**.
- 💿 [Class Audio CD1 track 6] Play or read the audio program again (see audio script, page T-155). Ss listen and check their answers. Repeat the audio program as needed.
- Write the chart on the board. Ask Ss to come to the board to write the answers.

Practice

- Focus Ss' attention on Exercise **2C**. Read the instructions aloud. Tell Ss that the story in this exercise is a summary of what happened in the pictures on page 6. Review with Ss the idea that a summary contains the most important (or key) points of a story.
- Direct Ss' attention to the words or phrases in the word bank. Say each word or phrase aloud. Ask Ss to repeat. Correct pronunciation as needed.
- Ask Ss if they know the meaning of each word in the word bank. Explain any new words. Explain the similarities between *aptitude for* (we say someone *has* an aptitude for a particular subject), *gifted in*, and *talented*

in, and how we use them. Have Ss note the different prepositions that are used with each word.
- Ss complete the exercise individually. Help as needed.

Comprehension check

- 💿 [Class Audio CD1 track 7] Play or read the audio program (see audio script, page T-155). Ss listen and check their answers. Repeat the audio program as needed.
- Write the numbers *1–8* on the board. Ask individual Ss to come to the board to write their answers.
- Ask the class: *Are these answers correct?* Make any corrections on the board.

Learner persistence (individual work)

- 💿 [Self-Study Audio CD tracks 4 and 5] Exercises **2A**, **2B**, and **2C** are recorded on the Ss' self-study CD at the back of the Student's Book. Ss can listen to the CD at home for reinforcement and review. They can also listen to the CD for self-directed learning when class attendance is not possible.

Application

- Focus Ss' attention on Exercise **2D**. Read the instructions aloud.
- Model the task. Ask a S the first question in the exercise. Have Ss listen to the answer.
- Ss complete the exercise in pairs. Help as needed.
- Ask several pairs to ask and answer the questions for the rest of the class.

Evaluation

- Direct Ss' attention to the lesson focus written on the board. Ask individual Ss to tell you about Nina and her personal strengths as well as those of her children. Ask other Ss to tell you about their own personal strengths.
- Check off each part of the lesson focus as Ss demonstrate an understanding of what they have learned in the lesson.

More Ventures (whole group, pairs, individual)
Assign appropriate exercises from the *Teacher's Toolkit Audio CD / CD-ROM, Add Ventures,* or the *Workbook.*

---

2 Listening

 **A** **Listen** and answer the questions.

1. Who are the speakers?
2. What are they talking about?

 **B** **Listen again.** Complete the chart.

Family member	Good at	Example
1. Brenda	*math*	*got first place in a math contest*
2. Gerry	*music*	*plays four instruments / sings really well*
3. Danny	*mechanics*	*fixed up an old car*
4. Nina	*cooking*	*cooking dinner for 14 people*

Listen again. Check your answers.

 **C** **Read.** Complete the story. Listen and check your answers.

aptitude	bright	gifted in	mechanical
brain	fixing up	mathematical	musical

Emily stops by Nina's house on her way home from jogging. They talk about Nina's three children. Brenda is very _mathematical_ (1). She's just won a math contest at school. When Emily calls Brenda a _brain_ (2), Nina says that all her children are _bright_ (3), but in different ways. Gerry isn't _gifted in_ (4) math, but he's very _musical_ (5). He plays and sings very well and even writes music. Danny is the _mechanical_ (6) one in the family. He's good at _fixing up_ (7) old cars. Emily thinks that Nina is also smart because she is such a good cook. Emily has no _aptitude_ (8) for cooking.

D **Discuss.** Talk with your classmates.

1. How are the three children different?
2. Do you think that one child is more intelligent than the others? Why or why not?
3. Do you think that Nina is a good parent? Why or why not?

Noun clauses

1 **Grammar focus:** noun clauses with *that*

Statements and questions

Emily realizes that Brenda has a good brain.
People say that Gerry plays the guitar very well.
Do you think that people are smart in different ways?
Do you feel that you're smart?

Introductory clauses

I think . . .	Do you think . . . ?
I feel . . .	Do you feel . . . ?
He realizes . . .	Does he realize . . . ?
People believe . . .	Do people believe . . . ?

For a grammar explanation, turn to page 146.

Useful language

When speaking, we frequently omit *that* before a noun clause.

*People think **that** she's smart.*
People think she's smart.

2 **Practice**

A **Write.** Write sentences with *that* and a noun clause.

1. There are many kinds of intelligence. (Do you believe . . . ?)
   Do you believe that there are many kinds of intelligence?

2. Nina has an interesting family. (Do you think . . . ?)
   Do you think that Nina has an interesting family?

3. She is very gifted in math. (Brenda's teacher agrees . . .)
   Brenda's teacher agrees that she is very gifted in math.

4. Gerry will be a famous musician someday. (Everyone believes . . .)
   Everyone believes that Gerry will be a famous musician someday.

5. Danny has an aptitude for fixing up cars. (I didn't realize . . .)
   I didn't realize that Danny has an aptitude for fixing up cars.

6. Mechanical skills are very important. (Do you feel . . . ?)
   Do you feel that mechanical skills are very important?

7. Nina is good at cooking. (Do you think . . . ?)
   Do you think that Nina is good at cooking?

Listen and check your answers.

Lesson objectives
- Introduce noun clauses with *that*
- Practice expressing opinions

Warm-up and review

- Before class. Write today's lesson focus on the board. *Lesson B:*
  Use noun clauses with that
  Express opinions
- Begin class. Books open. Direct Ss' attention to the pictures on page 6. Review key vocabulary from the unit by asking Ss questions about Nina and Emily. Ask Ss *Yes / No* questions using words to describe aptitudes, for example: *Does Nina have an aptitude for cooking? Is Emily athletic?*
- Point to the words on the board: *Express opinions*. Ask Ss to explain what this means (to say what your ideas are about a particular thing, person, or situation). Tell Ss that they will be learning about specific language we use to express opinions in English.

Presentation

- Direct Ss' attention to the *Statements and questions* list in the grammar chart in Exercise **1**. Read aloud each statement and question. Ask Ss to repeat.
- Read aloud the *Introductory clauses* list. Ask Ss to repeat.

Useful language

Read the tip box aloud. Ask Ss to repeat the two example sentences. Tell them that we sometimes omit *that* in questions, too. Start with the examples in Exercise **1** using *that*. Have one S ask a question starting with *Do you think that . . .* and another S answer: *I think that . . .* Continue until you have practiced all the introductory clauses. Write Ss' questions and answers on the board. Follow up by calling on Ss to read these examples, this time omitting *that*. Conclude by reminding Ss that the omission of *that* generally occurs in speaking as opposed to writing.

▼ Teaching tip

It might be helpful to refer Ss to the grammar explanation on page 146 in the Student's Book.

Practice

- Direct Ss' attention to Exercise **2A**. Read the instructions aloud. Ask a S to read aloud the example, and make sure that Ss understand the exercise.
- Ss complete the sentences individually. Walk around and help as needed.

Comprehension check

- Write the numbers *1–7* on the board. Ask volunteers to come to the board to write the correct answers to Exercise **2A** next to each number. Ask the class: *Are these answers correct?* Make any corrections on the board.
- [Class Audio CD1 track 8] Play or read the audio program (see audio script, page T-155). Have Ss check their answers as they listen.

Expansion activity *(student pairs)*

- Write two columns on the board with the headings: *Strengths* and *Job possibilities*.
- Ask Ss to work in pairs. Ss copy the headings and list the aptitudes that were discussed in class, along with jobs that would be a good match. Model and review job-related vocabulary as needed.
- Walk around and help as needed.
- After several minutes, ask Ss to share their answers.
- Lead a class discussion based on the information the class has gathered. Find out if Ss agree or disagree with the matching of certain skills and professions.

Learner persistence *(individual or whole group)*

- If some Ss have real-life interest in employment or career choices, you can have them read the "help-wanted" section in the local newspaper, visit the school employment office, or visit online employment Web sites. You can also use some of the ads as a basis for a lesson about the skills and talents needed for specific jobs.

Lesson B Noun clauses

Presentation

- Direct Ss' attention to the picture in Exercise **2B**. Ask Ss to look at the people in the picture. Ask: *What can you say about the man next to the car?* Elicit appropriate responses, such as: *I think he's athletic. I think he's about 30 years old.*
- Read the instructions aloud. Read the words in the word bank and have Ss repeat.
- Model the exercise. Ask two Ss to read aloud the first example conversation.
- Have Ss work in pairs to talk about the picture. Walk around and help as needed.
- Call on pairs to share their conversations with the class.

▼ **Teaching tip**
Ss may need clarification about the usage of these expressions. Explain that *I suppose* and *I'd say* are similar to saying *maybe*. Using them is a bit "softer" than *I'm sure, I believe*, and *I think*.

Practice

- Read aloud the second part of the instructions for Exercise **2B**.
- Ask a S to read the example sentence.
- Have Ss work individually to write their opinions. After several minutes, have Ss compare their sentences with a partner.
- Call on Ss to share their sentences with the class.

Application

- Direct Ss' attention to Exercise **3A**. Read the instructions aloud.

Useful language
Read the tip box aloud. Ask Ss to repeat the statements after you. Explain that *totally* and *strongly* make the statements much stronger. You can ask Ss if they have heard other words like this – adverbs – that make opinions stronger (*definitely, completely*).

- Ss work in small groups to complete the exercise. Encourage Ss to use language from the Useful language box when appropriate. Help as needed.

▼ **Teaching tip**
Ss from certain cultures may be unaccustomed to expressing opinions aloud, especially strong opinions. For these Ss, writing opinions is sometimes easier. Allow Ss the option of not using adverbs for emphasis if they do not feel comfortable doing so.

- After several minutes, read the instructions aloud for Exercise **3B**.
- Model the task. Ask Ss what they learned in Exercise **3A** about the opinions of the people in their group, for example: (Student's name) *doesn't believe that . . .*

Culture note
Read the culture note aloud. Ask Ss what they think happens concerning girls' and boys' aptitudes for math and science *after* elementary school. Ask Ss to share their opinions about this information.

Expansion activity (individual work, small groups)

- Tell Ss that they are going to give a presentation based on one of the beliefs they discussed in Exercise **3A**.
- Ask Ss to write down their "belief" statement and then several sentences to support their belief.
- Ask Ss to work in small groups to present their information to their classmates. After each presentation, Ss can agree or disagree with the presenter.
- When the groups are finished with the presentations, have some Ss share their belief statements with the class.

Evaluation

- Direct Ss' attention to the lesson focus written on the board.
- Write on the board: *I believe, I think, I'd say, I'm sure.* Then write: *mathematical, mechanical, musical,* and *gifted in art.* Then write: *I think that, I believe that, I strongly agree that, I disagree that.* Ask each S to make a sentence describing someone's aptitude or skill using the words on the board. Write some Ss' sentences on the board.
- Check off each part of the lesson focus as Ss demonstrate an understanding of what they have learned in the lesson.

More Ventures (whole group, pairs, individual)
Assign appropriate exercises from the *Teacher's Toolkit Audio CD / CD-ROM, Add Ventures,* or the *Workbook.*

B **Talk** with a partner. Look at the picture. Answer the questions. Use introductory clauses from the box.

| I believe . . . | I suppose . . . | I think . . . | I'd say . . . | I'm sure . . . |

> **A** I think (that) the young man is about 26.
> **B** I'd say (that) the young man is only 20.

1. How old are they?
2. Where are they going?
3. Where are they coming from?

4. What do they do for a living?
5. What are they good at?
6. What aren't they good at?

Write sentences about your opinions.

I think that the young man is about 26 years old.

3 Communicate

A **Work** in a small group. Give your opinions. Use *I believe*, *I think*, *I'd say*, *I don't believe*, and other introductory clauses.

1. Are women more talkative than men?
2. Are boys better at math and science than girls?
3. Are men more mechanical than women?
4. Are women more musical than men?
5. Are men more interested in sports than women?
6. Can women do the same jobs as men?

B **Share** your classmates' opinions.

Useful language
I (totally) agree with you.
I (strongly) disagree.

Culture note
Studies have shown that girls and boys in the United States have a similar aptitude for math and science when they start elementary school.

1 Grammar focus: contrasting adjectives and adverbs

Adjectives

Helen is an intelligent girl.
I am a slow driver.
You're a good dancer.
It was an easy game.

Adverbs

She talks very intelligently.
I drive slowly.
You dance well.
He won easily.

Irregular	
Adjectives	**Adverbs**
fast	fast
good	well
hard	hard

For a grammar explanation, turn to page 146.

2 Practice

A Write. Complete the sentences with adjectives or adverbs.

1. Carol speaks very ____*intelligently*____ . She's a ____*bright*____ girl.
   (intelligent) (bright)

2. That isn't a ____*bad*____ guitar, but he's playing it ____*badly*____ .
   (bad) (bad)

3. Benny is an ____*excellent*____ cook. His dinner last night was ____*fantastic*____ .
   (excellent) (fantastic)

4. The mechanic did a ____*good*____ job on my car. Now it runs ____*perfectly*____ .
   (good) (perfect)

5. You danced very ____*skillfully*____ in the dance contest. You were ____*wonderful*____ !
   (skillful) (wonderful)

6. I don't type very ____*fast*____ . I can't move my fingers very ____*quickly*____ .
   (fast) (quick)

7. That writing test was really ____*hard*____ . Writing is not an ____*easy*____
   (hard) (easy)

   subject for me.

8. You sang that song ____*beautifully*____ ! I didn't know you could sing
   (beautiful)

   so ____*well*____ !
   (good)

9. Your report is ____*great*____ . You wrote it very ____*clearly*____ .
   (great) (clear)

10. I work ____*slowly*____ . I have to be very ____*careful*____ .
    (slow) (careful)

Listen and check your answers.

Lesson objectives
- Contrast adjectives and adverbs
- Describe skills using adjectives and adverbs

Warm-up and review

- Before class. Write today's lesson focus on the board. *Lesson C: Contrasting adjectives and adverbs*
- Begin class. Books closed. Ask Ss to brainstorm a list of adjectives (*happy, quick, slow, careful,* etc.)
- Write on the board: *I am a quick eater. I eat quickly.*
- Start a separate column and write: *He is a good guitarist. He plays well.*
- Ask Ss to tell you the difference between the underlined words in each sentence, starting with *quick* and *quickly* (the meaning is the same, but *quick* is an adjective and *quickly* is an adverb). Tell Ss that in both sentences, the words *quick* and *quickly* are describing something. Adjectives describe nouns or other adjectives, and adverbs describe verbs or other adverbs. In the first sentence, *quick* describes the noun *eater,* and in the second sentence, the word *quickly* describes the verb *eat.* Tell Ss that most adverbs are formed by adding *-ly* to the adjective.
- Focus Ss' attention on the second set of sentences. Ask again what the difference is between the two underlined words (the meaning is very similar, but *good* describes the guitarist, and *well* describes how he plays). Tell Ss that irregular adverbs do not follow the same rule of adding *-ly* to the adjective and that they must be learned.
- Tell Ss that in this lesson, they will learn how to use adjectives and adverbs in English.

Presentation

- Books open. Direct Ss' attention to the grammar chart in Exercise **1**. Read each sentence under *Adjectives* and the corresponding sentences under *Adverbs*. Ask Ss to repeat.
- Ask Ss if they notice anything about changing *easy* to an adverb. Point out that the *y* changes into an *i* and then we add *-ly*.
- Read aloud the irregular adjectives and adverbs and have Ss repeat each one.
- Ask Ss if they notice any similarities or differences between the two categories (*fast* and *hard* are the same in the adjectival and adverbial form).

▼ **Teaching tip**
It might be helpful to refer Ss to the grammar explanation on page 146 in the Student's Book.

▼ **Teaching tip**
Point out the correct usage of *good* and *well.* Tell Ss that although *well* may be the "correct" response to *How are you?* or *How are you doing?,* many people use *good* as a response. Tell Ss that both *well* and *good* are accepted in daily conversation, but that *good* is informal and should not be used in formal situations or in writing.

Practice

- Direct Ss' attention to Exercise **2A**. Read the instructions aloud.
- Ask a S to read aloud the example sentence. Make sure Ss understand the exercise.
- Ss complete the exercise individually. Walk around and help as needed.

Comprehension check

- Read aloud the second part of the instructions for Exercise **2A**.
- 💿 [Class Audio CD1 track 9] Play or read aloud the audio program (see audio script, page T-155). Ss listen and check their answers.
- Write the numbers *1–10* on the board. Have Ss come to the board to write their answers.

Expansion activity *(small groups)*

- Tell Ss that adverbs and adjectives are useful when telling a story. Guide Ss to see that they are going to tell a story using the adjectives and adverbs from this lesson.
- Write on the board: *Once upon a time, there was a musician named Gerry. . . .*
- Tell Ss that they are going to finish the story, one sentence at a time, using as many adjectives and adverbs as they can from the lesson. Have Ss work in small groups. One person starts by reading the sentence on the board and creating a second sentence. The next S creates a third sentence, and so on. Each S should have a chance to say at least two sentences.
- After five minutes, stop the storytelling. Ask each group to share its story.
- You can have the Ss do a follow-up assignment of writing their group story (or a new story) for homework.

Lesson C Parts of speech

Practice

- Books open. Direct Ss' attention to the pictures in Exercise **2B**. Read the instructions aloud.
- Explain that Ss will use the words in the word bank and the words below the pictures to talk about the pictures. Make sure that Ss understand the exercise.
- Model the task. Ask two Ss to read aloud the example conversations. Then have Ss complete the exercise in pairs.
- Read aloud the second part of the instructions for Exercise **2B**. Ask a S to read the example sentence to the class.
- Ss complete this part of the exercise individually. Walk around and help as needed.
- Ask different Ss to write their sentences on the board. Ask other Ss to read aloud each sentence. Ask: *Is this sentence correct?* Make corrections on the board as needed.

Application

- Direct Ss' attention to Exercise **3A**. Read the instructions aloud.
- Model the task. Ask one S to read aloud the first question and another S to answer.
- Ss complete the exercise in small groups. Walk around and help as needed.
- Direct Ss' attention to Exercise **3B**. Read the instructions aloud.
- Ask different Ss to share information about their classmates with the class.

Expansion activity (small groups)

- **Materials needed** A set of index cards for each group, with a list of jobs, such as: *dancer, carpenter, mechanic, teacher, artist, dentist, truck driver*. Review occupations, if needed.

- Model the activity. Ask a S to choose one of the cards and use that information to make a sentence about himself or herself or a friend or family member (*I am a dancer. My sister is a teacher.*). Then call on another S to make a statement about the first S using an adjective and adverb, for example: *I think that you're a great dancer. I think you dance beautifully. I'm sure that your sister is a good teacher. I'm sure that your sister teaches well.*
- Ss in small groups. Have each group sit in a circle. Give each group a set of index cards, and ask Ss to distribute them. One S begins by making a sentence with the word on his or her card, and the next S in the circle should comment on the first S's sentence using both an adjective and an adverb. (*I think that he's a good carpenter. He works carefully.*)
- Continue for several minutes or until each S has had a chance to create sentences. Call on groups to share sample sentences. Write them on the board.

Learner persistence (whole group)

- Brainstorm different ways of keeping up with English lessons when Ss miss a class. Write ideas on the board, for example: *Practice the last lesson. Do Workbook exercises. Call a classmate and ask about class. Listen and repeat exercises on the Self-Study Audio CD. Call or e-mail your teacher for help.*

Evaluation

- Direct Ss' attention to the lesson focus written on the board. Ask Ss to tell you something about their skills and talents (or those of their classmates) using adjectives and adverbs.
- Check off each part of the lesson focus as Ss demonstrate an understanding of what they have learned in the lesson.

> **More Ventures** (whole group, pairs, individual)
> Assign appropriate exercises from the *Teacher's Toolkit Audio CD / CD-ROM, Add Ventures*, or the *Workbook*.

B **Talk** with a partner. Ask and answer questions about the pictures.
Use the adjective or adverb form of the words in the box.

> *A* What kind of artist is he?
> *B* He's a skillful artist.

> *A* How does he paint?
> *B* He paints beautifully.

beautiful	excellent	good	skillful
careful	fast	professional	wonderful

artist / paint

seamstress / sew

driver / drive

carpenter / work

singer / sing

dancers / dance

Write sentences about the people.

He's a skillful artist. He paints beautifully.

3 Communicate

A **Work** in a small group. Ask and answer the questions.

1. What kind of student are you?
2. How do you speak English?
3. What can you do very well?
4. What is difficult for you?
5. What can you do perfectly?
6. What do you do very fast?

B **Share** information about your classmates.

> Armando says he's an excellent student.

1 Before you read

Talk with a partner. Look at the reading tip. Answer the questions.

1. What is this article about?
2. How many ways are there to be smart, according to the article?

Before you begin reading, skim — look at the title, headings, and boldfaced words — to get a general idea of what the reading is about.

2 Read

SELF-STUDY AUDIO CD

 Read the magazine article. Listen and read again.

Many Ways to Be Smart

Josh is a star on the school baseball team. He gets Ds and Fs on all his math tests. His brother Frank can't catch, throw, or hit a baseball, but he easily gets As in math. Which boy do you think is more intelligent? Howard Gardner, a professor of education at Harvard University, would say that Josh and Frank are both smart, but in different ways. His theory of multiple intelligences identifies eight different "intelligences" to explain the way people understand, experience, and learn about the world around them.

Verbal / Linguistic
Some people are good with words. They prefer to learn by reading, listening, and speaking.

Bodily / Kinesthetic
Some people are "body smart." They are often athletic. Kinesthetic learners learn best when they are moving.

Logical / Mathematical
These people have an aptitude for math. They like solving logic problems and puzzles.

Interpersonal
Certain people are "group smart." They easily understand other people. They are good at communicating and interacting with others.

Musical / Rhythmical
These people are sensitive to sound, melodies, and rhythms. They are gifted in singing, playing instruments, or composing music.

Intrapersonal
Some people are "self smart." They can understand their own feelings and emotions. They often enjoy spending time alone.

Visual / Spatial
These "picture people" are often good at drawing or painting. They are sensitive to colors and designs.

Naturalist
These people are skilled in working with plants and animals in the natural world.

According to Gardner, many people have several or even all of these intelligences, but most of us have one or two intelligences that are primary, or strongest.

Lesson objectives

- Introduce and read "Many Ways to Be Smart"
- Practice using new topic-related vocabulary
- Skim to predict what a reading is about
- Discuss multiple intelligences

Warm-up and review

- Before class. Write today's lesson focus on the board.
  Lesson D:
  Read and understand "Many Ways to Be Smart"
  Learn new vocabulary about multiple intelligences
  Learn to skim to predict
- Begin class. Books closed. Write *intelligent* on the board. Draw a circle around it to create a word web. Ask Ss to brainstorm other words that explain or mean the same thing as *intelligent*. Write the words on the board around the circle, for example: *smart, talented, skillful, able to solve problems.*

Presentation

- Books open. Direct Ss' attention to Exercise **1**. Read the instructions aloud.

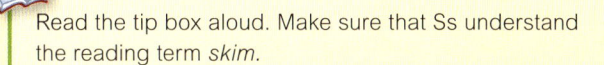

Read the tip box aloud. Make sure that Ss understand the reading term *skim*.

- Direct Ss' attention to the first question in Exercise **1**. Ask a S to read it aloud. Have the S read the title of the article. Remind Ss that the title is going to help them figure out what the reading is about. Elicit appropriate responses, such as: *It's about how people are smart. / It's about different ways that people are intelligent.*
- Ask a different S to read question number 2. Encourage Ss to skim the article and pay attention to the boldfaced headings in the reading before answering the question.

Practice

- Read aloud the instructions for Exercise **2**. Ask Ss to read the article silently before listening to the audio program.
- [Class Audio CD1 track 10] Play or read the audio program, and ask Ss to read along (see audio script, page T-155). Repeat the audio program as needed.
- While Ss are listening to and reading the article, ask them to write in their notebooks any new words they don't understand. When the audio program is finished, ask Ss to write the new vocabulary words on the board.

- Point to each word on the board. Say each word aloud and have Ss repeat. Give a brief explanation of each word, or ask Ss to explain the words if they are familiar with them. If Ss prefer to look up the new words in their dictionaries, allow them to do so.

▼ Teaching tip

If Ss come from the same language background, ask them to help each other translate unfamiliar words into their own language. This encourages a sense of community and ownership in the learning process.

- Encourage Ss to find the meaning of each new word from the context of the article. For example, if a S writes *kinesthetic* on the board, show how the meaning of the word is explained in the article: *Some people are "body smart." They are often athletic. Kinesthetic learners learn best when they are moving.*
- You may need to review the pronunciation of several of the vocabulary words, such as *kinesthetic* and *intrapersonal* versus *interpersonal*.

Learner persistence *(individual work)*

- [Self-Study Audio CD track 6] Exercise **2** is recorded on the Ss' self-study CD at the back of the Student's Book. Ss can listen to the CD at home for reinforcement and review. They can also listen to the CD for self-directed learning when class attendance is not possible.

Expansion activity *(small groups)*

- Tell Ss that they are going to discuss their opinions about the articles. Recycle the language learned in Lesson B, and review ways to begin a sentence that expresses an opinion. Write examples on the board: *I think that . . . , I believe that . . . , I strongly agree . . . ,* etc.
- Ss in small groups. Tell Ss that they should each take turns expressing their opinions about the article to other members of their group. They should support their opinions with examples.

Lesson D *Reading*

Comprehension check

- Direct Ss' attention to Exercise **3A**. Read the instructions aloud.
- Ask six Ss to read the statements aloud, one at a time. Make sure that all Ss understand them.
- Ss in pairs. Ask Ss to work with a partner to identify the primary intelligence of each person in the chart. Tell them that they can refer to the reading on page 12.
- Review by writing the numbers *1–6* on the board. Ask Ss to tell you the answers, and write each one next to the corresponding number.
- Review pronunciation as needed.

▼ **Teaching tip**
Using the dictionary may be new to some Ss. If so, spend some time reviewing dictionary usage. You can copy a dictionary page, review the components of each entry, and give a separate dictionary assignment for further practice if necessary.

Practice

- Direct Ss' attention to Exercise **3B**. Ask a S to read the instructions aloud. Make sure each S has a dictionary (or can share one with a partner).
- Write the words *prefix* and *root* on the board. Say each word aloud and have Ss repeat. Ask Ss if they have heard these words before. Tell Ss that a prefix is a letter or group of letters added to the beginning of a word to change the meaning or make a new word. Tell Ss that a root is the basic form of a word, and that we can add prefixes to roots to make new words.
- Model the exercise. Call on a S to read aloud the prefix for number 1 (*intra-*). Ask the S to read the information in the corresponding columns.
- Ss complete the exercise in pairs. Walk around and help as needed.
- Write a grid on the board as it appears on Student's Book page 13. Call on pairs to fill in the information. Correct as needed.

Expansion activity *(student pairs)*

- **Materials needed** One dictionary for each pair of Ss.
- Ask some pairs to find examples of words with the prefixes presented in Exercise **3B**. Ask other pairs in the class to find examples of words with the roots presented in Exercise **3B**.
- Write the words Ss find on the board.

  Option Follow up by having Ss write sentences with the new words discussed. Have Ss share their sentences with a partner or with the whole class.

Application

- Focus Ss' attention on Exercise **3C**. Read the instructions aloud.
- Ask a S to read aloud the questions in Exercise **3C**.
- Ss ask and answer the questions in pairs. Walk around and help as needed.

Evaluation

- Books closed. Direct Ss' attention to the lesson focus written on the board.
- Write on the board the intelligences from the article on page 12 (*Verbal / Linguistic, Logical / Mathematical,* etc.) Ask Ss to make sentences about the meaning of these words. For example: *Someone who is verbal / linguistic learns by reading, listening, and speaking.*
- Have Ss share their sentences with the class.
- Check off each part of the lesson focus as Ss demonstrate an understanding of what they have learned in the lesson.

Learner persistence *(individual)*

- You may wish to assign Extended reading worksheets from the *Teacher's Toolkit Audio CD / CD-ROM* for Ss to complete outside of class. The purpose of these worksheets is to encourage Ss to read for pleasure in English outside of English class. The worksheets can also be assigned as extended reading in class.

> **More Ventures** *(whole group, pairs, individual)*
> Assign appropriate exercises from the *Teacher's Toolkit Audio CD / CD-ROM, Add Ventures,* or the *Workbook*.

3 After you read

A Check your understanding.

Which primary intelligence do these people have?

1. Josh Dillon, age 16: A star on the school baseball team; loves all sports; plans to become a coach.	*bodily / kinesthetic*
2. Ida Grove, age 45: Knows the name of everything in her garden.	*naturalist*
3. Manisha Pari, age 22: Writes in her journal every day about her feelings; enjoys taking walks by herself.	*intrapersonal*
4. Joy Rhee, age 30: Writes short stories and enjoys poetry.	*verbal / linguistic*
5. Susana Ochoa, age 42: Vocational counselor at a community college; volunteers at her church every Sunday.	*interpersonal*
6. Amal Mohammed, age 27: Photographer; takes art classes.	*visual / spatial*

B Build your vocabulary.

Understanding prefixes and roots of words will help you learn new words.

1. Find an example in the reading of each prefix or root. Write it in the chart.

2. Use a dictionary. Write the meaning of the words.

3. Guess the meaning of the prefixes and roots in the chart.

	Example from reading	Meaning of word	Meaning of prefix or root
Prefixes			
1. *intra-*	*intrapersonal*	*inside a person's mind or self*	*in, inside*
2. *inter-*	*interpersonal*	*involving relationships between people*	*between*
3. *multi-*	*multiple*	*many things, people, or events*	*many*
Roots			
4. *kine*	*kinesthetic*	*relating to motion*	*motion, movement*
5. *log*	*logical*	*reasonable*	*word, reason*
6. *prim*	*primary*	*more important than anything else*	*first*
7. *vis*	*visual*	*relating to seeing*	*see*

C Talk with a partner.

1. What is your primary intelligence?
2. What are good jobs for people with the following intelligences: intrapersonal, interpersonal, kinesthetic, logical, and visual?

Writing

1 Before you write

A **Write** *1* through *4* next to your strongest intelligences. (Your primary intelligence should be number 1.) Compare with your classmates.

____ Verbal / Linguistic   ____ Bodily / Kinesthetic

____ Logical / Mathematical   ____ Interpersonal

____ Musical / Rhythmical   ____ Intrapersonal

____ Visual / Spatial   ____ Naturalist

B **Read** the writing tip. Then read the model paragraphs. Choose the best topic sentence for each paragraph. Write it on the line.

> A good paragraph has a topic sentence and supporting sentences. The topic sentence tells what the paragraph is about.

1. Topic sentence:
   a. I enjoy taking my flute to the park.
   b. My primary intelligence is musical.

> *My primary intelligence is musical.* All my life, I've enjoyed singing and playing the flute. While I was growing up, my favorite classes were always music classes. I've taken private music lessons and also attended special summer music camps. I think that I can play well, and I also like to write original songs. On weekends, I enjoy taking my flute to a nearby park. There, I sit on the grass and play my music for hours. If I'm not playing, I'm listening to the music of the birds and the wind in the trees.

2. Topic sentence:
   a. My strongest intelligence is mathematical.
   b. In school, my favorite subject was mathematics.

> *My strongest intelligence is mathematical.* My parents say that I started counting before I was two years old. I've always liked to play games with numbers. I never forget my friends' birthdays or telephone numbers. I like to keep track of my monthly expenses so that I stay within my budget. Other people complain that balancing their checkbooks is hard, but I enjoy it. My aptitude for mathematics helps me in every part of my life.

Warm-up and review

- Before class. Write today's lesson focus on the board.
  Lesson E:
  Discuss and write about personal intelligences
  Use a topic sentence and supporting details
  Write a paragraph about a primary intelligence
- Begin class. Books closed. Review vocabulary and grammar from the unit. Ask questions about the reading from Lesson D, for example: *What are the different types of intelligences?* (Verbal / Linguistic, Logical / Mathematical, Musical / Rhythmical, Visual / Spatial, Bodily / Kinesthetic, Interpersonal, Intrapersonal, Naturalist)
- Write the terms on the board and ask Ss to give definitions of each.

Presentation

- Books open. Direct Ss' attention to Exercise **1A**. Read the instructions aloud.
- Ask Ss to work individually to complete the exercise.
- Have Ss work in pairs to compare their answers with their classmates.

Practice

- Direct Ss' attention to Exercise **1B**. Read the instructions aloud.

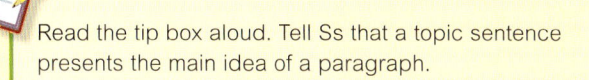

> Read the tip box aloud. Tell Ss that a topic sentence presents the main idea of a paragraph.

- Ss read the two paragraphs silently. Help them with vocabulary as needed.
- Give Ss time to choose the appropriate topic sentences.

- Call on two Ss to read aloud each paragraph and share the topic sentences they chose. Ask Ss why one choice is better than the other one for each paragraph. (*For paragraph 1, choice "a" is a supporting sentence, whereas choice "b" is the topic sentence. For paragraph 2, choice "a" is the topic sentence, and "b" is a supporting sentence.*)

Expansion activity *(small groups)*

- **Materials needed** Eight index cards, one for each type of intelligence.
- Form seven groups. Tell Ss that each group is going to develop a four-question questionnaire based on one of the intelligences to determine if it is their primary intelligence. Use the *Bodily / Kinesthetic* card as a model.
- Give each group one of the seven remaining index cards. Tell Ss: *What kinds of questions can you ask your classmates to find out if this intelligence is their primary intelligence? Write four different questions.* Write the following model on the board:
  Bodily / Kinesthetic
  Do you regularly participate in a sport or some physical activity?
  Do you enjoy working with your hands to create things?
  Do you like working with tools?
  Do you find it difficult to sit still?
- Walk around and help as needed.
- Read each intelligence and ask the group with that card to share its questions with the class.
- Tell Ss to think about the questions as they listen to them. This will also help them to determine their own primary intelligence.

Lesson E · Writing

Presentation

- Direct Ss' attention to Exercise **1C**. Read the instructions aloud.
- Ask four Ss to read each of the four sentences under *Supporting details*.
- Have Ss work individually to write a topic sentence.
- Ask Ss to share what they wrote. Write their answers on the board. For example: *My primary intelligence is kinesthetic,* or *My strongest intelligence is kinesthetic.*

Practice

- Direct Ss' attention to Exercise **1D**. Read the instructions aloud.
- Tell Ss they can start their outline by writing their topic sentence and then their supporting details.
- Have Ss work individually. Walk around and help as needed.

Application

- Focus Ss' attention on Exercise **2**. Read the instructions aloud.
- Ss complete the task individually. Walk around and help as needed.

Learner persistence (individual or pair work)

- If you have Ss who have difficulty writing, sit with them and help them while the other Ss are writing. Encourage them to review previous exercises to get ideas. If other Ss finish early, have them sit with and help the Ss who may be having difficulty with their writing.

Comprehension check

- Direct Ss' attention to Exercise **3A**. Read the instructions aloud. Ask a S to read the three checklist sentences to the class.
- This exercise asks Ss to review and edit their own writing. Ss check their own paragraphs individually. Walk around and help as needed. If any Ss check *No* for one or more of the checklist items, ask them to revise their paragraphs to include the missing information.

Evaluation

- Focus Ss' attention on Exercise **3B**. Read the instructions aloud.
- This exercise asks Ss to work together to peer-correct their writing. Reading aloud enables the writer to review his or her own writing. Reading to a partner allows the writer to understand the need to write clearly for an audience.

▼ **Teaching tip**
Self-editing may be difficult for some Ss. To help them, read aloud or write on the board the following tips for self-editing:

- Read your writing aloud. Sometimes reading aloud – even to yourself – will help you to find errors.
- Read your writing to a friend. This will also help you become aware of points that need more work.
- When in doubt, look it up! If you are not sure of how to spell a word, use your dictionary. Don't rely only on computer spell-checkers, which cannot correct the meaning of a word.

- Ss in pairs. Tell Ss to take turns reading their paragraphs to each other. Walk around and help as needed.
- Listen to Ss as they ask their partners questions about the paragraph and about one thing they learned.
- Remind Ss that even professional writers need to self-edit. Writing, like playing a sport or a musical instrument, is a skill – the more you do it, the better you will become.
- Books closed. Direct Ss' attention to the lesson focus written on the board. Ask Ss what two key points of paragraph writing were discussed (topic sentences and supporting details).
- Check off each part of the lesson focus as Ss demonstrate an understanding of what they have learned in the lesson.

> **More Ventures** (whole group, pairs, individual)
> Assign appropriate exercises from the *Teacher's Toolkit Audio CD / CD-ROM, Add Ventures,* or the *Workbook*.

C Complete the outline.

Read these supporting details about a person with kinesthetic intelligence.
Write a topic sentence.

Topic sentence: *My primary intelligence is kinesthetic. / My strongest intelligence is kinesthetic.*

Supporting details:
- Since I was a child, I have loved to move my body.
- I've taken many types of dance classes, including ballet, modern, jazz, swing, salsa, and African.
- I can dance to any kind of music that I hear.
- My friends say that I'm a great dancer.

D Plan a paragraph about your primary intelligence. Use the outline to make notes on your ideas.

Topic sentence: *(Answers will vary.)*

Supporting details:

- _____
- _____
- _____
- _____
- _____

2 Write

Write a paragraph about your primary intelligence. Use the paragraphs in Exercise 1B and the outlines in Exercises 1C and 1D to help you.

3 After you write

A Check your writing.

	Yes	No
1. I started my paragraph with a general topic sentence.	☐	☐
2. I gave specific details to support my topic sentence.	☐	☐
3. I used noun clauses, adjectives, and adverbs correctly.	☐	☐

B Share your writing with a partner.

1. Take turns. Read your paragraph to a partner.
2. Comment on your partner's paragraph. Ask your partner a question about the paragraph. Tell your partner one thing you learned.

1 Life-skills reading

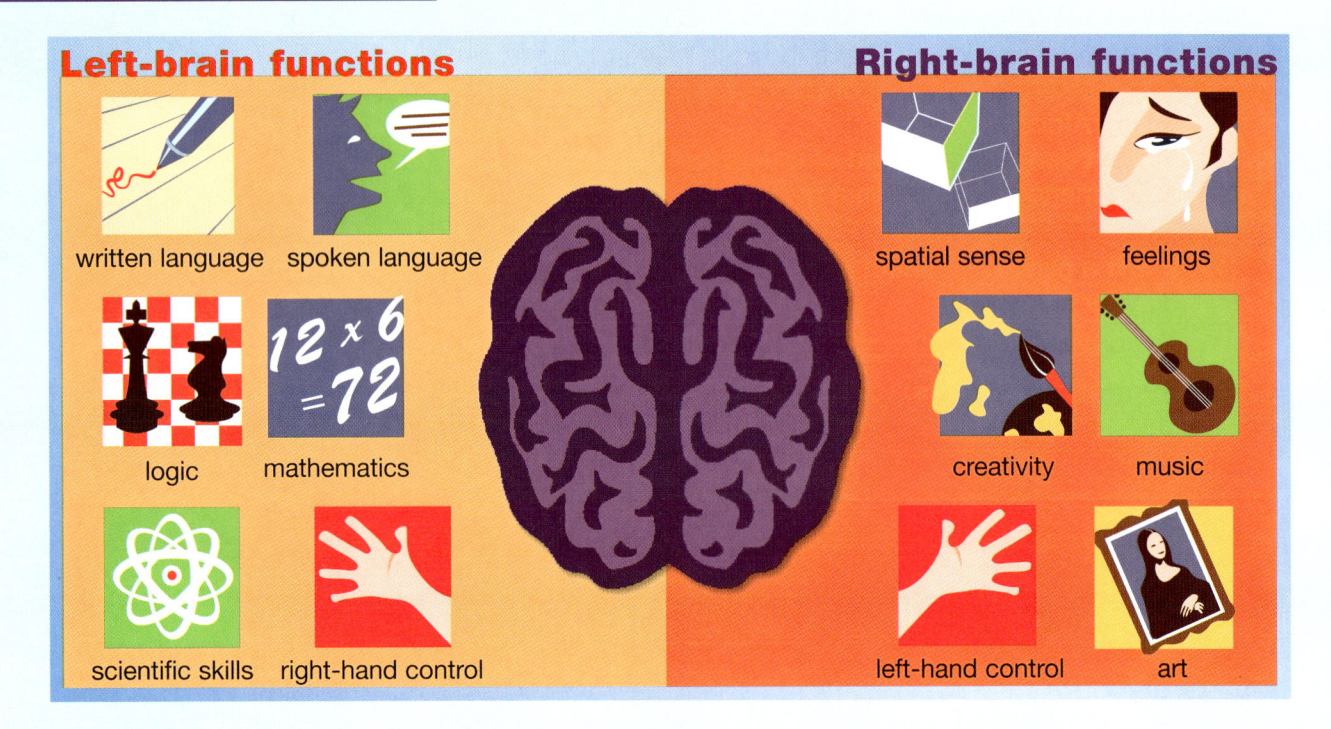

Left-brain functions   **Right-brain functions**

written language   spoken language   spatial sense   feelings

logic   mathematics   creativity   music

scientific skills   right-hand control   left-hand control   art

A Read the questions. Look at the diagram. Circle the answers.

1. Which side of the brain controls verbal ability?
   a. left side
   b. right side
   c. both sides
   d. none of the above

2. Which abilities are right-brain functions?
   a. art
   b. music
   c. creativity
   d. all of the above

3. Which ability is a left-brain function?
   a. spatial sense
   b. logic
   c. feelings
   d. none of the above

4. Which sentence is true?
   a. The left brain controls the left hand.
   b. The right brain controls the right hand.
   c. The left brain controls the right hand.
   d. none of the above

5. What can you say about "left-brained" people?
   a. They go to sleep easily.
   b. They are very musical.
   c. They are artistic.
   d. They are logical.

6. Which intelligence is a right-brain intelligence?
   a. musical / rhythmical
   b. logical / mathematical
   c. linguistic
   d. a and b

B Talk with a partner. Are you a right-brained or a left-brained person? What about the other people in your family?

Lesson objectives

- Practice reading and understanding a diagram of the brain
- Review vocabulary and grammar from the unit
- Introduce the project
- Complete the self-assessment

Warm-up and review

- Before class. Write today's lesson focus on the board.
  Lesson F:
  Read a diagram and answer questions about the brain
  Review vocabulary and discuss it in relation to famous people
  Complete the project and the self-assessment

- Begin class. Books closed. Write *the brain* on the board. Then write *left side* on one side and *right side* on the other. Ask Ss if they know which side of the brain is in charge of which functions. If they have any ideas, write them under the appropriate heading. (The left brain is responsible for written and spoken language, mathematics, logic, scientific skills, and right-hand control. The right brain is responsible for spatial sense, feelings, creativity, music, left-hand control, and art.)

- Say: *We are going to look at a diagram about the brain and answer questions about it.*

Presentation

- Books open. Direct Ss' attention to the diagram of the brain in Exercise **1**. Ask: *What do you see?* Elicit descriptions, such as: *left brain and right brain*.

- Have Ss focus on the icons and labels.

- Call on Ss to read the labels aloud.

- Ask other Ss to describe how each icon helps them to understand the brain function it represents.

Practice

- Read the instructions aloud for Exercise **1A**. This exercise helps prepare Ss for standardized-type tests they may have to take. Be sure that Ss understand the task and the vocabulary in the labels. Have Ss individually scan for and circle the answers.

- Check answers with the class. Ask Ss to read the questions and answers aloud. Ask: *Is that answer correct?* Make any necessary corrections.

Application

- Direct Ss' attention to Exercise **1B**. Read the instructions aloud.

- Ss work in pairs to ask and answer the questions. Walk around and help as needed.

Expansion activity *(individual work)*

- Have Ss write a paragraph about whether they are left-brained or right-brained people and why.

- Remind Ss of the writing tip from Lesson E. They can refer to page 15 in the Student's Book for help in outlining their paragraphs.

- Have Ss complete the writing in class or at home.

- Ask Ss to use the checklist in Exercise **3A** on page 15 to review their paragraphs prior to submitting them or sharing them with the class.

Expansion activity *(student pairs)*

- Write *left-brained person* and *right-brained person* on the board in two columns. Ask Ss to give you several examples based on the diagram (e.g. right-brained = artistic, left-brained = logical).

- Ask Ss: *How do left-brained or right-brained people react to certain situations? How would they talk about something like the weather?* Elicit appropriate responses, for example: a left-brained person might quote a weather report that he or she read or saw on television, whereas a right-brained person might say that he or she "feels" like rain is in the air.

- Ss in pairs. Ask pairs to create a short dialog between two people, one left-brained and one right-brained. The conversation can be about anything: home, school, the weather, or a combination of a few things. However, it should show the differences in right-brain and left-brain personalities based on what Ss learned from studying the diagram as well as any background knowledge they have about the subject. Encourage Ss to be creative and have fun with the activity.

- Ss work together. Walk around and help as needed.

- After several minutes, ask different pairs to share their dialogs with the class.

Lesson F Another view

Presentation

- Focus Ss' attention on Exercise **2A**. Read the instructions aloud.
- Ss work in small groups to complete the exercise. Help as needed.
- Write the numbers *1–6* on the board, along with the corresponding famous person's name.
- Ask Ss to come to the board to tell the class what the famous person is known for and to write the specific intelligence for each person.
- Direct Ss' attention to the second part of the instructions for Exercise **2A**. Read the instructions aloud.
- Ss discuss other famous people and their intelligences.
- Ss share information from their discussions with the class.

Expansion activity *(individual and pair work)*

- **Materials needed** Photos (from magazines or newspapers) of famous people from a variety of different backgrounds or fields.
- Distribute one photo to each S, and tell Ss that they are going to write a paragraph about that person.
- First, have pairs discuss their famous person; they should talk about the type of intelligence the famous person possesses and defend their statements with facts.
- Remind Ss to start their paragraph with a topic sentence about their famous person and to continue with supporting sentences.
- When each S has finished writing, Ss can share their paragraphs with their partners.

Application

- Direct Ss' attention to Exercise **2B**. Read the instructions aloud.
- Ss complete the activity with a partner. Help as needed.
- Check answers with the class. Call on individual Ss to read aloud each of the ten statements. For each statement, ask Ss to share whether it is true for them or not. Ask Ss to identify which kind of intelligence is related to each statement.

Expansion activity *(student pairs)*

- Have Ss work together to talk about the types of intelligences they most look for in a partner or best friend and to support their statements with examples.
- Give Ss time to ask and answer each other's questions and to compare information.
- Discuss with the class. Do an informal tally of how many Ss prefer someone like them (in terms of intelligences, etc.) and how many like someone who is different.

> **More Ventures** *(whole group, pairs, individual)*
> Assign appropriate exercises from the *Teacher's Toolkit Audio CD / CD-ROM, Add Ventures,* or the *Workbook.*

Application

Community building

- **Project** Ask Ss to turn to page 136 in their Student's Book to complete the project for Unit 1.

Evaluation

- Before asking Ss to turn to the self-assessment on page 141, do a quick review of the unit. Have Ss turn to Lesson A. Ask the class to talk about what they remember about this lesson. Prompt Ss, if necessary, with questions, for example: *What is the conversation about on this page? What vocabulary is in the pictures?* Continue in this manner to review each lesson quickly.
- **Self-assessment** Read the instructions for Exercise **3**. Ask Ss to turn to the self-assessment page and to complete the unit self-assessment. The self-assessments are also on the *Teacher's Toolkit Audio CD / CD-ROM*. If you prefer to collect the assessments and save them as part of each S's portfolio assessment, print out the unit self-assessment from the Toolkit, ask Ss to complete it, and collect and save it.
- If Ss are ready, administer the unit test on pages T-169–T-171 of this *Teacher's Edition* (or on the *Teacher's Toolkit Audio CD / CD-ROM*). The audio and audio script for the tests are on the *Teacher's Toolkit Audio CD / CD-ROM*.

2 Fun with language

A Work in a small group. What are these people famous for?
What are their intelligences?

Bodily / Kinesthetic	Intrapersonal	Musical / Rhythmical	Verbal / Linguistic
Interpersonal	Logical / Mathematical	Naturalist	Visual / Spatial

1 Princess Diana

2 the Dalai Lama

3 Venus Williams

4 Pablo Picasso

5 Christina Aguilera

6 Albert Einstein

Name some other famous people and describe their intelligences.

B Talk with your classmates. Which statements are true for you?
What kind of intelligence is related to each statement?

1. I'm an animal lover.
2. It's difficult for me to sit still for long.
3. I enjoy taking lots of photographs.
4. I'm very skillful with my hands.
5. I frequently play board games like chess or mah-jongg.
6. I like to go fishing.
7. I have many close friends.
8. I usually listen to music while I'm working or relaxing.
9. My checkbook is always balanced.
10. Other people think that I'm a good leader.

3 Wrap up

Complete the **Self-assessment** on page 141.

Get ready

1 Talk about the pictures

A What do you see?
B What is happening?

Lesson objectives

- Introduce students to the topic
- Find out what students know about the topic
- Preview the unit by talking about the pictures
- Practice key vocabulary
- Practice listening skills

Warm-up and review

- Before class. Write today's lesson focus on the board.
  Lesson A:
  Ask about courses and classes
  Discuss how to continue one's education
  Discuss obstacles and successes

- Begin class. Books closed. Direct Ss' attention to the lesson focus. Point to *Ask about courses and classes*. Ask Ss: *What classes have you taken? What classes are you taking now?* List Ss' responses on the board, for example: *I've taken several engineering classes in my country. I'm taking one English class right now.*

- Ask Ss: *What courses are you going to take in the future?* Elicit appropriate responses, such as: *I'm going to take another English course. I'm going to study nursing.*

▼ **Teaching tip**
By asking questions about the courses and classes they have taken, you can find out what your Ss' educational backgrounds are and, from time to time, call on their expertise.

Presentation

- Books open. Set the scene. Direct Ss' attention to the two pictures on page 18. Ask the question from Exercise **1A**: *What do you see?* Elicit and write on the board any vocabulary that Ss know, such as: *car, expressway (highway, freeway), class schedules, computer, poster.*

- Ask individual Ss to look at the two pictures and talk about the differences: *There's a young man in the first picture. He's in his car. He's meeting with a woman in the second picture. He's in an office.*

- Direct Ss' attention to the question in Exercise **1B**: *What is happening?* Read it aloud. Hold up the Student's Book. Point to the first picture. Ask: *What's he doing?* (He's driving and listening to the radio.)

- Hold up the Student's Book, and point to the young man in the second picture. Ask: *What's he doing here?* (He's sitting in Mrs. Ochoa's office.) Ask Ss to describe what is happening in the second picture. Write Ss' responses on the board. (They are probably talking about classes and schedules, etc.) Ask Ss who they think Mrs. Ochoa is (a counselor).

▼ **Teaching tip**
Encourage Ss to be creative. At this point, there is no single correct answer.

Culture tip
Tell Ss that in most colleges and universities, Ss can talk to counselors or advisors who can help them plan their class schedules. Tell Ss that counselors are specifically trained to help them figure out what classes they should take in order to achieve their educational and career goals.

- If you have counselors at your school, invite them to come to your class to talk to Ss about class advisement and goal-setting. Have Ss prepare questions about their areas of interest prior to the guests' visit.

Expansion activity (student pairs)

- Tell Ss to work in pairs to create a dialog between the young man and Mrs. Ochoa. Guide Ss to see that the characters are probably talking about classes the young man should take. Ask Ss to include in their conversations different suggestions about classes to take.

- Ask for volunteers to role-play their conversations for the class.

Presentation

- Tell Ss that they are going to hear two different audio segments. Direct Ss' attention to Exercise **2A**. Read the instructions aloud. Ask a S to read the questions to the class. Tell Ss to listen for the answers as the audio program is played or read.
- 💿 [Class Audio CD1 track 11] Play or read the audio program (see audio script, page T-156).
- Ask Ss if they have understood everything in the listening exercise. Write any unfamiliar words on the board and help Ss understand their meanings. Be sure that Ss understand the meaning of *certificate program* (an academic program, usually a series of classes, in which completion is recognized by the receipt of a certificate).
- Elicit answers to the questions; for example: *The speakers are a radio announcer, Mrs. Ochoa, and Vasili. They're talking about a Hospitality and Tourism certificate program at La Costa Community College.*
- Ask: *What do you think Vasili will do?* Elicit appropriate responses and write them on the board; for example: *I think Vasili will enroll in the program.*
- Focus Ss' attention on Exercise **2B**. Read the instructions aloud.
- 💿 [Class Audio CD1 track 12] Tell Ss to listen for details about the certificate program. Model the task. Play or read the audio program again. Pause the program after the announcer says in Part 1: *Then La Costa Community College's Hospitality and Tourism certificate program is for you.* Elicit: *Hospitality and Tourism.* Show Ss where on the chart *Hospitality and Tourism* is written. Encourage Ss to listen and complete the chart. Play or read the rest of the audio program.
- Direct Ss' attention to the second part of Exercise **2B**.
- 💿 [Class Audio CD1 track 12] Play or read the audio program again (see audio script, page T-156). Ss listen and check their answers.
- Write the numbers *1–6* on the board. Ask Ss to come to the board to write the answers. Have other Ss make corrections on the board as needed.

Practice

- Focus Ss' attention on Exercise **2C**. Read the instructions aloud. Tell Ss that the story in this exercise is a summary of the events shown in the pictures on page 18.
- Focus Ss' attention on the words in the word bank. Say each word aloud. Ask Ss to repeat. Correct pronunciation as needed. Explain any unfamiliar words.
- Ss complete the exercise individually. Walk around and help as needed.

Comprehension check

- 💿 [Class Audio CD1 track 13] Play or read the audio program (see audio script, page T-156). Ss listen and check their answers. Repeat the audio program as needed.
- Write the numbers *1–8* on the board. Ask Ss to come to the board to write their answers.

Learner persistence (individual work)

- 💿 [Self-Study Audio CD tracks 7 and 8] Exercises **2A**, **2B**, and **2C** are recorded on the Ss' self-study CD at the back of the Student's Book. Ss can listen to the CD at home for reinforcement and review. They can also listen for self-directed learning when class attendance is not possible.

Application

- Focus Ss' attention on Exercise **2D**. Read the instructions aloud.
- Ss complete the exercise in pairs. Help as needed.
- Ask several pairs to ask and answer the questions for the class. Discuss why or why not Ss in the class would also like this type of job.

Evaluation

- Direct Ss' attention to the lesson focus on the board. Ask individual Ss to look at the pictures on page 18 and make sentences using the words from the word bank in Exercise **2C**.
- Check off each part of the lesson focus as Ss demonstrate an understanding of what they have learned in the lesson.

> **More Ventures** (whole group, pairs, individual)
> Assign appropriate exercises from the *Teacher's Toolkit Audio CD / CD-ROM, Add Ventures*, or the *Workbook*.

2 Listening

 **A** **Listen** and answer the questions.

1. Who are the speakers?
2. What are they talking about?

 **B** **Listen again.** Complete the chart.

1. Type of certificate	Hospitality and Tourism
2. Places of employment	hotels, restaurants, airlines, travel agencies
3. Number of required classes	six
4. Time to complete the program	between one and two years
5. Cost per unit	$20
6. Estimated cost to earn the certificate	$1,000

Listen again. Check your answers.

 **C** **Read.** Complete the story. Listen and check your answers.

bilingual	high-paying	internship	qualify
deadline	industry	motivated	requirements

Vasili hears a radio ad about the Hospitality and Tourism certificate program at La Costa Community College. The ad says graduates can find ____high-paying____ jobs in the tourism ____industry____. Vasili goes to see his
1   2
ESL counselor, Mrs. Ochoa. She tells him about the program ____requirements____,
3
which include an ____internship____ in a local tourism business. She also tells
4
him about the ____deadline____ for registration, and she says there is financial
5
aid for students who ____qualify____. Vasili is concerned about his English,
6
but Mrs. Ochoa tells him not to worry. Vasili is ____bilingual____, he's very
7
____motivated____, and he has good interpersonal skills.
8

D **Discuss.** Talk with your classmates. Is hospitality and tourism a good industry for Vasili? Would you like this type of career? Why or why not?

1 Grammar focus: the present passive

Active	**Passive**
The college gives a placement test.	A placement test is given (by the college).
The college offers online classes every semester.	Online classes are offered (by the college) every semester.
Does the college offer financial aid?	Is financial aid offered (by the college)?
When does the college arrange internships?	When are internships arranged (by the college)?

For a grammar explanation, turn to page 147.
For a list of past participles, turn to page 154.

For a grammar explanation, turn to page 147.
For a list of past participles, turn to page 154.

> **Useful language**
> You can leave out the "by" phrase if the "doer" of the action is unknown or unimportant.

2 Practice

A Write. Complete the sentences. Use the present passive voice.

1. **A** When _____is_____ the English placement test _____given_____ to new students?
   (give)

   B The English placement test _____is administered_____ a week before the first day of class.
   (administer)

2. **A** _____Is_____ a math placement test also _____required_____ ?
   (require)

   B No, a math placement test _____is_____ not _____needed_____ .
   (need)

3. **A** Where _____is_____ the financial aid office _____located_____ ?
   (locate)

   B It _____is located_____ next to the admissions office.
   (locate)

4. **A** Where _____are_____ the classes _____held_____ ?
   (hold)

   B Most of the classes _____are held_____ in the business building.
   (hold)

5. **A** _____Are_____ classes _____offered_____ at different times?
   (offer)

   B Yes. Both day and evening classes _____are offered_____ .
   (offer)

6. **A** _____Are_____ job placement services _____provided_____ to graduates?
   (provide)

   B Yes. Job help _____is offered_____ to students who qualify.
   (offer)

Listen and check your answers. Then practice with a partner.

Warm-up and review

● Before class. Write today's lesson focus on the board.
Lesson B:
Use the present passive voice

● Begin class. Books open. Direct Ss' attention to the pictures on page 18. Review key vocabulary from the unit by asking Ss questions about Vasili:
What is Vasili interested in studying? (He is interested in studying hospitality and tourism.)
What information does Mrs. Ochoa give him? (She tells him the certificate program requirements at La Costa Community College.)
What is Vasili required to take? (He is required to take an English placement test.)
What is one of the program requirements? (One of the program requirements is an internship in a local tourist business.)
What does Mrs. Ochoa tell Vasili when he says he's worried about the cost of the program? (She says that there's financial aid for students who qualify.)

Presentation

● Books open. Direct Ss' attention to the grammar chart in Exercise **1**. Read aloud the first statements under the *Active* and *Passive* columns. Ask Ss to repeat.

● Direct Ss' attention to the second set of sentences. Read each sentence aloud. Have Ss repeat.

● Read aloud the remaining sentences.

● Ask: *What's the difference between the set of sentences under "Active" and the set of sentences under "Passive"?* Elicit an appropriate response, for example: *In the set under "Active," the sentences are about what the college does. In the set under "Passive," there is more focus on the action than on the college.*

● Write *active voice* and *passive voice* on the board. Tell Ss: *We use the active voice to focus on the person – or the doer – of the action. We use the passive voice to focus on the result of the action.*

● Ask Ss: *What do you notice about the verb forms in the present passive voice?* Elicit an appropriate response; for example: *They are formed by the verb "be" in the present tense plus the past participle, for example: "is given" or "are offered."*

Useful language
Read the tip box aloud. Refer Ss to the second set of sentences (under *Passive*), and have a S read the sentences aloud without including *by the college*. Ask Ss why they think the phrase *by the college* is in parentheses. Point out that *by the college* can be left out if it is not important to know who gives the placement test, for example, or if the giver of the placement test is unknown or obvious. Tell Ss that we use a *by* phrase when we want to clarify information or add emphasis, but that it is not always necessary.

▼ Teaching tip
It might be helpful to refer Ss to the grammar explanation on page 147 and to the list of past participles on page 154 of the Student's Book.

Practice

● Direct Ss' attention to Exercise **2A**. Read the instructions aloud. Have two Ss read the example aloud, and make sure that Ss understand the exercise.

● Ss complete the exercise individually. Walk around and help as needed.

Comprehension check

● [Class Audio CD1 track 14] Play or read the audio program (see audio script, page T-156). Ss listen and check their answers. Repeat the audio program as needed.

● Write the numbers *1–6* on the board. Ask several Ss to come to the board to write their answers in complete sentences. Make corrections on the board as needed.

● Have pairs practice the questions and answers.

Expansion activity *(student pairs)*

● **Materials needed** Copies of your program's course catalogs and/or information. If your school doesn't have a course catalog, you can find information for other programs and/or colleges through libraries or online at college Web sites. Give a catalog to each pair of Ss. Guide Ss to find examples of the present passive and to underline them.

● When Ss are finished, have volunteers read sentences with the present passive to the class. Explain any vocabulary that Ss do not understand.

Lesson B *The passive voice*

Presentation

- Books open. Direct Ss' attention to Exercise **2B**. Read the instructions aloud.
- Direct Ss' attention to the La Costa Community College Course Schedule. Have a S read the HOSP 100 entry.
- Ask another S to read the BUS 137 entry.
- Guide Ss to see that most listings in course catalogs consist of an abbreviation and a course number.

▼ **Teaching tip**
Ss may be unfamiliar with course-name abbreviations. Write HOSP and BUS on the board. Ask Ss what they stand for (hospitality and business). Ask Ss if they have seen other examples of abbreviations and what they were. If Ss have not seen others, write the following on the board: ENG, MAT, BIO. Ask Ss what they stand for (English, mathematics, biology). Have Ss look for other abbreviations in catalogs and on the Internet.

- Model the task. Ask two pairs of Ss to read the sample questions and answers to the class.
- Ss continue by asking and answering questions in pairs. Walk around and help as needed.

Practice

- Read aloud the second part of the instructions for Exercise **2B**.
- Ask a S to read the sample sentence to the class.
- Ss complete the exercise individually. Walk around and help as needed.

Comprehension check

- Ask individual Ss to come to the board to write their sentences. Ask Ss if the sentences are written correctly. Make corrections on the board as needed.

Application

- Direct Ss' attention to Exercise **3A**. Read aloud the instructions and the topics.
- Model the task. Ask two Ss to read the example conversation to the class.

- Ss work in pairs to complete the exercise. Help as needed.
- Direct Ss' attention to Exercise **3B**. Read the instructions aloud.
- Call on pairs to perform their role play for the class.

Expansion activity (small groups)

- Ask Ss: *What kinds of courses are you interested in?* Write the titles on the board.
- Use your college / program's course listings, or find listings for these classes from online sources. Give printouts or catalogs to each group and have Ss find listings for these classes.
- Ask Ss to ask and answer questions about the classes as they did in Exercise **2B**.
- Ss work in small groups to complete the activity. Walk around and help as needed.
- Call on groups to share the information they learned.

Evaluation

- Direct Ss' attention to the lesson focus on the board.
- Write the following sentence on the board: *The college offers four different levels of ESL classes.*
- Ask a S whether the statement is in the active or the passive voice (*active*), and then ask the S to come to the board to write the sentence in the passive voice. (*Four different levels of ESL classes are offered by the college.*) If you have time, repeat this activity, but call on Ss to give you examples (in either voice) for other Ss to write on the board.
- Check off each part of the lesson focus as Ss demonstrate an understanding of what they have learned in the lesson.

> **More Ventures** (whole group, pairs, individual)
> Assign appropriate exercises from the *Teacher's Toolkit Audio CD / CD-ROM, Add Ventures,* or the *Workbook*.

B Talk with a partner. Read about two courses in the Hospitality and Tourism Certificate Program. Ask and answer questions using the present passive. Use the past participles in the box.

given	held	located	offered	required

> **A** When is HOSP 100 offered?
> **B** It's offered in the fall and spring.

> **A** Are day and evening classes given?
> **B** Yes, they are.

La Costa Community College Course Schedule
Hospitality and Tourism Certificate Program

HOSP 100: Introduction to Hospitality and Tourism
Requirement: Pass an English placement test.
Fall and spring
T / Th 10:00–11:30 a.m.
M / W 6:00–7:30 p.m.
Room: T130

BUS 137: Customer Service
Requirement: Pass HOSP 100.
Spring
T / Th 8:00–9:30 a.m.
(Online course also available.)
Room: B480

Write sentences about the courses.

HOSP 100 is offered in the fall and spring.

3 Communicate

A Work with a partner. Role-play a conversation between a counselor and a student who wants to enroll in the Auto Mechanics Certificate Program. Ask and answer questions about the topics.

- online courses
- required courses
- English or math placement tests
- location of classes
- internships
- financial aid
- job counseling

> **Student** Are online courses offered in the Auto Mechanics Certificate Program?
> **Counselor** No. Online courses are not offered in that program.
> **Student** What about internships?
> **Counselor** Internships are arranged for each student in the program.

B Perform your role play for the class.

Lesson C *The passive voice*

1 Grammar focus: infinitives after passive verbs

Students are told to arrive early on the first day of class.

Everyone is encouraged to attend class regularly.

Are students expected to do homework every night?

How often are students expected to meet with their counselors?

For a grammar explanation, turn to page 147.

For a list of common infinitives after passive verbs, turn to page 147.

2 Practice

A Write complete statements or questions. Use the present passive with infinitives.

1. applicants / expect / meet / all application deadlines.

   Applicants are expected to meet all application deadlines.

2. new students / tell / come early / for registration.

   New students are told to come early for registration.

3. all new students / require / take / a writing test?

   Are all new students required to take a writing test?

4. some students / advise / enroll / in an English composition class.

   Some students are advised to enroll in an English composition class.

5. students / expect / attend / every class?

   Are students expected to attend every class?

6. students / encourage / meet / with a counselor regularly.

   Students are encouraged to meet with a counselor regularly.

7. when / participants / expect / complete / their internships?

   When are participants expected to complete their internships?

8. students / require / earn / a grade of C or better in each course.

   Students are required to earn a grade of C or better in each course.

9. students / tell / study / with a partner and to go to tutoring often.

   Students are told to study with a partner and to go to tutoring often.

Listen and check your answers.

Lesson objective

- Practice using infinitives after passive verbs

Warm-up and review

- Before class. Write today's lesson focus on the board.
  Lesson C:
  Use infinitives after passive verbs
- Begin class. Books closed. Write these sentences on the board: *La Costa Community College requires HOSP 100 students to pass an English placement exam. La Costa Community College expects BUS 137 students to pass HOSP 100.*
- Ask Ss to write the sentences in the passive voice. (*HOSP 100 students are required to pass an English placement exam. BUS 137 students are expected to pass HOSP 100.*)
- Ask two Ss to come to the board to write their answers. Have other Ss make corrections on the board as needed.
- Circle *pass* in the Ss' sentences on the board. Tell Ss that in this lesson they will learn about infinitives after passive verbs.

Presentation

- Books open. Direct Ss' attention to the grammar chart in Exercise **1**. Ask individual Ss to read aloud each of the sentences.
- Write the sentences on the board. Ask individual Ss to come to the board. Have each S underline the passive verb (both the form of the verb *to be* plus the past participle) and then circle the infinitive.
- Have Ss individually make up similar sentences or questions, using the verbs in this exercise, for example: *Everyone is expected to come to class every day. What time are students told to arrive on the first day of class?*
- Ask Ss to share their examples, and write them on the board.

▼ Teaching tip

It might be helpful to refer Ss to the grammar explanation on page 147 and the list of common infinitives after passive verbs on page 147 in the Student's Book.

Practice

- Direct Ss' attention to Exercise **2A**. Read the instructions aloud.
- Model the task. Ask a S to read aloud the example sentence. Remind Ss that the present passive is formed by using the present tense of *be* plus the past participle and that the infinitive is formed by *to* plus the base form of the verb. Tell Ss to continue the exercise by using the present passive with infinitives.
- Ss complete the exercise individually. Walk around and help as needed.

Comprehension check

- Read aloud the second part of the instructions for Exercise **2A**.
- [Class Audio CD1 track 15] Play or read the audio program (see audio script, page T-156). Ss listen and check their answers.
- Ask nine Ss to come to the board to write their answers. Make corrections on the board as needed.

Expansion activity *(student pairs)*

- Ask Ss to make up statements and questions, similar to the ones in Exercise **2A**, about their own school's program.
- Ss in pairs. Have partners discuss the statements and ask and answer each other's questions. Walk around and help as needed.

Lesson C *The passive voice*

Presentation
- Books closed. Write on the board: *college credit*. Ask Ss if they know what this means. Elicit appropriate responses, such as: *College credit is what you earn when you take certain courses. College certificate and degree programs require a specific amount of college credit.*

Practice
- Books open. Focus Ss' attention on Exercise **2B**. Read the instructions aloud. Read the past participles in the word bank.
- Direct Ss' attention to the advertisement. Ask a S to read the ad aloud. Explain vocabulary as needed, and write any new words on the board. Ask another S to read the example sentence above the ad.
- Ss complete the exercise in pairs. Walk around and help as needed.
- Read aloud the second part of the instructions for Exercise **2B**. Call on a S to read aloud the sample sentence.
- Ss complete the exercise individually. Walk around and help as needed.
- Ask several Ss to write their sentences on the board. Ask other Ss to read aloud each of the sentences on the board. Ask: *Is this sentence correct?* Have different Ss make corrections on the board as needed.

> **Culture note**
> Read the culture note aloud. Ask Ss if they have heard of work experience programs. Explain that these programs are designed to encourage Ss – especially adult Ss – to go to college or, in some cases, to return to college. Tell Ss that each college has its own rules regarding work for credit and that in most cases, evidence of work (either volunteer or paid) must be provided.

Expansion activity *(student pairs)*
- Role-play. Ask Ss to practice role-playing the activity of a S asking a school counselor information about work experience credit. Write an example of a conversation on the board, such as:

    S: I would like to try to get college credit for my work experience.
    Counselor: What kind of work experience do you have?
    S: I volunteered at the library last year. I gave people information about the library's programs.

Counselor: Very interesting! This is perfect because it's related to the program you are interested in.
S: If I get a letter from my boss, can I get credit for my work?
Counselor: I think so, but we need to know how many hours you worked.

- Ask two Ss to read the example conversation.
- Have pairs write and practice their own conversation. Walk around and help as needed.
- Ask several pairs to act out their conversation for the rest of the class.

Application
- Direct Ss' attention to Exercise **3A**. Read the instructions aloud. Call on a S to read the listed items.
- Ss in pairs. Ask two Ss to read aloud the example conversation.
- Ss complete the exercise. Walk around and help as needed.
- Direct Ss' attention to Exercise **3B**. Read the instructions aloud.
- Model the task. Ask a S from each pair to tell what he or she learned. Ask the S to make a sentence about the information his or her partner shared, for example: *In high schools in Freddy's country, students are not required to come to class every day.*
- Continue the exercise by asking different Ss to share information they learned from their classmates.

Evaluation
- Direct Ss' attention to the lesson focus on the board. Ask individual Ss to look at the ad on Student's Book page 23 and to make sentences using *allowed, encouraged, expected, required,* and *told.* Ss should say their sentences aloud.
- Check off the lesson focus as Ss demonstrate an understanding of what they have learned in the lesson.

> **More Ventures** *(whole group, pairs, individual)*
> Assign appropriate exercises from the *Teacher's Toolkit Audio CD / CD-ROM, Add Ventures,* or the *Workbook.*

B **Talk** with a partner. Read the ad. Make statements about the Work Experience Program. Use the past participles in the box.

allowed	encouraged	expected	required	told

Students are allowed to earn college credit for work experience.

Work Experience Program
at La Costa Community College

Earn college credit for the job you have.

You can earn up to 4 units of credit by participating in the program.

To enroll, attend an orientation session. Then work at least 75 paid hours or 60 volunteer hours. Questions?

Contact the Career Center at 777-555-2222, or visit our Web site.

www.lacosta.edu/workexperience

Write sentences about the Work Experience Program at La Costa Community College.

Students are allowed to earn college credit for work experience.

> **Culture note**
> Work experience programs exist in many U.S. colleges to help adult students get credit for past and present work experience.

3 Communicate

A **Work** with a partner. Ask and answer questions about the requirements at a school, course, or program that your partner knows. Discuss the items listed below.

- placement tests
- counselors
- dates and times of classes
- location
- registration fees
- attendance
- textbooks
- tutors
- homework

> **A** At high schools in your native country, are students given a placement test?
> **B** Yes. Every new student is required to take a placement test.

B **Share** information with your classmates.

Lesson D Reading

1 Before you read

Talk with a partner. Look at the reading tip. Answer the questions.

1. Who is the story about?
2. What was one obstacle to their success?
3. What places are mentioned in the reading?

2 Read

SELF-STUDY AUDIO CD **Read** the newspaper article. Listen and read again.

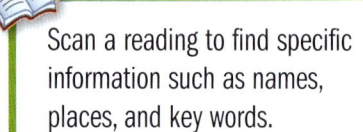

Scan a reading to find specific information such as names, places, and key words.

An Immigrant Family's Success Story

Choi and Lili Wei left China with their baby boy in the late 1980s. They were poor field workers in their native country, and they wanted their child to have the opportunities they lacked. They arrived in New York and found a one-bedroom apartment in a poor, unstable area. They could only afford a bicycle for transportation, yet they felt fortunate to have the chance to begin a new life in the United States.

Choi and Lili faced many obstacles because they couldn't speak English and had no skills. They found night work cleaning businesses and restaurants. They saved every penny, and after six years, they were able to buy a small restaurant of their own.

They were determined to learn English, get an education, and make a good life for their son. The couple sacrificed a great deal. They never went to a movie, never ate out, and hardly ever bought anything extra. In their free time, they attended English and citizenship classes. Both of them eventually earned their GED certificates. Choi then enrolled in college while Lili worked in the restaurant.

This past spring, Choi fulfilled a lifelong dream of graduating from college. Now he is registered in a master's degree program in business beginning this fall. And what about their "baby" boy? Their son, Peter, now 21, received a scholarship to a private university, where he is working on his own dream to become an architect.

Choi and Lili are proud to be models of the "American dream." Choi has this advice for other new immigrants: "Find your passion, make a plan to succeed, and don't ever give up."

Lesson objectives

- Introduce and read "An Immigrant Family's Success Story"
- Practice using new topic-related vocabulary
- Scan a reading to find specific information
- Identify words to describe obstacles and successes

Warm-up and review

- Before class. Write today's lesson focus on the board.
  Lesson D:
  Read and understand "An Immigrant Family's Success Story"
  Practice new vocabulary related to obstacles and successes
- Begin class. Books closed. Focus Ss' attention on the word *success* in the lesson focus. Write *success* on the board. Ask Ss: *How do you think most people define "success"? How do you define success?* Elicit appropriate responses and write them on the board. (Answers will vary.)
- Ask Ss to read the title of the story and tell what they think this story is about. Elicit responses, such as: *It's about a family from another country coming to the United States and doing well.* Write some of the Ss' predictions on the board.
- Some Ss may mention the "American dream." Ask Ss what they think this expression means.

Presentation

- Books open. Direct Ss' attention to Exercise **1**. Read the instructions aloud.

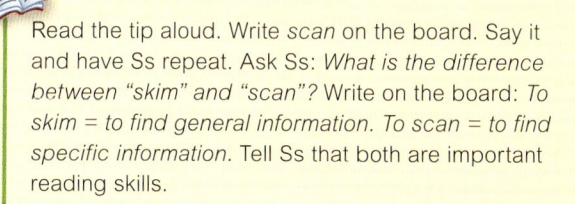

> Read the tip aloud. Write *scan* on the board. Say it and have Ss repeat. Ask Ss: *What is the difference between "skim" and "scan"?* Write on the board: *To skim = to find general information. To scan = to find specific information.* Tell Ss that both are important reading skills.

- Direct Ss' attention to the questions in Exercise **1**. Ask three Ss to read the questions aloud.
- Ss in pairs. Guide Ss to scan the article individually. Then ask Ss to answer the three questions with their partners. Have Ss indicate where in the article they found each of the three answers.

Practice

- Read the instructions aloud for Exercise **2**. Ask Ss to read the article silently before listening to the audio program.
- [Class Audio CD1 track 16] Play or read the audio program and ask Ss to read along (see audio script, page T-157). Repeat the audio program as needed.
- While Ss are listening and reading the article, ask them to write any words in their notebooks that they don't understand. When the audio program is finished, have Ss write the new vocabulary words on the board.
- Point to each word on the board. Say it and ask Ss to repeat. Give a brief explanation of each word, or ask Ss to explain the word if they know it. If Ss prefer to look up the new words in their dictionaries, allow them to do so.
- Encourage Ss to guess the meaning of unfamiliar words from the context of the article. For example, if a S writes *faced,* read the sentence aloud (*Choi and Lili faced many obstacles because they couldn't speak English and had no skills.*). Ask Ss to think about the meaning of the word *faced* based on the other information in the sentence. Tell Ss that *faced* is another way of saying *had to deal with* or *had to overcome obstacles.*

Learner persistence *(individual work)*

- [Self-Study Audio CD track 9] Exercise **2** is recorded on the Ss' self-study CD at the back of the Student's Book. Ss can listen to the CD at home for reinforcement and review. They can also listen to the CD for self-directed learning when class attendance is not possible.

Expansion activity *(student pairs)*

- Have Ss create a scanning exercise for their partners.
- Tell Ss to find a news article (suggest using a local publication that's accessible and not too difficult to follow) for homework. Have Ss read the article and make up three questions based on it.
- Ss in pairs. Ask partners to exchange articles and questions. Ss scan the articles for answers.
- Call on pairs to share the information they learned with the class.

Lesson D *Reading*

Comprehension check

- Books open. Direct Ss' attention to Exercise **3A**. Read the instructions aloud.
- Ask seven Ss to read the questions aloud, one at a time. Make sure that all Ss understand the questions.
- Ss in pairs. Have partners ask and answer the questions. Tell Ss that they can refer to the article on page 24.
- Discuss the answers to the questions with the class. Ask where in the reading the answers are found.

Practice

- **Materials needed** A dictionary for each S and index cards.
- Direct Ss' attention to Exercise **3B**. Ask a S to read aloud the instructions in number 1.
- Model the task. Read aloud the word *lacked* and have Ss scan the article on page 24 to find it. (It's in the first paragraph.) Call on a S to read the sentence with this word. Then ask Ss to underline the word in the article.
- Ss complete the exercise individually. Help as needed.
- Direct Ss to number 2 in Exercise **3B**. Ss complete the task individually.
- Direct Ss' attention to number 3 in Exercise **3B**. Ask a S to read the instructions aloud.
- Ask another S to read the model word and definition as well as the information about abbreviations below the example vocabulary cards.

> ▼ **Teaching tip**
> Remind Ss that when they look up a word in a dictionary, the word will appear in its base form and that there may be more than one definition for the word.

- Model the exercise by writing *faced* on the board. Ask a S what the base or root form is (*face*). Also ask what part of speech the word is (*verb*), and write the appropriate abbreviation on the board (*v*). Have a S read the definition, but adapt it since it is in the past tense (*dealt with a difficult situation*). Ask another S to give a sentence for the word. (*The new immigrants faced financial problems.*)
- Ss complete the exercise individually. Walk around and help as needed.
- Call on individual Ss to give examples of the words they chose in **3B** and to write their vocabulary card entries on the board. Have them read the entries aloud. Make corrections on the board as needed.

Learner persistence *(individual work)*

- Encourage Ss to make vocabulary cards when they learn new words and to review new words daily.

Application

- Read the instructions aloud for Exercise **3C**.
- Ask four Ss to read the questions to the class.
- Ss complete the exercise in pairs. Help as needed.
- Ask several pairs to ask and answer the questions for the class.

Expansion activity *(small groups)*

- Write *100 years ago* and *Today* on the board as headings for each of two separate columns. Write *Similarities* and *Differences* to the left of the columns. Ask Ss what the similarities and differences are between immigrants who come to the United States today and those who came 100 years ago. Write examples under each heading, such as: *Both groups followed / are following their dreams for a better life*.
- Using the language from Exercise **3B**, as well as that of the reading, Ss discuss the similarities and differences between the two immigrant groups. Ss should share information they discussed with the class.

Evaluation

- Books closed. Direct Ss' attention to the lesson focus on the board.
- Ask individual Ss to retell the main points of the article, "An Immigrant Family's Success Story."
- Focus Ss on the words that they wrote on vocabulary cards for number 3 of Exercise **3B**. Ask Ss to make a new sentence for each of these words to show that they understand the meaning.
- Check off each part of the lesson focus as Ss demonstrate an understanding of what they have learned in the lesson.

Learner persistence *(individual work, student pairs)*

- You may wish to assign Extended reading worksheets from the *Teacher's Toolkit Audio CD / CD-ROM* for Ss to complete outside of class. The purpose of these worksheets is to encourage Ss to read for pleasure in English outside of the English class. The worksheets can also be assigned as extended reading in class.

> ***More Ventures*** *(whole group, pairs, individual)*
> Assign appropriate exercises from the *Teacher's Toolkit Audio CD / CD-ROM, Add Ventures*, or the *Workbook*.

3 After you read

A Check your understanding.

1. What was Choi and Lili's native country?
2. What kind of work did they do before they came to the United States?
3. Why did they decide to come to the United States?
4. What kind of job did they find in the United States?
5. What did Choi and Lili do when they weren't working?
6. What is Peter's dream?
7. What is Choi's advice for people who want to succeed?

B Build your vocabulary.

1. Find and underline the following words in the story: *lacked*, *unstable*, *fortunate*, *obstacles*, *determined*, and *passion*.

2. Find three more words that you do not know. Write them here:

_____   _____   _____

3. Look up all the words in a dictionary. Make a vocabulary card for each word. On one side of the card, write the word and the part of speech. On the other side, write the definition and your own sentence using the word.

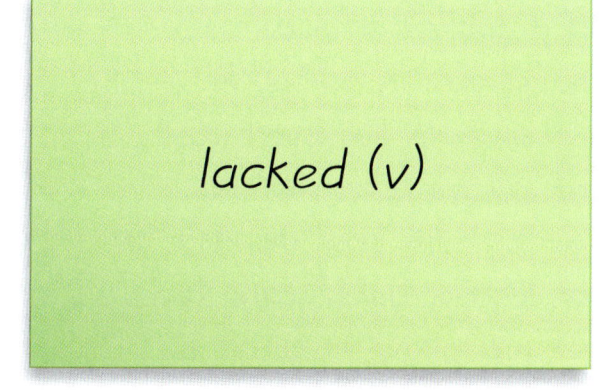

lacked (v)

Definition: missed, did not have

I lacked the requirements to get into college.

Abbreviations for parts of speech: v = verb; adj = adjective; n = noun; adv = adverb

C Talk with a partner.

1. Do you believe that you are fortunate? Why or why not?
2. What are you determined to do?
3. Have you found your passion? What is it?
4. What is one obstacle you have faced?

1 Before you write

A Talk with your classmates. Answer the questions.

1. Do you know a successful person?
2. Why is this person successful?
3. What did the person do to become successful?
4. What was one obstacle to this person's success?

B Read the paragraph.

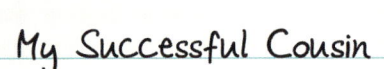

My Successful Cousin

My cousin, Daniel, is the most successful person I know. However, he has had many obstacles on his road to success. First of all, his parents died in an automobile accident when he was 17 years old. Daniel needed to take care of his two younger brothers, so he quit school and found a job at a local supermarket. When his brothers were in school, he worked. At night, he helped them with homework and did all the chores. Even with all his responsibilities, Daniel was a very reliable worker. His boss decided to help him go to college. It took Daniel eight years, but finally he graduated. Now Daniel plans to enroll in a business management course. If he is accepted, he hopes to open his own business someday. Daniel has a dream, and he is working hard to achieve his dream. He is my hero!

> Use specific details such as facts, examples, and reasons to support your topic sentence.

C Talk with a partner.

1. What is one fact about Daniel's life?
2. What is one example of an obstacle in Daniel's life?
3. What is a reason for that obstacle?
4. What is Daniel's dream or goal?

Lesson objectives
- Write about a successful person
- Practice using specific details to support ideas

Warm-up and review

- Before class. Write today's lesson focus on the board.
  Lesson E:
  Write a paragraph about a successful person
  Use facts, examples, and reasons to support ideas

- Begin class. Books closed. Review vocabulary from the unit. Write the words *success* and *obstacle* on the board. Ask Ss what the difference is between a success and an obstacle. Elicit appropriate responses, such as: *A success is something that you accomplish or do well. An obstacle is an event or situation that makes it harder to succeed.*

- Remind Ss about the Wei family story. Ask Ss:
  Did Choi and his wife face many obstacles? (Yes, they did.)
  What were they? (They lacked money and English skills. They didn't have job skills.)
  Did they have successes? (Yes, they did.)
  What were they? (They were able to save enough money to buy a small restaurant. They earned their GED certificates, and Choi graduated from college – and he is still studying. Their son received a scholarship to a private university, where he is studying to become an architect.)
  What advice does Choi give to new immigrants? (He says that they should find their passion, make a plan to succeed, and never give up.)

Presentation

- Books open. Direct Ss' attention to Exercise **1A**. Read the instructions aloud.

- Ask four Ss to read aloud the four questions in Exercise **1A**.

- Ss ask and answer the questions with a partner. Help as needed.

Practice

- Direct Ss' attention to Exercise **1B**. Read the instructions aloud.

- Ss read the paragraph silently. Ask Ss to underline any words in the paragraph with which they are unfamiliar.

- Have Ss tell you the words they underlined. Write them on the board. Go over the meaning of each word.

> Read the tip box aloud. Tell Ss that the topic sentence is the main idea of the paragraph and that the other sentences they write should support the topic sentence. Ask Ss why it is important to use facts, examples, and reasons to support the topic sentence. Elicit responses, such as: *Facts, examples, and reasons that support the topic sentence make a paragraph more interesting and convincing.*

Application

- Focus Ss' attention on Exercise **1C**. Read the instructions aloud.

- Ask four Ss to read the questions in Exercise **1C**.

- Ss ask and answer the questions with a partner. Help as needed.

- Call on pairs to share their answers with the class.

Expansion activity *(student pairs)*

- Ask Ss to brainstorm a list of obstacles that immigrants face today and write them on the board.

- Ss in pairs. Tell Ss to write down the personal qualities people need to have in order to overcome each of these obstacles.

- Model the activity. Ask: *What qualities are most important for new immigrants to have?* Elicit appropriate responses, such as: *New immigrants need to be patient because goals and success can take a long time to achieve.*

- Ask Ss to share their examples with the class.

Lesson E *Writing*

Presentation

- Direct Ss' attention to Exercise **1D**. Read the instructions aloud.
- Ask a S to read the headings in the chart and the example answers.
- Remind Ss of the strategy they learned in the last lesson. Ask Ss to scan the paragraph for this specific information.
- Ss complete the chart individually.
- Write a chart on the board similar to the one in the Student's Book.
- Call on Ss to come to the board, one at a time, to fill in the chart. Make corrections on the board as needed.

▼ **Teaching tip**
Before Ss begin to write, have them talk about the topic in a prewriting activity. Speaking about the topic with a partner will help Ss to focus on the person they are going to write about in Exercise **2**.

Practice

- Direct Ss' attention to Exercise **1E**. Read the instructions aloud.
- Point out to Ss that a graphic organizer, such as a chart, will help them organize their ideas for writing.
- Ss complete the exercise individually. Walk around and help as needed.
- Focus Ss' attention on Exercise **2**. Read the instructions aloud.
- Ss complete the task individually. Walk around and help as needed.

Learner persistence (individual work)

- If you have any Ss who have difficulty writing, sit with them and help them as the other Ss are writing. Encourage them to use their notes from Exercise **1E** to add facts and other details to support their topic sentence.

Comprehension check

- Direct Ss' attention to Exercise **3A**. Read the instructions aloud.
- Ss complete the task individually. Walk around and help as needed.
- Ss check their own paragraphs against the writing checklist. If any Ss check *No* for one or more of the checklist items, ask them to revise and edit their paragraphs to include the missing information.

Evaluation

- Focus Ss' attention on Exercise **3B**. Read the instructions aloud. Make sure that Ss understand the task.
- This exercise enables Ss to work together to peer-correct their writing. Reading aloud enables the writer to review his or her own writing. Reading to a partner allows the writer to understand the need to write clearly for an audience.
- Ss complete the exercise in pairs. Tell Ss to take turns reading their paragraphs to each other. Walk around and help as needed.
- Listen to Ss as they ask their partner a question about the paragraph and tell their partner one thing they learned from the paragraph.
- Ask several Ss to read aloud the paragraphs they wrote for Exercise **2**. Have other Ss ask questions and mention something they learned from the paragraph.
- Direct Ss' attention to the lesson focus written on the board.
- Check off each part of the lesson focus as Ss demonstrate an understanding of what they have learned in the lesson.

> *More Ventures* (whole group, pairs, individual)
> Assign appropriate exercises from the *Teacher's Toolkit Audio CD / CD-ROM, Add Ventures,* or the *Workbook*.

D Complete the chart with Daniel's obstacles and successes. *(Answers may vary.)*

Daniel's obstacles	Daniel's successes
His parents died.	*He found a job in a local supermarket.*
He had to quit school.	*He was a very reliable worker.*
He needed to take care of his two younger brothers.	*He graduated from college.*

E Plan a paragraph about a successful person you know. Use the chart to make notes on your own ideas.

_____'s obstacles	_____'s successes
(Answers will vary.)	

2 Write

Write a paragraph about someone you know who is successful. Use the paragraph in Exercise 1B and the charts in Exercises 1D and 1E to help you.

3 After you write

A Check your writing.

	Yes	No
1. My topic sentence identifies a successful person.	☐	☐
2. I included examples of obstacles and successes.	☐	☐
3. I used active and passive verbs correctly.	☐	☐

B Share your writing with a partner.

1. Take turns. Read your paragraph to a partner.
2. Comment on your partner's paragraph. Ask your partner a question about the paragraph. Tell your partner one thing you learned.

1 Life-skills reading

Location of Vocational Classes	North Center	South Center	West Center	Downtown Center	East Center
Auto Mechanics	■	■	■		
Certified Nursing Assistant	■	■	■	■	■
Food Service Worker	■	■	■		■
Hospitality and Tourism	■				
Office Systems	■	■	■		■
Retail		■		■	
Welding	■		■		
Workplace Readiness	■	■	■	■	■

A **Read** the questions. Look at the chart. Circle the answers.

1. Where are the most vocational classes offered?
   a. Downtown Center
   b. North Center
   c. South Center
   d. West Center

2. Where are the fewest vocational classes offered?
   a. Downtown Center
   b. North Center
   c. South Center
   d. West Center

3. Workplace Readiness is offered at which of the following sites?
   a. Downtown Center only
   b. East Center and West Center only
   c. North Center and South Center only
   d. all sites

4. Which vocational class is only offered at one site?
   a. Certified Nursing Assistant
   b. Hospitality and Tourism
   c. Retail
   d. Welding

5. You want to work in a hotel. Which class is appropriate for you?
   a. Hospitality and Tourism
   b. Office Systems
   c. Retail
   d. Welding

6. You want to study computers. Which class is appropriate for you?
   a. Auto Mechanics
   b. Food Service Worker
   c. Hospitality and Tourism
   d. Office Systems

B **Talk** with a partner. Ask and answer your own questions about the chart.

Lesson objectives
- Practice reading and understanding a chart about the location of classes
- Review vocabulary and grammar from the unit
- Introduce the project
- Complete the self-assessment

Warm-up and review
- Before class. Write today's lesson focus on the board.
  Lesson F:
  Read and understand a chart about course locations
  Review topic vocabulary and grammar from Unit 2
  Complete the project and the self-assessment
- Begin class. Books closed. Write *location* on the board. Say the word and ask Ss to repeat.
- Ask Ss: *What does "location" mean?* Elicit answers, such as: *Location is where something happens or takes place.*
- Ask Ss: *When and why do you need to check information about course locations?* Elicit responses, such as: *You should check the course locations so that you know where to go on the first day of class. This is important to do before the first day of class.*

Presentation
- Write *vocation* on the board and ask Ss what this word means. If Ss don't know, tell them that it means the same thing as *occupation,* and write that word on the board. Ask Ss what *vocational classes* are (classes for specific training in an occupation).
- Tell Ss that they will practice reading and understanding a chart of course locations for vocational classes.
- Books open. Call on individual Ss to read the names and locations of the eight vocational classes. Explain new vocabulary as needed.

▼ **Teaching tip**
Tell Ss that learning to read these kinds of charts is a useful skill for everyday life. Ask Ss if they have used similar types of charts. If no one says yes, explain that Ss may have jobs or be in situations in the future in which they will need to use charts like this.

Practice
- Direct Ss' attention to Exercise **1A**. Read the instructions aloud. This task helps prepare Ss for standardized-type tests they may have to take. Be sure that Ss understand the task. Have Ss individually scan for and circle the answers.

Comprehension check
- Check answers to Exercise **1A** with the class. Make sure that Ss have followed the instructions and circled their answers.
- Have Ss read aloud the questions and the answers they circled. Ask Ss: *Is that answer correct?* Make corrections as needed.

Application
- Direct Ss' attention to Exercise **1B**. Read the instructions aloud.
- Model the exercise. Ask one S to ask a question about the chart and another S to answer the question.
- Ss work in pairs. Walk around and help as needed.
- After pairs have asked and answered their own questions about the chart, call on individual Ss to share their questions with the class.

Presentation

- Books closed. Write on the board: *careers*. Read the word aloud and have Ss repeat.

▼ **Teaching tip**
Because the word *career* is similar to a word in Spanish that has a slightly different meaning (*carrera* – which most frequently means "major," as in course of study), Spanish-speaking Ss may be confused by the term. Tell them that in English, *career* is similar to *occupation*.

- Ask Ss if they can give you examples of careers in English. Elicit appropriate responses, such as *teacher, writer, singer, doctor, nurse*. Write responses on the board.

Practice

- Books open. Direct Ss' attention to Exercise **2A**. Read the instructions aloud.
- Ask a S to read aloud the words in the word bank. Make sure that Ss understand these words. Ask them to mime the meaning to confirm comprehension.
- Ss work in small groups to complete the exercise. Walk around and help as needed.
- Have six Ss read their answers aloud. Make corrections as needed.

Expansion activity (small groups)

- **Materials needed** Photographs of famous people from magazines. (Check that the careers of the people match those in this lesson.)
- Write *ballet dancer, musician, singer / actor, soccer player, statesman,* and *writer* on the board as headings for columns.
- Distribute several photos to each group. Tell Ss that they need to match the people in the photos with the appropriate career.
- Ss work in small groups to complete the activity. Walk around and help as needed.
- Ask Ss from each group to come to the board and write the person they discussed under the appropriate heading.

> **More Ventures** (whole group, pairs, individual)
> Assign appropriate exercises from the *Teacher's Toolkit Audio CD / CD-ROM, Add Ventures,* or the *Workbook*.

Application

- Direct Ss' attention to Exercise **2B**. Read the instructions aloud.
- Write *p-l-a-n f-o-r s-u-c-c-e-s-s* on the board in large letters.
- Model the exercise. Ask Ss to make as many words as they can from the letters in the phrase. Examples might include: *force, plane, seal, soup, place.*
- Ss complete the exercise in pairs. Walk around and help as needed.

Expansion activity (individual work)

- Encourage each S to write a plan for his or her own success. Goal-setting might include taking more English classes, getting a GED certificate, and attending vocational classes.
- Have volunteers share their plans with the class.
- Leave time for Ss to ask and answer questions about their plans for success.

Application

Community building

- **Project** Ask Ss to turn to page 136 in their Student's Book and complete the project for Unit 2.

Evaluation

- Before asking Ss to turn to the self-assessment on page 141, do a quick review of the unit. Have Ss turn to Lesson A. Ask the class to talk about what they remember about this lesson. Prompt Ss, if necessary, with questions, for example: *What is the conversation about on this page? What vocabulary is in the pictures?* Continue in this manner to review each lesson quickly.
- **Self-assessment** Read the instructions for Exercise **3**. Ask Ss to turn to the self-assessment page to complete the unit self-assessment. The self-assessments are also on the *Teacher's Toolkit Audio CD / CD-ROM*. If you prefer to collect the assessments and save them as part of each S's portfolio assessment, print out the unit self-assessment from the Toolkit, ask Ss to complete it, and collect and save it.
- If Ss are ready, administer the unit test on pages T-172–T-174 of this *Teacher's Edition* (or on the *Teacher's Toolkit Audio CD / CD-ROM*). The audio and audio script for the tests are on the *Teacher's Toolkit Audio CD / CD-ROM*.

2 Fun with language

A **Work** in a small group. Complete the sentences with careers from the box. Discuss other successful people from your culture who are known for each of these careers.

ballet dancer	singer / actor	statesman
musician	soccer player	writer

Isabel Allende is known as a _____*writer*_____ .

David Beckham is known as a _____*soccer player*_____ .

Nelson Mandela is known as a _____*statesman*_____ .

Yo-Yo Ma is known as a _____*musician*_____ .

Mikhail Baryshnikov is known as a _*ballet dancer*_ .

Jennifer Lopez is known as a _____*singer / actor*_____ .

B **Work** with a partner. How many new words can you make with the letters from the phrase *plan for success*?

p-l-a-n f-o-r s-u-c-c-e-s-s

3 Wrap up

Complete the **Self-assessment** on page 141.

Review

1 Listening

🔊 **Listen.** Take notes on a conversation.

1. Type of certificate	*Automotive Technology*
2. Number of required classes	*eight*
3. Total number of courses	*10*
4. Time to complete the program	*four semesters*
5. Cost per course	*$60*

Talk with a partner. Check your answers.

2 Grammar

A Write. Complete the story.

A Famous Athlete

Sammy Sosa ___*is considered*___ one of the world's great baseball players.

1. considers / is considered

Raised in the Dominican Republic, he was so _____*poor*_____ that he made a

2. poor / poorly

bat out of a tree branch. After he picked up a real baseball bat at the age of 14, he

learned _____*quickly*_____ . He had great kinesthetic intelligence. In 1989, he got

3. quick / quickly

a contract with a major league baseball team. He didn't play _____*well*_____ in

4. good / well

the beginning, but he hit 66 home runs in 1998. Sosa _____*is admired*_____ for his

5. admires / is admired

generous donations to education and health in the Dominican Republic.

B Write. Look at the words that are underlined in the answers. Write the questions.

1. **A** *Where did Sammy Sosa grow up?*

   B Sammy Sosa grew up <u>in the Dominican Republic</u>.

2. **A** *When did he get a contract with the major leagues?*

   B He got a contract with the major leagues <u>in 1989</u>.

3. **A** *What is he admired for?*

   B He is admired <u>for his generous donations</u>.

Talk with a partner. Ask and answer the questions.

Lesson objectives
• Review vocabulary and grammar from Units 1 and 2
• Practice pronunciation of -ed verb endings

Warm-up and review

• Before class. Write today's lesson focus on the board.
  Review unit:
  Review vocabulary and grammar from Units 1 and 2
  Pronounce -ed verb endings
• Begin class. Books closed. Review vocabulary and grammar from Units 1 and 2. Ask Ss:
  Do you think that you have an aptitude for learning languages?
  What are the names of some of the intelligences?
• Review the passive voice. Ask a S: *Where is this class held?* Elicit: *This class is held in _____.* Ask another S: *Is a placement test required to take this class?* Elicit: *Yes, a placement test is required to take this class. / No, a placement test is not required to take this class.*

Presentation

• Books open. Direct Ss' attention to Exercise **1**. Read the instructions aloud. Tell Ss that they will hear a conversation between two friends, Faisal and Angela.
• [Class Audio CD1 track 17] Model the task. Play or read the first part of the conversation on the audio program (see audio script, page T-157). Pause the program after Faisal says, *He gave me some information about a certificate program in automotive technology.*
• Direct Ss' attention to number 1 in the chart (*Type of certificate*) and ask: *What is the type of certificate Faisal spoke to his career counselor about?* (Automotive Technology)
• Have four Ss read the remaining phrases in the chart. Say: *Now listen and fill in the information in the chart.*
• [Class Audio CD1 track 17] Play or read the complete audio program (see audio script, page T-157). Ss listen and complete the chart. Repeat the audio program as needed.

▼ **Culture tip**
Automotive technology is an important and changing industry in the United States. It includes many types of certificate programs in areas such as transmission (automatic and manual), brakes, electronics, and much more. Because the average American family owns at least two vehicles, and because there is so much to learn as the automotive industry rapidly changes, many schools offer specialized automotive certificate programs.

Comprehension check

• Read aloud the second part of the instructions for Exercise **1**.
• Ss complete the exercise in pairs. Walk around and help as needed.

Practice

• Direct Ss' attention to Exercise **2A**. Ask: *What is the title of this story?* ("A Famous Athlete")
• Read the instructions aloud for Exercise **2A**.
• Ask a S to read aloud the first sentence in the story and to explain the choice of word needed to complete the sentence. Tell Ss to continue reading the story and filling in the blanks.
• Ss complete the exercise individually. Help as needed.

▼ **Teaching tip**
In multilevel classes, some Ss may have little difficulty with this review of grammar. Others may find this review more challenging. Create small groups of mixed ability. Encourage the Ss who are comfortable with these grammar points to help those who are less comfortable.

• Write the numbers *1–5* on the board. Ask Ss to come to the board to write only the answers.
• Read the story aloud using Ss' answers. Correct on the board as needed.

Comprehension check

• Direct Ss' attention to Exercise **2B**. This exercise reviews question formation by asking questions related to the story, "A Famous Athlete."
• Read the instructions aloud. Model the exercise. Ask a S to read the answer to number 1. Ask: *What is the question for this answer?* Elicit: *Where did Sammy Sosa grow up?*
• Ss complete the exercise individually. Help as needed.
• Check answers with the class. Ask for volunteers to read their questions. Write the correct questions on the board.
• Read aloud the second part of the instructions for Exercise **2B**.
• Pairs ask and answer the questions. Walk around and help as needed.

Review

Presentation

- Write on the board: <u>-ed verb endings</u>. Explain that the regular past tense in English has three different-sounding endings. Write /t/, /d/, and /ɪd/ as column heads in a chart on the board. Pronounce each sound.
- Write several words on the board that have different -ed verb endings (e.g., *watched, lived,* and *wanted*) and ask Ss to add additional words. Say each word on the board. Have Ss repeat and indicate in which column each word belongs.
- Direct Ss' attention to Exercise **3A**. Read the instructions aloud.
- 💿 [Class Audio CD1 track 18] Play or read the complete audio program (see audio script, page T-157).
- Have a S read aloud the second part of the instructions for Exercise **3A**.
- 💿 [Class Audio CD1 track 19] Play the audio program again. Pause after each phrase to give Ss time to repeat. Play the audio program as many times as needed. Focus Ss' attention on the pronunciation of the words in bold in Exercise **3A**.

▼ **Teaching tip**
Some Ss may find it difficult to think beyond the spelling of words with final *d* when working on pronunciation for these exercises. If possible, take extra time with these Ss to review the sounds. Exaggerate the final sounds.

Practice

- Direct Ss' attention to Exercise **3B**. Read the instructions aloud.
- 💿 [Class Audio CD1 track 20] Model the task. Play or read the first sentence on the audio program (see audio script, page T-157). Ask Ss to tell you the -ed word (*located*) and in which column the word belongs (/ɪd/).
- Tell Ss to pay attention to the sounds of the verbs with the -ed endings as they listen and repeat. Play or read the audio program, stopping as needed for Ss to repeat the sentences.
- 💿 [Class Audio CD1 track 20] Play or read the complete audio program again. Ss identify the pronunciation of the -ed endings by marking the appropriate column.
- Read aloud the second part of the instructions for Exercise **3B**.
- Ss complete the exercise in pairs. Listen to Ss' pronunciation. Help Ss pronounce the -ed endings correctly.

Application

- Direct Ss' attention to Exercise **3C**. Read the instructions aloud.
- Ss complete the exercise in pairs. Walk around and listen to Ss' pronunciation. Write any words on the board that Ss had trouble pronouncing. Point to each word. Say it and ask Ss to repeat.
- Ask Ss to write the words with -ed verb endings on the board in the appropriate columns: /t/, /d/, or /ɪd/. Correct pronunciation and have Ss repeat as needed.
- Focus Ss' attention on Exercise **3D**. Read the instructions aloud.
- Model the exercise. Ask a S to make up a question using *administered* and write it on the board. Ask another S to answer the question. Correct pronunciation as needed.
- Ss complete the exercise in pairs. Listen to Ss' pronunciation as they ask and answer the questions.

Evaluation

- Direct Ss' attention to the lesson focus written on the board.
- Write on the board:
  Venus Williams is a great athlete.
  Mathematical skills are very important.
- Ask Ss to make up questions with *that* and a noun clause using the statements on the board. (*Do you think that Venus Williams is a great athlete?*)
- Write *adjectives* and *adverbs* on the board. Ask Ss to give you examples of each (e.g., *quick / quickly, skillful / skillfully, good / well*).
- Write the following on the board:
  The college gives a placement test to all new students.
  Does the college arrange internships for students?
- Ask Ss to read each sentence and then change each sentence into the present passive voice. (*A placement test is given to all new students. Are internships arranged for students?*)
- Ask Ss to make sentences about their school's program using the following past participles and the infinitive: *encouraged, expected, required,* and *told.* (*Students are encouraged to arrive early,* etc.)
- Focus Ss' attention on the sentences in Exercise **3A**. Ask Ss to read the sentences aloud, and check that they pronounce the final -ed verb endings correctly.
- Check off each part of the lesson focus as Ss demonstrate an understanding of what they have learned in the lesson.

3 Pronunciation: *-ed* verb endings

A 💿 **Listen** to the *-ed* verb endings in these sentences.

/t/
1. He has always **liked** playing number games.
2. She has **worked** as an accountant for ten years.

/d/
3. Emily has **realized** that Brenda has a good brain.
4. Naturalists are **skilled** in working with plants.

/ɪd/
5. The little boy **started** counting when he was two.
6. She is **gifted** in singing and dancing.

💿 **Listen again and repeat.** Pay attention to the *-ed* verb endings.

B 💿 **Listen and repeat.** Then check (✓) the correct pronunciation for each *-ed* verb ending.

	/t/	/d/	/ɪd/
1. Classes are located at various elementary schools.			✓
2. All students are advised of the school rules.		✓	
3. An application is required for admission.		✓	
4. A math test is needed as well.			✓
5. The test is administered once a week.		✓	
6. The students are expected to pay their fees soon.			✓
7. Lucas hasn't talked with a counselor yet.	✓		
8. But he is finished with all his tests.	✓		

Talk with a partner. Compare your answers.

C **Talk** with a partner. Practice the conversations. Pay attention to the pronunciation of the *-ed* verb endings: /t/, /d/, or /ɪd/.

1. *A* Are classes offered on Saturday?
   B Yes, classes are offered from 9:00 to 12:00.
2. *A* What are we expected to bring to class?
   B You are expected to bring a notebook, the textbook, and a pen.
3. *A* How did she cook?
   B She cooked very well.
4. *A* How did he paint?
   B He painted skillfully.

D **Write** five questions. Use the following words: *administered*, *required*, *located*, *expected*, and *provided*. Then ask your partner.

Lesson **A** *Get ready*

1 Talk about the pictures

A What do you see?

B What is happening?

Lesson objectives
- Introduce students to the topic
- Find out what students know about the topic
- Preview the unit by talking about the pictures
- Practice key vocabulary
- Practice listening skills

Warm-up and review

- Before class. Write today's lesson focus on the board. *Lesson A:*
  Ask about rules at home and at school
  Ask questions indirectly
  Talk about past events and experiences
- Begin class. Books closed. Direct Ss' attention to the lesson focus. Point to the first item: *Ask about rules at home and at school*. Write *rules* on the board. Ask Ss: *What are rules?* Elicit appropriate responses, such as: *statements that tell what is allowed or not allowed in a certain place or situation.* Ask: *What's an example of a school rule?* List Ss' responses on the board, for example: *At school, eating in the classroom is against the rules. Ss are not allowed to miss more than three classes per semester.*
- Ask Ss: *What happens if you don't follow rules?* (You will be asked to leave class; you will have family arguments; etc.)

Presentation

- Books open. Set the scene. Direct Ss' attention to the first picture on page 32. Ask the question from Exercise **1A**: *What do you see?* Elicit and write on the board as much vocabulary about the picture as possible. Explain any unfamiliar words. Continue eliciting words to describe the two remaining pictures.
- Direct Ss' attention to the question in Exercise **1B**: *What is happening?* Read it aloud. Focus on Picture 1. Hold up the Student's Book. Point to the first picture. Ask: *What are Lan and Mary doing?* (They're leaving school early on a school day.)
- Have Ss focus on Picture 2. Hold up the Student's Book and point to the second picture. Ask: *What are they doing in this picture?* (They're walking around a shopping mall.)
- Direct Ss' attention to Picture 3. Ask Ss to describe what is happening in the picture. (An older woman, probably Lan's mother, is arguing with her about something.)
- Brainstorm and list on the board things that Lan and Mrs. Lee might be saying to each other.

▼ Teaching tip
Encourage Ss to be creative. At this point, there is no single correct answer.

▼ Culture tip
Share with Ss the idea that in high schools in the United States, Ss are expected to be present every day that school is in session. In many places it is against the law to miss school, and in some schools Ss cannot return to classes without a note from a parent or a doctor explaining the reason for the absence. Many school systems now have computer phone systems that notify parents when children are not in school. You may wish to compare school attendance rules in the United States with those in your Ss' home countries.

Practice

- Ss in pairs. Have Ss develop their visual literacy skills by working with a partner to create a story from the pictures. One S writes the story as pairs work together.

▼ Teaching tip
If you have a multilevel class, this would be a good time to pair a S who feels more confident with speaking skills with a S who feels more comfortable with writing skills. Encourage pairs to be supportive as they work together to create a story.

- Invite a S to begin the story. Write several suggestions or sentence-starters on the board. Then have partners work together to continue the story.
- Ask Ss from several pairs to share their stories with the class.

Expansion activity (student pairs)

- Tell Ss to work in pairs to create conversations. Divide the class into three groups: the first group should work on the conversation between the girls in the first picture (where they are leaving school), the second group should work on the conversation between the girls at the mall, and the third group should work on a conversation between the mother and her daughter.
- Have several pairs role-play their conversations for the class.

Lesson A · Get ready

Presentation

- Books open. Direct Ss' attention to Exercise **2A**. Tell Ss that they are going to listen to three audio segments, one for each of the pictures on page 32. Ss should listen for the main ideas. Then read the instructions aloud.
- [Class Audio CD1 track 21] Play or read the audio program (see audio script, page T-157). Ask a S to read the questions in Exercise **2A**. Tell Ss to listen for the answers.
- Elicit answers to the questions, for example: *In the first segment, there's a recorded message from the school for Mrs. Lee. The message from the school states that Lan was absent from her 7th period class.*
- Focus Ss' attention on Exercise **2B**. Read the instructions aloud. Tell Ss to listen and complete the chart based on the information they hear.
- [Class Audio CD1 track 22] Have Ss listen for details about Lan, her absence, and what her mother says. Model the task. Play or read the audio program again. Pause it after the person calling from Lan's school in Part 1 says: *Please call the office at 619-555-2300 to explain why your daughter missed class. Thank you.* Call on a S to read the example under Part 1 of the chart (*Lan absent from class*). Tell Ss to listen to the audio and complete the chart based on the information they hear. Play or read the rest of the audio program.
- Direct Ss' attention to the second part of Exercise **2B**. Read the instructions aloud.
- [Class Audio CD1 track 22] Play or read the audio program again (see audio script, page T-157). Ss listen and check their answers. Repeat as needed.
- Write the chart on the board. Have several Ss come to the board to write their answers.

Practice

- Focus Ss' attention on Exercise **2C**. Read the instructions aloud. Tell Ss that the story in this exercise is a summary of what happened in the three pictures on page 32.
- Direct Ss' attention to the words or expressions in the word bank. Say each and have Ss repeat. Correct pronunciation as needed. Explain the meaning of any words that are new to Ss.
- Model the exercise. Ask a S to read aloud the first three sentences of the story, including the answer in the example blank. Have Ss fill in the remaining blanks with the words from the word bank.
- Ss complete the exercise individually. Help as needed.

Comprehension check

- [Class Audio CD1 track 23] Play or read the audio program (see audio script, page T-158). Ss listen and check their answers. Repeat the audio program as needed.
- Write the numbers *1–8* on the board. Have Ss come to the board to write only the answers.
- Ask Ss: *Are the answers correct?* Have Ss make corrections on the board as needed.

Learner persistence (individual work)

- [Self-Study Audio CD tracks 10 and 11] Exercises **2A**, **2B**, and **2C** are recorded on the Ss' self-study CD at the back of the Student's Book. Ss can listen to the CD at home for reinforcement and review. They can also listen to the CD for self-directed learning when class attendance is not possible.

> **Culture note**
> Read the culture note aloud. Ask Ss if they have ever heard of a school calling parents to talk about a problem with a student. Explain that this is common practice in many schools in the United States and that sometimes the school will request that the parents come to school for a meeting to discuss the problem. Ask Ss how parents might respond to such a meeting.

Application

- Focus Ss' attention on Exercise **2D**. Read the instructions aloud.
- Model the task. Ask a S the question: *Do you think Lan's mother is too strict?* Call on another S to respond, who should support his or her answer with reasons.
- Ss complete the exercise in pairs. Walk around and help as needed.

Evaluation

- Direct Ss' attention to the lesson focus written on the board. Ask individual Ss to look at the pictures on page 32 to tell you the story about Lan. Encourage Ss to make sentences using the words and expressions from the word bank in Exercise **2C**.
- Check off each part of the lesson focus as Ss demonstrate an understanding of what they have learned in the lesson.

> **More Ventures** (whole group, pairs, individual)
> Assign appropriate exercises from the *Teacher's Toolkit Audio CD / CD-ROM, Add Ventures,* or the *Workbook.*

2 Listening

 **A**  **Listen** and answer the questions.

1. Who are the speakers?
2. What are they talking about?

 **B**  **Listen again.** Take notes.

Part 1	Part 2	Part 3
Reason for call:	Mother's rules:	Reason mother is upset:
Lan absent from class	*Lan can't go anywhere*	*Lan broke the school rules.*
Action to take:	*without her parents or brother.*	Lan's punishment:
Call the office		*grounded for the next two weekends*

Listen again. Check your answers.

 **C**  **Read.** Complete the story. Listen and check your answers.

bring (someone) up	chaperone	permitted	strict
broke (the) rules	grounded	raised	trust

    Mrs. Lee received a phone message from her daughter's school saying Lan missed her 7th period class. Lan left school early to go to the mall with her friend Mary. At the mall, Lan tells Mary that her mother is too _____*strict*_____ .
1

Lan thinks it's because her mother wants to _____*bring*_____ her _____*up*_____
    2   2

the same way she was _____*raised*_____ in China. That's why Lan needs a
              3

_____*chaperone*_____ to go out on a date. At home, Lan and her mother have an
    4

argument. Lan is angry because she's not _____*permitted*_____ to go to the mall alone.
                5

She thinks her mother doesn't _____*trust*_____ her. Mrs. Lee is upset because

Lan _____*broke*_____ the _____*rules*_____ . As a punishment, she says Lan is
    7

_____*grounded*_____ for two weeks.
    8

D **Discuss.** Talk with your classmates. Do you think Lan's mother is too strict? Give reasons for your opinion.

> **Culture note**
> When a child gets into trouble at school, the school staff calls the parents to help enforce the school rules.

1 Grammar focus: indirect *Wh-* questions

Direct *Wh-* questions	Indirect *Wh-* questions
Why is she so strict?	I wonder why she is so strict.
How is everything at home?	I'd like to know how everything is at home.
Where did you go?	Can you tell me where you went?
When did they leave?	Do you know when they left?

Introductory clauses

I'd like to know . . .	Tell me . . .	Can you tell me . . . ?
I don't know . . .	I wonder . . .	Do you know . . . ?

For a grammar explanation, turn to page 148.

2 Practice

Culture note
Indirect questions are often more polite than direct questions. Use "please" to make the questions even more polite.

A Write. Change the direct questions to indirect *Wh-* questions.

1. What is the student's name?

   A Do you know _what the student's name is_____ ?

   B Her name is Lan.

2. What class did she miss?

   A Can you please tell me _what class she missed_____ ?

   B Mr. Latham's 7th period English class.

3. Why did she break the rules?

   A I would like to know _why she broke the rules_____ .

   B I don't know why. Perhaps she was bored in class.

4. When did she and her friend leave the school?

   A I wonder _when she and her friend left the school_____ .

   B They left after 6th period.

5. What did they do at the mall?

   A I want to know _what they did at the mall_____ .

   B They talked and went window-shopping.

6. What was Lan's punishment?

   A Can you please tell me _what Lan's punishment was_____ ?

   B Her mother grounded her for two weeks.

Listen and check your answers. Then practice with a partner.

Lesson objective
- Introduce indirect *Wh-* questions

Warm-up and review
- Before class. Write today's lesson focus on the board.
  Lesson B:
  Ask and answer Wh- questions
- Begin class. Books open. Direct Ss' attention to the three pictures on page 32. Review key vocabulary by asking Ss questions about Lan and her mother. Point to Picture 1. *What are Lan and her friend doing?* (They're leaving school in the middle of the school day.) Point to Picture 2. *Where are they?* (They're at the mall, talking and eating.) Point to Picture 3. *Why is Lan's mother upset?* (She's upset because the school called to tell her that her daughter had broken the rules and had left school when she wasn't permitted.) *What is the school rule?* (Students are not allowed to leave school during school hours.) *How is Lan punished?* (She's grounded for the next two weeks.)

Presentation
- Direct Ss' attention to the grammar chart in Exercise **1**. Read aloud the first direct *Wh-* question. Ask Ss to repeat.
- Ask a S to read aloud the first indirect *Wh-* question. Have Ss repeat. Continue in this way for each pair of *Wh-* questions in the chart.
- Point out that with indirect *Wh-* questions, we do not invert the subject and the verb as we do with direct *Wh-* questions.
- Read aloud the list under *Introductory clauses*. Ask Ss to repeat. Point out that when using introductory clauses such as *I'd like to know . . . , Tell me . . . , I don't know . . .* , and *I wonder . . .* , the questions become indirect. *Wh-* questions with *can* or *do* in front of them (e.g., *Can you tell me . . . ?* and *Do you know . . . ?*) also become indirect.
- Ask Ss to write direct and indirect *Wh-* questions about the three pictures on page 32. Give examples: *Why did the school call Lan's mother? Do you know what Lan's mother said when Lan came home?*
- Ss work individually. Walk around and help as needed.

Teaching tip
It might be helpful to refer Ss to the grammar explanation on page 148 in the Student's Book.

Culture note
Call on a S to read the culture note aloud. Tell Ss that the direct forms of the *Wh-* questions can be softened by adding *please*, for example: *Can you please tell me where you went?*

Practice
- Focus Ss' attention on Exercise **2A**. Read the instructions aloud.
- Model the task. Ask two Ss to read aloud the first conversation. Make sure that Ss understand the exercise.
- Ss complete the exercise individually. Walk around and help as needed.

Comprehension check
- Focus Ss' attention on the second part of the instructions for Exercise **2A**, and read it aloud.
- [Class Audio CD1 track 24] Play or read the audio program (see audio script, page T-158). Ss listen and check their answers. Repeat the audio program as needed.
- Have Ss practice the conversation in pairs. Correct pronunciation as needed.
- Write the numbers *1–6* on the board. Ask several Ss to come to the board to write the corresponding set of sentences. Make corrections on the board as needed.
- Point out the use of *please* in questions 2 and 6.
- Call on a S to explain why the word *please* is added to these two indirect questions. (*Please* makes these two questions even more polite.)

Presentation

- Direct Ss' attention to the school report card in Exercise **2B**. Ask Ss what information is on the card. (The semester, the name of the student, the advisor's name, the subject, the grade, and the teacher.)
- Ask a S to read the school subjects. Define or explain any unfamiliar subjects.

▼**Teaching tip**
Ss may be unfamiliar with report cards and with grading systems in the United States. Tell Ss that grading systems vary according to schools and states. Some high schools, for example, don't use letters but number equivalents from 1 to 100. (An A might equal 90% to 100%.) Many high schools include short evaluations along with the grades. (If you have a sample report card, bring it to class.) Ask Ss about grading systems in their countries. You might also want to talk about grades and evaluations for noncredit adult programs.

Practice

- Read the instructions aloud for Exercise **2B**.
- Model the task. Ask two Ss to read the example question and answer to the class.
- Ss complete the exercise with a partner. Walk around and help as needed.
- Call on pairs to share the indirect questions they asked each other.
- Read aloud the instructions for the second part of Exercise **2B**. Refer Ss to the introductory clauses in the chart on page 34 of the Student's Book.
- Call on a S to read the example question.
- Ss complete the exercise individually. Walk around and help as needed.

Comprehension check

- Ask several Ss to come to the board to write their indirect questions.
- Have other Ss read the questions aloud. Ask Ss if the indirect questions are written correctly.

Application

- Direct Ss' attention to Exercise **3A**. Read the instructions aloud.
- Model the task. Invite two Ss to read the example conversation between the parent and the teenager.
- Call on Ss to read Situations 1 and 2 to the class.

- Ask Ss to think of some direct questions they could ask for Situation 1, such as: *Why are you so late? Where were you?* Write Ss' questions on the board.
- Have Ss think of some indirect questions they could ask for Situation 1, such as: *Can you tell me why you are so late? I'd like to know where you were.* Write Ss' suggestions on the board.
- Ss work in pairs to complete the exercise. Walk around and help as needed.
- Direct Ss' attention to Exercise **3B**. Read the instructions aloud.
- Call on pairs to perform their role play for the class.

Expansion activity (student pairs)

- Have Ss role-play conversations outside of the school context. Suggest that they role-play the following conversations using indirect questions with *who, what, where, when, why,* and *how.*
  Situation 1
  A driver gets lost while trying to find the mall.
  The driver stops at a gas station and asks the gas station attendant for detailed directions.
  Situation 2
  A customer in a bookstore can't find the book that he or she wants.
  The customer asks the salesperson for help.
- Ss work in pairs to complete the activity. Walk around and help as needed.
- Call on pairs to perform their role play for the class.

Evaluation

- Direct Ss' attention to the lesson focus written on the board.
- Write the following questions on the board: *Where were you last night? Why didn't you go to class?* Ask Ss if these are direct or indirect *Wh-* questions (direct). Have three Ss come to the board to write the indirect form for each of the questions.
- Check off the lesson focus as Ss demonstrate an understanding of what they have learned in the lesson.

> ***More Ventures*** (whole group, pairs, individual)
> Assign appropriate exercises from the *Teacher's Toolkit Audio CD / CD-ROM, Add Ventures,* or the *Workbook.*

B **Talk** with a partner about Lan's report card. Ask indirect questions.

> **A** Do you know what grade Lan got in World History?
> **B** She got a B.

School Report Card – First Semester

Student's name: LAN SUZI LEE   Advisor: MR. GREEN

Subject	Grade	Teacher
WORLD HISTORY	B	LOPEZ
ADVANCED ENGLISH	A	LATHAM
ALGEBRA	B+	SMITH
P.E.	C	CHIN
CHEMISTRY	C	HOGAN
CERAMICS	A	AZARI

Write indirect questions about Lan's report card.

Do you know what grade Lan got in World History?

3 Communicate

A **Work** with a partner. Role-play conversations between a parent and a teenager. Use indirect questions with *who*, *what*, *where*, *when*, and *why*.

> **Parent** I'd like to know why you're late.
> **Teenager** I stayed after class to talk to my math teacher.
> **Parent** OK. But next time, call me if you're going to be late. All right?

Situation 1
The teenager is two hours late coming home from school.
The parent is worried.

Situation 2
The teenager's report card arrived in the mail. He or she got one A, two Bs, two Cs, and a D. Normally, the teenager gets all As and Bs. The parent is shocked.

B **Perform** your role play for the class.

Lesson C *Indirect questions*

1 Grammar focus: indirect *Yes / No* questions

Direct *Yes / No* questions	**Indirect *Yes / No* questions**
Did you finish your homework?	I'd like to know if (whether) you finished your homework.
Do they have a test tomorrow?	Can you tell me if (whether) they have a test tomorrow?

For a grammar explanation, turn to page 148.

For a grammar explanation, turn to page 148.

Useful language
In indirect *Yes / No* questions, *if = whether*.

2 Practice

A Write. Complete the conversation. Use indirect *Yes / No* questions with *if*.

Son Can I go to a party at Joe's house?

Father Maybe. First I need to know <u>*if you finished your homework*</u> .
1. Did you finish your homework?

Son Yes, I finished it an hour ago.

Father OK. Can you tell me <u>*if his parents will be home*</u> ?
2. Will his parents be home?

Son Yes, his parents will be there.

Father That's good. I wonder <u>*if you need to take a birthday gift*</u> .
3. Do you need to take a birthday gift?

Son No, I don't. It's not a birthday party.

Father I wonder <u>*if they are going to serve dinner*</u> .
4. Are they going to serve dinner?

Son Yes. They're going to barbecue chicken for us.

Father What about your friend John?

Do you know <u>*if he is invited to the party*</u> ?
5. Is he invited to the party?

Son Yes, I think so.

Father Do you know <u>*if John's parents can bring you home*</u> ?
6. Can John's parents bring you home?

Son I'll ask them.

Listen and check your answers. Then practice with a partner.

Lesson objective
- Introduce indirect *Yes / No* questions

Warm-up and review
- Before class. Write today's lesson focus on the board.
  Lesson C:
  Ask and answer indirect Yes / No questions
- Begin class. Books closed. Write these questions on the board: *What did she do yesterday? Can you tell me what she did yesterday?*
- Ask Ss: *What's the difference between these two questions?* (The first is direct; the second is indirect.)
- Underline the *Wh-* word (*What*) and the introductory clause for the indirect question (*Can you tell me . . . ?*). Ask Ss to tell you other ways to change the direct *Wh-* question to an indirect question. (*I'd like to know what she did yesterday. I wonder what she did yesterday. I don't know what she did yesterday,* etc.) Write these indirect questions on the board.
- Tell Ss that in this lesson they will learn about another type of indirect question.

Presentation
- Books open. Direct Ss' attention to the grammar chart in Exercise **1**. Ask a S to read the sentences under *Direct "Yes / No" questions*. Then have another S read the sentences under *Indirect "Yes / No" questions*.
- Ask Ss to identify the introductory clauses under *Indirect "Yes / No" questions*. (*I'd like to know . . .* and *Can you tell me . . . ?*)
- Remind Ss that when forming indirect *Wh-* questions, the introductory clause is followed by *who, what, when, where, why,* or *how.* When forming indirect *Yes / No* questions, the introductory clause is followed by *if* or *whether.*
- Remind Ss that when you write direct questions in the past beginning with *Did,* you do not use the past participle of the main verb. *Finish* is the main verb in the first direct question. However, when you write indirect questions, you use the past participle of the main verb, for example, *finished.* Offer additional examples, such as: *Did you <u>watch</u> TV last night?* (direct) *I'd like to know if you <u>watched</u> TV last night.* (indirect)
- Point out that when direct questions begin with *Do,* you do not use inversion. For example, *Do they have a test tomorrow? Do they know all the answers?* However, direct questions with an auxiliary (a helping verb) require inversion. Write additional examples on the board and underline the inversion: <u>*Are you*</u> *going to the picnic?* <u>*Will she*</u> *go to the movies this weekend?* <u>*Can you*</u> *go to the party tonight?*

- Say: *When direct questions with helping verbs become indirect questions, you do not use inversion.* Write the following indirect questions on the board next to the corresponding direct questions, and underline the uninverted subject and helping verb: *Can you tell me if <u>you are</u> going to the picnic? I wonder if <u>she will</u> go to the movies this weekend. I'd like to know if <u>you can</u> go to the party tonight.*

> ### ▼ Teaching tip
> It might be helpful to refer Ss to the grammar explanation on page 148 in the Student's Book.

> ### Useful language
> Read the tip box aloud. Explain to Ss that in indirect *Yes / No* questions, *if* and *whether* share the same meaning, so either one can be used. Remind Ss that the first *h* is silent in *whether*. If necessary, distinguish between *whether* and *weather*.

Practice
- Direct Ss' attention to Exercise **2A**. Read the instructions aloud.
- Model the task. Ask two Ss to read the first two lines of the conversation between a father and son.
- Ss complete the exercise individually. Walk around and help as needed.

Comprehension check
- Read aloud the second part of the instructions for Exercise **2A**.
- [Class Audio CD1 Track 25] Play or read the audio program (see audio script, page T-158). Ss listen and check their answers.
- Ask six Ss to come to the board to write their answers. Make corrections on the board as needed.

  Option Have Ss read aloud the answers to Exercise **2A** using *whether* instead of *if*. Ss can also work in pairs to take turns reading the completed conversation.

Presentation

- Books closed. Write *dating* on the board. Ask Ss if they know what this term means. Elicit appropriate responses, such as: *Dating is regularly going out with a person you like in a romantic way.*

Practice

- Books open. Direct Ss to Exercise **2B**. Read the instructions aloud. Direct Ss' attention to the pictures. Ask: *What do you see?* Elicit appropriate responses, such as: *The girl's parents are asking her questions. The parents are meeting the girl's boyfriend for the first time. The boyfriend is nervous. The daughter wants to leave.*
- Model the task. Ask a S to read the example indirect *Yes / No* question to the class. Ask other Ss to read aloud the bulleted points. Explain vocabulary as needed.

▼ **Teaching tip**
Review introductory clauses from the previous lesson, such as:

I'd like to know . . .	Tell me . . .
I wonder . . .	Do you know . . . ?

Remind Ss that they can use these introductory clauses to make indirect *Yes / No* questions.

- Ss complete the exercise in pairs. Walk around and help as needed.
- Direct Ss' attention to the second part of the instructions for Exercise **2B**, and read it aloud. Call on a S to read the example indirect question to the class.
- Ss complete the exercise individually. Walk around and help as needed.
- Ask several Ss to come to the board to write their indirect questions. Ask other Ss to read aloud each of the sentences on the board. Ask: *Is this sentence correct?* Work with the class to correct the indirect questions as needed.

Expansion activity (student pairs)

- Tell Ss to imagine that they are going to have a conversation with the boy or girl who is about to go on a date with their teenage son or daughter. Have Ss use the questions they wrote in Exercise **2B** and any other indirect questions they think of to create a conversation between a parent and the boy or girl.

- Ss work together in pairs. One S plays the parent, and the other S plays the boy or girl who is about to go on a date with the parent's child.
- Walk around and help as needed.
- Ask several pairs to act out their conversations for the rest of the class.

Application

- Direct Ss' attention to Exercise **3A**. Read the instructions aloud. Call on a S to read the items listed.
- Have one S read the first bulleted item. Ask three Ss to read the example conversation.
- Ss complete the exercise in small groups. Walk around and help as needed.
- Direct Ss' attention to Exercise **3B**. Read the instructions aloud.
- Have volunteers share information about their classmates with the rest of the class.

   Option Follow up by having a class discussion about different dating practices. Talk about the differences between dating in the United States and in Ss' own cultures.

Evaluation

- Direct Ss' attention to the lesson focus written on the board. Write the following *Yes / No* questions on the board: *Do you have plans this weekend? Will you be home late tonight?*
- Ask a S to read the questions aloud. Then ask Ss to write the same questions as indirect *Yes / No* questions. (*I'd like to know if you have plans this weekend. Can you tell me if you will be home late tonight?*, etc.)
- Check off the lesson focus as Ss demonstrate an understanding of what they have learned in the lesson.

More Ventures (whole group, pairs, individual)
Assign appropriate exercises from the *Teacher's Toolkit Audio CD / CD-ROM*, *Add Ventures*, or the *Workbook*.

B **Talk** with a partner. Imagine you are a parent. Read the information you want to ask your daughter about the young man she is dating. Make indirect questions. Use a variety of introductory clauses.

> Can you tell me if he's a good student?

- is a good student
- has a job
- has nice friends
- has a good relationship with his parents

- lives alone or at home
- is polite
- drives carefully

Write the parents' indirect questions.

Can you tell me if he's a good student?

3 Communicate

A **Work** in a small group. Ask and answer questions about your lives when you were teenagers. Use indirect *Yes / No* questions. Discuss the items listed below.

- dating experience
- relationship with parents
- grades in school
- school activities
- things you were required to do at home
- things you were permitted to do
- things you weren't permitted to do

> **A** I'd like to know if you dated in high school.
> **B** Yes, I did. But only in a group.
> **C** I didn't date until after high school.

B **Share** information about your classmates.

1 Before you read

Talk with your classmates. Answer the questions.

1. How many generations of your family are living in the United States? Which generation are you?

2. What are some of the differences between you and the other generations in your family?

3. Look at the reading tip. Look up the meaning of *barrier*, and predict what the story will be about.

2 Read

SELF-STUDY AUDIO CD

Read the magazine article. Listen and read again.

> Pay attention to words that repeat in a reading. They may give you an idea of what the reading is about.

Barriers Between Generations

In immigrant families, language differences and work schedules often create barriers to communication between the generations. Dolores Suarez, 42, and her son Diego, 16, face both kinds of barriers every day. Dolores is an immigrant from Mexico who works seven days a week as a housekeeper in a big hotel. She doesn't use much English in her job, and she has never had time to study it. Consequently, her English is limited. Her son, on the other hand, was raised in the United States. He understands Spanish, but he prefers to speak English. When his friends come over to visit, they speak only English. "They talk so fast, I can't understand what they are saying," says Dolores. To make the situation more complicated, Diego and Dolores live with Dolores's father, who speaks Nahuatl, a native language spoken in Mexico. Diego can't understand anything his grandfather says.

Dolores's work schedule is the second barrier to communication with Diego. Because she rarely has a day off, Dolores isn't able to spend much time with him. She doesn't have time to help him with his homework or attend parent-teacher conferences at his school. In 1995, when Dolores immigrated to the United States, her goal was to bring up her son with enough money to avoid the hardships her family suffered in Mexico. Her hard work has permitted Diego to have a comfortable life and a good education. But she has paid a price for this success. "Sometimes I feel like I don't know my own son," she says.

Lesson objectives

- Introduce and read "Barriers Between Generations"
- Practice using new topic-related vocabulary
- Locate words that repeat in a reading
- Learn about word families

Warm-up and review

- Before class. Write today's lesson focus on the board.
  Lesson D:
  Read and understand "Barriers Between Generations"
  Practice new vocabulary related to word families
- Begin class. Books closed. Direct Ss' attention to the title of the reading in the lesson focus.
- Write *generations* on the board. Ask Ss: *What is a generation?* Elicit responses, such as: *All the people of about the same age within a particular family or society.*
- Write *barriers* on the board. Ask: *What do you think "barriers" are?* Remind Ss of the word *obstacle* they learned in Unit 2. Say: *"Barrier" is a synonym of "obstacle."*

Presentation

- Books open. Direct Ss' attention to Exercise **1**. Read the instructions aloud.
- Direct Ss' attention to the three questions in Exercise **1**. Ask three Ss to read them aloud.
- Ss in small groups. Have Ss discuss the questions together. Call on a S from each group to share some of the information that the group discussed.

> Read the tip box aloud. Write *words that repeat* on the board. Tell Ss that words that repeat can be an aid to reading comprehension. Point out that repeating words may include words in the title as well.

- Guide Ss to scan the article for words that repeat. Point out that *barriers* repeats in the title, in the first and second sentences of the first paragraph, and in the first sentence of the second paragraph.
- Ask Ss to tell you what other repeating words they found (*immigrant, communication, English,* etc.). Write the words on the board.

Practice

- Read the instructions aloud for Exercise **2**. Ask Ss to read the magazine article silently before listening to the audio program.
- [Class Audio CD1 track 26] Play or read the audio program, and ask Ss to read along (see audio script, page T-158). Repeat the audio program as needed.

- While Ss are listening and reading the article, ask them to write any words they don't know in their notebooks. When the audio program is finished, have Ss write the new vocabulary words on the board.
- Point to each word on the board. Say it and ask Ss to repeat. Give a brief explanation of each word, or ask Ss who are familiar with the word to explain it. Allow Ss to look up new words in their dictionaries.
- Encourage Ss to guess the meaning of the unfamiliar words they listed from the context clues in the article. For example, if a S writes *hardships,* show how the S can figure out the meaning of the word from context clues in the article. Read this sentence aloud: *In 1995, when Dolores immigrated to the United States, her goal was to bring up her son with enough money to avoid the **hardships** her family suffered in Mexico.* Ask Ss to think about the meaning of *hardships* based on the surrounding words, such as *suffered,* and information in the sentence. Tell Ss that *hardships,* such as the lack of money, cause people to suffer.

Learner persistence *(individual work)*

- [Self-Study Audio CD track 12] Exercise **2** is recorded on the Ss' self-study CD at the back of the Student's Book. Ss can listen to the CD at home for reinforcement and review. They can also listen to the CD for self-directed learning when class attendance is not possible.

Expansion activity *(whole group)*

- Books closed. Point to the new vocabulary words from Exercise **2** that you elicited from Ss and wrote on the board. Say each word and have Ss repeat.
- Invite Ss to summarize the article in Exercise **2**, using the new vocabulary words on the board as a guide to citing only the most important points.
- Ask as many Ss as possible to say at least one sentence about the article. Listen closely to monitor how well Ss have comprehended the reading.

Lesson D Reading

Comprehension check

- Read the instructions aloud for Exercise **3A**.
- Ask six Ss to read the questions aloud, one at a time. Make sure that Ss understand all the questions.
- Ss complete the exercise individually. Walk around and help as needed.
- Ss in pairs. Ask Ss to compare answers with their partner.
- Discuss the answers with the class. Ask Ss to say where in the reading they found each of the answers.

Practice

- **Materials needed** A dictionary for each S.
- Direct Ss' attention to Exercise **3B**. Have a volunteer read the instructions for number 1.
- Ss complete the task individually.
- Direct Ss to number 2 of Exercise **3B**, and read it aloud.
- Model the task. Find *immigrant* in the dictionary and show Ss how to find the part of speech of the word. (The word is a noun and an adjective.)
- Ss complete the task individually. Walk around and help as needed.
- Write the chart in number 2 on the board. Call on Ss to fill in the missing words in the word families and write these words on the board. Say each word and have Ss repeat.
- Ask Ss if they notice patterns in certain word-form endings (e.g., noun endings with *-tion*, verb endings with *-ate*, adjective endings with *-ive, -ful,* or *-al*).
- Call on a S to read aloud the three categories in the chart. Have another S read the examples in the top row. Point out that most words will change depending on their part of speech, but in this case, *immigrant* is the same in its noun and adjectival form. Ask Ss: *If "immigrant" looks the same when it is a noun and an adjective, how can you tell what part of speech it is?* Elicit appropriate responses, such as: *You have to look at the word in context to figure out the part of speech.*
- Direct Ss' attention to number 3 in Exercise **3B**. Ask a S to read the instructions aloud.
- Ss complete the exercise individually by filling in the correct form of the word from the chart in number 2 of Exercise **3B**. Walk around and help as needed.
- Ask six Ss to read their answers aloud. As they do, point to the chart on the board to indicate which word form the S used. Have other Ss make corrections on the board as needed.

Application

- Direct Ss' attention to Exercise **3C**, and read the instructions aloud.
- Ask a S to read the questions in Exercise **3C** to the class.
- Ss complete the exercise in pairs. Walk around and help as needed.
- Ask several pairs to ask and answer the questions for the rest of the class.

Expansion activity (individual work)

- Refer Ss to the questions in Exercise **3C**. Ask them to choose one of the questions and write a paragraph based on it. Remind them to start with a topic sentence and to use facts, examples, reasons, and other details to support their topic sentence and ideas.

Evaluation

- Direct Ss' attention to the lesson focus written on the board.
- Books closed. Ask individual Ss to summarize the article, "Barriers Between Generations."
- Books open. Write on the board several of the words from the chart in number 2 of Exercise **3B**. Ask Ss to identify whether each word is a noun, verb, adjective, or noun and adjective.
- Check off each part of the lesson focus as Ss demonstrate an understanding of what they have learned in the lesson.

Learner persistence (individual work)

- You may wish to assign Extended reading worksheets from the *Teacher's Toolkit Audio CD / CD-ROM* for Ss to complete outside of class. The purpose of these worksheets is to encourage Ss to read for pleasure in English outside of the English class. The worksheets can also be assigned as extended reading in class.

> ***More Ventures*** (whole group, pairs, individual)
> Assign appropriate exercises from the *Teacher's Toolkit Audio CD / CD-ROM*, *Add Ventures*, or the *Workbook*.

3 After you read

A Check your understanding.

1. What are the two barriers to communication between Dolores and her son?
2. Why is Dolores's English limited?
3. Which language does Diego prefer?
4. Why can't Diego communicate with his grandfather?
5. What was Dolores's goal when she came to the United States?
6. How do you think Dolores and her son could communicate better?

B Build your vocabulary.

1. Find and underline the following words in the reading: *immigrant*, *differences*, *create*, *communication*, *education*, and *success*.

2. Use a dictionary. Fill in the chart with the missing word forms.

Noun	Verb	Adjective
immigrant	*immigrate*	*immigrant*
differences	*differ*	*different*
creation	create	*creative*
communication	*communicate*	*communicative*
education	*educate*	*educative*
success	*succeed*	*successful*

3. Complete the sentences. Write the correct form of the word from Exercise B2.

a. My family decided to _____*immigrate*_____ to the United States because there was a war in my country.

b. Parents and teenagers almost always _____*differ*_____ in the kind of music they prefer.

c. Shosha paints beautiful and unusual oil paintings. She's very _____*creative*_____ .

d. Debra's son isn't very _____*communicative*_____ . It's hard to know what he's thinking.

e. It's a parent's responsibility to _____*educate*_____ children about right and wrong behavior.

f. You need two things to be _____*successful*_____ in life: motivation and luck.

C Talk with a partner.

1. What are some ways that you and your parents are different?
2. How can parents help children to be more creative?
3. How can people communicate if they don't speak the same language?
4. Is it necessary to go to school to be an educated person? Explain your answer.

1 Before you write

A **Talk** with a partner. What are some differences between you and your parents or you and your children? Write your information in the charts.

Me	My parents
like salads and sandwiches	like lamb and rice
(Answers will vary.)	

Me	My children
play cards	play video games

B **Read** the paragraph.

Different Eating Habits

One difference between my parents and me is that we don't have the same eating habits anymore. My family is Iranian, but I was brought up in the United States. Since most of my friends are American, I enjoy eating "American style." For example, I like to eat salads and sandwiches instead of meat and rice. Because of my job, I don't have time to cook, so I like fast food. I also love to eat in restaurants. On the other hand, my parents still eat like they did back home. They eat rice with every meal, and they eat a lot of lamb and vegetables. They don't like to eat in restaurants because my father thinks my mother is the best cook in the world. Actually, I agree with him. That's why I try to come home for dinner at least twice a week!

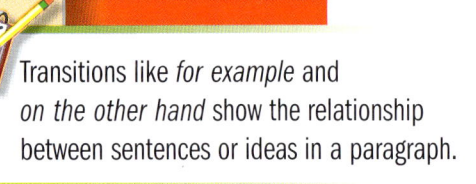

Transitions like *for example* and *on the other hand* show the relationship between sentences or ideas in a paragraph.

Warm-up and review

- Before class. Write today's lesson focus on the board.
  Lesson E:
  Write a paragraph about differences between you and your parents or you and your children
  Use transitions to show the relationship among sentences and ideas
- Begin class. Books closed. Review vocabulary from the unit. Write the words *Barriers between generations* on the board. Ask Ss to give some examples of these barriers. Elicit appropriate responses, such as: *differences in language, in schedules, in tastes.*

Presentation

- Books open. Direct Ss' attention to Exercise **1A** and read the instructions aloud.
- Ask two Ss to read the column headings and the examples in the charts. Tell Ss that if they want, they can fill in both charts and then decide later which one they will use for their writing.

> ▼ **Teaching tip**
> It is important to be sensitive to the fact that some Ss may not have parents and may have been raised by guardians and/or other family members.

- Ask Ss to discuss the information with a partner. Then have Ss work individually to complete the chart.
- Have volunteers share some of the differences between themselves and their parents or between themselves and their children.

Practice

- Direct Ss' attention to Exercise **1B** and read the instructions aloud. Tell Ss that they are going to read about a man who has eating habits that are different from those of his parents.
- Focus Ss' attention on the photographs. Ask Ss what type of meal they prefer – fast food or home-cooked.

- Have Ss read the paragraph silently. Tell them to underline any unfamiliar words.
- Ask Ss to write any new words on the board. Have other Ss explain the words if they know them, or encourage Ss to try to guess the meaning of the words from context.

> Read the tip box aloud. Tell Ss that transitions (or transitional words and phrases) are good for both the writer *and* the reader because they make the relationships among sentences and ideas clear. Ask Ss if they know other transitional words or phrases in English. Elicit responses, such as: *also, finally, in addition, in contrast.*

Expansion activity *(student pairs)*

- Write a chart on the board similar to the one on page 40 in the Student's Book but with the headings *My parents and my grandparents* and *My children and my grandchildren.*
- Tell Ss that they should choose the situation that is most appropriate for them. Encourage Ss to work independently to make a list of differences between their parents and their grandparents or between their children and their grandchildren.
- Model the activity. Ask: *What are some differences between your parents and your grandparents?* Elicit appropriate responses, such as: *My parents travel; my grandparents never left their native country.*
- Ss work individually at first. Tell Ss to write down their ideas.
- Ss then work in pairs. Have Ss take turns asking and answering questions about the information in their charts.
- If both Ss feel comfortable, have partners share with the class the information they learned in their discussions.

Practice

- Direct Ss' attention to Exercise **1C**. Read the instructions aloud.
- Ask a S to read the sample topic sentence to the class.
- Ask another S to read aloud Part A of the informal outline. Make sure that Ss understand that the outline is based on the model paragraph on the previous page.
- Direct Ss' attention to Part B of the outline. Ss work individually to complete this part. Walk around and help as needed.
- Have Ss share the examples they wrote with the class. Write them on the board.
- Direct Ss' attention to Exercise **1D**. Read the instructions aloud.
- Write the skeleton of an outline on the board:

  Topic Sentence:
  A (Me):
     1. Example:
     2. Example:
     3. Example:
  Transition: On the other hand
  B (My parents / my children)
     1. Example:
     2. Example:
     3. Example:

- Ss work independently to complete their outline before writing.

▼ **Teaching tip**
Before Ss begin to write, encourage them to discuss the topic with a partner or a small group. Such prewriting discussions will help Ss focus their ideas for writing and may give them additional ideas they may not have considered.

Application

- Focus Ss' attention on Exercise **2**. Read the instructions aloud.
- Guide Ss to see that they will be writing a contrast paragraph in which they will be showing the differences between two items – here, two groups of people.
- Ss complete the task individually. Walk around and help as needed.

Learner persistence (individual work)

- If you have any Ss who have difficulty writing, sit with them and help them as the other Ss are writing. Work through the outline from Exercise **1D** to show Ss how to use it as a guide for their writing.

Comprehension check

- Direct Ss' attention to Exercise **3A**. Read the instructions aloud.
- This exercise asks Ss to develop skills to revise and edit their own writing.
- Ss check their own paragraphs against the writing checklist. Walk around and help as needed. If any Ss checked *No* for one or more of the checklist items, ask them to revise and edit their paragraphs to include the missing information.

Evaluation

- Focus Ss' attention on Exercise **3B**. Read the instructions aloud. This exercise enables Ss to work together to peer-correct their writing. Reading aloud enables the writer to review his or her own writing. Reading to a partner allows the writer to understand the need to write clearly for an audience.
- Ss complete the exercise in pairs. Tell Ss to take turns reading their paragraphs to each other. Walk around and help as needed.
- Listen to Ss as they ask their partner a question about the paragraph and tell their partner one thing they learned from it.
- Ask several Ss to read their paragraphs to the class. Have other Ss ask questions and mention something they learned from the paragraph.
- Have Ss tell you examples of transitions they used or heard.
- Direct Ss' attention to the lesson focus written on the board.
- Check off each part of the lesson focus as Ss demonstrate an understanding of what they have learned in the lesson.

More Ventures (whole group, pairs, individual)
Assign appropriate exercises from the *Teacher's Toolkit Audio CD / CD-ROM, Add Ventures,* or the *Workbook.*

C **Work** with a partner. Complete the outline of the model paragraph.

Topic sentence: *One difference between my parents and me is that we don't have the same eating habits anymore.*

A Me: *I enjoy eating "American style."*

   1. Example: *I like to eat salads and sandwiches.*

   2. Example: *I don't eat a lot of meat and rice.*

   3. Example: *I like fast food.*

Transition: *On the other hand*

B My parents: *They still eat like they did back home.*

   1. Example: *They eat rice with every meal.*

   2. Example: *They eat a lot of lamb and vegetables.*

   3. Example: *They don't like to eat in restaurants.*

D **Plan** a paragraph about a difference between you and your parents or you and your children. Include examples to support your main idea. Make an outline. Use your own paper. *(Answers will vary.)*

2 Write

Write a paragraph about a difference between you and your parents or you and your children. Use the paragraph in Exercise 1B and the outlines in Exercises 1C and 1D to help you.

3 After you write

A **Check** your writing.

	Yes	No
1. My topic sentence states the difference between my parents and me or my children and me.	☐	☐
2. I gave examples to support the main idea.	☐	☐
3. I used a transition between the two parts of my paragraph.	☐	☐

B **Share** your writing with a partner.

1. Take turns. Read your paragraph to a partner.
2. Comment on your partner's paragraph. Ask your partner a question about the paragraph. Tell your partner one thing you learned.

1 Life-skills reading

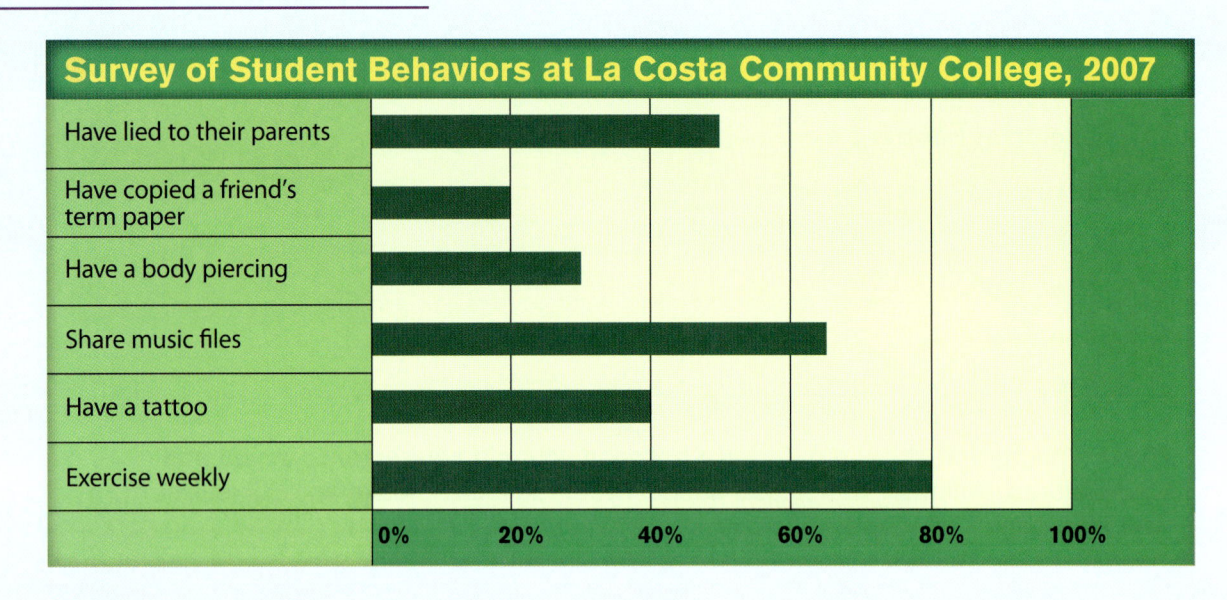

Survey of Student Behaviors at La Costa Community College, 2007

Have lied to their parents	
Have copied a friend's term paper	
Have a body piercing	
Share music files	
Have a tattoo	
Exercise weekly	

0%   20%   40%   60%   80%   100%

A **Read** the questions. Look at the survey results. Circle the answers.

1. What was the population surveyed in this study?
   a. high school students
   b. college students *(circled)*
   c. adult school students
   d. none of the above

2. What percentage of the people in the survey said they exercise weekly?
   a. 35%
   b. 40%
   c. 65%
   d. 80% *(circled)*

3. What percentage of the people in the survey have a tattoo?
   a. 10%
   b. 35%
   c. 40% *(circled)*
   d. 65%

4. According to the survey, the highest percentage of students _____ .
   a. exercise weekly *(circled)*
   b. have lied to their parents
   c. share music files
   d. have copied a friend's term paper

5. According to the survey, the lowest percentage of students _____ .
   a. have copied a term paper *(circled)*
   b. have a body piercing
   c. have a tattoo
   d. have lied to their parents

6. Which of the following statements is true?
   a. More students share music files than exercise weekly.
   b. More students have a body piercing than a tattoo.
   c. More students have copied a friend's term paper than lied to their parents.
   d. More students have a tattoo than a body piercing. *(circled)*

B **Talk** with a partner. What do you think about these survey results? Does anything surprise you?

Warm-up and review

- Before class. Write today's lesson focus on the board.
  Lesson F:
  Read and understand a bar graph
  Review topic vocabulary and grammar from Unit 3
  Complete the project and the self-assessment
- Begin class. Books closed. Write *survey* on the board. Say the word and ask Ss to repeat.
- Ask Ss: *What's a "survey"?* Elicit answers, such as: *A survey asks people questions to gather information (or data), usually to find out how people live or to get their opinion about different things.*
- Ask Ss: *When would you need to read a survey?* Elicit responses, such as: *You would need to read a survey if you were taking a business class, or if you were working in a business and trying to get information about a certain group or groups of people.*

Presentation

- Books open. Direct Ss' attention to the bar graph in Exercise **1**.
- Tell Ss that they will practice reading and understanding a bar graph that presents the results of a survey about student behaviors. Explain to Ss that a bar graph compares items and represents data visually by using horizontal or vertical bars.
- Ask individual Ss to read the title of the graph and the categories on the left-hand side (the Y-axis) of the graph. Explain vocabulary as needed.
- Ask a S to read the percentages along the bottom (the X-axis) of the graph.

▼ **Teaching tip**
Tell Ss that learning to read bar graphs is a useful tool for everyday life. Ask Ss if they have used similar types of graphs, such as line graphs or pie charts. If no one says *yes,* explain that as technology increases in the workplace, Ss may have jobs or be in situations in the future in which they will need to read graphs.

Practice

- Direct Ss' attention to Exercise **1A**. Read the instructions aloud. This exercise helps prepare Ss for standardized-type tests they may have to take. Make sure that Ss understand the exercise. Have Ss individually scan for and circle the answers.

Comprehension check

- Check answers to Exercise **1A** with the class. Make sure that Ss have followed the instructions and circled their answers.
- Have Ss read aloud the questions and the answers they circled.

Application

- Direct Ss' attention to Exercise **1B**. Read the instructions aloud.
- Ss work in pairs to discuss the results of the survey and any surprising aspects of it. Walk around and help as needed.
- After pairs have discussed the survey results, open up the discussion to the entire class.

Expansion activity (small groups)

- Ss in small groups. Ss should develop their own surveys for S behaviors in their class. (If you have a small class, you can have Ss ask other Ss in the program or in the school.) Ask Ss to write a list of six different types of S behaviors. Have Ss write corresponding questions, for example: For a category such as *Have broken a school rule,* the questioner would ask: *Have you ever broken a school rule?*
- Walk around and help as needed.
- Review Ss' categories and questions with the class.
- Have Ss work together to coordinate asking Ss in other groups the questions they prepared. Encourage them to speak with as many Ss as possible (ideally, at least ten).
- Once Ss have gathered their information, they should create a bar graph modeled after the bar graph in Exercise **1**. Walk around and help as needed.
- Ss present their bar graphs to the class.
- Allow time for a question-and-answer session.

Another view

Presentation

- Books closed. Write on the board: *House rules*. Read the words aloud.
- Ask Ss to tell you some of the rules in their own homes or mention some that they may have grown up with as children. Ask if there are differences in these rules for girls and boys. Elicit appropriate responses, such as: *Girls need to have a chaperone when going out on a date. Boys can go out without a chaperone.*

Practice

- Books open. Direct Ss' attention to Exercise **2A**. Read the instructions aloud.
- Ask ten Ss in turn to read aloud the categories. Explain vocabulary as needed.
- Ss complete the first part of the exercise individually. Walk around and help as needed.
- Have Ss interview a partner to complete the survey.

Application

- Direct Ss' attention to Exercise **2B**. Read the instructions aloud.
- Ss share the results of their surveys in small groups.
- Ask a S from each group to present to the class the conclusions about generational or cultural differences among their classmates.

Expansion activity *(small groups)*

- **Materials needed** Index cards, at least one for each S.
- Write the following "house rules" on sets of index cards: *allowance, attending family events, chores, computer/video games, dating, driving, having friends over, home alone, messy room, money, movie rules, parties, phones, privacy, rock concerts.*
- Distribute at least one card to each S. Help with word recognition.
- Tell Ss that they should look at their card and develop a "house rule" for a teenage son or daughter based on that topic. Model first. Write *allowance* on the board, and then present a sample rule, such as: *My son / daughter will receive an allowance of $20 a week.*

- Ss complete the activity in small groups. Each S should present his or her card and rule to the group. Walk around and help as needed. Encourage Ss to ask each other questions about the rules that they make, such as: *Is this a rule you grew up with? Do you know other people who follow this rule?*
- Ask Ss from each group to share some of the rules they discussed.

> **More Ventures** *(whole group, pairs, individual)*
> Assign appropriate exercises from the *Teacher's Toolkit Audio CD / CD-ROM, Add Ventures,* or the *Workbook.*

Application

Community building

- **Project** Ask Ss to turn to page 137 in their Student's Book to complete the project for Unit 3.

Evaluation

- Before asking Ss to turn to the self-assessment on page 142, do a quick review of the unit. Have Ss turn to Lesson A. Ask the class to talk about what they remember about this lesson. Prompt Ss, if necessary, with questions, for example: *What are the conversations about on this page? What vocabulary is in the pictures?* Continue in this manner to review each lesson quickly.
- **Self-assessment** Read the instructions for Exercise **3**. Ask Ss to turn to the self-assessment page to complete the unit self-assessment. The self-assessments are also on the *Teacher's Toolkit Audio CD / CD-ROM.* If you prefer to collect the assessments and save them as part of each S's portfolio assessment, print out the unit self-assessment from the Toolkit, ask Ss to complete it, and collect and save it.
- If Ss are ready, administer the unit test on pages T-175–T-177 of this *Teacher's Edition* (or on the *Teacher's Toolkit Audio CD / CD-ROM*). The audio and audio script for the tests are on the *Teacher's Toolkit Audio CD / CD-ROM.*

2 Fun with language

A Work with a partner. Pretend you have a 16-year-old daughter and a 16-year-old son. What would you permit her or him to do? Complete the survey for yourself. Then interview a classmate.

	You		Your partner: _____	
	Daughter **Yes / No**	**Son** **Yes / No**	**Daughter** **Yes / No**	**Son** **Yes / No**
1. go to the mall with friends				
2. go out on a date with no chaperone				
3. spend the night at a friend's house				
4. stay out after midnight				
5. get a tattoo				
6. get a body piercing				
7. get a driver's license				
8. have a cell phone				
9. dye hair a strange color				
10. wear the same clothes other teenagers are wearing				

B Work in a group. Compare your responses. Choose two or three interesting results and report them to the class. What conclusions can you make about generational differences or cultural differences among students in your class?

3 Wrap up

Complete the **Self-assessment** on page 142.

Lesson A · Get ready

1 Talk about the pictures

A What do you see?

B What is happening?

Warm-up and review

- Before class. Write today's lesson focus on the board.
  Lesson A:
  Ask about stress
  Discuss ways to cope with stress
  Give advice about past actions

- Begin class. Books closed. Direct Ss' attention to the lesson focus. Point to the first item: *Ask about stress.* Ask Ss: *What is stress?* List Ss' responses on the board, for example: *nervousness, tension, uneasy feelings,* etc.

- Ask Ss: *What causes stress?* List Ss' responses on the board, for example: *lack of money, problems with spouse / children, problems with a boss or other job difficulties.*

Presentation

- Books open. Set the scene. Direct Ss' attention to the first picture on page 44. Ask the question from Exercise **1A**: *What do you see?* Elicit and write on the board as much vocabulary about the picture as possible: *bus stop, people chatting, MP3 player (iPod),* etc. Explain any unfamiliar words. Continue eliciting words to describe the two remaining pictures.

- Ask individual Ss to look at the three pictures and talk about the similarities: *She's nervous in all of them. She's waiting for something to happen. She looks stressed out.*

- Direct Ss' attention to the question in Exercise **1B**: *What is happening?* Read it aloud. Focus on Picture 1. Hold up the Student's Book. Ask: *What's Sara doing here? How is she different from the other people waiting at the bus stop?* (She's waiting for the bus. She looks more nervous than the other people waiting at the bus stop.)

- Focus on Picture 2. Hold up the Student's Book and point to Sara in the second picture. Ask: *What's Sara doing here?* (She's listening to her boss. He is angry at her for being late.)

- Focus on Picture 3. Ask Ss to describe what is happening. (Sara's waiting to take her driving test, and she's nervous. Her friend Mike is trying to calm her down.) Check if Ss understand the meaning of DMV (Department of Motor Vehicles). Ask how Ss felt when they took their road tests.

- Ask Ss to guess who the man in the background is. (He will decide whether she passes or fails her road test.)

▼**Teaching tip**
Encourage Ss to be creative. At this point, there is no single correct answer.

▼**Culture tip**
Tell Ss that in the United States, punctuality is very important. Many bosses interpret lateness as a sign of lack of interest in a job – or even disrespect.

- Ask Ss what Sara should do if her bus is usually late and prevents her from getting to work on time. Elicit responses, such as: *Sara should leave home earlier / take an earlier bus / take a train / join a carpool.*

Expansion activity (student pairs)

- Ss in pairs. Assign pairs one of the pictures, and have them create a dialog between the people in the picture (i.e., between Sara and a person waiting for the bus; between Sara and her boss; or between Sara and her friend Mike as Sara waits to take her road test).

- Pairs should write and then practice their dialog until they know it well.

- Invite several pairs to role-play their dialog for the class.

Presentation

- Books open. Direct Ss' attention to Exercise **2A**. Have Ss listen for the main ideas. Read the instructions aloud. Tell Ss that they are going to hear two different audio segments.
- [Class Audio CD1 track 27] Play or read the audio program (see audio script, page T-158).
- Ask Ss if they have understood everything in the listening exercise. Write any unfamiliar words on the board and help Ss understand the meanings. Make sure that Ss understand the meaning of *unreliable*.
- Elicit answers to the questions. For example: *The speakers are Sara, Cindy (Sara's co-worker), Mr. Stanley (Sara's boss), and Mike (Sara's friend). In the first audio segment, Mr. Stanley asks Cindy where Sara is. Then, after Sara arrives, Mr. Stanley tells Sara that if she's late to work again, she'll be fired. In the second audio segment, Sara tells Mike about her nervousness as she waits to take her driving test.*
- Focus Ss' attention on Exercise **2B**, and read the instructions aloud. Tell Ss to listen and complete the chart based on the information they hear. Ask Ss what *symptoms* means. Elicit responses, such as: *Symptoms are signs of illness that a person might show or feel.*
- [Class Audio CD1 track 28] Tell Ss to listen for details about Sara's symptoms and Mike's advice. Model the task. Play or read the audio program again. Pause the program after Sara says in Part 2: *I'm so worried about losing my job, I can't sleep.* Ask a S to read the example written under Sara's symptoms (*can't sleep*). Tell Ss to listen and complete the chart. Then play or read the rest of the audio program.
- Read aloud the second part of the instructions for Exercise **2B**.
- [Class Audio CD1 track 28] Play or read the audio program again (see audio script, page T-158). Ss listen and check their answers. Repeat the audio program as needed.
- Write the numbers *1–6* on the board. Ask Ss to come to the board to write the answers. Have other Ss make corrections on the board as needed.

Practice

- Direct Ss' attention to Exercise **2C**, and read the instructions aloud. Tell Ss that the story in this exercise is a summary of what happened in the pictures on page 44.
- Focus Ss' attention on the words or expressions in the word bank. Say each word and ask Ss to repeat. Correct pronunciation. Explain any new words.

- Model the task. Ask a S to read aloud the first two sentences in the story, including the example answer.
- Ss complete the exercise individually. Walk around and help as needed.
- [Class Audio CD1 track 29] Play or read the audio program (see audio script, page T-159). Ss listen and check their answers. Repeat the audio program as needed.
- Write the numbers *1–8* on the board. Ask Ss to come to the board to write their answers. Work with the class to correct any answers as necessary.

Learner persistence *(individual work)*

- [Self-Study Audio CD tracks 13 and 14] Exercises **2A**, **2B**, and **2C** are recorded on the Ss' self-study CD at the back of the Student's Book. Ss can listen to the CD at home for reinforcement and review. They can also listen to the CD for self-directed learning when class attendance is not possible.

Application

- Focus Ss' attention on Exercise **2D** and read the instructions aloud.
- Ss complete the exercise in pairs. Help as needed.
- Ask several pairs to share their answers with the class.

Community building *(whole group)*

- Because Ss may face a wide range of stress-inducing situations, it is important to discuss resources in your community that may be available to help alleviate stress. If your program is affiliated with a college, find out what the college has to offer in the way of counseling or stress-management classes. Ask Ss if they can recommend any stress-reduction classes they may have taken. Compile a list of places in your community that offers such classes or techniques and distribute it to the class. Your local librarian may also be helpful in finding resources that you can pass on to Ss.

Evaluation

- Direct Ss' attention to the lesson focus on the board. Ask individual Ss to look at the three pictures on page 44 and make sentences using the words in Exercise **2C**.
- Check off each part of the lesson focus as Ss demonstrate an understanding of what they have learned in the lesson.

> **More Ventures** *(whole group, pairs, individual)*
> Assign appropriate exercises from the *Teacher's Toolkit Audio CD / CD-ROM, Add Ventures,* or the *Workbook.*

2 Listening

 **A**  **Listen** and answer the questions.

1. Who are the speakers?
2. What are they talking about?

 **B**  **Listen again.** Complete the chart.

Sara's symptoms	Mike's advice
1. _can't sleep_	4. _take a few deep breaths_
2. _can't eat_	5. _think positive thoughts_
3. _can't concentrate_	6. _meditate every day_

Listen again. Check your answers.

 **C**  **Read.** Complete the story. Listen and check your answers.

anxiety	calm down	cope with	stressed out
breathing	concentrate	meditation	tense

> Mike is driving Sara to the Department of Motor Vehicles (DMV) to take her driving test. He notices that she's very _____tense_____ .
> $\frac{}{1}$
> Sara says she's _____stressed out_____ because she was late to work again.
> $\frac{}{2}$
> She's worried that her boss will fire her if she's late one more time. She's so afraid of losing her job that she can't eat, she can't sleep, and she can't
> _____concentrate_____ . Mike says that she has to _____calm down_____
> $\frac{}{3}$ $\frac{}{4}$
> if she wants to pass her driving test. He suggests three techniques to help
> her _____cope with_____ her _____anxiety_____ . One is deep
> $\frac{}{5}$ $\frac{}{6}$
> _____breathing_____ . The second one is thinking positive thoughts, and
> $\frac{}{7}$
> the third one is _____meditation_____ .
> $\frac{}{8}$

D **Discuss.** Talk with your classmates.

1. Do you ever feel stressed out? What are your symptoms?
2. What helps you when you feel stressed?

1 Grammar focus: *ought to, shouldn't, have to, don't have to*

Advice

Sara ought to learn how to meditate.
She shouldn't get stressed out.

Necessity

Sara has to take public transportation because she doesn't have a car.

Lack of necessity

She doesn't have to take her driving test today. She can take it next week.

For a grammar explanation, turn to page 148.

> **Useful language**
> *ought to = should*

2 Practice

A **Write.** Complete the story. Use *ought to*, *shouldn't*, *have to*, and *don't have to*.

Ana and Bill just got engaged, and they are planning to get married in four weeks. Because the wedding is so soon, they are feeling a lot of pressure. Ana's mother wants a big wedding, but Ana and Bill don't. Because they are paying for the wedding themselves, they believe they ____ought to____ do
                                                          1
what they want. Another pressure is all the things Ana and Bill ____have to____ do before the wedding. For example, Ana ____has to____ buy
        2   3
a dress, choose her bridesmaids, and send out the invitations. Bill ____has to____
                                                                      4
plan the reception and order the food. Most importantly, they ____have to____
                                                                   5
decide where the wedding will be. Ana wants to get married outdoors, but Bill thinks they ____shouldn't____ plan an outdoor wedding because it might rain. Now Bill
              6
has a different idea. He realizes that they ____shouldn't____ get married so soon.
                                                  7
Maybe they ____ought to____ postpone the wedding until the spring. That way, they
               8
____don't have to____ feel so much pressure.
        9

🔘 **Listen** and check your answers.

Lesson objective

- Introduce modals: *ought to, shouldn't, have to, don't have to*

Warm-up and review

- Before class. Write today's lesson focus on the board.
  Lesson B:
  Use ought to, shouldn't, have to, and don't have to
- Begin class. Books open. Direct Ss' attention to the pictures on page 44. Ask Ss: *Why is Sara tense in the car?* (She's on her way to take her driving test.) *What advice does her friend Mike give her?* (He suggests three techniques to help her relax: deep breathing, thinking positive thoughts, and meditating.)
- Ask: *What other advice could you give Sara to help her relax?* Elicit appropriate responses, such as: *She should exercise, practice yoga, or take a hot bath.*
- Tell Ss that in this lesson, they are going to learn about different ways to give advice.

Presentation

- Direct Ss' attention to the grammar chart in Exercise **1**. Read aloud the first two statements under *Advice*. Ask Ss to repeat.
- Read aloud the statement under *Necessity*. Have Ss repeat.
- Read the statements under *Lack of necessity*. Tell Ss to repeat after you.
- Ask: *What's the difference between the sentences under "Advice" and the sentence under "Necessity"?* Elicit an appropriate response, such as: *The sentences under "Advice" make suggestions for Sara or tell her how she should act. The sentence under "Necessity" says what is necessary, or what Sara **must** do.*
- Ask Ss: *What do the sentences under "Lack of necessity" express?* Elicit an appropriate response, for example: *These sentences say that it is not necessary for Sara to do a particular thing at a certain time.*
- Explain that we use the language under *Advice* to make suggestions; we use the language under *Necessity* when we talk about the way something *must* be; and we use the language under *Lack of necessity* when we want to say that someone doesn't have to do something.

Useful language

Read the tip box aloud. Refer Ss to the sentences under *Advice,* and have a S read them aloud. Ask a S to read the first sentence aloud but to substitute *should* for *ought to.* Tell Ss that they can use *should* and *ought to* interchangeably. Point out that *shouldn't* and *ought not* are the negative forms and that *ought not* is not used as often as *shouldn't*.

▼ **Teaching tip**
It might be helpful to refer Ss to the grammar explanation on page 148 in the Student's Book.

Practice

- Direct Ss' attention to Exercise **2A** and read the instructions aloud. Have Ss look at the picture on page 46 to predict what the story will be about.
- Model the task. Ask a S to read aloud the first four sentences, including the example sentence. Tell Ss to complete the exercise by filling in the blanks with *ought to, shouldn't, have to,* and *don't have to.*
- Ss complete the exercise individually. Walk around and help as needed.

Comprehension check

- Direct Ss' attention to the second part of the instructions for Exercise **2A** and read it aloud.
- [Class Audio CD1 track 30] Play or read the audio program (see audio script, page T-159). Ss listen and check their answers.
- Write the numbers *1–9* on the board. Ask several Ss to come to the board to write the answers in complete sentences. Call on other Ss to make corrections on the board as needed.

Expansion activity *(student pairs)*

- **Materials needed** Index cards.
- Brainstorm with the class a list of stress-inducing situations and write them on the board. For example: *taking a test, going on a job interview, starting a new job, going out on a date.*
- Write the situations on index cards and distribute them to Ss.
- Ss in pairs. Explain that one S describes the situation on the card. The other S responds with suggestions using *ought to* or *should.*
- Model the activity with a S. Then have pairs work together. After several minutes, ask partners to switch roles.
- Invite several pairs to share their role play with the class.

Lesson B Modals

Presentation

- Tell Ss that they are going to read and talk about different situations in which people need advice. Read the instructions aloud for Exercise **2B**.
- Books open. Direct Ss' attention to the pictures in Exercise **2B**.
- Call on three Ss to read the descriptions under the pictures.
- Ask individual Ss to read one piece of advice from the box. Explain the meaning of any phrases that are unclear to Ss.
- Model the task with a S. Read the two examples above the pictures.
- Ss complete the exercise in pairs. Walk around and help as needed.

Practice

- Direct Ss' attention to the second part of the instructions for Exercise **2B**. Read the instructions aloud.
- Ask a S to read the sample sentence to the class.
- Ss work individually to complete the exercise. Walk around and help as needed.
- Have Ss come to the board to write their sentences. Work with the class to make corrections on the board as needed.

Application

- Direct Ss' attention to Exercise **3A** and read the instructions aloud.
- Model the task. Ask a S to read the first situation aloud. Have another S read the sample advice.
- Ss work in small groups to complete the exercise. Walk around and help as needed.
- Direct Ss' attention to Exercise **3B** and read the instructions aloud.
- Have groups share with the class the advice they gave for each situation.

Expansion activity (small groups)

- Ask Ss if they have ever heard of "Dear Abby" or a similar advice column. If not, explain that "Dear Abby" is a newspaper column that advises people about how to handle personal problems or difficult situations.

- Have each group brainstorm ideas to create a list of personal problems that might make a person write for advice. Write a sample letter on the board. For example:

  Dear Abby,

  I have a friend whose boyfriend ignores her. Even though she is so nice, he doesn't return her calls. I think that he has another girlfriend. What should I do to help my friend?

  Sincerely,
  Worried Friend

- Explain that sometimes the letter writer will use a descriptive name to sign the letter rather than his or her real name. Ask Ss why the person might do this. (to hide his or her identity)
- Call on a S to use the grammatical structures they learned in this unit (*ought to, shouldn't, have to, don't have to*) to respond to *Worried Friend's* request for advice.
- Have Ss in each group work together to write a group letter of advice. Walk around and help as needed.
- When groups have finished, invite a member from each group to read the group letter to the class.
- Allow time for questions and answers so that Ss can discuss some of the advice that was given.

Evaluation

- Books closed. Direct Ss' attention to the lesson focus on the board.
- Write the following sentences on the board:
  1. You ought to go to the meeting tonight.
  2. You have to go to the meeting tonight.
- Ask a S what the difference is in the meaning of the two sentences. Elicit an appropriate response: *The first sentence gives advice. The second sentence shows necessity, or what you must do.* Ask a S for another way to say the first sentence. (*You should go to the meeting tonight.*)
- Check off the lesson focus as Ss demonstrate an understanding of what they have learned in the lesson.

> **More Ventures** (whole group, pairs, individual)
> Assign appropriate exercises from the *Teacher's Toolkit Audio CD / CD-ROM, Add Ventures*, or the *Workbook*.

B **Talk** with a partner. Discuss what the people in the pictures *ought to*, *shouldn't*, *have to*, and *don't have to* do. Use the items from the box in your discussion.

> Carmela and Hugo ought to try to meet new people.

> Kevin doesn't have to follow his parents' advice.

Carmela and Hugo
- just got married
- just moved to a new town

Chul and Sun Mi
- just had a baby
- live in a studio apartment

Kevin
- just started his first job
- still lives with his parents

try to meet new people	ask lots of questions
call parents whenever they have (he has) a problem	find a new place to live
	follow their (his) parents' advice
learn how to manage money	make decisions by themselves (himself)
try to do everything perfectly	be responsible

Write sentences about the people in the pictures.

Carmela and Hugo ought to try to meet new people.

3 Communicate

A **Work** in a small group. Discuss the following situations, and give advice. Use *ought to*, *shouldn't*, *have to*, and *don't have to*.

1. The Wong family has just bought a house. The house has no furniture at all. Also, it is far from Mr. Wong's job, and the family doesn't have a car.

> They have to buy furniture.

> They ought to check the newspaper for furniture sales.

2. Etsuko and Hiro have just immigrated to the United States. They are anxious because there are so many things to do. They don't have a big enough place to live, they aren't enrolled in English classes, and their children aren't registered for school.

3. Boris is very nervous about his new job. He doesn't know anyone at the company yet, and he doesn't know his duties yet, either. His boss is a woman. He has never worked for a woman before.

B **Share** your group's advice with your classmates.

Lesson C Modals

1 Grammar focus: *should have, shouldn't have*

Regret in the past

I hate my new job.
I should have kept my old job.
I shouldn't have changed jobs.

Advice in the past

Robert is late to work.
He should have left the house earlier.
He shouldn't have read the newspaper before work.

For a grammar explanation, turn to page 149.
For a list of past participles, turn to page 154.

2 Practice

A Write. Read about Imelda. Write sentences with *should have* and *shouldn't have*.

Imelda left the Philippines last year and immigrated to the United States.
None of her family came with her. She got homesick and depressed.

1. She didn't talk to anyone about her problems.

   She should have talked to someone about her problems.

2. She didn't go out.

   She should have gone out.

3. She stayed home alone all the time.

   She shouldn't have stayed home alone all the time.

4. She didn't make new friends.

   She should have made new friends.

5. She didn't exercise.

   She should have exercised.

6. She didn't eat regular, balanced meals.

   She should have eaten regular, balanced meals.

7. She ate lots of junk food.

   She shouldn't have eaten lots of junk food.

8. She slept a lot.

   She shouldn't have slept a lot.

9. She didn't call her family.

   She should have called her family.

Listen and check your answers.

Lesson objective
• Introduce and practice the modals *should have* and *shouldn't have*

Warm-up and review
• Before class. Write today's lesson focus on the board.
• *Lesson C:*
• *Use should have and shouldn't have*
• Begin class. Books closed. Ask a S: *When your friend is stressed or tense, what advice can you give your friend using "ought to," "shouldn't," "have to," or "don't have to"?* Elicit appropriate responses, such as: *You should relax. You ought to meditate. You have to calm down. You don't have to worry about that now.*
• Write answers on the board and underline the modals (*should, ought to, have to, don't have to*).
• Ask Ss: *What are some things that you have to do every day?* Elicit appropriate responses, such as: *eat, sleep, take care of my family, do my homework, practice English.*
• Ask Ss: *What are some things that you don't have to do every day?* Elicit appropriate responses, such as: *watch TV, do the laundry.*

Presentation
• Books open. Direct Ss' attention to the grammar charts in Exercise **1**. Read aloud each of the statements under the *Regret in the past* column. Ask Ss to repeat.
• Ask Ss what *regret* means. Elicit an appropriate response, such as: *a bad feeling about an action taken or not taken in the past.* You can have Ss look up *regret* in the dictionary. Explain that it is being used as a noun here, but that it can also be used as a verb.
• Direct Ss' attention to the statements under *Advice in the past.* Read each statement aloud. Have Ss repeat. Point out that the first sentence in each column presents the situation, but the actual grammar point of the lesson appears in the two sentences that follow.
• Point out that when expressing regret in the past, or when giving advice in the past, *should have* and *shouldn't have* are followed by the past participle form of a verb (e.g., *I should have gone to that party. He shouldn't have eaten the whole pizza.*). Write *should have / shouldn't have* + *past participle* on the board and explain.
• Have Ss make up similar sentences, using *should have* and *shouldn't have.* For example: *I am not happy with my grade on this test. I shouldn't have gone out last night. I should have stayed home and studied.* Or, *Sally has a stomachache. She should have eaten less for dinner. She shouldn't have eaten all that ice cream for dessert.*
• Ask Ss to share their examples, and write them on the board.

Teaching tip
It might be helpful to refer Ss to the grammar explanation on page 149 and to the list of past participles on page 154 in the Student's Book.

Practice
• Direct Ss' attention to Exercise **2A** and read the instructions aloud.
• Ask a S to read the background information about Imelda.
• Model the task. Ask another S to read aloud the first sentence and the example sentence.
• Ss complete the exercise individually. Walk around and help as needed.

Comprehension check
• Read aloud the second part of the instructions in Exercise **2A**.
• [Class Audio CD1 track 31] Play or read the audio program (see audio script, page T-159). Ss listen and check their answers.
• Write the numbers *1–9* on the board. Ask Ss to come to the board to write the two sentences for each item.

Expansion activity *(student pairs)*
• Ask Ss to think of a situation in a story, a book, or a movie in which the main character should have done something differently. Have them use *should* and *shouldn't have.*
• Write this template on the board:
In (name of book or movie), *the main character shouldn't have _____ . He should have _____ .*
• Model the activity. For example, tell Ss: *In Aesop's fable "The Tortoise and the Hare," the hare shouldn't have taken a nap during the race. He should have continued to run the race without stopping.*
• Ss in pairs. Have Ss work together to think of situations from stories, books, or movies to complete the template using *should* and *shouldn't have.*
• Invite pairs to share their situations with the class.

Lesson C Modals

Practice

- Direct Ss' attention to the six pictures in Exercise **2B**. Ask Ss: *What is the man doing in the first picture?* Elicit an appropriate response, such as: *The man has overslept (slept for too long).* Focus Ss' attention on the second picture and ask: *What happened?* Elicit an appropriate response, such as: *The man forgot his briefcase.* Continue in this manner with the four remaining pictures.
- Read the instructions aloud.
- Ask a S to read the example sentence aloud.
- Ss complete the exercise in pairs. Walk around and help as needed.
- Read the instructions aloud for the second part of Exercise **2B**. Ask a S to read the sample sentence to the class.
- Ss complete the exercise individually. Walk around and help as needed.
- Ask several Ss to write their sentences on the board.
- Have other Ss read aloud each of the sentences on the board. Ask: *Is this sentence correct?* Make corrections on the board as needed.

Expansion activity *(student pairs)*

- Ask Ss to role-play Nikolai arriving late to his meeting. Write an example of a conversation on the board, such as:

  Nikolai: Hello, everyone. I'm sorry to keep you waiting!
      Boss: Nikolai, you should have been here an hour ago!
  Nikolai: I know. I should have arrived earlier. It won't happen again.

- Ask two Ss to role-play the example conversation.
- Ss in pairs. Have partners write and practice their own conversations. Walk around and help as needed.
- Ask several pairs to act out their role play for the class.

Application

- Direct Ss' attention to Exercise **3A**. Read the instructions aloud. Ask a S to read the three questions.
- Ss work in small groups to complete the exercise. Walk around and help as needed.
- Direct Ss' attention to Exercise **3B** and read the instructions aloud.
- Model the task. Ask a S to use *should have* or *shouldn't have* to share a situation discussed in his or her group. For example: *One day when Ted went to work, he forgot his uniform. He should have remembered it. He should have gone home to get it before he went to work.*
- Continue the exercise by asking Ss from each group to share information they learned about their classmates.

Evaluation

- Direct Ss' attention to the lesson focus on the board.
- Write on the board:
  1. I watched five hours of television last night.
  2. I went to bed at 3:00 a.m. I'm tired.
  3. I didn't eat breakfast this morning.
  4. I didn't take out the trash.
- Ask four Ss to read the sentences on the board. Ask other Ss to write sentences with *should have* and *shouldn't have*. For example: *You shouldn't have watched television for five hours last night. You shouldn't have gone to bed at 3:00 a.m. You should have eaten breakfast. You should have taken out the trash.*
- Check off the lesson focus as Ss demonstrate an understanding of what they have learned in the lesson.

> **More Ventures** *(whole group, pairs, individual)*
> Assign appropriate exercises from the *Teacher's Toolkit Audio CD / CD-ROM*, *Add Ventures*, or the *Workbook*.

B **Talk** with a partner. Look at the pictures. What should Nikolai and his boss have done differently? Use *shouldn't have*.

Nikolai shouldn't have overslept.

oversleep

forget (one's) briefcase

arrive late

criticize (someone) in public

leave the meeting

lose (one's) temper

Write sentences about what Nikolai and his boss should have done instead.

Nikolai should have gotten up on time.

3 Communicate

A **Work** in a small group. Think about a past situation in your life that didn't go well. Take turns asking and answering questions about it.

1. What was the situation?
2. What did you do that you shouldn't have?
3. What didn't you do that you should have?

B **Share** information about your classmates.

1 Before you read

Talk with your classmates. Answer the questions.

1. When you are in a stressful situation, what happens to your body?
2. Read the **boldfaced** questions in the article. Share your answers to these questions before you read the article.

2 Read

  **Read** the magazine article. Listen and read again.

STRESS: What You Ought to Know

What is stress?

Stress is our reaction to changing events in our lives. The reactions can be mental – what we *think* or *feel* about the changes – and physical – how our body *reacts* to the changes.

What causes stress?

Stress often comes when there are too many changes in our lives. The changes can be positive, like having a baby or getting a better job, or they can be negative, such as an illness or a divorce. Some stress is healthy. It motivates us to push forward. But too much stress over time can make us sick.

What are the signs of stress?

There are both physical and emotional signs of stress. Physical signs may include tight muscles, elevated blood pressure, grinding your teeth, trouble sleeping, an upset stomach, and back pain. Common emotional symptoms are anxiety, nervousness, depression, trouble concentrating, and nightmares.

How can you manage stress?

To prevent stress, you should eat right and exercise regularly. When you know there will be a stressful event in your day – such as a test, a business meeting, or an encounter with someone you don't get along with – it is really important to eat a healthy breakfast and to limit coffee and sugar.

When you find yourself in a stressful situation, stay calm. Take a few deep breaths to help you relax. Roll your shoulders or stretch to loosen any tight muscles. And take time to think before you speak. You don't want to say something you will regret later!

Lesson objectives

- Introduce and read "Stress: What You Ought to Know"
- Practice using new topic-related vocabulary
- Practice the reading strategy of relating what students read to their own experiences
- Identify suffixes that change the part of speech of a word

Warm-up and review

- Before class. Write today's lesson focus on the board.
  Lesson D:
  Read and understand "Stress: What You Ought to Know"
  Practice new vocabulary related to stress and managing stress
  Identify suffixes that change the part of speech of a word

- Begin class. Books closed. Focus Ss' attention on the word *stress* in the lesson focus. Write *stress* on the board. Remind Ss about Sara and her situation. Ask Ss: *Why is Sara so stressed out?* Elicit appropriate responses, for example: *She's worried about losing her job.*

- Ask Ss if they are familiar with health magazines or newspaper columns that offer health advice. If possible, bring to class a few examples and show to Ss.

- Write on the board: *"Stress: What You Ought to Know."* Have Ss read the title and use it as a clue to predict what the magazine article is about. Elicit responses, such as: *The article is about things you should know about stress. It's about how to help yourself when you're stressed out.* Write Ss' predictions on the board.

Presentation

- Books open. Direct Ss' attention to Exercise **1**. Read the instructions aloud.

- Ask two Ss to read the questions to the class.

- Have Ss focus on the second question. Ask: *What does "boldfaced" mean?* Guide Ss to look at the boldfaced questions. Ask Ss: *Why do you think the questions in this magazine article are boldfaced?* Elicit appropriate responses, such as: *The questions are boldfaced because they introduce the topic of the information that follows. They also make the reader want to read the paragraph to learn the answer.* Ask Ss what the benefit of boldfaced questions is. Elicit an appropriate response, such as: *It makes it easier for the reader to find specific information.*

- Ss in pairs. Ask Ss to answer the questions with a partner. Walk around and help as needed.

Practice

- Read the instructions aloud for Exercise **2**. Ask Ss to read the article silently before listening to the audio program.

- [Class Audio CD1 track 32] Play or read the audio program, and ask Ss to read along (see audio script, page T-159). Repeat the audio program as needed.

- While Ss are listening and reading the article, ask them to write in their notebooks any words or expressions they don't understand. When the audio program is finished, have Ss write the new vocabulary words on the board.

- Point to each new word on the board. Say it aloud and ask Ss to repeat. Give a brief explanation of each word, or ask other Ss to explain the word if they know it. If Ss prefer to look up the new words in their dictionaries, allow them to do so.

Learner persistence (individual work)

- [Self-Study Audio CD track 15] Exercise **2** is recorded on the Ss' self-study CD at the back of the Student's Book. Ss can listen to the CD at home for reinforcement and review. They can also listen to the CD for self-directed learning when class attendance is not possible.

Expansion activity (small groups)

- **Materials needed** Poster board and markers.

- Have Ss work in small groups to create a poster entitled "Low-stress Lifestyle Tips."

- Encourage group members to brainstorm ideas to make a list of tips for their poster.

- Point out to Ss that the list should be based on what they have read in the article and their personal experiences.

- Suggest that Ss take notes during the brainstorming session and the group discussion. Guide Ss to use their notes and the grammar from the unit to discuss low-stress lifestyle tips with their group.

- Invite each group to present its poster to the class. Write some of the tips on the board, and engage in a class discussion.

Lesson D Reading

Comprehension check

- Direct Ss' attention to Exercise **3A**, and read the instructions aloud.

> Read the tip aloud. Write *relate* on the board. Say it and have Ss repeat. Ask Ss what they think the word means. Write on the board: *relate = connect.* Tell Ss that good readers relate the information they read to their own experience to help them understand what they are reading. If Ss have experienced some kind of stress, or if they know of someone who has, they will find the article easier to understand if they relate it to their personal experiences.

- Ask five Ss to read the questions aloud, one at a time. Make sure that all Ss understand the questions.
- Ss complete the exercise in pairs. Remind Ss that they can refer to the magazine article on page 50.
- Discuss the answers to the five questions with the class. Ask Ss to locate in the reading where some of the answers are found.

Practice

- **Materials needed** A dictionary for each S.
- Direct Ss' attention to Exercise **3B**. Call on a S to read the instructions in number 1.
- Have Ss scan the article on page 50, and then underline the words with the suffixes that are shown in the left column in the chart.
- Direct Ss to number 2 of Exercise **3B**. Ss work individually to fill in the chart. Walk around and help as needed. Point out that Ss may use a dictionary, if needed, to complete the chart.
- Direct Ss' attention to number 3 of Exercise **3B**. Ask a S to read the instructions aloud.
- Have another S read the model sentence. Ss work in pairs to complete the exercise. Walk around and help as needed.
- Focus Ss' attention on number 4 of Exercise **3B**.
- Model the task by writing *react* on the board. Ask a S: *What suffix could you add to make "react" into a noun?* (-ion) Write *reaction* on the board. Ask another S to give you an example sentence using the new word. (*It's important to control your reaction to stressful situations.*)

- Ss work in pairs to complete the exercise. Walk around and help as needed.
- Ask pairs to come to the board. One S should write the new words with the suffixes; the other S should write the sentence for each of the words. Have other Ss read the sentences aloud. Work with the class to make corrections on the board as needed.

Application

- Direct Ss' attention to Exercise **3C** and read the instructions aloud.
- Ask Ss to read aloud each of the five questions in Exercise **3C**.
- Ss complete the exercise in pairs. Walk around and help as needed.
- Ask several pairs to share the answers they discussed with the class.

Evaluation

- Direct Ss' attention to the lesson focus on the board.
- Ask individual Ss to retell the main points of the article, "Stress: What You Ought to Know."
- Have Ss focus on the words they wrote in the chart for number 2 of Exercise **3B**. Ask Ss to make sentences with these words to show that they understand their meanings.
- Check off each part of the lesson focus as Ss demonstrate an understanding of what they have learned in the lesson.

Learner persistence (individual work, student pairs)
- You may wish to assign Extended reading worksheets from the *Teacher's Toolkit Audio CD / CD-ROM* for Ss to complete outside of class. The purpose of these worksheets is to encourage Ss to read for pleasure in English outside of the English class. The worksheets can also be assigned as extended reading in class.

> **More Ventures** (whole group, pairs, individual)
> Assign appropriate exercises from the *Teacher's Toolkit Audio CD / CD-ROM, Add Ventures,* or the *Workbook.*

3 After you read

A **Check** your understanding.

1. What are some physical signs of stress?
2. What are some emotional signs of stress?
3. What should you eat when you know there will be a stressful event in your life? What foods should you avoid?
4. Do you have a favorite exercise that you do to reduce stress? If so, what is it?
5. Think of a time when there were many changes in your life. Were the changes positive or negative? How did you feel? How did your body react?

> Good readers relate what they are reading to their own experience.

B **Build** your vocabulary.

1. English uses suffixes to change the part of speech of a word. Underline words in the reading that end with the suffixes in the left column.

2. Complete the chart. Use a dictionary if necessary.

Suffix	Example	Part of speech	Main word	Part of speech
-ful	stressful	adj	stress	noun
-en	loosen	verb	loose	adj
-ly	regularly	adv	regular	adj
-ness	illness	noun	ill	adj
-ion	depression	noun	depress	verb

3. Work with a partner. Compare the examples from the reading with the main words. How does each suffix change the main word?

The suffix -ful changes a noun to an adjective.

4. Work with a partner. On your own paper, write more words with each suffix. Write a sentence for each new word.

C **Talk** with a partner.

1. What's a stressful situation you've been in recently?
2. Why is it important to exercise regularly?
3. What are some physical habits that can show nervousness?
4. Is it a good idea to take medicine for depression? Why or why not?
5. Do your muscles often get tight? How do you loosen them?

1 Before you write

A Talk with a partner. Look at the pictures. Answer the questions.

1. How do the people in the pictures cope with stress?
2. What are some healthy ways of coping with stress?
3. What are some unhealthy ways of coping with stress?
4. What makes you feel stressed?

B Read the paragraph.

How I Cope with Stress

When I feel stressed, I like to curl up with my cat, listen to classical music, and read an interesting book. Stroking my cat's soft fur helps my body relax, and soon I feel less tense. The sound of classical music with piano and string instruments shuts out the noises around me and reduces my anxiety. I like to listen with my eyes closed until my muscles start to relax. Then I open my eyes and pick up a book. I usually choose stories about people and the difficult events in their lives because they help me forget about all the stressful things I have to do in my own life.

> One way to organize details in a paragraph is to write about actions and the results of those actions.
>
> *I like to listen with my eyes closed* (action) *until my muscles start to relax* (result).

Lesson objectives
- Write about coping with stress
- Practice writing about actions and the results of those actions

Warm-up and review
- Before class. Write today's lesson focus on the board.
  Lesson E:
  Write a paragraph about coping with stress
  Use actions and their results to organize and support ideas
- Begin class. Books closed. Write the words *Cope with stress* on the board. Ask Ss to define the words. Elicit appropriate responses, such as: *"Cope" means "to deal with" or "to handle."*
- Ask Ss to refer to the magazine article on page 50 and to use some of their own ideas to answer the following questions:
  How did the article define stress? (Stress is how we react to the changing events in our lives.)
  What are some signs of stress? (Physical signs: tight muscles, elevated blood pressure, teeth grinding, trouble sleeping, upset stomach, and back pain; emotional signs: anxiety, nervousness, depression, trouble concentrating, and nightmares.)
  What are some ways to manage stress? (Eat right and exercise regularly.)
  What are some suggestions for coping with stress? (Stay calm, take deep breaths, roll your shoulders and stretch, take time to think before you speak.)

Presentation
- Books open. Direct Ss' attention to Exercise **1A**. Read the instructions aloud.
- Ask Ss to read aloud the five questions in Exercise **1A**.
- Ss work in pairs to ask and answer the questions. Walk around and help as needed.
- Have partners share with the class some of the information they discussed.

Practice
- Direct Ss' attention to Exercise **1B** and read the instructions aloud.
- Ss read the paragraph silently. Ask them to underline any unfamiliar words.
- Have Ss tell you the words that they underlined. Write them on the board. Go over the meaning of each of the words.

Read the tip aloud. Point out that there are also other ways to organize details in a paragraph (by chronological order, by cause and effect, by comparing and contrasting, etc.). Tell Ss that organizing details will help the writer to write more clearly and the reader to follow the ideas more easily.

Expansion activity *(small groups)*
- Ask Ss to work in small groups to brainstorm ideas for a list of some of their goals (e.g., travel, become a teacher, own a business). Elicit Ss' goals and write them on the board. Ask Ss to tell the steps (actions) they would have to take in order to reach each of those goals (results); write some goal-setting examples on the board:
  save money → travel
  take education courses → become a teacher
  take business classes → own a business
- Have groups discuss their goals and give advice related to the actions group members have to take in order to achieve their goals.
- Model the task. Write on the board and have two Ss role-play this dialog:
  A: What's your goal?
  B: I want to travel abroad.
  A: You should (or ought to) get a job and then save some money!
- Call on groups to write and perform role plays based on their goal-setting discussions.

Lesson E — Writing

Presentation

- Direct Ss' attention to Exercise **1C** and read the instructions aloud. Tell Ss that they will need to refer to the model paragraph on page 52 in order to complete this exercise.
- Ask a S to read aloud the first part of the topic sentence.
- Call on another S to read the next heading (*Ways of reducing stress*) and the sample action and result.
- Ss work with a partner to fill in the missing information in Exercise **1C**. Walk around and help as needed.
- Copy the outline from the Student's Book on the board.
- Have Ss come to the board, one at a time, to fill in the chart. Make corrections on the board as needed.

Practice

- Direct Ss' attention to Exercise **1D** and read the instructions aloud. Tell Ss that taking the time to plan a paragraph makes it easier for the writer to write the paragraph and easier for the reader to understand it.
- Ss complete their outlines individually. Walk around and help as needed.

▼**Teaching tip**
Before Ss begin to write, encourage them to engage in a prewriting discussion about the topic of coping with stress. Talking about the topic with a partner or a small group will help Ss narrow their topic and gather ideas for writing.

Application

- Direct Ss' attention to Exercise **2** and read the instructions aloud.
- Ss complete the task individually. Walk around and help as needed.

Learner persistence (individual work)

- If you have any Ss who have difficulty writing, sit with them and help them as the other Ss are writing. Encourage them to use their notes from Exercise **1D** to create supporting facts and details for their topic sentence.

Expansion activity (student pairs)

- Encourage Ss to speak with a partner about coping with illness. Using the same outline as in Exercise **1D**, have Ss talk to their partners about actions and results.
- Model the task. Ask Ss what action they might take if they had a cold and were trying to feel better. For example:
  action: drink hot tea with lemon → result: throat feels better, body feels warmer
- Have Ss discuss the task with a partner.
- **Option** Give Ss the option of writing a paragraph about ways of treating a specific physical illness. Remind Ss to write about actions and results.

Comprehension check

- Direct Ss' attention to Exercise **3A** and read the instructions aloud. This exercise asks Ss to develop skills to review and edit their own writing.
- Ss check their own paragraphs against the writing checklist. Walk around and help as needed. If any Ss check *No* for one or more of the checklist items, ask them to revise and edit their paragraphs to include the missing information.

Evaluation

- Focus Ss' attention on Exercise **3B**, and read the instructions aloud. This exercise enables Ss to work together to peer-correct their writing. Reading aloud enables the writer to review his or her own writing. Reading to a partner allows the writer to understand the need to write clearly for an audience.
- Listen to Ss as they ask their partner a question about the paragraph and tell their partner one thing they learned from it.
- Direct Ss' attention to the lesson focus on the board.
- Check off each part of the lesson focus as Ss demonstrate an understanding of what they have learned in the lesson.

More Ventures (whole group, pairs, individual)
Assign appropriate exercises from the *Teacher's Toolkit Audio CD / CD-ROM, Add Ventures*, or the *Workbook*.

C **Work** with a partner. Complete the outline of the model paragraph.

Topic sentence: When I feel stressed, _I like to curl up with my cat, listen to classical_ _music, and read an interesting book_ .

Ways of reducing stress:

action: _stroke my cat's fur_ → result: _body relaxes, feel less tense_

action: _listen to music with my eyes closed_ → result: _muscles start to relax_

action: _read stories_ → result: _helps me forget about the stress in my life_

D **Plan** a paragraph about how you cope with stress. Use the outline to make notes on your ideas.

Topic sentence: When I feel stressed, _(Answers will vary.)_

_____ .

Ways of reducing stress:

action: _____ → result: _____

action: _____ → result: _____

action: _____ → result: _____

2 Write

Write a paragraph about how you cope with stress. Use the paragraph in Exercise 1B and the outlines in Exercises 1C and 1D to help you.

3 After you write

A **Check** your writing.

	Yes	No
1. My topic sentence identifies actions for coping with stress.	☐	☐
2. For each action, I described a result.	☐	☐
3. I used modals and verb tenses correctly.	☐	☐

B **Share** your writing with a partner.

1. Take turns. Read your paragraph to a partner.
2. Comment on your partner's paragraph. Ask your partner a question about the paragraph. Tell your partner one thing you learned.

1 Life-skills reading

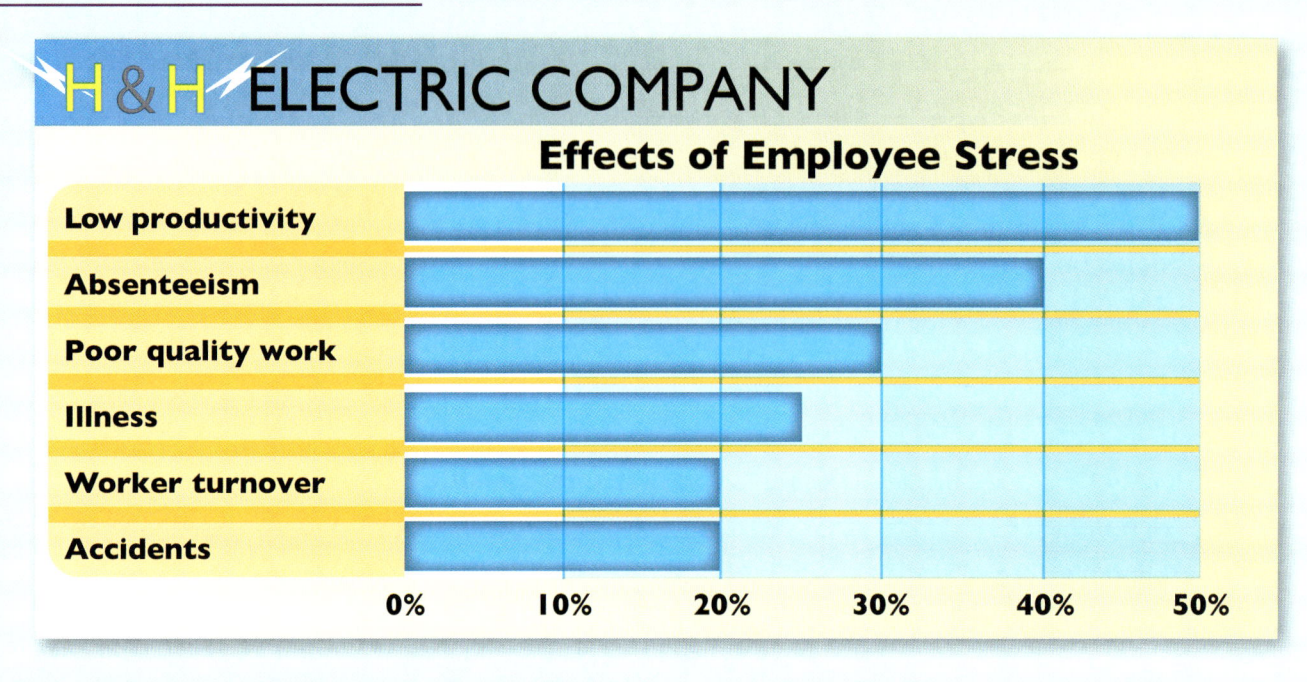

H & H ELECTRIC COMPANY

Effects of Employee Stress

Low productivity
Absenteeism
Poor quality work
Illness
Worker turnover
Accidents

0%   10%   20%   30%   40%   50%

A **Read** the questions. Look at the bar graph. Circle the answers.

1. This chart is about _____ .
   a. how stress affects employees
   b. how stress affects a business
   c. both a and b
   d. neither a nor b

2. Employee stress is the cause of _____ .
   a. 30 percent of poor quality work
   b. 20 percent of worker turnover
   c. both a and b
   d. neither a nor b

3. Employee stress contributes to worker turnover less than it contributes to _____ .
   a. productivity
   b. work quality
   c. illness
   d. all of the above

4. Employee stress affects accidents as much as it affects _____ .
   a. absenteeism
   b. worker turnover
   c. both a and b
   d. neither a nor b

5. Employee stress affects _____ the most.
   a. productivity
   b. work quality
   c. illness
   d. absenteeism

6. Employee stress affects illness more than it affects _____ .
   a. productivity
   b. absenteeism
   c. both a and b
   d. neither a nor b

B **Talk** with your classmates. Should employers do something to relieve stress in the workplace? Why or why not? What could they do?

Lesson objectives

- Practice reading and understanding a graph related to employee stress
- Review vocabulary and grammar from the unit
- Introduce the project
- Complete the self-assessment

Warm-up and review

- Before class. Write today's lesson focus on the board.
  Lesson F:
  Read and understand a bar graph that shows the effects of employee stress
  Review topic vocabulary and grammar from Unit 4
  Complete the project and the self-assessment

- Begin class. Books closed. Write *Effects of employee stress* on the board. Say the words and have Ss repeat.

- Ask Ss: *What does "effects" mean?* Elicit: *consequences* or *results*.

- Say: *Today we will practice reading and understanding a bar graph about the effects of stress on workers and the company where they work.* Ask Ss: *What do you think the effects of employee stress are?* Elicit responses, such as: *poor quality of work, illness, absenteeism, job turnover, accidents.*

Presentation

- Books open. Direct Ss' attention to the bar graph in Exercise **1**. Ask a S to read the names of six effects of employee stress on a business along the left side of the graph (the Y-axis). Explain new vocabulary as needed.

- Ask a S to read the different percentages listed along the bottom of the graph (the X-axis). Make sure that Ss understand what these percentages refer to. For example, employee stress is the cause of 40 percent of all worker absences.

▼ **Teaching tip**
Tell Ss that learning to read these kinds of graphs is a useful life skill. Explain that as technology increases in the workplace, Ss may have jobs in the future that will require them to create, read, interpret, and analyze graphs.

Practice

- Read the instructions aloud for Exercise **1A**. This task helps prepare Ss for standardized-type tests they may have to take. Make sure that Ss understand the task. Have Ss individually scan for and circle the answers.

Comprehension check

- Check the answers with the class. Make sure that Ss have followed the instructions and circled their answers.

- Have Ss read aloud the questions and the answers they circled. Ask Ss: *Is that answer correct?* Correct Ss' answers as needed.

Application

- Direct Ss' attention to Exercise **1B** and read the instructions aloud. Make sure that Ss understand the meaning of the questions.

- Ss in pairs. Have partners discuss whether or not employers should do something to relieve employee stress. Encourage Ss to give strong reasons for their opinions. Walk around and help as needed.

- After Ss have asked and answered the questions, open up the discussion to the entire class.

Expansion activity (small groups)

- Have Ss work together in small groups to write a list of suggestions for employers about how to relieve employee stress.

- Tell Ss to use *ought to, should, shouldn't, have to,* and *don't have to* in their recommendations. Refer Ss to page 46 in the Student's Book as needed.

- Model the activity. Write an example on the board:
  Employers should communicate with their employees in regular meetings.
  Employers should discuss any problems employees are having with their work.

- Walk around and help groups as needed.

- Call on groups to write their recommendations on the board, and engage the class in a discussion.

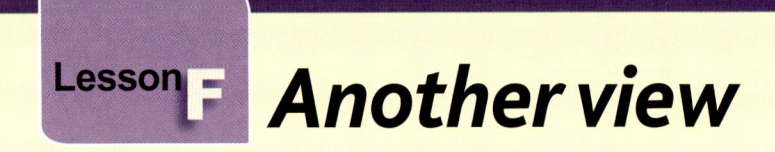

Lesson F — Another view

Presentation

- Books closed. Write on the board: *stress test*. Read the phrase aloud and have Ss repeat.
- Ask Ss if they know what a stress test is. Some Ss may be familiar with the test that is done in the doctor's office in which the heart rate is monitored. Elicit appropriate responses, such as: *a kind of test that determines how much stress you have in your life.*

Practice

- Books open. Direct Ss' attention to Exercise **2A** and read the instructions aloud.
- Call on individual Ss to read the 12 statements. Explain vocabulary as needed.
- Ss complete the activity individually. Walk around and help as needed.
- After Ss have finished giving each of the 12 statements a score, direct Ss to total the numbers in the right-hand column and to circle the corresponding numbers at the bottom of the test to determine how much stress they have.

Application

- Direct Ss' attention to Exercise **2B** and read the instructions aloud.
- Ss work in small groups and share their test results with the other members of the group.
- Ask individual Ss to share their results with the class.

Expansion activity *(small groups)*

- Among the many recommendations for stress reduction is an exercise called "A Minute Vacation." Read this description to Ss:
  Unfortunately, you can't always run away or escape from problems and stress, but you can use your dreams as a means of getting away. Close your eyes. Imagine a calm place, like a beautiful beach where there are no other people, and you feel comfortable and relaxed. As you imagine this place, be aware of all the details, including sounds, smells, and temperature.

- Have Ss sit in small groups to discuss and try this visualization technique to reduce stress. Encourage Ss to share details about their stress-free dream vacation destinations. Ask Ss: *Did visualizing this "dream place" help you reduce stress?*

> **More Ventures** *(whole group, pairs, individual)*
> Assign appropriate exercises from the *Teacher's Toolkit Audio CD / CD-ROM, Add Ventures,* or the *Workbook.*

Application

Community building

- **Project** Ask Ss to turn to page 137 in their Student's Book to complete the project for Unit 4.

Evaluation

- Before asking Ss to turn to the self-assessment on page 142, do a quick review of the unit. Have Ss turn to Lesson A. Ask the class to talk about what they remember about this lesson. Prompt Ss, if necessary, with questions, for example: *What are the conversations about on this page? What vocabulary is in the pictures?* Continue in this manner to review each lesson quickly.
- **Self-assessment** Read the instructions for Exercise **3**. Ask Ss to turn to the self-assessment page to complete the unit self-assessment. The self-assessments are also on the *Teacher's Toolkit Audio CD / CD-ROM.* If you prefer to collect the assessments and save them as part of each S's portfolio assessment, print out the unit self-assessment from the Toolkit, ask Ss to complete it, and collect and save it.
- If Ss are ready, administer the unit test on pages T-178–T-180 of this *Teacher's Edition* (or on the *Teacher's Toolkit Audio CD / CD-ROM*). The audio and audio script for the tests are on the *Teacher's Toolkit Audio CD / CD-ROM.*

2 Fun with language

A **Write** your answers to this test about stress.

STRESS TEST

Directions: Give each statement a score of 1 to 5 to indicate how true the statement is about you.

1 = Always   2 = Often   3 = Sometimes   4 = Rarely   5 = Never

1. I eat at least one balanced meal a day. _____
2. I get seven to eight hours of sleep a night. _____
3. I am in good health. _____
4. I am the correct weight for my height. _____
5. I have fewer than three caffeinated drinks (coffee, tea, or soda) a day. _____
6. I have enough money to pay for necessary things. _____
7. I have someone I talk to when I have personal problems. _____
8. When I am angry or worried, I am able to talk about it. _____
9. I organize my time effectively. _____
10. I make some time for myself each day. _____
11. I do something for fun at least once a week. _____
12. I exercise or walk at least three times a week. _____

Total _____

Add the numbers in the right-hand column. How much stress do you have?
Little or no stress 12–24   A lot of stress 37–48
Some stress 25–36   Too much stress 49–60

B **Talk** with your classmates about your test results.

1. How much stress do you have in your life?
2. Is there anything you ought to change? If so, what?
3. Is there anything you don't have to change? If not, why not?

3 Wrap up

Complete the **Self-assessment** on page 142.

Review

1 Listening

Listen. Take notes on a phone conversation.

Yesenia's symptoms	Sue's suggestions
1. *tense*	4. *take a parenting class*
2. *quiet*	5. *call Yesenia's school counselor*
3. *can't concentrate on schoolwork*	6. *take an exercise class together*

Talk with a partner. Check your answers.

2 Grammar

A Write. Complete the story. Use indirect questions.

Ann's Night Out

Ann is 16 years old. It's midnight, and she isn't home yet. She went out

with her friend Liz. Ann's mom doesn't know _____*where they went*_____ . She
1. Where did they go?

wonders _*if / whether Ann and Liz are safe*_ . Ann's mother wants to call Liz's house, but
2. Are Ann and Liz safe?

she doesn't know _*what the phone number is*_ . Ann's father is worried, too. He
3. What is the phone number?

wonders _*if / whether he can find them*_ . Then he hears a sound. For a minute, he
4. Can he find them?

doesn't know _____*who it is*_____ . It's Ann! Her father says, "We had no
5. Who is it?

idea _____*where you were*_____ , but we're glad you're home."
6. Where were you?

B Write. Look at the words that are underlined in the answers. Write
the questions.

1. **A** *When should Ann have been home?*

   B Ann should have been home <u>at 11:00</u>.

2. **A** *Who should she have called?*

   B She should have called <u>her parents</u>.

3. **A** *What should Ann's parents do?*

   B Ann's parents should <u>ground her</u>.

Talk with a partner. Ask and answer the questions.

Lesson objectives
- Review vocabulary and grammar from Units 3 and 4
- Practice intonation in questions

Warm-up and review

- Before class. Write today's lesson focus on the board. *Review unit:*
  Review vocabulary and grammar from Units 3 and 4
  Practice using intonation in questions
- Begin class. Books closed. Ask Ss questions to review vocabulary from Units 3 and 4, for example: *What are some barriers between generations of immigrant families? What are some differences between your parents and you? What is stress? What are some stressful situations? How can you cope with stress?*

Presentation

- Books open. Direct Ss' attention to Exercise **1** and read the instructions aloud. Tell Ss that they will hear a conversation between two friends, Blanca and Sue.
- [Class Audio CD2 track 2] Model the task. Play or read only the first part of the conversation on the audio program (see audio script, page T-159). Pause after Blanca says *I'm really worried about Yesenia. Lately she's been different. She seems tense and too quiet.*
- Direct Ss' attention to number 1 in the chart (*Yesenia's symptoms*), and ask: *How does Blanca describe Yesenia's behavior to her friend Sue?* Elicit: *tense.*
- Ask a S to read aloud the other chart heading (*Sue's suggestions*). Say: *Now listen and fill in the information in both columns of the chart.*
- [Class Audio CD2 track 2] Play or read the complete audio program (see audio script, page T-159). Ss listen and complete the chart. Repeat the audio program as needed.

Comprehension check

- Read aloud the second part of the instructions for Exercise **1**.
- Ss complete the exercise in pairs. Walk around and help as needed.
- Play the audio program again if needed.

▼ **Culture tip**
Parenting classes are not uncommon in the United States. They are often held in schools or in local libraries. These classes help parents learn everything from helping children with homework to handling discipline issues. Point out that school counselors are also excellent resources for parents – and children – when it comes to coping with many different kinds of situations both inside and outside of school.

Practice

- Direct Ss' attention to Exercise **2A**. Ask Ss: *What is the title of this story?* ("Ann's Night Out")
- Read the instructions aloud for Exercise **2A**. Point out that Ss should use the information below the blank to complete each sentence with an indirect question. Call on a S to read the first three sentences in the story, including the sample indirect question in the blank. Review how the sample direct question was changed into an indirect question. Have Ss continue reading the story and filling in the blanks.
- Ss complete the exercise individually. Walk around and help as needed.
- Write the numbers *1–6* on the board. Ask Ss to come to the board to write the answers. Have Ss write only the words that are missing from the blanks, not the entire sentence.
- Read the story aloud using Ss' answers. Make corrections on the board as needed.

▼ **Teaching tip**
In multilevel classes, some Ss may have little difficulty with this review of grammar. Others may find this review more challenging. Create small groups of mixed ability. Encourage the Ss who are comfortable with these grammar points to help those who are less comfortable.

Comprehension check

- Direct Ss' attention to Exercise **2B**. This exercise reviews question formation by asking questions related to the reading "Ann's Night Out."
- Read the instructions aloud. Model the task. Direct Ss' attention to Speaker B's answer in number 1. Ask Ss: *What question can you write to get this answer?* Elicit this response: *What time should Ann have been home?*
- Ss complete the exercise individually. Walk around and help as needed.
- Check answers with the class. Ask for volunteers to read their questions. Write the questions on the board and correct as needed.
- Read aloud the second part of the instructions for Exercise **2B**.
- Ss work in pairs to ask and answer the questions. Help as needed.

Presentation

- Books closed. Write on the board: *intonation in questions*. Then write these two questions on the board: *How are you? Can you tell me if you did your homework?* Tell Ss that you are going to say these questions aloud and that you want them to pay attention to the tone, or intonation, of your voice at the end of each question. Explain that the tone – or *intonation* – is a change in pitch when speaking. Say: *In English, when we ask direct questions, our intonation falls: it goes down.* Draw a falling arrow above *you* in the first question. Then say: *In English, when we ask indirect questions, our intonation rises: it goes up.* Draw a rising arrow above *homework* in the second question.
- Write a few examples of direct and indirect questions on the board. Say each one aloud, and ask Ss to repeat. Ask Ss if the intonation rises or falls, and indicate the correct intonation with up-or-down arrows.

▼ **Teaching tip**
Some Ss may find it difficult to differentiate between rising and falling intonation. Exaggerate the intonation so that these Ss can hear the differences clearly.

- Books open. Direct Ss' attention to Exercise **3A**. Read the instructions aloud.
- 💿 [Class Audio CD2 track 3] Play or read the complete audio program (see audio script, page T-159).
- Have a S read the second part of the instructions for Exercise **3A**.
- 💿 [Class Audio CD2 track 4] Repeat the audio program. Pause after each sentence to give Ss time to repeat.

Practice

- Direct Ss' attention to Exercise **3B** and read the instructions aloud.
- 💿 [Class Audio CD2 track 5] Model the task. Play or read the first sentence on the audio program (see audio script, page T-159). Ask Ss to tell you whether the intonation is rising or falling (falling).
- Tell Ss to pay attention to the intonation in each question as they listen and repeat. Play or read the audio program, stopping as needed for Ss to repeat the sentences.
- 💿 [Class Audio CD2 track 5] Play or read the complete audio program again. Ss identify the intonation of each question by drawing rising or falling arrows. Repeat the audio program as needed.
- Read aloud the second part of the instructions for Exercise **3B**.

- Ss complete the task in pairs. Listen to Ss' pronunciation, helping with intonation.

Comprehension check

- Direct Ss' attention to Exercise **3C**, and read the instructions aloud.
- Ss work in pairs to complete the exercise. Walk around and listen to Ss' intonation.
- Call on individual Ss to read aloud the questions. Ask Ss whether each question is direct or indirect. Also ask if the intonation is rising or falling.

Application

- Focus Ss' attention on Exercise **3D** and read the instructions aloud.
- Ask a S to read aloud the example question. Ask Ss if it is a direct or an indirect question (indirect). Ask Ss to repeat the question. Correct intonation as needed.
- Ss work in pairs to complete the exercise. Walk around and help as needed.

Evaluation

- Direct Ss' attention to the lesson focus on the board.
- Write the following direct *Wh-* questions on the board: *Where did you go? When did he leave? How is everything at school? Why is she so strict?* Ask Ss to change the questions to indirect *Wh-* questions using introductory clauses.
- Write this question on the board: *Did you finish your homework?* Have Ss tell you what the indirect (*Yes / No*) form of the question is. For example: *I wonder if / whether you finished your homework.*
- Write on the board: *ought to, shouldn't, have to, don't have to.* Ask Ss to write four sentences, one for each modal.
- Write these two sentences on the board:
  1. *I don't like the way this soup tastes. It's too salty.*
  2. *Ed didn't do well on the test because he went to a party last night.*
- Ask Ss to read each sentence. Have Ss change number 1 into a sentence that shows regret (e.g., *I shouldn't have put so much salt in the soup. / I should have put less salt in the soup.*) and number 2 into a sentence that gives advice in the past (e.g., *Ed should have studied last night. He shouldn't have gone to the party*).
- Focus Ss' attention on the questions in Exercise **3B**. Ask Ss to read the questions aloud, using rising or falling intonation correctly.
- Check off each part of the lesson focus as Ss demonstrate an understanding of what they have learned in the lesson.

3 Pronunciation: intonation in questions

A 🔊 **Listen** to the intonation in these questions.

Direct question

Where did he go?

Indirect question

Can you tell me where he went?

🔊 **Listen again and repeat.** Pay attention to the intonation.

B 🔊 **Listen and repeat.** Then draw arrows to show rising or falling intonation in the questions.

1. *A* What does Ann do to reduce stress?
   B She listens to music.

2. *A* Why are you so tense?
   B I have my driver's test today.

3. *A* Do you know what Rodolfo does to calm down?
   B He walks or jogs.

4. *A* When did Ivan miss his class?
   B He missed his class on Tuesday.

5. *A* Can you tell me where Andy lives?
   B He lives on East Fifth Street.

6. *A* Do you know why they're always late?
   B No, I don't know.

Talk with a partner. Compare your answers.

C **Talk** with a partner. Ask and answer the questions. Use the correct intonation.

1. What is one thing you should have done today or yesterday?
2. What is a common punishment for teenagers when they come home late?
3. What were your favorite things to do when you were growing up?
4. Can you tell me what you do to reduce stress?
5. Do you know why it's important to exercise regularly?
6. Do you know if meditation is difficult to do?

D **Write** five questions. Make at least three indirect questions. Ask your partner.

Can you tell me how you cope with stressful situations?

1. _____
2. _____
3. _____
4. _____
5. _____

Lesson A *Get ready*

1 Talk about the pictures

A What do you see?

B What is happening?

Lesson objectives
- Introduce students to the topic
- Find out what students know about the topic
- Preview the unit by talking about the pictures
- Practice key vocabulary
- Practice listening skills

Warm-up and review

- Before class. Write today's lesson focus on the board. *Lesson A:*
  Ask about volunteer activities
  Discuss personal experiences with volunteering or with helping people
- Begin class. Books closed. Direct Ss' attention to the lesson focus. Point to *Ask about volunteer activities.* Ask Ss: *What does "volunteer activities" mean?* List Ss' responses on the board, for example: *activities that help people, work that you don't receive money for.*
- Ask Ss: *What are some examples of volunteer activities?* List Ss' responses on the board, for example: *working in a shelter, working at a school or a public library, helping in a soup kitchen, helping in a church program, helping at a community center.*

Presentation

- Books open. Set the scene. Direct Ss' attention to the two pictures on page 58. Ask the question from Exercise **1A**: *What do you see?* Elicit and write on the board as much vocabulary as possible: *elderly people, a walker, a wheelchair, nursing home, Bingo, a volunteer,* etc. Explain any unfamiliar words. Point to each word on the board and have Ss repeat.

▼**Culture tip**

 Draw or show an example of this sign to your Ss. Ask Ss: *Where have you seen this sign?* Write Ss' responses on the board, for example: *on doors to public bathrooms, on parking spaces, in buses, at airports, on entrances to some public buildings.* Ask what the sign indicates (that a place can be used by – or is reserved for – handicapped people). Tell Ss that seating for the disabled and elderly is often indicated on public transportation. Emphasize that it is culturally understood that elderly people and people with physical disabilities have seating priority.

- Direct Ss' attention to the question in Exercise **1B**: *What is happening?* Draw two columns on the board, one for each picture.
- Hold up the Student's Book. Ask Ss to say a few sentences about what is happening in each picture. Elicit responses such as: *In the first picture, some elderly people are walking with walkers, others are sitting in wheelchairs, someone is delivering mail. In the second picture, Almaz is talking to Steve in an office.*
- Brainstorm and list on the board things that Almaz and Steve might be saying to each other.
- Discuss Ss' ideas and make suggestions. For example, say: *Have they met before, or is this the first time they are meeting each other?*

▼**Teaching tip**
Encourage Ss to be creative. At this point, there is no single correct answer.

Expansion activity (student pairs)

- Invite Ss to work in pairs to write and perform a dialog based on the situation they see in one of the two pictures. Ss' dialogs should be between two people; for example, between an elderly person and a volunteer in the first picture or between Almaz and Steve in the second picture.
- Encourage partners to develop their visual literacy skills by looking closely at the details in both pictures and talking about what they see.
- When partners have completed writing and practicing their dialog, call on several pairs to act it out for the class.

  Option Pairs may choose to write a story based on the situation they see in one of the pictures.

Presentation

- Books open. Direct Ss' attention to Exercise **2A** and read the instructions aloud.
- Ask a S to read aloud the two questions in Exercise **2A**. Tell Ss to listen for the answers as the audio program is played or read.
- [Class Audio CD2 track 6] Play or read the audio program (see audio script, page T-160). Repeat the audio program as needed.
- Ask Ss if they have understood everything in the listening exercise. Elicit any unfamiliar words and write them on the board. Help Ss understand the meanings. Be sure that they understand the definition of *worthwhile* (a good use of time or effort).
- Elicit answers to the questions in Exercise **2A**. For example: *The speakers are Almaz and Steve. They are talking about Almaz's interest in volunteering at the nursing home.*
- Focus Ss' attention on Exercise **2B** and read the instructions aloud. Tell Ss to listen to the audio program and to complete the chart based on the information they hear. Ask Ss to define *responsibilities*. Elicit responses, such as: *Responsibilities are duties that a person has at work or at home.*
- [Class Audio CD2 track 7] Tell Ss to listen for details about Almaz's responsibilities when she volunteered at the public library and what her responsibilities will be at the nursing home. Model the task. Play or read the audio program again. Pause the program after Almaz says: *I worked with adults who wanted to learn how to read.* Ask a S to read the example in the chart, under the heading *Almaz's responsibilities at the library* (*worked with adults learning to read*). Play or read the rest of the audio program. Ss listen and complete the chart.
- Read aloud the second part of the instructions for Exercise **2B**.
- [Class Audio CD2 track 7] Play or read the audio program again (see audio script, page T-160). Ss listen and check their answers.
- Write the numbers *1–6* on the board. Ask Ss to come to the board to write their answers.

Practice

- Focus Ss' attention on Exercise **2C**. Read the instructions aloud. Tell Ss that the story in this exercise is a summary of what happened in the pictures on the previous page.
- Direct Ss' attention to the words in the word bank. Say each word aloud and have Ss repeat. Correct pronunciation as needed. Explain any words that are new to Ss.

- Model the task. Ask a S to read aloud the first two sentences in the story. Point out that Ss need to fill in the remaining blanks with the words from the word bank.
- Ss complete the exercise individually. Walk around and help as needed.

Comprehension check

- [Class Audio CD2 track 8] Play or read the audio program (see audio script, page T-160). Ss listen and check their answers. Repeat the audio program as needed.
- Write the numbers *1–8* on the board. Ask eight Ss to come to the board to write only the answers. Have other Ss read the sentences using the words on the board to fill in the blanks.

Learner persistence (individual work)

- [Self-Study Audio CD tracks 16 and 17] Exercises **2A**, **2B**, and **2C** are recorded on the Ss' self-study CD at the back of the Student's Book. Ss can listen to the CD at home for reinforcement and review. They can also listen to the CD for self-directed learning when class attendance is not possible.

> **Culture note**
> Read the culture note aloud. Be sure that Ss understand the term *nursing home*. Ss may not be familiar with nursing homes since many may come from cultures in which elderly family members are cared for at home.

Application

- Read the instructions aloud for Exercise **2D**.
- Ss complete the exercise in pairs. Help as needed.
- Ask several pairs to share their ideas with the class.

Evaluation

- Direct Ss' attention to the lesson focus on the board. Check Ss' understanding of the key vocabulary by asking them to use the words in the word bank in Exercise **2C** to make sentences about why Almaz wants to volunteer at the nursing home, Quiet Palms.
- Check off each part of the lesson focus as Ss demonstrate an understanding of what they have learned in the lesson.

> **More Ventures** (whole group, pairs, individual)
> Assign appropriate exercises from the *Teacher's Toolkit Audio CD / CD-ROM, Add Ventures,* or the *Workbook*.

2 Listening

 **A** Listen and answer the questions.

1. Who are the speakers?
2. What are they talking about?

 **B** **Listen again.** Complete the chart.

Almaz's responsibilities at the library	Volunteer responsibilities at Quiet Palms
1. *worked with adults learning to read*	4. *help residents with meals*
2. *taught writing*	5. *deliver mail and flowers*
3. *read stories to kids*	6. *take residents for walks*

Listen again. Check your answers.

 **C** **Read.** Complete the story. Listen and check your answers.

can't wait	compassionate	orientation	residents
commitment	coordinator	patient	worthwhile

Last summer, Almaz volunteered at the public library downtown. She liked

working with the older people because she felt that she was doing something

_____*worthwhile*_____ . Today, she is meeting with Steve, the volunteer
          1

_____*coordinator*_____ at Quiet Palms, a nursing home. She wants to volunteer
          2

there to find out if she likes working in the health-care field. Steve tells her

about some of her responsibilities at Quiet Palms. He says it's very important

for volunteers to be _____*compassionate*_____ and _____*patient*_____ when
                                3   4

they are working with the _____*residents*_____ . He asks Almaz to make a
                                      5

_____*commitment*_____ to volunteer at least three hours per week. Almaz agrees
          6

to attend an _____*orientation*_____ . She says she _____*can't wait*_____ to
                      7   8

start volunteering.

Culture note
A *nursing home* is a place where elderly people live when their families can't take care of them.

D **Discuss.** Talk with your classmates. Is the nursing home a good place for Almaz to volunteer? Why or why not?

1 Grammar focus: clauses with *until* and *as soon as*

Almaz **will stay** with Mr. Shamash **until** he **finishes** his lunch.
Until Mr. Shamash **finishes** his lunch, Almaz **will stay** with him.

Almaz **will leave** Quiet Palms **as soon as** Mr. Shamash **finishes** his lunch.
As soon as Mr. Shamash **finishes** his lunch, Almaz **will leave** Quiet Palms.

For a grammar explanation, turn to page 149.

2 Practice

A Write. Complete the sentences with *until* or *as soon as*.

1. **A** Mr. Shamash is in pain. When will he start to feel better?

   B He'll feel better _____*as soon as*_____ he takes his medication.

2. **A** How long will Mr. Shamash stay at Quiet Palms?

   B He'll stay _____*until*_____ his broken hip heals.

3. **A** When can Mr. Shamash begin exercising again?

   B _*As soon as*_____ Mr. Shamash feels stronger, he can start doing moderate exercise.

4. **A** When does Mr. Shamash get ready for his walk?

   B He gets ready _____*as soon as*_____ Almaz arrives.

5. **A** How long will Mr. Shamash and Almaz play cards?

   B They'll play cards _____*until*_____ it is time for lunch.

6. **A** How long will Almaz stay with Mr. Shamash?

   B She'll stay _____*until*_____ his family arrives to visit him.

7. **A** When is Mr. Shamash going to go to sleep?

   B _*As soon as*_____ his visitors leave, he'll take his medicine and go to sleep.

   Listen and check your answers. Then practice with a partner.

Warm-up and review

- Before class. Write today's lesson focus on the board.
  Lesson B:
  Use time clauses with <u>until</u> and <u>as soon as</u>
- Begin class. Books open. Direct Ss' attention to the two pictures on page 58. Ask Ss to imagine what the people in the pictures will do in one hour, using the future with *will*. Elicit responses, such as: *Almaz will go home. Steve will meet with another volunteer. The people in the nursing home will eat.*

Presentation

- Books open. Direct Ss' attention to the grammar chart in Exercise **1**. Read the first two statements aloud. Ask Ss to repeat.
- Direct Ss' attention to the second set of statements. Read them aloud. Have Ss repeat.
- Write on the board:
  as soon as = when (at the moment that something happens)
  She will let us know as soon as she arrives at the train station.
  until = up to a specific time
  Until he finishes his homework, he has to stay in his room.
- Explain that *as soon as* is very similar to *when*, but it emphasizes that one event will occur immediately after the other. *Until* means "up to a certain time."
- Ask Ss if they notice anything about the verb forms in these sentences. Explain that although both sentences are about the future, the future with *will* is used only in the main clause. The simple present is used in the subordinate clause with *until* and *as soon as*.
- Explain that when *until* and *as soon as* begin a sentence, a comma is used after the clause that is introduced by those words.
- Ask Ss to rewrite the sentences on the board but to keep the meaning the same, for example:
  She will let us know as soon as she arrives at the train station.
  As soon as she arrives at the train station, she will let us know.
  Until he finishes his homework, he has to stay in his room.
  He has to stay in his room until he finishes his homework.

Practice

- Direct Ss' attention to Exercise **2A** and read the instructions aloud.
- Model the task. Ask a S to read number 1 to the class. Make sure that Ss understand the task.
- Ss complete the exercise individually. Walk around and help as needed.

Comprehension check

- Focus Ss' attention on the second part of the instructions for Exercise **2A**.
- [Class Audio CD2 track 9] Play or read the audio program (see audio script, page T-160). Ss listen and check their answers. Then they practice the dialog with their partner.
- Write the numbers *1–7* on the board. Ask seven Ss to come to the board to write the questions and answers. Work with the class to make corrections on the board as needed.
- Invite partners to read aloud the *A* and *B* sentences on the board.

Expansion activity *(student pairs)*

- Write the following clauses on the board:
  As soon as she serves dinner, . . .
  As soon as I get home, . . .
  Until we pay all our bills, . . .
- Tell Ss that they should first complete the sentences and then write each sentence in another way. For example:
  As soon as I get home, I will make dinner.
  I will make dinner as soon as I get home.
- Call on volunteers to write their sentences on the board.
- Review answers with the class and make corrections as needed.

Time clauses

Presentation

- Books open. Tell Ss they are going to read and talk about different volunteer activities. Read the instructions aloud for Exercise **2B**.
- Direct Ss' attention to the pictures and descriptions on page 61.
- Call on six Ss to read the words under each picture.
- Model the task. Ask a S to read the example sentence.
- Ss complete the exercise with a partner. Walk around and help as needed.

Culture note

Read the culture note aloud. Write on the board: *to volunteer* and *a volunteer,* explaining that the first is a verb and the second is a noun. Explain that Americans of all ages often use some of their free time to help people or to support a political campaign or a social cause. Ask Ss for some example volunteer activities and write them on the board. Discuss each one.

Practice

- Direct Ss' attention to the second part of Exercise **2B**. Read the instructions aloud.
- Ask a S to read the example sentence to the class.
- Ss work individually to complete the exercise. Walk around and help as needed.

Comprehension check

- Write the numbers *1–6* on the board. Ask individual Ss to come to the board to write their answers for Exercise **2B**.
- Have other Ss read the sentences aloud. Ask Ss if the sentences are written correctly. Have different Ss correct them on the board as needed.

Application

- Direct Ss' attention to Exercise **3A**. Read the instructions aloud.
- Ss work individually to make a list of activities. Walk around and help as needed.
- Direct Ss' attention to Exercise **3B**. Read the instructions aloud.
- Model the task. Ask a pair of Ss to read aloud the sample dialog.
- Ss work in pairs to complete the exercise, using *as soon as* and *until* to explain their activities. Walk around and help as needed.

- Read the instructions aloud for Exercise **3C**. Call on pairs to share information with the class about any volunteer activities in which their partners participated or participate.

Expansion activity (student pairs)

- Ask Ss to talk about their responsibilities at work or at home, using *until* and *as soon as*. Partners should begin by telling each other whether they want to talk about work or home so that their partner will know what questions to ask.
- Model the activity. Ask Ss: *What questions can you ask your partner about his or her responsibilities at home?* Write some examples on the board:
  What do you do as soon as you get home?
  What do you do until dinner is ready?
  What are some things you need to do as soon as you finish dinner?
- Tell Ss they can use these questions or make up others, depending on which situation they decide to discuss. Ss work in pairs to ask and answer each other's questions.
- Have pairs share the information they discussed.

Evaluation

- Books closed. Direct Ss' attention to the lesson focus on the board.
- Write the following sentences on the board:
  He helps his brother with his homework as soon as he gets home.
  He helps his brother until it's time for dinner.
- Ask Ss: *What is the difference in the meaning of the two sentences?* Elicit an appropriate response, such as: *The first sentence means that when he gets home, he helps his brother. The second sentence means that he helps his brother before dinner, but once it's time for dinner, he stops.*
- Check off the lesson focus as Ss demonstrate an understanding of what they have learned in the lesson.

More Ventures (whole group, pairs, individual)
Assign appropriate exercises from the *Teacher's Toolkit Audio CD / CD-ROM, Add Ventures,* or the *Workbook*.

B Talk with a partner. Discuss Charles's volunteer activities at another nursing home. Use *as soon as* or *until*.

As soon as Charles arrives at work, he puts on his name tag.

arrive / put on name tag

walk with Mrs. Halliday / time to deliver mail

read to Mrs. Halliday / lunchtime

stop reading / lunch is delivered

talk to Mrs. Halliday / finish eating

go home / finish playing a game with Mrs. Halliday

Write sentences about Charles's volunteer activities.

As soon as Charles arrives at work, he puts on his name tag.

3 Communicate

A Choose one time when you helped someone or volunteered. Make a list of your activities. Use Exercise 2B to help you.

B Work with a partner. Ask questions about each other's activities. Use *as soon as* and *until*.

> *A* What did you do as soon as you arrived at the animal shelter?
> *B* I checked the board for my duties.
> *A* How late did you stay?
> *B* I stayed until the shelter closed for the day.

C Share information about your partner.

> **Culture note**
> Volunteering is a popular activity among Americans of all ages, from children to senior citizens.

Verb tense contrast

1 Grammar focus: repeated actions in the present and past

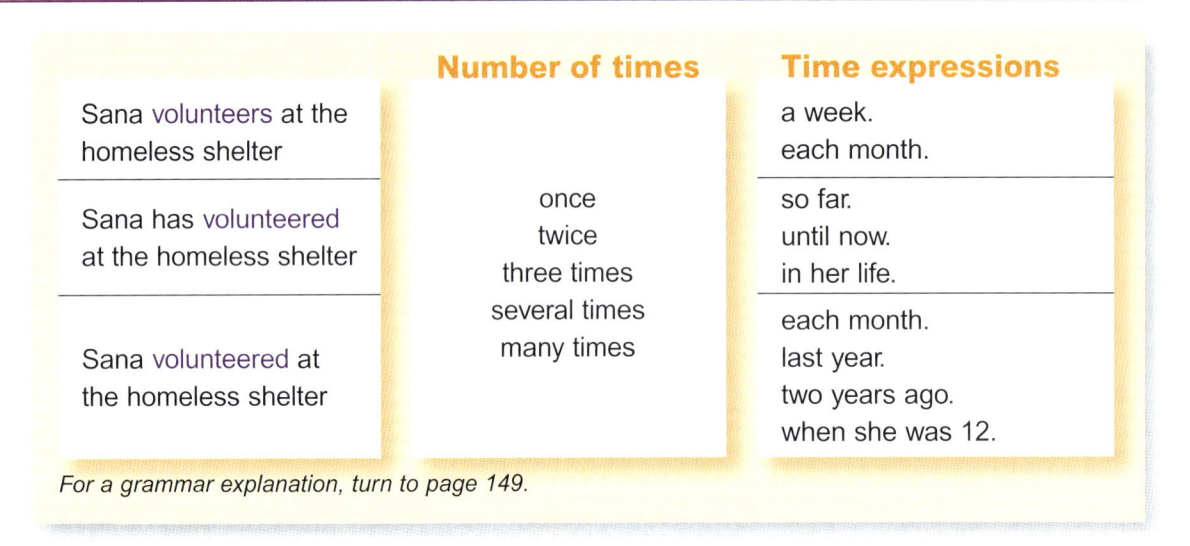

	Number of times	Time expressions
Sana volunteers at the homeless shelter		a week. each month.
Sana has volunteered at the homeless shelter	once twice three times several times many times	so far. until now. in her life.
Sana volunteered at the homeless shelter		each month. last year. two years ago. when she was 12.

For a grammar explanation, turn to page 149.

2 Practice

A Write. Complete the story with the present, present perfect, or past forms of the verbs.

Sharing with Sally

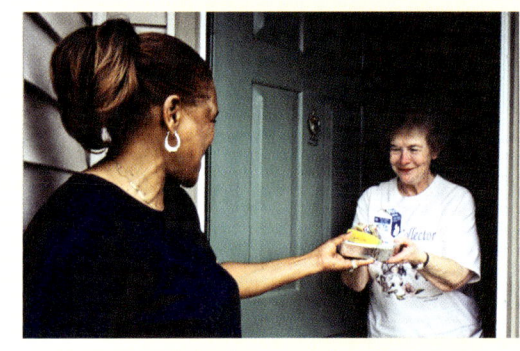

Sally Sutherland created "Sharing with Sally," a volunteer organization that helps seniors stay connected with the outside world. The organization *has delivered* over 5,000
1. deliver
dinners to seniors so far. Sharing with Sally

____*began*____ six years ago. Every week, Sally and her volunteers ____*deliver*____
2. begin 3. deliver
meals, ____*talk*____ to seniors on the phone, and ____*visit*____ the ones who
4. talk 5. visit
can't leave their homes. Over 200 people volunteer at Sharing with Sally. Jake, a

college student, ____*volunteered*____ all last year. He ____*called*____ elderly people on the
6. volunteer 7. call
phone once a week and ____*talked*____ to each person. He said it was a very valuable
8. talk
experience. Betsy, a 35-year-old mother of two, *has volunteered* for two years so far and
9. volunteer
loves it.

Listen and check your answers.

Warm-up and review

- Before class. Write today's lesson focus on the board. *Lesson C:*
  Discuss repeated actions in the present and past
- Write on the board: *repeated actions*. Ask Ss what the phrase means. Elicit an appropriate response, for example: *Repeated actions are things that are done over and over again.*
- Ask Ss: *Has anyone ever volunteered? Does anyone volunteer now?* If you have no volunteers in the class, vary the question to include paid jobs. Elicit responses, such as: *Manny has volunteered (or worked) at the hospital. Mariko works at the elementary school.* Ask Ss how often they volunteered or worked in the past (or how often they volunteer or work now, depending on what Ss say).

Presentation

- Books open. Direct Ss' attention to the grammar chart in Exercise **1**. Read the title: *repeated actions in the present and past*. Read aloud the first sentence in the left-hand column: *Sana volunteers at the homeless shelter.*
- Read aloud the words and phrases under *Number of times* and ask Ss to repeat.

▼**Teaching tip**
The pronunciation of *once* may be difficult for some Ss. You may want to write on the board: *won + s* and explain to Ss that this is how the word *once* sounds. Have Ss repeat the word several times until they can pronounce it correctly.

- Direct Ss' attention to the phrases under *Time expressions*. Read each one aloud and have Ss repeat. Tell Ss that when talking about repeated actions in the present and past, certain time expressions correspond to certain tenses.
- Write the following headings on the board: *Present, Present perfect,* and *Past*. Ask Ss to tell the verb tenses used in the three sentences in the grammar focus (present – *volunteers*; present perfect – *has volunteered*; past – *volunteered*). Write the correct form of the verb under the appropriate heading on the board.
- Ask a S to make a sentence using information from each of the three columns (the beginning of the sentence + the number of times + one of the corresponding time expressions). Model the task, for example: *Sana volunteers at the homeless shelter three times each month.*

- Encourage Ss to make up their own sentences using the present, the present perfect, or the past; the number of times; and a corresponding time expression. Model the task, if needed. For example: *I go to school three times a week. I have visited Chicago twice so far.*
- Call on Ss to share their sentences. Write them on the board. Correct on the board as needed.

▼**Teaching tip**
It might be helpful to refer Ss to the grammar explanation on page 149 in the Student's Book.

Practice

- Direct Ss' attention to Exercise **2A** and read the instructions aloud.
- Model the task. Call on a S to read the first two sentences, including the example answer.
- Ss complete the exercise individually. Walk around and help as needed.

Comprehension check

- Read aloud the second part of the instructions for Exercise **2A**.
- [Class Audio CD2 track 10] Play or read the audio program (see audio script, page T-160). Ss listen and check their answers.
- Write the numbers *1–9* on the board. Invite nine Ss to come to the board to write the word or words they have written on the blanks. Ask other Ss to read the answers aloud. Ask the class: *Are these sentences correct?* Work with the class to make corrections on the board as needed.

Community building (small groups)

- Write on the board: *Questionnaire*. Elicit a definition, such as: *A questionnaire is a list of questions that you answer.* Ask if any Ss have ever responded to a questionnaire.
- Tell Ss that they are going to write a five-question questionnaire to get information about the volunteer experiences of people who are *not* in the class. On the board, write two example sentences for the questionnaire: *Have you ever volunteered? Do you volunteer now?*
- Ss work in small groups to prepare a questionnaire with their group. Walk around and check that each group has used the present, the present perfect, or the past form correctly.
- Ask Ss to interview people for homework and to report their findings in a later class.

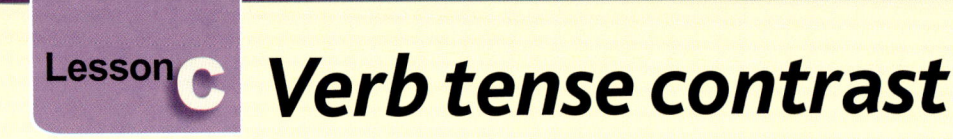
Practice

- Direct Ss' attention to Exercise **2B** and read the instructions aloud.
- Ask five Ss to read aloud the activities in the chart along with the corresponding numbers under the columns *Number of times last year* and *Number of times this year*. Explain vocabulary as needed, and write any new words on the board.
- Call on two Ss to read the two example sentences.
- Ss complete the exercise in pairs. Walk around and help as needed.
- Read the instructions aloud for the second part of Exercise **2B**. Call on a S to read the example sentence.
- Ss complete the exercise individually. Walk around and help as needed.
- Ask several Ss to write their sentences on the board.
- Call on other Ss to read each sentence on the board. Ask: *Is this sentence correct?* Make corrections on the board as needed.

Application

- Direct Ss' attention to Exercise **3A**. Read the instructions aloud. Ask a S to read aloud the first item in each list.
- Ss complete the chart individually. Walk around and help as needed.
- Direct Ss' attention to Exercise **3B**. Read the instructions aloud.
- Model the task. Ask two Ss to read the example conversation.
- Ss work with a partner to ask and answer each other's questions. Walk around and help as needed.
- Read the instructions aloud for Exercise **3C**. Ss take turns sharing information they learned from their partner.

Expansion activity *(whole class)*

- **Materials** Index cards.
- On separate index cards, write the words from the last two columns in the grammar chart at the top of page 62 (*Number of times* and *Time expressions*). Make a set of cards for each group of three or four Ss in the class. Place the cards in two different piles.

- Have Ss look at the chart on page 62 and note which tenses correspond to which time expressions.
- Books closed. Form teams of three to four Ss. Have each S on a team choose a card from each pile (e.g., *several times* from the first pile, *in her life* from the second pile) and say the two phrases aloud. Ss write sentences on the board using the correct tense and phrases, and they check with their team to see if the sentence makes sense.
- Once Ss from all teams have finished writing their sentences on the board, each S then reads his or her sentence to the class. Each S who has written and read aloud a correct sentence earns a point for his or her team.
- Tally the number of points for each team. The team with the most points wins.

Evaluation

- Direct Ss' attention to the lesson focus on the board.
- Ask Ss to refer to the grammar chart on page 62 and to write a sentence in the present tense using the time expression *a week*. Elicit responses, such as: *I work three times a week.* Call on individual Ss to read their sentences aloud.
- Ask Ss to write a sentence in the present perfect using the time expression *in my life*. Elicit responses, such as: *I have been on a plane twice in my life.* Call on individual Ss to read their sentences aloud.
- Then ask Ss to write a sentence in the past tense using *many times* and *last year*. Elicit responses, such as: *I went to Riverside Park many times last year. I went to English class many times last year.* Call on individual Ss to read their sentences aloud.
- Check off the lesson focus as Ss demonstrate an understanding of what they have learned in the lesson.

More Ventures *(whole group, pairs, individual)*
Assign appropriate exercises from the *Teacher's Toolkit Audio CD / CD-ROM, Add Ventures,* or the *Workbook*.

B Talk with a partner. Make sentences about Betsy's volunteer experience. Include the number of times and time expressions.

> A Betsy visited seniors at their homes 30 times last year.
> B And she's visited them 15 times so far this year.

Activity	Number of times last year	Number of times this year
Visit seniors at their homes	30	15
Deliver meals	25	10
Call seniors on the phone	45	25
Help Sally put meals in the truck	5	1
Take her children with her to the seniors' homes	10	3

Write sentences about Betsy's activities.

Betsy visited seniors at their homes 30 times last year.

3 Communicate

A Make a list of your experiences volunteering or helping people.

Last year	This year
• *took my grandmother to the hairdresser*	• *babysit my nephew while my sister is at work*
• _____	• _____
• _____	• _____
• _____	• _____

B Work with a partner. Share your lists. Ask questions about your partner's activities. Use *How often . . . ?* or *How many times . . . ?*

> A How often did you take your grandmother
>   to the hairdresser last year?
> B I took her every week.
> A How many times a week do you babysit
>   your nephew?
> B I babysit once or twice a week.
> A How many times have you babysat
>   your nephew so far?
> B About six times so far this year.

C Share information about your partner.

1 Before you read

Talk with your classmates. Answer the questions.

1. Look at the picture. What is unusual about it?
2. Read the title. What do you think the story will be about?

2 Read

 **Read** the newspaper article. Listen and read again.

A WORTHWHILE COMMITMENT

Imagine running with your eyes closed. How do you feel? Insecure? Afraid? Justin Andrews knows these feelings very well. Justin is a former long-distance runner who lost his vision because of a grave illness. For the past six months, he has been running twice a week with the help of volunteer runners at Running with Ropes, an organization that assists blind and visually impaired runners. "Running with Ropes has changed my life," Justin says. "Until I heard about it, I thought I'd never run outside again."

Volunteers at Running with Ropes make a commitment to volunteer two to four hours a week. Scott Liponi, one of the running volunteers, explains what they do. "We use ropes to join ourselves to the blind runners and guide them around and over obstacles, such as holes in the road and other runners." Scott has learned how to keep the rope loose so the blind runner has more freedom. He deeply respects the blind runners' tenacity. "They are incredibly determined," he says. "It doesn't matter if it's hot, raining, or snowing – they are going to run." Scott says it is gratifying to share in the joy of the runners and to feel that they trust him. "The four hours I spend at Running with Ropes are the most rewarding part of my week," he says. "It's really a worthwhile commitment."

Warm-up and review

- Before class. Write today's lesson focus on the board.
  Lesson D:
  Read and understand "A Worthwhile Commitment"
  Practice using new topic-related vocabulary
  Identify positive and negative words

- Begin class. Books closed. Focus Ss' attention on the word *worthwhile* in the lesson focus. Write the word on the board. Ask: *What does "worthwhile" mean?* Elicit appropriate responses, such as: *useful, important, beneficial.* Write the words on the board.

- Point to *"A Worthwhile Commitment"* on the board and ask Ss what they think this title means. Write some of the Ss' ideas on the board, for example: *doing something important on a regular basis, helping someone regularly, volunteering.*

Presentation

- Books open. Direct Ss' attention to Exercise **1**. Read the instructions aloud.

- Have Ss focus on the two questions in Exercise **1**. Ask two Ss to read them aloud.

- Ss in pairs. Have Ss answer the questions with a partner.

Practice

- Read the instructions aloud for Exercise **2**. Ask Ss to read the newspaper article silently before listening to the audio program.

- [Class Audio CD2 track 11] Play or read the audio program, and ask Ss to read along (see audio script, page T-160). Repeat the audio program as needed.

- While Ss are listening and reading the article, ask them to write in their notebooks any words or expressions they don't understand. When the audio program is finished, have Ss write the new vocabulary words on the board.

- Point to each word on the board. Say it aloud. Ask Ss to repeat. Give a brief explanation of each word, or ask Ss to explain the word if they know it. If Ss prefer to look up the new words in their dictionaries, allow them to do so.

- Encourage Ss to guess the meaning of unfamiliar words from the context of the article. For example, if a S writes *tenacity,* read aloud the sentence containing the word and any related sentences: *He deeply respects the blind runners' tenacity. "They are incredibly determined,"* *he says.* Ask Ss to think about the meaning of the word *tenacity* based on the information in the surrounding sentences. Tell Ss that *tenacity* is another way of saying being determined, or of continuing to do something even when faced with obstacles.

Learner persistence (individual work)

- [Self-Study Audio CD track 18] Exercise **2** is recorded on the Ss' self-study CD at the back of the Student's Book. Ss can listen to the CD at home for reinforcement and review. They can also listen to the CD for self-directed learning when class attendance is not possible.

Community building (student pairs)

- Tell Ss to do some research about volunteer activities in their neighborhood. They can use the Internet, contact the Chamber of Commerce, or talk to storeowners or other people in their neighborhood.

- For each volunteer activity, Ss should find out what the responsibilities are and what kind of commitment (if any) is required. Ss should decide which activity they think would be a worthwhile commitment for them and present their research findings orally to the class.

- Write some of the volunteer activities on the board and discuss them with Ss.

Comprehension check

- Direct Ss' attention to Exercise **3A** and read the instructions aloud.
- Ss work with a partner to ask and answer the questions. Walk around and help as needed.
- Discuss the answers with the class. Ask Ss to say where in the reading they found each of the answers.

Practice

- Direct Ss' attention to Exercise **3B**. Ask a S to read aloud the instructions in number 1.

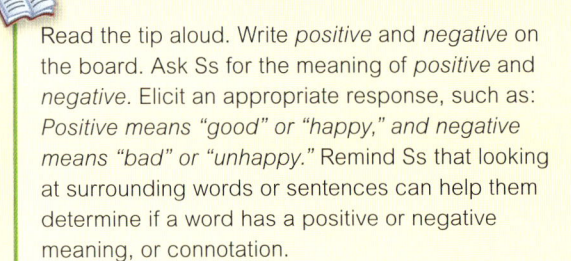

Read the tip aloud. Write *positive* and *negative* on the board. Ask Ss for the meaning of *positive* and *negative*. Elicit an appropriate response, such as: *Positive means "good" or "happy," and negative means "bad" or "unhappy."* Remind Ss that looking at surrounding words or sentences can help them determine if a word has a positive or negative meaning, or connotation.

- Model the task. Ask Ss to find *grave* in the first paragraph of the article. Have a S read the sentence in which *grave* appears. Ask other Ss whether the word has a positive or negative meaning in the sentence. Tell Ss to place a check mark in the negative column and write the clue that helped them figure out the connotation of the word. Make sure that all Ss understand the task.
- Ss fill in the chart individually. Walk around and help as needed.
- Write the chart on the board and ask seven Ss to fill in their answers. Work with the class to make corrections on the board as needed.
- Direct Ss' attention to number 2 of Exercise **3B** and read the instructions aloud.
- Ss complete the task in a small group. Examples from the text include: *commitment* (P), *obstacles* (N), *determined* (P), *worthwhile* (P). Invite Ss to say their answers to the class. Correct as needed.

Expansion activity *(small groups)*

- Ss in small groups. Give Ss a time limit (3–5 minutes). Ask groups to brainstorm words to create a list of as many positive and negative words as they can think of without using a dictionary.

- Walk around and correct Ss' work if they have misspelled a word or categorized it incorrectly.
- Ask each group to write two sentences, one in which the word has a positive connotation or meaning, the other in which the word has a negative one. One representative from each group writes the group's two sentences on the board, underlining the positive or negative word without telling the class which is which.
- Ss from other groups have to guess whether the underlined word is positive or negative based on the words around it in the sentence.

Application

- Direct Ss' attention to Exercise **3C** and read the instructions aloud.
- Ask four Ss to read aloud the questions in Exercise **3C**.
- Partners take turns asking and answering the questions. Walk around and help as needed.
- Ask several pairs to share the answers they discussed with the class. (Ss discuss the response to number 1 only if they feel comfortable in doing so.)

Evaluation

- Books closed. Direct Ss' attention to the lesson focus on the board. Write on the board the words in number 1 from Exercise **3B**. Ask Ss to use these words to retell the main points of the newspaper article "A Worthwhile Commitment."
- Check off each part of the lesson focus as Ss demonstrate an understanding of what they have learned in the lesson.

Learner persistence *(individual work, student pairs)*

- You may wish to assign Extended reading worksheets from the *Teacher's Toolkit Audio CD / CD-ROM* for Ss to complete outside of class. The purpose of these worksheets is to encourage Ss to read for pleasure in English outside of the English class. The worksheets can also be assigned as extended reading in class.

More Ventures *(whole group, pairs, individual)*
Assign appropriate exercises from the *Teacher's Toolkit Audio CD / CD-ROM, Add Ventures,* or the *Workbook*.

---

3 After you read

A Check your understanding.

1. Who is Justin Andrews? What happened to him?
2. What is Running with Ropes?
3. How is Justin able to run?
4. Who is Scott Liponi?
5. How does Scott feel about his volunteer commitment?

> When you see a new word, look at the words around it to guess if the meaning is positive or negative.
>
> *He lost his vision because of a* **grave** *illness.*
>
> You can guess that *grave* has a negative meaning.

B Build your vocabulary.

1. Look at the reading tip. Then underline the words from the chart in the reading passage. Decide if their meanings are positive or negative. Fill in the clues that helped you guess.

Word	Positive	Negative	Clue
1. grave		✓	*He lost his vision because of an illness.*
2. insecure		✓	*Afraid*
3. impaired		✓	*blind / visually*
4. freedom	✓		*loose*
5. tenacity	✓		*deeply respects; incredibly determined*
6. gratifying	✓		*share in the joy of the runners and to feel that they trust him*
7. rewarding	✓		*worthwhile commitment*

2. Work with your classmates. Write four more words in the reading that have a positive or negative meaning. Write *P* next to positive words. Write *N* next to negative words. *(Answers may vary.)*

a. _____ *obstacles – N* _____   c. _____ *joy – P* _____

b. _____ *determined – P* _____   d. _____ *trust – P* _____

C Talk with a partner.

1. When do you feel most insecure?
2. Tell about something that takes tenacity.
3. Describe a gratifying experience.
4. What do visually impaired people use to help them? What about hearing-impaired people?

Lesson E Writing

1 Before you write

A Talk with your classmates. Look at the picture. Answer the questions.

1. Who are the people in the picture? Where are they? What are they doing?
2. Do you think the young woman is doing something unusual? Why or why not?

B Read the paragraph.

> Story Lady
>
> My friend Vivianne is one of the most compassionate people I have ever met. After college, she wanted to do something truly worthwhile, so she spent a year working as a literacy volunteer in northeastern Brazil. At the time, this area didn't have any libraries, so Vivianne traveled to different schools in a mobile library van. As soon as she arrived at a school, the children would run outside and shout, "Story Lady! Story Lady!" Then everyone went inside, sat down, and listened quietly while she read them a story. Vivianne made a huge difference in these children's lives. She introduced them to literature and taught them to love reading. Today, she still gets letters from children who remember her generosity and kindness.

Make your writing more interesti
by including specific details that
answer the questions *who*, *what*,
when, *where*, *why*, and *how*.

Warm-up and review

- Before class. Write today's lesson focus on the board. *Lesson E:*
  Write a paragraph about someone you know who made a difference
  Use specific details to make your writing more interesting
- Begin class. Books closed. Review vocabulary from the unit. Write the words *someone who makes a difference,* and ask Ss what they think the expression means. Elicit an appropriate response, such as: *someone who changes something for the better.* Ask Ss if they can give you some examples of famous people who have made a difference (e.g., Mahatma Gandhi, Mother Teresa, Martin Luther King Jr., Cesar Chávez, Harriet Tubman).
- Ask Ss to explain to the class how the famous person they mentioned has made a difference.

Presentation

- Books open. Focus Ss' attention on the picture in Exercise **1A**. Ask: *What do you see?* Elicit an appropriate response, such as: *a woman telling a story to children.*
- Read the instructions aloud for Exercise **1A**.
- Ask two Ss to read the two questions to the class.
- Ss work with a partner to ask and answer the questions. Walk around and help as needed.
- Have two pairs answer the questions for the rest of the class.
- Ask Ss which stories they liked listening to when they were children, and why. Ask Ss: *Who used to tell you your favorite stories?* (Answers may include a teacher, a parent or another family member, a neighbor, or a friend.)
- If your Ss have children, ask those Ss whether they read to their children, and if so, what kinds of books or stories they read. Encourage Ss to read to their children in English or in their native language.

Practice

- Direct Ss' attention to Exercise **1B** and read the instructions aloud.
- Have Ss focus on the title of the paragraph, "Story Lady." Ask Ss to use the title to predict what the story is about.

- Tell Ss to read the paragraph silently. Have them underline any words they don't know. Write the new words on the board. Encourage Ss to use context clues to try to figure out the meaning of each new word.

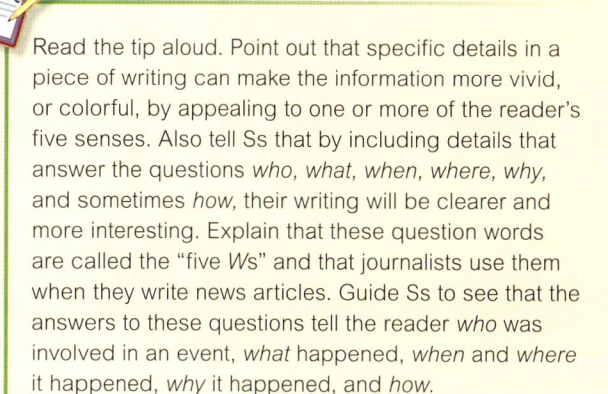

Read the tip aloud. Point out that specific details in a piece of writing can make the information more vivid, or colorful, by appealing to one or more of the reader's five senses. Also tell Ss that by including details that answer the questions *who, what, when, where, why,* and sometimes *how,* their writing will be clearer and more interesting. Explain that these question words are called the "five *W*s" and that journalists use them when they write news articles. Guide Ss to see that the answers to these questions tell the reader *who* was involved in an event, *what* happened, *when* and *where* it happened, *why* it happened, and *how.*

Expansion activity (small groups)

- Invite Ss to write a story for Vivianne, the Story Lady, to tell the Brazilian children. The story can be about any topic that the children might enjoy. Encourage Ss to be creative and to think of stories they liked to hear when they were young.
- Have Ss work in small groups to brainstorm a list of story ideas. Then encourage each group to choose a story idea as well as a recorder to write the group's story on a piece of paper.
- Walk around and help as needed.
- Have each group choose a reader (someone different from the recorder) to read the story aloud or to tell it to the class, using oral storytelling skills such as reading loudly and clearly and using appropriate emphasis, intonation, and gestures.
- After each group finishes reading its story aloud, ask Ss from other groups to assess the story they have just heard, evaluating it both for content and oral presentation.

Lesson E Writing

Presentation

- Focus Ss' attention on Exercise **1C**. Read the instructions aloud. Tell Ss to refer to page 66 to complete this exercise.
- Model the task. Ask a S to read aloud the first detail from the paragraph and to read the example answer.
- Ss complete the exercise with a partner. Walk around and help as needed.
- Check answers with the class.

Practice

- Direct Ss' attention to Exercise **1D** and read the instructions aloud.
- Ss complete their charts individually. Walk around and help as needed.

▼**Teaching tip**
Before Ss get ready to write, encourage them to talk about their topics in a prewriting activity. Talking with a partner or a small group will help Ss focus on their subject and on the specific details they can use in the paragraph they will be writing in Exercise **2**.

Application

- Focus Ss' attention on Exercise **2**. Read the instructions aloud.
- Ss complete the task individually, using the model paragraph in Exercise **1B** on page 66 and the chart in Exercise **1D** on page 67 to help them write their own paragraph. Walk around and help as needed.

Learner persistence (pairs)

- If more proficient writers finish early, ask them to sit with Ss who need help with their writing.

Comprehension check

- Direct Ss' attention to Exercise **3A**.
- This exercise asks Ss to develop skills to review and edit their own writing.
- Ss check their own paragraphs against the writing checklist. Walk around and help as needed. If any Ss check *No* for one or more of the checklist items, ask them to revise and edit their paragraphs to include the missing information.

Evaluation

- Direct Ss' attention to Exercise **3B** and read the instructions aloud. This exercise asks Ss to work together to peer-correct their writing. Reading aloud enables the writer to review his or her own writing. Reading to a partner allows the writer to understand the need to write clearly for an audience.
- Ss complete the exercise in pairs. Have Ss take turns reading their paragraphs to each other. Walk around and help as needed.
- Listen to Ss as they ask their partner one question about the paragraph and tell their partner one thing they learned from it.
- Ask several Ss to read their paragraphs aloud. Tell the other Ss in the class to listen for descriptive details that appeal to one or more of their five senses. For example, ask Ss: *Which details in the story could you see, hear, touch, taste, and/or smell? How did these details make the writing more colorful and interesting?*
- Have Ss also listen for details that answer the questions: *who, when, where, why, what,* and *how*. The writer of the paragraph can confirm that the information is correct.
- Direct Ss' attention to the lesson focus on the board.
- Check off each part of the lesson focus as Ss demonstrate an understanding of what they have learned in the lesson.

> **More Ventures** (whole group, pairs, individual)
> Assign appropriate exercises from the *Teacher's Toolkit Audio CD / CD-ROM, Add Ventures,* or the *Workbook.*

C **Work** with a partner. Write the words *who*, *when*, *where*, *why*, *what*, or *how* next to the details from the paragraph.

1. _____*who*_____ my friend Vivianne
2. _____*when*_____ after college
3. _*what / who*_ a literacy volunteer
4. _____*where*_____ northeastern Brazil
5. _____*why*_____ because the area didn't have any libraries
6. _*how / where*_ in a mobile library van
7. _____*what*_____ She read stories to the children.
8. _____*what*_____ She introduced them to literature and taught them to love reading.

D **Plan** a paragraph about someone you know who made a difference. Use the chart to make notes.

Who made a difference?	*(Answers will vary.)*
What did he or she do?	
Why did this person do it?	
Where did it happen?	
When did it happen?	
How did this person make a difference?	

2 Write

Write a paragraph about someone you know who made a difference. Use the paragraph in Exercise 1B and the chart in Exercise 1D to help you.

3 After you write

A **Check** your writing.

	Yes	No
1. My topic sentence names the person who made a difference.	☐	☐
2. I included details that answer *Wh-* questions.	☐	☐
3. I used verb tenses correctly with time words and expressions.	☐	☐

B **Share** your writing with a partner.

1. Take turns. Read your paragraph to a partner.
2. Comment on your partner's paragraph. Ask your partner a question about the paragraph. Tell your partner one thing you learned.

1 Life-skills reading

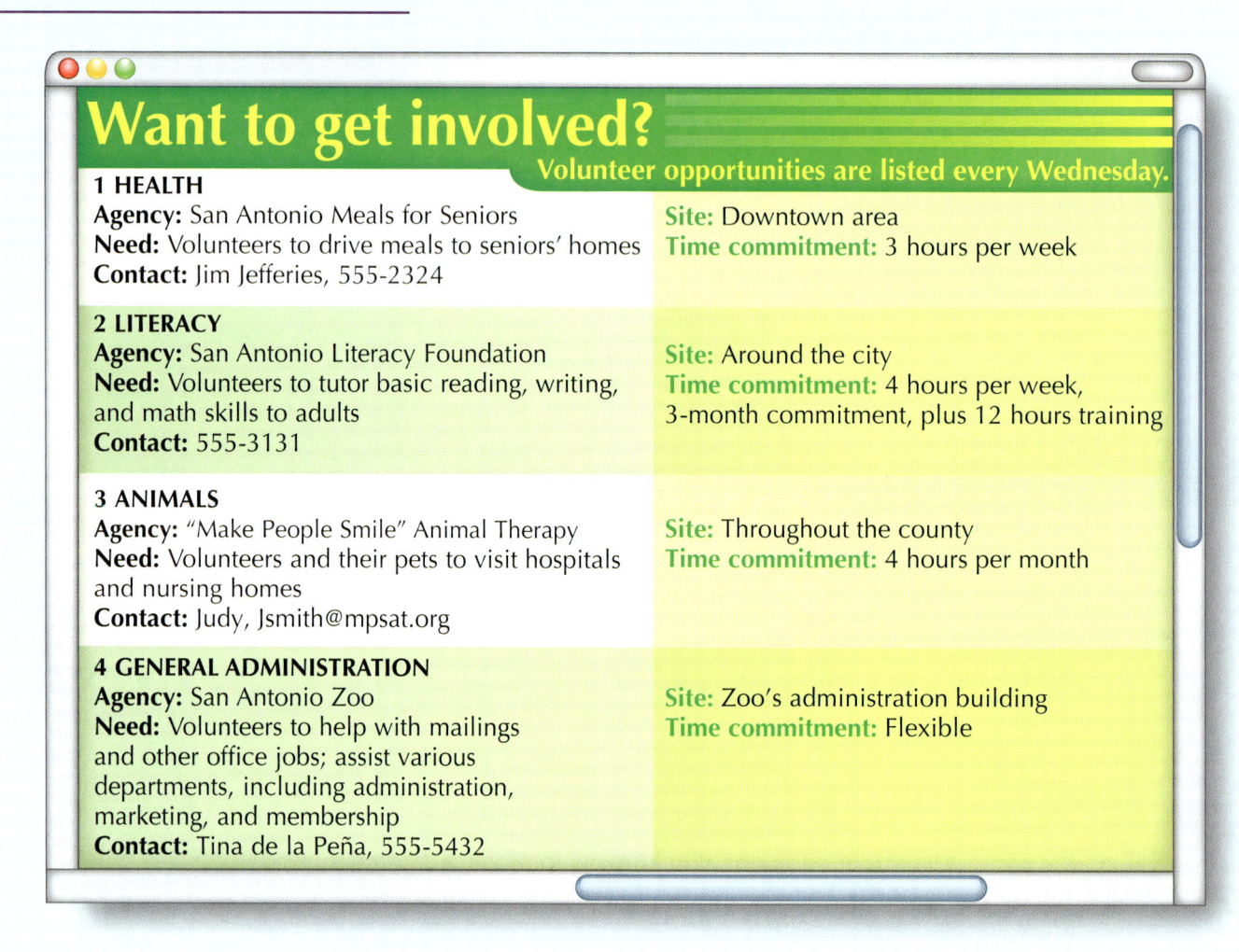

Want to get involved?
Volunteer opportunities are listed every Wednesday.

1 HEALTH
Agency: San Antonio Meals for Seniors
Need: Volunteers to drive meals to seniors' homes
Contact: Jim Jefferies, 555-2324
Site: Downtown area
Time commitment: 3 hours per week

2 LITERACY
Agency: San Antonio Literacy Foundation
Need: Volunteers to tutor basic reading, writing, and math skills to adults
Contact: 555-3131
Site: Around the city
Time commitment: 4 hours per week, 3-month commitment, plus 12 hours training

3 ANIMALS
Agency: "Make People Smile" Animal Therapy
Need: Volunteers and their pets to visit hospitals and nursing homes
Contact: Judy, Jsmith@mpsat.org
Site: Throughout the county
Time commitment: 4 hours per month

4 GENERAL ADMINISTRATION
Agency: San Antonio Zoo
Need: Volunteers to help with mailings and other office jobs; assist various departments, including administration, marketing, and membership
Contact: Tina de la Peña, 555-5432
Site: Zoo's administration building
Time commitment: Flexible

A **Read** the questions. Look at the advertisements for volunteer positions. Circle the answers.

1. Which volunteer position requires the biggest time commitment?
   a. 1   c. 3
   b. 2   d. 4

2. Which ad wants you to e-mail your response?
   a. 1   **c. 3**
   b. 2   d. 4

3. Which position requires math skills?
   a. 1   c. 3
   b. 2   d. none of the positions

4. Which position requires office skills?
   a. 1   c. 3
   b. 2   **d. 4**

5. Which position requires a driver's license?
   a. 1   c. 3
   b. 2   d. 4

6. Which position requires some training?
   a. 1   c. 3
   b. 2   d. none of the positions

B **Talk** with your classmates. Discuss the ads. Which ones are interesting to you? Why?

Lesson objectives

- Practice reading and understanding ads for volunteer positions
- Review vocabulary and grammar from the unit
- Introduce the project
- Complete the self-assessment

Warm-up and review

- Before class. Write today's lesson focus on the board.
  Lesson F:
  Read and understand ads for volunteer positions
  Review topic vocabulary and grammar from Unit 5
  Complete the project and the self-assessment
- Begin class. Books closed. Write on the board: *Want to get involved? Volunteer opportunities are listed every Wednesday.*
- Ask Ss: *What does "get involved" mean?* Elicit responses, such as: *do something to make a difference, help a person or an organization.*
- Tell Ss that in this lesson, they will practice reading and understanding several advertisements looking for volunteers.
- Ask Ss where they can find ads for volunteer positions, for example: *in community newspapers, online, on bulletin boards at schools, in places of religious worship, in community centers, in supermarkets.*
- Ask Ss what kind of information they expect to see in an ad looking for volunteers. Elicit responses, such as: *the name of the company or organization looking for volunteers, where volunteers would work, how many hours a week or month they would work (time commitment), and who to contact for more information.*

Presentation

- Books open. Direct Ss' attention to the four ads in Exercise **1**.
- Divide the class into four groups. Assign one of the advertisements to each group. Tell each group to read the advertisement and discuss the meaning of any new words. Allow Ss to use dictionaries to look up any words they don't understand. Walk around and help as needed.
- Tell Ss that they are going to explain their advertisement to another group without looking at the ad as they are explaining. Ask each group to write down any key words that will help them remember the advertisement.
- Give each S a number according to how many Ss are in each group. For example, if there are three Ss in a group, number each S from 1 to 3.
- Ask all number ones to get together in a new group, as well as all number twos and threes.

- Books closed. Tell Ss to describe their ad to their new group.
- Walk around and help as needed. If Ss can't remember something about their advertisement, give them clues to help them recall the content.

Practice

- Read aloud the instructions for Exercise **1A**. This exercise helps prepare Ss for standardized-type tests they may have to take. Be sure that Ss understand the task. Have Ss individually scan for and circle the answers.

Comprehension check

- Check answers with the class. Make sure that Ss have followed the instructions and circled their answers.
- Have Ss read aloud the questions and answers they circled. Make corrections as needed.

Application

- Direct Ss' attention to Exercise **1B** and read the instructions aloud.
- Ss work in small groups to discuss the ads.
- Ask several Ss to share their opinions with the class.

Expansion activity (student pairs)

- Ss in pairs. Tell Ss that they are going to write the advertisement that motivated Almaz to apply for the volunteer job in the nursing home at the beginning of the unit.
- Encourage Ss to look at the pictures on page 58. Ask Ss: *What information should you include in the ad?* (name of the nursing home, responsibilities, time commitment, contact information, etc.).
- Tell Ss that they should talk about the information with their partner and then write the ad together. Have Ss use the ads on page 68 as models. Encourage Ss to be creative.
- Walk around and help as needed. When Ss have finished, have volunteers read their ads to the class.

Another view

Presentation

- Books closed. Write on the board: *sayings*. Ask Ss if they know what *sayings* are. Elicit an appropriate response, such as: *a well-known expression or a wise statement*.
- Tell Ss that there are sayings in many different cultures and that we usually learn sayings from our parents or grandparents. Tell Ss that they are going to learn some popular sayings in English about giving.

Practice

- Books open. Direct Ss' attention to the photographs in Exercise **2A**. Ask individual Ss to describe what they see in each photograph.
- Read the instructions aloud for Exercise **2A**.
- Divide the class into four groups, assigning each group one of the four sayings to discuss. Then have one S in each group read the saying aloud. Ask groups if they have heard or used these sayings before.
- Ss work with their group to complete the activity. Walk around and help as needed.
- Check answers with the class.

Application

- Direct Ss' attention to Exercise **2B**. Read the instructions aloud.
- Call on six Ss to read the six volunteer categories.
- Model the exercise. Ask Ss: *Have you ever volunteered to serve food to homeless people?* Go through the list of volunteer situations until you get a *yes* answer. Show Ss where they should write the name of the person who answers *yes*.
- Ss complete the exercise by walking around and talking to their classmates.
- Direct Ss' attention to the second part of Exercise **2B**. Call on Ss to paraphrase and share information they learned about their classmates.

Expansion activity (student pairs)

- Write the following chart on the board:

Saying	Origin (where it's from)	Meaning
Tell me who you walk with, and I'll tell you who you are.	*Mexico / my grandmother*	*Your friends say a lot about your character.*

- Invite a S to read the saying. Ask Ss if they have heard it before. You can tell Ss that although this saying comes from the Spanish language, there is a similar saying in English: *Birds of a feather flock together*.
- Ss in pairs. Ask partners to tell each other some of the sayings (or proverbs) they know in English or in their native language if they are able to translate the sayings into English.
- Open up the discussion to the class. Invite Ss to come to the board to add examples to the chart. Ask Ss if they have similar sayings in their native language. Encourage Ss to compare those that are similar in meaning but slightly different in translation.

> **More Ventures** (whole group, pairs, individual)
> Assign appropriate exercises from the *Teacher's Toolkit Audio CD / CD-ROM, Add Ventures,* or the *Workbook*.

Application

Community building

- **Project** Ask Ss to turn to page 138 in their Student's Book to complete the project for Unit 5.

Evaluation

- Before asking Ss to turn to the self-assessment on page 143, do a quick review of the unit. Have Ss turn to Lesson A. Ask the class to talk about what they remember about this lesson. Prompt Ss, if necessary, with questions, for example: *What are the conversations about on this page? What vocabulary is in the pictures?* Continue in this manner to review each lesson quickly.
- **Self-assessment** Read the instructions for Exercise **3**. Ask Ss to turn to the self-assessment page to complete the unit self-assessment. The self-assessments are also on the *Teacher's Toolkit Audio CD / CD-ROM*. If you prefer to collect the assessments and save them as part of each S's portfolio assessment, print out the unit self-assessment from the Toolkit, ask Ss to complete it, and collect and save it.
- If Ss are ready, administer the unit test on pages T-181–T-183 of this *Teacher's Edition* (or on the *Teacher's Toolkit Audio CD / CD-ROM*). The audio and audio script for the tests are on the *Teacher's Toolkit Audio CD / CD-ROM*.

2 Fun with language

A **Work** in a group. Read the list of popular sayings about giving. Discuss the meanings. Then look at the pictures. Match the sayings with the pictures.

a. From small beginnings come great things.   c. The best things in life are free.
b. Many hands make light work.   d. It's better to give than to get.

1. _c_

2. _a_

3. _d_

4. _b_

B **Talk** with your classmates. Find someone who has volunteered to do the activities in the chart.

Find someone who has volunteered . . .	Name
to serve food to homeless people	Hector
to play music for others	
to tutor a child	
to coach a team	
to sell items to raise money for charity	
to help elderly people	

Share information about your classmates.

3 Wrap up

Complete the **Self-assessment** on page 143.

Lesson A Get ready

1 Talk about the pictures

A What do you see?

B What is happening?

Mrs. Rosen

Mr. Chung

Mail

Ms. Morales

Warm-up and review

- Before class. Write today's lesson focus on the board.
  Lesson A:
  Talk about time-saving devices
  Discuss the advantages and disadvantages of technology
- Begin class. Books closed. Direct Ss' attention to the lesson focus. Point to *time-saving devices*. Ask Ss to guess the meaning of this phrase. Help Ss come to an understanding by asking: *What things do you use to help you save time?*
- Ask Ss: *What are some examples of time-saving devices?* List Ss' responses on the board, for example: *dishwashers, washing machines, copy machines, cell phones, computers.*
- Ask Ss: *What are advantages and disadvantages?* Elicit appropriate answers, such as: *positive and negative points about something.*
- Underline the prefix *dis-* in *disadvantages* (from the lesson focus). Point out that *dis-* is a prefix meaning "not," so the literal meaning of the word is "not advantages." Ask Ss if they can think of other words that begin with *dis-*. Elicit appropriate answers, such as: *disrespect, disappear, dishonest, dislike, disagree, disorganized.*

Presentation

- Books open. Set the scene. Direct Ss' attention to the pictures on page 70. Ask the question from Exercise **1A**: *What do you see?* Elicit and write on the board as much vocabulary as Ss know, such as: *reporter, journalist, microphone, interview, post office, cell phone, letters.* Explain any unfamiliar words.
- Direct Ss' attention to the question in Exercise **1B**: *What is happening?* Read it aloud. Hold up the Student's Book. Point to the picture of Mrs. Rosen. Ask: *What's Mrs. Rosen doing here?* (She's being interviewed, and she's showing an address stamper to the man who is interviewing her.)

- Point to the picture of Mr. Chung. Ask: *What's Mr. Chung doing here?* (He's talking to the reporter and showing him a stack of letters.)
- Point to the picture of Ms. Morales. Ask: *What's Ms. Morales doing here?* (She's showing her cell phone to the reporter.)

▼**Culture tip**
Ask Ss if they notice anything about the titles on the female characters' name labels (*Mrs.* and *Ms.*). Tell Ss that there are three possible titles for a woman in English: *Miss, Mrs.,* and *Ms.* Explain that *Miss* is used for an unmarried woman and that *Mrs.* is used for a married woman. Point out that unlike *Miss* and *Mrs., Ms.* does not identify a woman's marital status. Lead Ss to see that the title *Ms.* is now the most common way to address a woman you don't know and that the best way to find out which title a woman prefers is to ask her.

Practice

- Have Ss work in groups of three to write an interview between the person in each of the pictures and the reporter. Assign Ss in each group a number: *1, 2,* or *3.* Suggest that all the ones write an interview between Mrs. Rosen and the reporter; all the twos write an interview between Mr. Chung and the reporter; and all the threes write an interview between Ms. Morales and the reporter.

▼**Teaching tip**
Encourage Ss to be imaginative. At this point, there is no single correct answer.

- Walk around and help as needed.
- Ask for volunteers to role-play their interview for the class.

Presentation

- Books open. Direct Ss' attention to Exercise **2A**. Read the instructions aloud. Tell Ss that they are going to hear three different conversations. Have Ss listen for the main ideas.
- [Class Audio CD2 track 12] Play or read the audio program (see audio script, page T-161).
- Ask Ss if they have understood everything in the listening exercise. Write any unfamiliar words on the board and help Ss understand the meaning of each. Be sure that Ss understand the meaning of *spam* ("junk e-mail," or unwanted e-mail advertising).
- Partners complete Exercise **2A**. Elicit answers to the questions in the exercise.
- Direct Ss to Exercise **2B**, and read the instructions aloud. Tell Ss to listen and complete the chart.
- [Class Audio CD2 track 13] Model the task. Play or read the audio program again. Pause the program after Mrs. Rosen says in Conversation 1: *Let me see. . . . I guess it's this – my address stamper.* Ask a S to read the example written under *Time-saving device* (address stamper). Play or read the audio again. Pause after Mrs. Rosen says: *The address stamper just takes seconds, even though it's not electronic.* Ask Ss: *What would you fill in for Mrs. Rosen under "Opinion about time-saving device" in the chart?* (She thinks the address stamper is very useful.) Tell Ss that even though Mrs. Rosen's opinion is not stated directly, we can guess her opinion from what she says. Play or read the rest of the audio program. Ss listen and complete the chart.
- Read aloud the second part of the instructions for Exercise **2B**.
- [Class Audio CD2 track 13] Play or read the audio program again (see audio script, page T-161). Ss listen and check their answers. Repeat the audio as needed.

Practice

- Direct Ss' attention to Exercise **2C**. Read the instructions aloud. Tell Ss that the story is a summary of what happened in the pictures on page 70. Remind Ss that a summary retells only the most important points of a story.
- Direct Ss' attention to the words in the word bank. Say each word aloud. Ask Ss to repeat. Correct pronunciation as needed. Make sure that Ss understand the meaning of each word. Explain any words that are new to Ss.
- Model the exercise. Call on a S to read the first sentence in the story, including the example answer.
- Ss complete the exercise individually. Walk around and help as needed.

Comprehension check

- [Class Audio CD3 track 14] Play or read the audio program (see audio script, page T-161). Ss listen and check their answers. Repeat the audio program as needed.
- Write the numbers *1–8* on the board. Ask eight Ss to come to the board to write their answers.
- Make corrections on the board as needed.

Learner persistence (individual work)

- [Self-Study CD tracks 19 and 20] Exercises **2A**, **2B**, and **2C** are recorded on the Ss' self-study CD at the back of the Student's Book. Ss can listen to the CD at home for reinforcement and review. They can also listen to the CD for self-directed learning when class attendance is not possible.

Application

- Focus Ss' attention on Exercise **2D**. Read the instructions aloud.
- Ss complete the exercise in pairs. Help as needed.
- Ask several pairs to ask and answer the questions for the class. Discuss Ss' opinions about technology.

Expansion activity (small groups)

- Ask Ss: *Have you ever thought of a time-saving device that hasn't been invented yet? What's something that could be invented that would save you time and energy?*
- Ask small groups to brainstorm a list of time-saving devices that have not yet been invented (to the best of their knowledge) but that they would like to have. After each S has had a chance to share his or her device, the group should decide on the one device that it will present to the class.
- One S in each group should present that group's favorite device to the class. The representative should say what it is, what it does, how it works, and why his or her group chose it.

Evaluation

- Direct Ss' attention to the lesson focus on the board. Ask individual Ss to look at the pictures on page 70 and make sentences using the words in Exercise **2C**.
- Check off each part of the lesson focus as Ss demonstrate an understanding of what they have learned in the lesson.

> **More Ventures** (whole group, pairs, individual)
> Assign appropriate exercises from the *Teacher's Toolkit Audio CD / CD-ROM*, *Add Ventures*, or the *Workbook*.

2 Listening

 **A** **Listen** and answer the questions.

1. Who are the speakers?
2. What are they talking about?

 **B** **Listen again.** Complete the chart.

	Time-saving device	Opinion about time-saving device
1. Mrs. Rosen	*address stamper*	*It saves her time.*
2. Mr. Chung	*e-mail*	*It's distracting and interrupts his work.*
3. Ms. Morales	*cell phone*	*She loves it.*

Listen again. Check your answers.

 **C** **Read.** Complete the story. Listen and check your answers.

convenient	distracting	innovative	spam
devices	electronic	manual	text message

Today, a reporter from KESL Radio asked three people about technology and their favorite time-saving ___*devices*___ . Mrs. Rosen's favorite
1

device is ___*manual*___ . She says it saves time, even though it isn't
2

___*electronic*___ . Mr. Chung isn't a fan of technology. In fact, he says
3

technology wastes more time than it saves. For example, he says he doesn't like

e-mail because he gets lots of ___*spam*___ . He also finds e-mail
4

___*distracting*___ . He doesn't think it is ___*convenient*___ .
5   6

Ms. Morales loves technology. She uses the camera on her cell phone in a very

___*innovative*___ way – to send her daughter pictures of clothes that
7

are on sale. Her daughter sends a ___*text message*___ back: "Buy" or
8

"Don't buy."

D **Discuss.** Talk with a partner.

1. Do you agree with the people interviewed? Why or why not?
2. In general, do you think technology saves time or wastes time? Give examples.

Clauses of concession

1 Grammar focus: *although, even though*

> Although (Even though) e-mail is fast, Mr. Chung doesn't like to use it.
> Mr. Chung doesn't like to use e-mail although (even though) it is fast.
>
> *For a grammar explanation, turn to page 150.*

2 Practice

A Write. Combine the sentences. Use *even though*.

1. Mr. Gormet doesn't want a microwave. He knows microwaves save time.

   Mr. Gormet doesn't want a microwave even though he knows they save time.

2. Ms. Honig's car has a GPS system. She gets lost all the time.

   Even though Ms. Honig's car has a GPS system, she gets lost all the time.

3. Mr. Wang doesn't have a laptop computer. He travels constantly.

   Mr. Wang doesn't have a laptop computer even though he travels constantly.

4. Mrs. Sanchez can't operate her digital camera. She read the instructions three times.

   Mrs. Sanchez can't operate her digital camera even though she read the instructions three times.

5. Mrs. Belcanto doesn't want a dishwasher. She has six children.

   Mrs. Belcanto doesn't want a dishwasher even though she has six children.

6. Ms. Kaye had urgent business in another state. She refused to travel by plane.

   Even though Ms. Kaye had urgent business in another state, she refused to travel by plane.

7. My house has central air-conditioning. I prefer to use a fan when it's hot.

   Even though my house has central air-conditioning, I prefer to use a fan when it's hot.

8. My grandmother doesn't use e-mail. She has an e-mail address.

   My grandmother doesn't use e-mail even though she has an e-mail address.

9. DVD movies are very popular. I still watch movies on videocassettes.

   Even though DVD movies are very popular, I still watch movies on videocassettes.

Listen and check your answers.

Warm-up and review

- Before class. Write today's lesson focus on the board.
  Lesson B:
  Practice using although *and* even though
- Begin class. Books open. Direct Ss' attention to the three pictures on page 70. Review key vocabulary from the unit.
- Say: *It takes only a minute to write a return address on an envelope, but Mrs. Rosen tells the reporter that her address stamper is her favorite time-saving device. Why do you think she feels this way?*
- Say: *Many people think e-mail is convenient. Mr. Chung doesn't agree. He thinks it's distracting. Does his opinion of e-mail surprise you?*
- Tell Ss that in today's lesson, they will look at words to use when they want to add new or surprising information to a statement.

Presentation

- Direct Ss' attention to the grammar chart in Exercise **1**. Read the two statements aloud.
- Point to *Although (Even though)* in the first statement. Tell Ss that in this sentence, the *although* clause gives us information that adds a surprising contrast: *We expect that since e-mail is fast, Mr. Chung will like to use it.*
- Tell Ss that the second statement is just a different way of writing the first statement. The meaning is the same.
- Explain to Ss that *although* and *even though* have almost the same meaning, but *even though* can be a bit stronger (more emphatic) than *although*.
- Ask: *What do you notice about using commas with "although" and "even though"?* Elicit an appropriate response, such as: *A comma is used when the "although / even though" clause is at the beginning of a sentence.*
- Write an additional statement on the board: *Although Mary studied for three hours, she did not do well on the test.* Tell Ss that in this sentence, the *although* clause gives information that adds a surprising contrast to the main clause. We expect that, after studying for three hours, Mary would do well on the test.

▼**Teaching tip**
It might be helpful to refer Ss to the grammar explanation on page 150 in the Student's Book.

Practice

- Direct Ss' attention to Exercise **2A**. The purpose of this exercise is to check comprehension of the grammar focus and to combine sentences using *even though*. Read the instructions aloud.
- Call on a S to read the example. Make sure that Ss understand the exercise.
- Ss complete the exercise individually. Walk around and help as needed.

Comprehension check

- Focus Ss' attention on the second part of the instructions for Exercise **2A**, and read it aloud.
- ⊙ [Class Audio CD2 track 15] Play or read the audio program (see audio script, page T-161). Ss listen and check their answers. Repeat the audio program as needed.
- Write the numbers *1–9* on the board. Ask nine Ss to come to the board to write their combined sentences. Make corrections on the board as needed.

Expansion activity (small groups)

- On the board, write the following clauses:
  Although she's not feeling well, . . .
  Even though we have a lot of money, . . .
  Even though they love movies, . . .
  Although he liked her at first, . . .
  She likes to climb mountains . . .
  He tried to fix the car . . .
- Tell Ss to work with their classmates to complete each of the sentences with an *although / even though* clause. Walk around and help as needed.
- Ask Ss to share their sentences with the class. Write (or have Ss write) several examples on the board. Make corrections on the board as needed.

Lesson B Clauses of concession

Presentation

- Books open. Direct Ss' attention to the pictures in Exercise **2B**. Hold up the Student's Book. Point to each picture and make sure that Ss know the vocabulary words for each illustration (e.g., *vacuum cleaner, broom, dishwasher*.
- Tell Ss that they are going to talk and write about which devices or technology Mr. Chung prefers.

Practice

- Read the instructions aloud for Exercise **2B**.
- Ask a S to read the words in the word bank. Ask another S to read the example sentence above the pictures. Tell Ss that they should imagine which devices or technology Mr. Chung likes best.
- Ss complete the exercise in pairs. Walk around and help as needed.
- Direct Ss' attention to the second part of Exercise **2B**. Read the instructions aloud.
- Call on a S to read the example sentence. Tell Ss that their sentences must include a clause with *although* or *even though*.
- Ss work individually to complete the exercise. Walk around and help as needed.
- Ask Ss to come to the board to write their sentences. Make corrections on the board as needed.

Application

- Direct Ss' attention to Exercise **3A** and read the instructions aloud.
- Model the task. Ask two Ss to read the example dialog to the class.
- Ss work in small groups to complete the exercise. Walk around and help as needed.
- Direct Ss' attention to Exercise **3B** and read the instructions aloud.
- Ask Ss to share with the class information they learned about the time-saving devices and tools that their classmates own but don't use.

> ### Culture note
> Call on a S to read the culture note to the class. Ask Ss if they have ever been to a garage, yard, or tag sale. Ss who have been to these sales can say what the sale was like and what items they bought. Have Ss suggest how they can find out about garage sales in their community (*by reading the local newspaper, by looking at signs that are posted around town*, etc.).

Expansion activity *(student pairs)*

- Ask Ss if they know somebody like Mr. Chung, who prefers to do things the "old-fashioned way." If so, they know it is sometimes difficult to convince someone to change his or her ways. Explain to Ss that in this activity, they will attempt to change Mr. Chung's mind.
- Tell Ss that they are going to write a conversation with a partner in which one of them is Mr. Chung, and the other is Mrs. Rosen or Ms. Morales. In the conversation, the other person should try to convince Mr. Chung to try a new way of doing something. Ss must use *even though* or *although* at least twice.
- Model the task. Write the following on the board:

Ms. Morales: Even though you prefer to listen to your cassette player, you should try an MP3 player!

Mr. Chung: But why? Although I know they're very popular, I prefer my cassette player. It's less expensive.

Ms. Morales: Even though it is less expensive, it's more difficult to carry.

- Ss work in pairs to write their short dialog. Then have them practice their conversation a few times, taking turns to play each role. Walk around and help as needed.
- Ask several pairs to perform their dialog for the class.

Evaluation

- Books closed. Direct Ss' attention to the lesson focus on the board.
- Write the following sentence on the board: *Although it's raining hard, I want to go to the football game.* Ask a S to say this sentence in another way. Tell the S that he or she can change the word order but not the words. Elicit an appropriate response: *I want to go to the football game although it's raining hard*.
- Ask a S to tell another way of saying that same sentence without using *although*. Elicit: *Even though it's raining hard, I want to go to the football game. I want to go to the football game even though it's raining hard*.
- Check off the lesson focus as Ss demonstrate an understanding of what they have learned in the lesson.

> **More Ventures** *(whole group, pairs, individual)*
> Assign appropriate exercises from the *Teacher's Toolkit Audio CD / CD-ROM*, *Add Ventures*, or the *Workbook*.

B **Talk** with a partner. Choose pairs of pictures and make sentences about Mr. Chung. Use *although* and *even though* with verbs from the box.

clean	find information	have	listen	use	wash	write

> Although Mr. Chung has a computer, he prefers to write letters by hand.

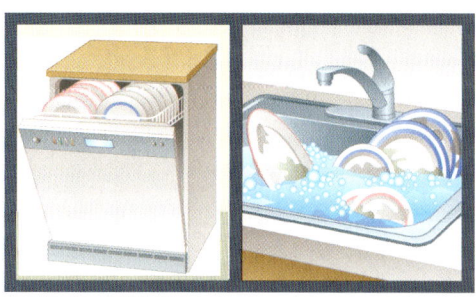

Write sentences about Mr. Chung.

Although Mr. Chung has a computer, he prefers to write letters by hand.

3 Communicate

A **Work** in a small group. Talk about time-saving devices or tools that you own but don't use. Use *although* and *even though*.

> **A** Although I have a food processor, I almost never use it.
> **B** Why?
> **A** It's too hard to clean.

Culture note
In the United States, many people hold garage or yard sales to sell their household items that they no longer use.

B **Share** information about your classmates.

Lesson C *Clauses of reason and concession*

1 Grammar focus: contrasting *because* and *although*

Because wireless technology is fast, many schools have it.
Although wireless technology is fast, my school cannot afford it.

For a grammar explanation, turn to page 150.

2 Practice

A Write. Complete the story. Use *because* or *although*.

Pam   Beth

_____Although_____ Pam and Beth are sisters, they are very different. Pam is
        1

very modern. She loves electrical appliances _____because_____ they are fast and
                                                   2

convenient. For example, she loves her microwave _____because_____ she can
                                                        3

use it to thaw meat quickly. She enjoys shopping for the latest kitchen devices,

_____although_____ some of them are very expensive.
        4

Beth has a different attitude about modern technology. She prefers not to use

electrical appliances. For instance, she never uses a microwave _____because_____ she
                                                                     5

thinks the radiation is bad. She dries her clothes outside on a line _____because_____
                                                                          6

she likes their smell after they've been in the fresh air. She washes her dishes by hand

_____because_____ she says dishwashers waste energy. Pam doesn't understand why
        7

Beth is so old-fashioned. But _____although_____ the sisters have different lifestyles,
                                      8

they appreciate and enjoy one another very much.

Listen and check your answers.

Lesson objective
- Contrast *because* and *although*

Warm-up and review

- Before class. Write today's lesson focus on the board.
  Lesson C:
  Contrast because and although
- Begin class. Books closed. Write on the board: *although* and *even though*. Then write this sentence: *Although I have a food processor, I almost never use it. Even though I have a food processor, I almost never use it.* Read the sentences aloud.
- Ask Ss to make up similar sentences using *although* and *even though* and a device that they have but don't use. Write some examples on the board.
- Ask Ss: *Why don't you use your _____ ?* Give an example: *I don't use my food processor because it's so hard to clean.*

Presentation

- Books open. Direct Ss' attention to the grammar chart in Exercise **1**. Read the two statements aloud.
- Ask Ss what *because* means. Elicit an appropriate response, such as: *for the reason that.*
- Tell Ss that although they are very similar, *because* is used to explain a statement (usually an expected result), and *although* is used to qualify or clarify a statement (usually for an unexpected result).
- Point out that when *because* and *although* begin a sentence, a comma is needed before the main clause.

▼ **Teaching tip**
Refer Ss to the grammar explanation on page 150 in the Student's Book.

Practice

- Direct Ss' attention to Exercise **2A** and read the instructions aloud.
- Ask a S to read aloud the first sentence containing the sample answer.
- Ss complete the exercise individually. Walk around and help as needed.

Comprehension check

- Read aloud the second part of the instructions for Exercise **2A**.
- [Class Audio CD2 track 16] Play or read the audio program (see audio script, page T-161). Ss listen and check their answers.

- Write the numbers *1–8* on the board. Ask eight Ss to come to the board to write and then read the sentences by filling in the answers. Make corrections on the board as needed.

Expansion activity (small groups)

- Write the following incomplete story on the board. You can also type the following and give each small group one copy to share.
  _____ the ground was freezing cold, we had a picnic in the park.
  _____ it was so cold, we decided to bring some hot soup to warm us up.
  _____ the soup was very spicy, I ate it all.
  _____ the soup was very spicy, I drank a lot of water.
  _____ it was so chilly, we decided to pack up our things and go to the movies.
  _____ the movie was very scary, I really enjoyed it.
  _____ it was getting late, we decided to go to another friend's house.
  _____ we were hungry, we ordered some pizza.
  _____ I didn't get home until late, I was really tired in class today.
  _____ I was very sleepy in class today, I got an A on the grammar quiz!
- Tell Ss that they have to decide whether to use *Although* or *Because* to complete the story.
- Ss work in small groups to complete the sentences. Walk around and help as needed.
- Check answers with the class.

Expansion activity (student pairs)

- Ask Ss to think about someone they know who is different from them. Tell Ss to use *because* and *although* to talk about the differences.
- Model the task. Say: *Although Karen is my best friend, she and I are very different. For example, she enjoys spending a lot of time at home because she has a cozy apartment. Although I have a nice apartment, I like to go out.*
- Ss in pairs. Ss take turns telling each other about themselves and their relatives or friends who are different from them.
- Call on several pairs to share their discussions with the class.

Practice

- Direct Ss' attention to the two pictures in Exercise **2B**. Ask Ss to compare what is happening in each picture. Elicit an appropriate response, such as: *The first man is driving a fast car. The second man is taking the subway.*

- Direct Ss' attention to the two headings in the chart in Exercise **2B**. Ask: *What does "speedy" mean?* Elicit an appropriate response: *"Speedy" describes someone who does everything quickly.* Then ask: *What does "thrifty" mean?* Elicit: *"Thrifty" describes someone who is careful about spending money.*

- Read the instructions aloud. Call on two Ss to read the first item in each column of the chart. Call on two other Ss to read the example sentences above the two pictures.

- Have Ss complete the exercise with a partner. Be sure that each pair understands the task. Walk around and help as needed.

- Read the instructions aloud for the second part of Exercise **2B**. Call on two Ss to read the two example sentences.

- Ss complete the exercise individually. Remind Ss to use *because* or *although* in each sentence. Walk around and help as needed.

- Ask several Ss to come to the board to write their sentences.

- Have other Ss read aloud each of the sentences on the board. Ask: *Is this sentence correct?* Work with the class to make corrections on the board as needed.

Expansion activity *(student pairs)*

- Ask Ss to role-play a conversation between Mr. Speedy and Mr. Thrifty. Ss can ask and answer questions about Mr. Speedy's and Mr. Thrifty's preferences using the information from Exercise **2B** as a guide.

- Model the task. Write this example on the board.

    Mr. Speedy: I just don't understand why you take the subway!
    Mr. Thrifty: I take the subway because it's convenient – and inexpensive!

- Encourage Ss to have fun with this activity. Ask several pairs to act out their conversations for the class, using appropriate stress, intonation, and gestures.

Application

- Direct Ss' attention to Exercise **3A** and read the instructions aloud.

- Ss in pairs. Model the task. Ask two Ss to read the example dialog aloud.

> **Useful language**
> Read the tip box aloud. Ask two Ss to read the example dialog. Write the word *neither* on the board. Tell Ss that we can pronounce the *ei* in *neither* in two ways: /i/ and /ɑɪ/. Pronounce both ways and have Ss repeat. Ask Ss what the opposite of *neither* is (*both*).

- Ss complete the exercise in pairs. Walk around and help as needed.

- Direct Ss' attention to Exercise **3B**. Read the instructions aloud.

- Ask several Ss to share information they learned about their partner.

Evaluation

- Direct Ss' attention to the lesson focus on the board. Ask Ss to tell the class three sentences about themselves using *although* and *because*.

- Check that Ss have used *although* and *because* correctly. Make corrections on the board as needed.

- Check off the lesson focus as Ss demonstrate an understanding of what they have learned in the lesson.

> **More Ventures** *(whole group, pairs, individual)*
> Assign appropriate exercises from the *Teacher's Toolkit Audio CD / CD-ROM, Add Ventures,* or the *Workbook.*

B **Talk** with a partner. Compare Mr. Speedy and Mr. Thrifty. Use *because* and *although*.

> Mr. Speedy drives to work because it's fast.

> Although driving is faster, Mr. Thrifty takes the subway to work because it's cheaper.

Mr. Speedy	Mr. Thrifty
drives to work	takes the subway to work
shops online	shops in stores
buys his lunch	brings lunch from home
travels by plane	travels by train
calls directory assistance for a phone number	uses the phone book
buys cakes at a bakery	bakes his own cakes

Write sentences about Mr. Speedy and Mr. Thrifty.

Mr. Speedy drives to work because it's fast.
Although driving is faster, Mr. Thrifty takes the subway to work because it's cheaper.

3 Communicate

A **Work** with a partner. Ask and answer questions about the items in Exercise 2B. Give reasons for your answers.

> *A* Do you drive to work or take the subway?
> *B* Well, although driving is faster, I take the subway.
> *A* Why?
> *B* Because I don't have a car!

> **Useful language**
> Use *neither* when both answers to a question are negative.
>
> *A* Do you drive to work or take the subway?
> *B* Neither. I ride my bike.

B **Share** information about your partner.

Lesson D *Reading*

1 Before you read

Talk with your classmates. Answer the questions.

1. How do you stay in touch with friends and family in your native country?
2. What is a *blog*? Do you write or read one?

2 Read

 **Read** the blog. Listen and read again.

SELF-STUDY
AUDIO CD

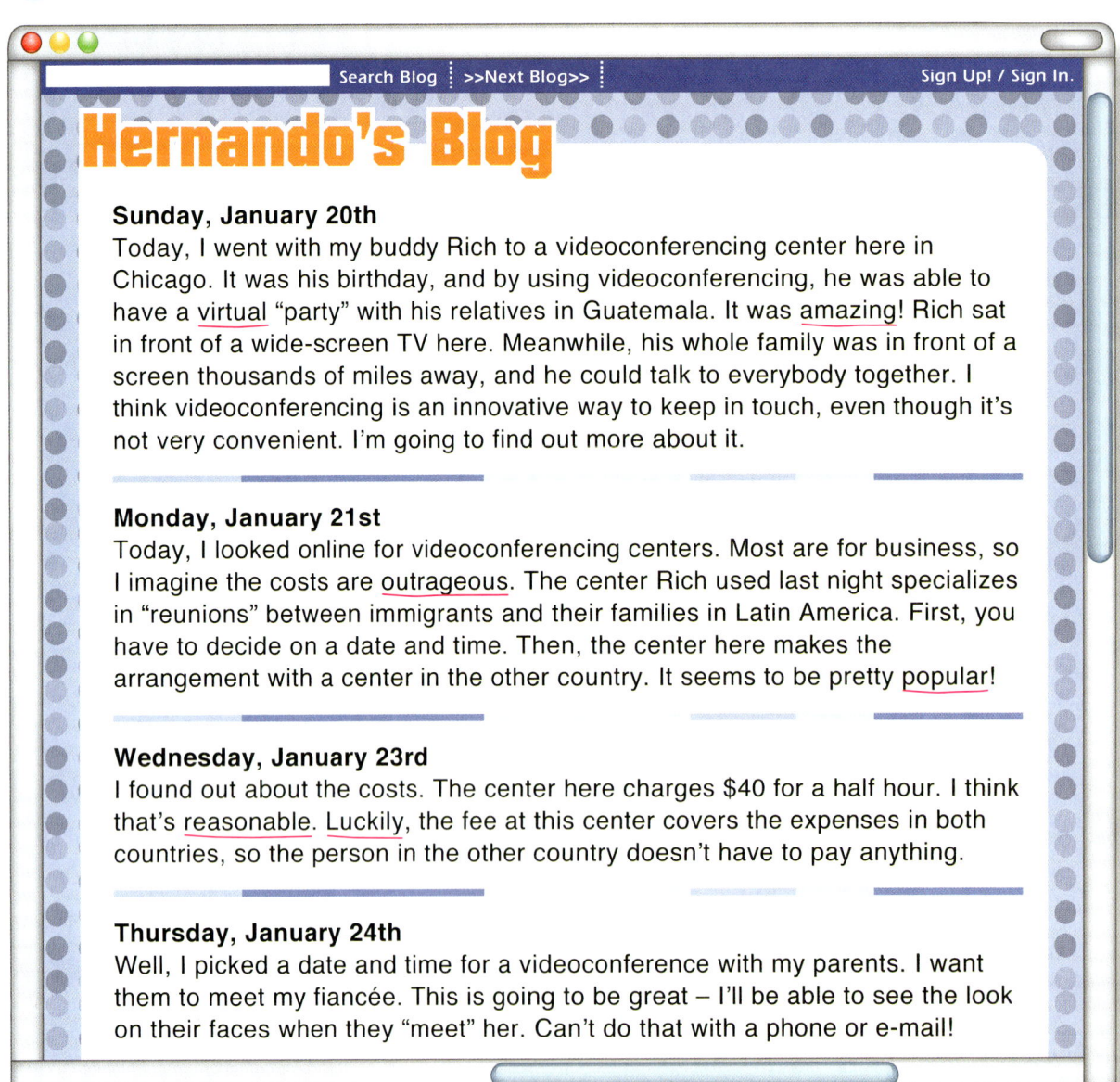

Hernando's Blog

Sunday, January 20th
Today, I went with my buddy Rich to a videoconferencing center here in Chicago. It was his birthday, and by using videoconferencing, he was able to have a virtual "party" with his relatives in Guatemala. It was amazing! Rich sat in front of a wide-screen TV here. Meanwhile, his whole family was in front of a screen thousands of miles away, and he could talk to everybody together. I think videoconferencing is an innovative way to keep in touch, even though it's not very convenient. I'm going to find out more about it.

Monday, January 21st
Today, I looked online for videoconferencing centers. Most are for business, so I imagine the costs are outrageous. The center Rich used last night specializes in "reunions" between immigrants and their families in Latin America. First, you have to decide on a date and time. Then, the center here makes the arrangement with a center in the other country. It seems to be pretty popular!

Wednesday, January 23rd
I found out about the costs. The center here charges $40 for a half hour. I think that's reasonable. Luckily, the fee at this center covers the expenses in both countries, so the person in the other country doesn't have to pay anything.

Thursday, January 24th
Well, I picked a date and time for a videoconference with my parents. I want them to meet my fiancée. This is going to be great – I'll be able to see the look on their faces when they "meet" her. Can't do that with a phone or e-mail!

Search Blog   >>Next Blog>>   Sign Up! / Sign In.

Lesson objectives

- Introduce and read "Hernando's Blog"
- Practice using new topic-related vocabulary
- Recognize the difference between facts and opinions
- Use multiple-meaning words

Warm-up and review

- Before class. Write today's lesson focus on the board.
  Lesson D:
  Read and understand "Hernando's Blog"
  Practice new vocabulary related to technology
  Understand the difference between facts and opinions
  Use multiple-meaning words

- Begin class. Books closed. Direct Ss' attention to the title of the reading, "Hernando's Blog," and ask Ss to predict what they think the reading is about. Write some of the Ss' predictions on the board. If Ss don't know the word *blog*, tell them that the word comes from a combination of two words: *Web* and *log*. Explain that *Web* is another word for the Internet and that *log* is another word for journal or diary – writing that contains ideas or information updated regularly.

Presentation

- Books open. Direct Ss' attention to Exercise **1** and read the instructions aloud.
- Have two Ss read aloud the questions in Exercise **1**.
- Ss in small groups. Ss discuss their answers to the questions. Walk around and help as needed.
- Call on individual Ss to share their answers with the class.

Practice

- Read the instructions aloud for Exercise **2**. Ask Ss to read the blog silently before listening to the audio program.
- [Class Audio CD2 track 17] Play or read the audio program and ask Ss to read along (see audio script, page T-161). Repeat the audio program as needed.
- While Ss are listening and reading the blog, ask them to underline any words they don't know. When the audio program is finished, have Ss write the new vocabulary words on the board.
- Point to each word on the board. Say it and have Ss repeat. Give a brief explanation of each word, or ask Ss who know the word to explain it. If Ss prefer to look up the new words in their dictionaries, allow them to do so.
- Point out that unlike "Hernando's Blog," most blogs are actually presented in reverse chronological order. In other words, the entry dated "Thursday, January 24th" would appear first in many blogs.

Learner persistence *(individual work)*

- [Self-Study Audio CD track 21] Exercise **2** is recorded on the Ss' self-study CD at the back of the Student's Book. Ss can listen to the CD at home for reinforcement and review. They can also listen to the CD for self-directed learning when class attendance is not possible.

Expansion activity *(small groups)*

- **Materials needed** Blog samples for each group.
- Find some interesting blog samples online. For example, look for short blog entries about food, certain hobbies, or celebrities. Print them out and bring them to class.
- Distribute the blog samples to small groups. Ask group members to read and discuss them.
- Write the following questions on the board:
  What similarities do the blogs have?
  What differences do they have?
  Which one would you like to read more of? Why?
- Have Ss compare "Hernando's Blog" and their blog sample to answer the questions on the board. Walk around and help as needed.
- Invite a spokesperson from each group to share the group's comparison with the class. Ask Ss what they would write about if they had a blog. Write Ss' suggestions on the board and discuss.

Community building *(small groups)*

- Ask Ss to work in small groups to design a questionnaire to ask people outside the class about their use of blogs. You can start by brainstorming ideas with the class to create a list of questions for the questionnaire and then have Ss write questions with their groups. Write example questions on the board, such as: *How often do you read blogs on the Internet? Which ones do you usually read?*
- Ss work in small groups to prepare questionnaires of four to five questions.
- Have Ss interview people about their blog use. Invite Ss to report their findings in a later class.
- Leave time for a question-and-answer session when Ss report their findings.

Comprehension check
- Direct Ss' attention to Exercise **3A** and read the instructions aloud.

> Read the tip to the class. Write on the board: *critical reader.* Ask Ss what they think this term means. Elicit and write: *A critical reader is someone who reads carefully.* Tell Ss that all the tips in this book are designed to help them become better critical readers. Then write on the board: *facts* and *opinions.* Ask Ss: *Where do you usually find facts and opinions?* Elicit appropriate responses, such as: *Facts are usually found in news articles and encyclopedias. Opinions are found in editorial sections of newspapers or in blogs.*

- Ask a S to read the example item in Exercise **3A** to the class.
- Call on five other Ss to read the remaining items, one at a time. Make sure that Ss understand the statements and task.
- Ss complete the exercise individually. Walk around and help as needed.
- Check answers with the class.
- Ask Ss how they determined which statements were fact and which were opinions. Tell Ss that when an adjective accompanies a statement, it is often an opinion. Ask Ss to name the adjectives that were used in these statements (*convenient* in number 2, *outrageous* in number 4, *reasonable* in number 6).

Practice
- **Materials needed** A dictionary for each S.
- Direct Ss' attention to number 1 of Exercise **3B**. Read the instructions aloud. Have a S read the sample dictionary entry. Ask Ss how many definitions there are in the entry. (two)
- Have Ss focus on number 2 in Exercise **3B** and read the instructions aloud. Ask a S to read the three headings. Call on another S to read the example in the chart.
- Ss work individually to underline the words in the reading and then complete the chart. Walk around and help as needed.
- Encourage Ss to use their dictionaries.

- Copy the chart on page 77 on the board. Ask six Ss to come to the board to complete the chart, writing the definition of each word as it is used in the reading and listing related words and their part of speech. Make corrections on the board as needed.

Learner persistence (individual work)
- Encourage Ss to use their notebook or vocabulary cards to write the related words and part of speech. Also encourage Ss to review new words daily and to practice them as much as possible.

Application
- Focus Ss' attention on Exercise **3C** and read the instructions aloud.
- Call on three Ss to read the questions.
- Ss complete the exercise in pairs, stating their opinions clearly.
- Ask several pairs to share their answers with the class.

Evaluation
- Books closed. Direct Ss' attention to the lesson focus on the board.
- Ask individual Ss to retell the main points of the reading, "Hernando's Blog."
- Books open. Focus Ss' attention on the words that they wrote in the chart for number 2 in Exercise **3B**. Ask Ss to make sentences with these words to show that they understand the meanings.
- Check off each part of the lesson focus as Ss demonstrate an understanding of what they have learned in the lesson.

Learner persistence (individual work, student pairs)
- You may wish to assign Extended reading worksheets from the *Teacher's Toolkit Audio CD / CD-ROM* for Ss to complete outside of class. The purpose of these worksheets is to encourage Ss to read for pleasure in English outside of the English class. The worksheets can also be assigned as extended reading in class.

> ***More Ventures*** (whole group, pairs, individual)
> Assign appropriate exercises from the *Teacher's Toolkit Audio CD / CD-ROM, Add Ventures,* or the *Workbook*.

3 After you read

A Check your understanding.
Look at the reading tip. Then write *F* for fact or *O* for opinion, based on the reading.

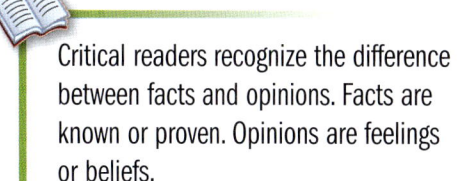

Critical readers recognize the difference between facts and opinions. Facts are known or proven. Opinions are feelings or beliefs.

_F_ 1. Videoconferences can connect people who are thousands of miles apart.

_O_ 2. Videoconferencing is not convenient.

_F_ 3. Videoconferencing centers are listed online.

_O_ 4. The cost of business videoconferences is probably outrageous.

_F_ 5. The Chicago center charges $40 for a half hour of videoconferencing.

_O_ 6. The cost for a half hour is reasonable.

B Build your vocabulary.

1. Read the dictionary entry. How many definitions are there?

> **virtual** /*adj*/ **1** almost a particular thing or quality **2** occurring or existing online, not as a physical reality – **virtually** /*adv*/

2. Underline the words from the chart in the reading. Use a dictionary. Write the correct definition to fit the reading. Write related words and their part of speech.

Vocabulary	Definition	Related words and part of speech
1. virtual	*occurring or existing online, not as a physical reality*	*virtually (adverb)*
2. amazing	*very good, especially in a surprising way*	*amazement (noun); amaze (verb)*
3. outrageous	*shocking or very unusual*	*outrage (verb or noun)*
4. popular	*liked or enjoyed by most people in a particular group*	*popularity (noun); popularize (verb); popularly (adv)*
5. reasonable	*fair and practical*	*reason (verb or noun); reasonably (adv)*
6. luckily	*fortunately*	*luck (noun); lucky (adj)*

C Talk with a partner.

1. Give an example of an amazing new technology.
2. What do you think is a reasonable price for a computer?
3. Do you think videoconferencing will become more popular? Why or why not?

1 Before you write

A Work in a small group. Make a list of time-saving devices you and your classmates use. Write one advantage and one disadvantage of each.

Device	Advantage	Disadvantage
electronic calculator	does math quickly	breaks easily
1. (Answers will vary.)		
2.		
3.		
4.		
5.		
6.		
7.		
8.		

B Read the paragraph.

My Favorite Time-saving Device

Voice mail is my favorite time-saving device. It has several advantages. Before I had voice mail, I used to answer my phone every time it rang, even if I was busy. But with voice mail, I don't have to interrupt my work. The caller can just leave a message, and I can get it later. Another benefit of voice mail is that it allows me to avoid talking to people I don't want to talk to. But, of course, that is also a disadvantage because they can avoid talking to me! Another problem is that not only friends leave messages. Sometimes there are voice-mail messages from salespeople. So even though voice mail is very convenient, it has drawbacks as well.

One way of organizing a paragraph is by describing advantages and disadvantages.

Lesson objective

- Use advantages and disadvantages to organize a paragraph

Warm-up and review

- Before class. Write today's lesson focus on the board.
  Lesson E:
  Write a paragraph about the advantages and disadvantages of a time-saving device or activity

- Begin class. Books closed. Review vocabulary from the unit. Write the words *time-saving devices* on the board. Ask Ss for several examples. Elicit appropriate responses, such as: *dishwashers, washing machines, dryers, cars, calculators, cell phones, computers.*

- Have Ss recall the blog they read in Lesson D. Ask: *What was Hernando's blog about?* (It was mostly about videoconferencing.)
  What does Hernando say were some of the advantages of videoconferencing? (It gives people the chance to see family members who live far away, and the cost is reasonable.)
  What are some of the disadvantages? (Some videoconferencing centers are very expensive, and they are not always convenient.)

Presentation

- Books open. Direct Ss' attention to Exercise **1A**. Read the instructions aloud.

- Ask a S to read the three headings in the chart in Exercise **1A**: *Device, Advantage, Disadvantage*. Call on another S to read the example in the chart.

- Ss work in small groups to complete the chart. Walk around and help as needed.

- Write the chart from Exercise **1A** on the board. Call on Ss from each group to fill in one row at a time with an example from their group work.

Practice

- Direct Ss' attention to Exercise **1B** and read the instructions aloud.

- Ss read the paragraph silently. Tell them to underline words they do not understand.

- Have Ss write the new words on the board. Point to each word. Say it and ask Ss to repeat.

- Remind Ss of the reading strategies they have learned for finding clues to help them figure out the meaning of an unfamiliar word. For example, if a S writes *drawbacks* on the board, ask the S to look at the sentence in which it appears (the last sentence of the paragraph). The words *even though* in the sentence indicate that there will be a contrast in the sentence. Something *convenient* is positive, so a *drawback* has to be something negative.

Read the tip aloud. Have Ss refer to the model paragraph in Exercise **1B**. Ask Ss: *According to the paragraph, how many advantages of voice mail are there? Read the examples from the paragraph.* (There are two: 1. I don't have to interrupt my work. 2. It allows me to avoid talking to people I don't want to talk to.) Ask Ss: *How many disadvantages are there? Tell what are they in your own words.* (There are two: 1. People can also avoid talking to the writer. 2. Salespeople, not just friends, leave messages.) Tell Ss that by showing both sides of a topic (advantages and disadvantages), their argument or opinion is presented in a more balanced and convincing way.

Expansion activity *(student pairs)*

- Ask Ss if they know some synonyms of the word *drawbacks* (e.g., disadvantages, problems, weak points, negative aspects, bad points). Write the synonyms on the board.

- Tell Ss that the concluding sentence of a paragraph can sometimes be more effective if it mentions that there are drawbacks as well as advantages.

- Direct Ss' attention to the concluding sentence in the paragraph in Exercise **1B**. Have a S read it aloud. Ask if there is another way that the sentence could have been worded. Elicit an appropriate response and write it on the board. For example: *Although voice mail is very convenient, it has drawbacks as well.*

- Ss in pairs. Have partners write several examples of possible concluding sentences for a paragraph about the advantages and disadvantages of a time-saving device, using *although* and *even though* to show that a contrast between advantages and drawbacks is being presented.

- Model the task. Ask a S to use the sample entry in the chart as the basis for a concluding sentence. Elicit an appropriate sentence and write it on the board. (*Although an electronic calculator does math quickly, it also has some drawbacks.*)

- When pairs have finished writing their sentences, have several volunteers write their concluding sentences on the board. Make corrections on the board as needed.

Presentation

- Focus Ss' attention on Exercise **1C** and read the instructions aloud. Tell Ss that using this kind of diagram or graphic organizer is a good way of organizing ideas before writing.
- Ask a S to read the example advantage of voice mail.
- Ss work in pairs to fill in the diagram with supporting information based on the model paragraph on page 78.
- Write a diagram or web on the board similar to the one in the Student's Book.
- Have Ss come to the board, one at a time, to fill in the diagram. Make corrections on the board as needed.

Practice

- Direct Ss' attention to Exercise **1D** and read the instructions aloud. Guide Ss to see that the information they use to fill in this diagram will be useful for planning their own paragraphs.
- Ss complete their diagrams individually. Tell them that they can add more spokes and ovals to their diagrams if they have additional ideas. Walk around and help as needed.

Application

- Focus Ss' attention on Exercise **2** and read the instructions aloud.
- Ss complete the task individually. Walk around and help as needed.

Learner persistence (individual work)

- If you have Ss who have difficulty writing, sit with them and help them as the other Ss are writing. Help Ss use their notes from the model paragraph in Exercise **1B** on page 78 and the diagrams in Exercises **1C** and **1D** on page 79 to help them write a paragraph.

Comprehension check

- Direct Ss' attention to Exercise **3A**.
- This exercise asks Ss to develop skills to review and edit their own writing.
- Ss check their own paragraphs against the writing checklist. Walk around and help as needed. If any Ss check *No* for one or more of the checklist items, ask them to revise and edit their paragraphs to include the missing information.

Evaluation

- Focus Ss' attention on Exercise **3B**. Read the instructions aloud. This exercise enables Ss to work together to peer-correct their writing. Reading aloud enables the writer to review his or her own writing. Reading to a partner allows the writer to understand the need to write clearly for an audience.
- Ss complete the exercise in pairs. Tell Ss to take turns reading their paragraphs to each other. Walk around and help as needed.
- Listen to Ss as they ask their partner one question about the paragraph and tell their partner one thing they learned from it.
- Ask several Ss to read their paragraphs aloud. Have other Ss ask questions and mention one thing they learned from the paragraph.
- Direct Ss' attention to the lesson focus on the board.
- Check off the lesson focus as Ss demonstrate an understanding of what they have learned in the lesson.

Expansion activity (small groups)

- **Materials needed** Several magazine pictures or online illustrations from advertisements for time-saving devices discussed in this unit (calculators, answering machines, cell phones, cars, washing machines, etc.).
- Tell Ss to imagine that they are having a garage sale and that they are trying to sell the devices in the pictures you give them. Remind Ss that Americans hold garage or yard sales to sell household items that they no longer use.
- Ss in small groups. Ss take turns being sellers and buyers. The sellers should present the advantages of the device, and the buyers can point out the disadvantages (especially if they want a lower price!).
- Distribute several pictures to each group. Tell Ss that there should be one seller, but there can be more than one buyer. Encourage Ss to use *although, even though,* and *because* in their conversations.
- Encourage several Ss to have fun role-playing their conversations for the class.

> ### *More Ventures* (whole group, pairs, individual)
> Assign appropriate exercises from the *Teacher's Toolkit Audio CD / CD-ROM, Add Ventures,* or the *Workbook*.

C **Work** with a partner. Complete the diagram of the model paragraph.

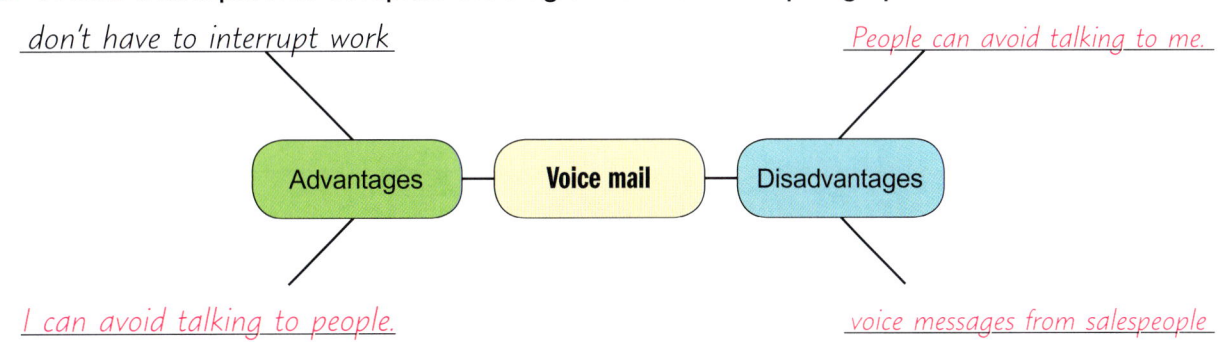

don't have to interrupt work

People can avoid talking to me.

Advantages — **Voice mail** — Disadvantages

I can avoid talking to people.

voice messages from salespeople

D **Plan** a paragraph that discusses the advantages and disadvantages of a time-saving device or activity. Use the diagram to make notes on your ideas.

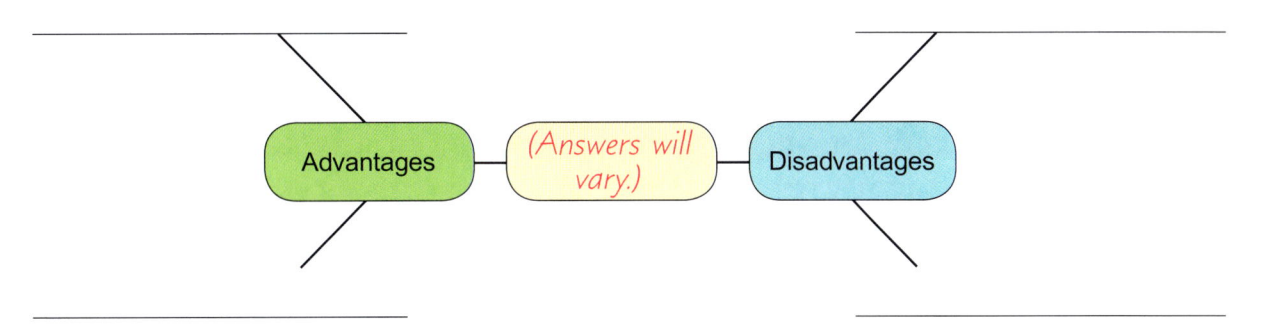

Advantages — *(Answers will vary.)* — Disadvantages

2 Write

Write a paragraph about the advantages and disadvantages of a time-saving device or activity. Use the paragraph in Exercise 1B and the diagrams in Exercises 1C and 1D to help you.

3 After you write

A **Check** your writing.

	Yes	No
1. My topic sentence names the time-saving device or activity.	☐	☐
2. I described at least two advantages and two disadvantages.	☐	☐
3. I used *because*, *even though*, and *although* when it was appropriate.	☐	☐

B **Share** your writing with a partner.

1. Take turns. Read your paragraph to a partner.
2. Comment on your partner's paragraph. Ask your partner a question about the paragraph. Tell your partner one thing you learned.

Another view

1 Life-skills reading

DAILY INTERNET ACTIVITIES OF GREEN COUNTY RESIDENTS

What activities do you do on the Internet on an average day?	Percent of Individuals		
	2005	2006	2007
Chat or online discussion	18	22	24
Electronic banking	14	23	30
Download music	24	18	16
Get information	30	32	35
Play games	24	26	28
Shopping	21	29	37
Send and receive e-mail	51	58	72
Watch videos on a video-sharing site	9	11	15

A Read the questions. Look at the table. Circle the answers.

1. In 2005, the most popular use of the Internet was _____ .
   a to get information
   b. to do electronic banking
   c. to send and receive e-mail
   d. none of the above

2. In 2005, fewer than 20 percent of the people in the survey used the Internet _____ .
   a. to do electronic banking
   b. to watch videos
   c. to chat
   d. all of the above

3. In 2007, getting information was less popular than _____ .
   a. shopping
   b. sending e-mail
   c. both a and b
   d. neither a nor b

4. From 2005 to 2007, there was a decline in the percentage of people who used the Internet _____ .
   a. to watch videos
   b. to download music
   c. to chat
   d. all of the above

5. From 2005 to 2007, the greatest increase was in _____ .
   a. sending and receiving e-mail
   b. chatting
   c. playing games
   d. none of the above

6. In 2006, playing games was more popular than _____ .
   a. downloading music
   b. watching videos
   c. shopping
   d. both a and b

B Talk with your classmates. Which activities in the table do you think will become more popular or less popular in the future? Why?

Lesson objectives

- Practice reading and understanding a table about daily Internet activities
- Review vocabulary and grammar from the unit
- Introduce the project
- Complete the self-assessment

Warm-up and review

- Before class. Write today's lesson focus on the board.
  Lesson F:
  Read and understand a table that shows people's daily Internet activities
  Review topic vocabulary and grammar from Unit 6
  Complete the project and the self-assessment
- Begin class. Books closed. Write on the board: *daily Internet activities.*
- Ask Ss: *What are examples of Internet activities?* Elicit: *chatting, banking, shopping, blogging,* etc. Write the examples on the board.
- Say: *The table that you're going to read shows the Internet activities of people living in Green County, from 2005 to 2007. What changes do you think might have taken place from 2005 to 2007 in Internet usage?* Elicit: *An increase in Internet usage, more chatting, more shopping online, more downloading of music,* etc.

Presentation

- Books open. Ask a S to read aloud the question in the table: *What activities do you do on the Internet on an average day?*
- Call on eight Ss to read the listed activities. Explain vocabulary as needed.
- Make sure that Ss understand what the heading *Percent of Individuals* refers to. For example, say: *In 2005, 18 percent of Green County residents chatted online or participated in an online discussion group.*

Practice

- Read the instructions aloud for Exercise **1A**. This task helps prepare Ss for standardized-type tests they may have to take. Make sure that Ss understand the task. Have Ss individually scan for and circle the answers.

Comprehension check

- Check answers with the class. Be sure that Ss have followed the instructions and circled their answers.

- Have Ss read aloud the questions and answers they circled. Ask: *Is that answer correct?* Correct Ss' answers as needed.

Application

- Direct Ss' attention to Exercise **1B** and read the instructions aloud.
- Ss in small groups. Ss discuss which activities will become more popular or less popular in the future. Walk around and help as needed.
- Open up the discussion to the entire class.

Expansion activity *(student pairs)*

- Ask Ss: *Do you know someone who doesn't like the Internet or who has never tried to use it? How could you convince him or her to use the Internet?* Elicit: *By telling him or her about the advantages of using the Internet.*
- Ss in pairs. Ss fold a piece of paper in half. On one side they write a list of advantages of using the Internet, and on the other side they write a list of disadvantages.
- Invite Ss to perform a role play between a person who doesn't like to use the Internet and a person who likes it and is trying to convince the first person to change his or her opinion. Ss should support their statements with information from the unit as well as from their own experience.
- Have several pairs perform their conversation for the class.
- Invite Ss to discuss the advantages and disadvantages of the Internet as a class.

Lesson F Another view

Presentation

- Books closed. Write on the board: *Class Internet Survey*. Read the phrase aloud and have Ss repeat.
- Ask Ss what they think the top-ten uses for the Internet would be among their classmates. Write their guesses on the board.

Practice

- Books open. Direct Ss' attention to Exercise **2A** and read the instructions aloud.
- Call on individual Ss to read the ten categories. Explain vocabulary as needed.
- Ask Ss if they can think of another use (the last category), and write that use on the board as an example (e.g., *checking the weather*).
- Ss complete the activity individually but compare information with their partner. Walk around and help as needed.
- Direct Ss' attention to the second part of the instructions for Exercise **2A**. Ask Ss to raise their hands if they marked *1* as you call out each activity. Tally the results on the board. Compare the results to the class's original prediction.

Application

- Direct Ss' attention to the pictures in Exercise **2B**. Make sure that Ss can identify all the time-saving devices.
- Read the instructions aloud.
- Model the task. Have a conversation with two Ss using the questions and the pictures. For example:

    T: *Which time-saving device do you think changed the world the most? Why?*
    S1: *I think the telephone changed the world the most. People could only meet in person or send letters before the telephone was invented.*
    T: *What are some of the disadvantages of telephones?*
    S2: *People don't always take the time to meet in person. Phone bills can be expensive.*

- Ss work in groups of three to complete the exercise. Walk around and help as needed.
- Focus Ss' attention on the second part of the instructions for Exercise **2B**. Ask groups to share information they learned.

Expansion activity *(small groups)*

- Tell Ss that this next activity will help them realize how technology affects their lives. Ask Ss to identify the time-saving devices they use at home.
- Have Ss sit in small groups to discuss what their lives would be like without these machines or devices. Encourage Ss to share details about what they would do instead of using a particular time-saving device.
- Call on Ss to share information from their group discussion.

> **More Ventures** *(whole group, pairs, individual)*
> Assign appropriate exercises from the *Teacher's Toolkit Audio CD / CD-ROM, Add Ventures*, or the *Workbook*.

Application

Community building

- **Project** Ask Ss to turn to page 138 in their Student's Book to complete the project for Unit 6.

Evaluation

- Before asking Ss to turn to the self-assessment on page 143, do a quick review of the unit. Have Ss turn to Lesson A. Ask the class to talk about what they remember about this lesson. Prompt Ss, if necessary, with questions, for example: *What are the conversations about on this page? What vocabulary is in the pictures?* Continue in this manner to review each lesson quickly.
- **Self-assessment** Read the instructions for Exercise **3**. Ask Ss to turn to the self-assessment page to complete the unit self-assessment. The self-assessments are also on the *Teacher's Toolkit Audio CD / CD-ROM*. If you prefer to collect the assessments and save them as part of each S's portfolio assessment, print out the unit self-assessment from the Toolkit, ask Ss to complete it, and collect and save it.
- If Ss are ready, administer the unit test on pages T-187–T-189 of this *Teacher's Edition* (or on the *Teacher's Toolkit Audio CD / CD-ROM*). The audio and audio script for the tests are on the *Teacher's Toolkit Audio CD / CD-ROM*.

2 Fun with language

A Write the numbers 1 to 10 to show how you use the Internet. Write *1* next to the activity you do the most and *10* for the activity you do the least. Then talk with a partner. Compare your information.

What activities do you do on the Internet?			
Participate in an online discussion		Shop	
Electronic banking		Read the news	
Download music		Send and receive e-mail	
Get information		Watch videos on a video-sharing site	
Play games		Other use:	

Survey your class about the activities. What is the most common use for the Internet in your class?

B Work in a small group. Discuss. What are the advantages and disadvantages of the time-saving devices below? Which ones changed the world the most in your opinion? Why do you think so?

Share your ideas with your classmates.

3 Wrap up

Complete the **Self-assessment** on page 143.

Review

1 Listening

Listen. Take notes on a radio interview.

Characteristics of tutors	Requirements to be a tutor
1. compassionate – care about helping	4. 12 hours of training
2. generous with their time	5. meet for at least 1½ hours per week
3. patient	6. minimum commitment of 6 months

Talk with a partner. Check your answers.

2 Grammar

A Write. Complete the story.

A Love of Technology

My friend Bob loves technology. _____As soon as_____ a new computer
1. As soon as / Until

comes out, he buys it. The same is true with his cell phone. He doesn't wait

_____until_____ the end of the contract. _____Even though_____ his cell phone is
2. as soon as / until   3. Because / Even though

still good, he buys a new one. _____Because_____ he loves the latest technology,
4. Because / Even though

his house is filled with new devices. _____Although_____ he has the newest devices,
5. Although / Until

he keeps the old ones. His wife is unhappy. She has told him, "No more electronic

gadgets _____until_____ you get rid of the old ones."
6. as soon as / until

B Write. Look at the words that are underlined in the answers. Write the questions.

1. **A** _Who loves technology?_____

   B <u>Bob</u> loves technology.

2. **A** _How often / When does he buy a new cell phone?_____

   B He buys a new cell phone <u>as soon as a new one comes out</u>.

3. **A** _What is his house filled with?_____

   B His house is filled with <u>new devices</u>.

4. **A** _Why is Bob's wife unhappy?_____

   B <u>Because of all the electronic gadgets</u>, Bob's wife is unhappy.

Talk with a partner. Ask and answer the questions.

Lesson objectives
- Review vocabulary and grammar from Units 5 and 6
- Practice the pronunciation of stressed and unstressed words

Warm-up and review

- Before class. Write today's lesson focus on the board.
  Review unit:
  Review vocabulary and grammar from Units 5 and 6
  Practice pronouncing stressed and unstressed words

- Begin class. Books closed. Ask Ss questions to review vocabulary and grammar from Units 5 and 6, for example: *What do you do as soon as you get home? What do you do until dinner is ready?*

- Review repeated actions in the present and past. Ask Ss questions about their activities using *How often . . . ?* or *How many times . . . ?*

- Review *although* and *even though*. Encourage Ss to talk about time-saving devices or tools that they own but don't use, using *although* and *even though*.

- Review the difference between *although* and *because*. Write these two sentences on the board, and ask Ss to fill in each blank with *Although* or *Because*.
  _____ it was a beautiful day, we stayed inside and watched TV. _____ we stayed inside, we didn't get to enjoy the sunny weather.

Presentation

- Books open. Direct Ss' attention to Exercise **1** and read the instructions aloud. Tell Ss that they will hear a radio interview between an interviewer and Rebecca Ford, a woman who works with volunteer literacy tutors.

- [Class Audio CD2 track 18] Model the task. Play or read only the first part of the conversation on the audio program (see audio script, page T-162). Pause after Rebecca says: *But in one way, they're all the same: they're very compassionate. They really care about helping other people.*

- Direct Ss' attention to the first heading in the chart (*Characteristics of tutors*). Tell Ss that *characteristics* is another word for *personal qualities*. Ask Ss: *How does Rebecca describe the tutors?* (She says that they're compassionate, which means that they care about helping other people.)

- Ask a S to read aloud the second chart heading (*Requirements to be a tutor*). Say: *Now listen and complete the information in the chart.*

- [Class Audio CD2 track 18] Play or read the complete audio program (see audio script, page T-162). Ss listen and complete the chart individually. Repeat the audio program as needed.

Comprehension check

- Read aloud the second part of the instructions for Exercise **1**.

- Ss check their answers with their partner. Walk around and help as needed.

Practice

- Direct Ss' attention to Exercise **2A**. Ask Ss: *What is the title of this story?* ("A Love of Technology")

- Read the instructions aloud for Exercise **2A**. Point out that Ss should select one of the choices below each blank to complete each sentence. Ask a S to read aloud the first two sentences in the story, including the example. Tell Ss to continue reading the story and filling in the blanks to complete the story.

- Ss complete the exercise individually. Walk around and help as needed.

- Write the numbers *1–6* on the board. Have six Ss come to the board to write only the answers.

- Invite other Ss to read the story aloud, filling in the blanks with the answers on the board. Make corrections as needed.

▼ **Teaching tip**
Encourage the Ss who are comfortable with these grammar points to help those who are less comfortable. Have Ss turn to the appropriate lessons in the book to work together to review the grammar presentation and exercises.

Comprehension check

- Direct Ss' attention to Exercise **2B**. This exercise reviews question formation related to the reading, "A Love of Technology."

- Read the instructions aloud. Model the task. Direct Ss to speaker B's answer in number 1. Say: *What question can you ask to get this answer?* Tell Ss that the underlined word is their clue for the *Wh-* question word they need to use. Ask Ss to think about the question word they would use for a person (Who).

- Ss complete the exercise individually. Walk around and help as needed.

- Check answers with the class. Ask for volunteers to read their questions. Write the questions on the board. Work with the class to make corrections on the board as needed.

- Read aloud the second part of the instructions for Exercise **2B**.

- Ss work in pairs to ask and answer the questions. Walk around and help as needed.

Review

Presentation

- Books closed. Write on the board: *stressed and unstressed words*. Then write this sentence on the board: *Bob buys a new cell phone as soon as a new one comes out.* Ask Ss if they can tell which words are stressed (have more emphasis) and which are unstressed (have less emphasis). Tell Ss that you are going to say the sentence aloud, and you want them to pay attention to the stresses.
- Write on the board:
  content words = stressed   function words= unstressed
- Say this sentence, stressing the underlined words: *Bob buys a new cell phone as soon as a new one comes out.*

> ▼ **Teaching tip**
> Some Ss may find it difficult to differentiate between stressed and unstressed words when working on pronunciation. If possible, take extra time with these Ss to review the sounds. Exaggerate the stress in stressed words so that Ss can clearly hear the difference between words that are stressed and unstressed.

- Books open. Direct Ss' attention to the top of page 83. Call on a S to read the information about content and function words.
- Read the instructions aloud for Exercise **3A**.
- 💿 [Class Audio CD2 track 19] Play or read the complete audio program (see audio script, page T-162).
- Have a S read aloud the second part of the instructions for Exercise **3A**.
- 💿 [Class Audio CD2 track 20] Repeat the audio program. Pause after each phrase to give Ss time to repeat. Play the audio program as many times as needed. Focus Ss' attention on the pronunciation of the underlined words in Exercise **3A**.

Practice

- Direct Ss' attention to Exercise **3B**. Read the instructions aloud.
- 💿 [Class Audio CD2 track 21] Model the task. Play or read the first sentence on the audio program (see audio script, page T-162). Ask Ss to tell you which words are stressed, and have them underline those content words in the sentence.
- Tell Ss to pay attention to the stressed words in each sentence as they listen and repeat. Play or read the audio program, stopping as needed for Ss to repeat the sentences.
- Play or read the complete audio program again. Ss identify the stressed words by underlining them. Repeat the audio program as needed.

- Read aloud the second part of the instructions for Exercise **3B**.
- Ss complete the exercise in pairs. Walk around and listen to Ss' pronunciation. Help Ss pronounce the stressed words correctly.

Comprehension check

- Direct Ss' attention to Exercise **3C** and read the instructions aloud.
- Ss complete the exercise individually. Walk around and help as needed.
- Read aloud the second part of the instructions for Exercise **3C**.
- Ss work in pairs to compare their answers. Ss take turns reading the paragraph to each other.
- Call on individual Ss to read the paragraph aloud. Ask Ss which words are stressed in the paragraph.

Application

- Focus Ss' attention on Exercise **3D** and read the instructions aloud.
- Have Ss write four sentences from Units 5 and 6 to complete the exercise.
- Ss work individually to write the sentences but then exchange papers to underline the stressed words in their partner's sentences.

Evaluation

- Direct Ss' attention to the lesson focus on the board.
- Write these two sentences on the board, and ask Ss to fill in the blanks with *until* or *as soon as*.
  He'll feel better _____ he takes his medicine.
  The volunteer will stay with him _____ his family comes to visit.
- Write these three questions on the board: *How often did Maria volunteer at the homeless shelter? How often has Maria volunteered at the homeless shelter? When did Maria volunteer at the homeless shelter?* Then refer Ss to the grammar chart on page 62. Ask Ss to make up answers to the questions using both the number of times and an appropriate time expression.
- Write the words *advantage* and *disadvantage* on the board. Ask Ss to describe one advantage and one disadvantage of a time-saving device. Have Ss use *even though, although,* or *because*.
- Check off each part of the lesson focus as Ss demonstrate an understanding of what they have learned in the lesson.

3 Pronunciation: stressed and unstressed words

Content words (nouns, main verbs, adverbs, adjectives, negatives, and question words) are usually stressed. Function words (pronouns, prepositions, conjunctions, articles, *to be* verbs, and auxiliary verbs) are usually not stressed.

A **Listen** to the stressed and unstressed words in each sentence. The stressed words are underlined.

1. <u>Pam</u> <u>loves</u> <u>electrical</u> <u>appliances</u> because they <u>save</u> her <u>time</u>.
2. She <u>wants</u> to <u>volunteer</u> in the <u>health-care</u> <u>field</u>.
3. Even though <u>computers</u> are <u>time-savers</u>, <u>some</u> <u>people</u> <u>don't</u> <u>use</u> them.
4. Will he <u>go</u> to <u>sleep</u> as soon as his <u>visitors</u> <u>leave</u>?

Listen again and repeat. Stress the underlined content words.

B **Listen and repeat.** Then underline the stressed content words.

1. She <u>delivers</u> <u>meals</u> to <u>seniors</u>.
2. <u>Volunteers</u> should be <u>patient</u> and <u>compassionate</u>.
3. Do you <u>walk</u> to <u>work</u> or <u>drive</u>?
4. <u>Mr. Chung</u> isn't a <u>fan</u> of <u>e-mail</u>.

Read your sentences to a partner. Compare your answers.

C **Read** the paragraph. Underline the stressed words.

   <u>Ingrid</u> <u>worked</u> with <u>computers</u> in her <u>native</u> <u>country</u>, so that's the <u>job</u> she <u>wants</u> here. She's been <u>looking</u> for <u>several</u> <u>months</u>, but she hasn't <u>found</u> one yet. <u>Finally</u>, she <u>decided</u> to do some <u>volunteer</u> <u>work</u> until she could find a <u>paying</u> <u>job</u>. <u>Ingrid</u> <u>volunteers</u> at the <u>local</u> <u>zoo</u>. She does <u>office</u> <u>work</u> on the <u>computer</u>.

Talk with a partner. Compare your answers. Read the paragraph to your partner.

D **Write** four sentences from Units 5 and 6. Then work with a partner. Underline the stressed words in your partner's sentences.

1. *(Answers will vary.)* _____
2. _____
3. _____
4. _____

Lesson A Get ready

1 Talk about the pictures

A What do you see?
B What is happening?

Shopping

Rosa

Lesson objectives

- Introduce students to the topic
- Find out what students know about the topic
- Preview the unit by talking about the pictures
- Practice key vocabulary
- Practice listening skills

Warm-up and review

- Before class. Write today's lesson focus on the board.

  Lesson A:

  Ask about returning merchandise

  Ask about store policies

  Talk about shopping mistakes

  Identify store personnel

  Describe people, places, and things

- Begin class. Books closed. Direct Ss' attention to the lesson focus. Point to *Ask about returning merchandise.* Ask Ss: *What is merchandise?* List Ss' responses on the board, for example: *clothes, shoes, electronic devices.*

- Point to *Ask about store policies.* Ask Ss: *What are store policies?* List Ss' responses on the board, for example: *rules for store employees and customers.*

- Point to *Identify store personnel.* Ask Ss: *What does "store personnel" mean?* List Ss' responses on the board, for example: *staff, people who work in the store, salesclerks, managers.*

Presentation

- Books open. Set the scene. Direct Ss' attention to the main picture on page 84. Ask the question from Exercise **1A:** *What do you see?* Elicit and write on the board as much vocabulary about the picture as possible: *cameras, customers, clerks, customer service desk, checkout counters, aisles,* etc. Explain any unfamiliar words. Elicit words to describe the second picture on page 84, such as: *customer service desk* and *returns.* Ask Ss what type of store is featured in the pictures.

- Direct Ss' attention to the question in **1B**: *What is happening?* Read it aloud. Hold up the Student's Book. Point to the first picture. Ask: *What's Rosa doing here?* (She's talking to a salesclerk to try to find out where she should go to return her camera.)

- Point to Rosa in the second picture. Ask: *What's Rosa doing here?* (She's trying to return her camera.)

- Brainstorm and list on the board possible reasons why Rosa wants to return the camera.

▶ **Teaching tip**

Encourage Ss to be creative. At this point, there is no single correct answer.

▶ **Culture tip**

Tell Ss that in the United States, they can return or exchange items that don't work. Usually, the store will require a receipt in order to take back the item, but different stores have different policies. Ask Ss what they would do if they were in Rosa's situation. Elicit responses, such as: *go to the customer service department of the store; call the store; bring the item, receipt, and packaging to the store.*

Practice

- Ss in pairs. Ask Ss to write a role play between Rosa and the first clerk she meets or between Rosa and the clerk at the customer service desk. In either role play, Rosa should give details about the problem she is having, and the clerk should offer advice.

- Walk around and listen to Ss as they role-play the situation.

- Ask several pairs to perform their role play for the class.

▶ **Teaching tip**

Encourage Ss to avoid reading their lines when they act out their role play. Suggest that Ss first read the line to themselves, then look up and say the line. This strategy helps foster fluency and confidence in speaking English.

Presentation

- Books open. Direct Ss' attention to Exercise **2A**. Read the instructions and questions aloud. Explain that after listening to the conversation, Ss in pairs will ask and answer the two questions in the exercise. Tell Ss to listen for the answers to these two questions as the audio program is played or read.
- 🔘 [Class Audio CD2 track 22] Play or read the audio program (see audio script, page T-162).
- Ask Ss if they have understood everything in the listening exercise. Write any unfamiliar words on the board and help Ss understand the meaning of each new word. Be sure that Ss understand *defective*.
- Elicit answers to the questions. For example: *The speakers are Rosa and different store personnel. In Part 1, Rosa asks a clerk who she should speak to about getting a refund. In Part 2, Rosa asks for a refund. The clerk in customer service tells her about the store refund and exchange policy. In the end, the clerk offers her a store credit.*
- Focus Ss' attention on Exercise **2B** and read the instructions aloud. Tell Ss to listen to the audio program and complete the chart based on the information they hear.
- 🔘 [Class Audio CD2 track 23] Tell Ss to listen for details about Rosa's conversation with the clerk in customer service. Model the task. Play or read the audio program again. Pause the program after Rosa says in Part 1: *It's a camera, a digital camera.* Ask a S to read the example answer written next to *kind of camera Rosa bought* (*a digital camera*). Play or read the rest of the audio program. Ss listen and complete the chart. Draw the chart on the board.
- Read aloud the second part of the instructions for Exercise **2B**.
- 🔘 [Class Audio CD2 track 23] Play or read the audio program again (see audio script, page T-162). Ss listen and check their answers.
- Write the numbers *1–6* on the board. Ask Ss to come to the board to write their answers in the chart. Make corrections on the board as needed.

Practice

- Direct Ss' attention to Exercise **2C** and read the instructions aloud. Tell Ss that the story is a summary of what happened in the pictures on the previous page.
- Focus Ss' attention on the words in the word bank. Say each word and have Ss repeat. Correct pronunciation as needed. Explain any words that are new to Ss.

- Model the task. Ask a S to read aloud the first sentence in the story, including the example answer.
- Ss complete the exercise individually. Walk around and help as needed.

Comprehension check

- 🔘 [Class Audio CD2 track 24] Play or read the audio program (see audio script, page T-163). Ss listen and check their answers. Repeat the audio program as needed.
- Write the numbers *1–8* on the board. Ask Ss to come to the board to write only the answers.

Learner persistence (individual work)

- 🔘 [Self-Study Audio CD tracks 22 and 23] Exercises **2A**, **2B**, and **2C** are recorded on the Ss' self-study CD at the back of the Student's Book. Ss can listen to the CD at home for reinforcement and review. They can also listen to the CD for self-directed learning when class attendance is not possible.

Application

- Focus Ss' attention on Exercise **2D** and read the instructions aloud.
- Ss complete the exercise in pairs. Help as needed.
- Ask several pairs to ask and answer the questions for the class. Discuss Ss' experiences with trying to return or exchange merchandise.

▼ **Teaching tip**

Ss with limited confidence in speaking English may be reluctant to return defective products or merchandise they don't really want. However, it is important to encourage them to do so. Remind Ss to always keep their receipts so that they can get a refund or an exchange. Emphasize that it is important for returns or exchanges to be done as soon as possible.

Evaluation

- Direct Ss' attention to the lesson focus on the board. Ask individual Ss to look at the pictures on page 84 to make sentences using the words from Exercise **2C**.
- Check off each part of the lesson focus as Ss demonstrate an understanding of what they have learned in the lesson.

More Ventures (whole group, pairs, individual)
Assign appropriate exercises from the *Teacher's Toolkit Audio CD / CD-ROM, Add Ventures,* or the *Workbook.*

2 Listening

 **A** **Listen** and answer the questions.

1. Who are the speakers?
2. What are they talking about?

 **B** **Listen again.** Complete the chart.

1. kind of camera Rosa bought	*a digital camera*
2. problem	*screen is too small*
3. date purchased	*the 5th*
4. today's date	*the 20th*
5. store policy for refunds	*return within 10 days for a refund*
6. store policy for exchanges	*30 days if the merchandise is in perfect condition*

Listen again. Check your answers.

 **C** **Read.** Complete the story. Listen and check your answers.

| condition | defective | merchandise | store credit |
| customer service | exchanges | refund | warranty |

Rosa wants to return the camera that she bought and get a ___*refund*___ .
1

She is told that she needs to speak with someone in ___*customer service*___ . The clerk
2

there asks Rosa if the camera is ___*defective*___ . Rosa says that it's not broken, but
3

she doesn't like the screen. The clerk tells her about the store policy for returns and

___*exchanges*___ . It's too late for Rosa to return the camera, but she can exchange
4

it if the ___*merchandise*___ is in perfect ___*condition*___ . Rosa still has the camera
5   6

box with the instruction book and the ___*warranty*___ card. Since Rosa is in a hurry,
7

she decides to get a ___*store credit*___ , and she will use it at a later time.
8

D **Discuss.** Talk with your classmates.

1. What are some reasons that people may want to return merchandise to a store?
2. What are some situations where it may be impossible to return merchandise?
3. Do you think it is right for people to get their money back for something that they have used? Why or why not?

1 Grammar focus: *who* and *that* as the subject of a dependent clause

Simple sentences	Sentences with an adjective clause
The camera costs only $99. It is on sale.	The camera that is on sale costs only $99.
The manager helped the customer. She lost her receipt.	The manager helped the customer who lost her receipt.

For a grammar explanation, turn to page 150.

2 Practice

A Write. Combine the sentences. Change the second sentence into an adjective clause with *that* or *who*.

> **Useful language**
> Adjective clauses that describe people may begin with *that* or *who*.

1. I want to buy a camera. It's not too expensive.
   I want to buy a camera that's not too expensive.

2. I'd like to get a good camera. It will last for many years.
   I'd like to get a good camera that will last for many years.

3. Many people shop online. They are looking for cameras.
   Many people who / that are looking for cameras shop online.

4. My friend told me about a camera store. It sells used merchandise.
   My friend told me about a camera store that sells used merchandise.

5. Customers like to shop at Super Camera. They appreciate good service.
   Customers who / that appreciate good service like to shop at Super Camera.

6. The clerk is very helpful. He works in customer service.
   The clerk who / that works in customer service is very helpful.

7. These days, most people want a digital camera. It holds a lot of pictures.
   These days, most people want a digital camera that holds a lot of pictures.

8. Digital cameras are sometimes difficult to use. They have small screens.
   Digital cameras that have small screens are sometimes difficult to use.

Listen and check your answers.

Warm-up and review

- Before class. Write today's lesson focus on the board.
  Lesson B:
  Practice using who and that as the subject of a dependent clause
- Begin class. Books closed. Point to the word *clause* in the lesson focus. Ask Ss what the word means. Elicit an appropriate answer, such as: *a group of words containing a subject and a verb.*
- Ask Ss if they know what a dependent clause is. Elicit appropriate responses, such as: *A dependent clause is not a complete sentence. It must be connected to an independent clause. It cannot stand alone.*
- Explain that there are different kinds of dependent clauses but that the focus of today's lesson is on adjective clauses.
- Write the word *adjective* on the board. Ask Ss to explain what an adjective is. Elicit appropriate responses, such as: *a word that describes, or modifies, a noun or a pronoun.*
- Ask Ss if they can guess what an adjective clause is. (a dependent clause that gives additional information about a noun.)

Presentation

- Books open. Direct Ss' attention to the grammar chart in Exercise **1**. Read each of the headings aloud.
- Direct Ss' attention to the statements under *Simple sentences*. Read each of the sentences aloud.
- Read aloud the statements under *Sentences with an adjective clause.*
- Ask: *What's the difference between the sentences on the left and the sentences on the right?* Elicit an appropriate response, for example: *In each of the sentences on the right, two of the simple sentences from the left are combined to make one sentence.*
- Explain to Ss that an adjective clause gives additional information about a noun and needs to follow the noun it is modifying. Call on a S to read the two example sentences and then the combined example sentence about the camera. Ask Ss: *What is the noun that is being described?* (the camera) Show Ss that when we combine sentences to create a new sentence with an adjective clause, we omit the subject of the second simple sentence (in this case, *it*) and use a relative pronoun (in this case, *that*).
- Point out that when we combine the other simple sentences about the manager and the customer, we omit *she* and use the relative pronoun *who* to form the new sentence with an adjective clause.

▼ **Teaching tip**
It might be helpful to refer Ss to the grammar explanation on page 150 in the Student's Book.

Useful language
Read the tip box aloud. Direct Ss' attention to the second sentence under *Sentences with an adjective clause*. Ask a S to read it aloud but to say *that* instead of *who*. Tell Ss that they can use *that* or *who* to describe people.

- Focus Ss' attention on Exercise **2A** and read the instructions aloud.
- Model the exercise. Ask a S to read the example answer to the class. Make sure that Ss understand the task of combining two sentences using an adjective clause.
- Ss complete the exercise individually. Walk around and help as needed. Tell Ss that the combined sentences for numbers 3, 5, 6, and 8 have a change in word order. The adjective clauses in these sentences must immediately follow the nouns that they are modifying.

Comprehension check

- 🔘 [Class Audio CD2 track 25] Play or read the audio program (see audio script, page T-163). Ss listen and check their answers.
- Write the numbers *1–8* on the board. Call on Ss to write the combined sentence for each item. Make corrections on the board as needed.

Expansion activity *(student pairs)*

- **Materials needed** Magazine pictures of people doing different activities.
- Ss in pairs. Bring in a group picture of several people, ideally doing different things. Distribute one copy to each pair of Ss.
- Ask Ss to tell you several simple sentences about the people in the photo, and write the sentences on the board. For example:
  The dark-haired woman is very athletic. She is riding a bicycle.
- Have pairs combine the sentences and change the second sentence into an adjective clause with *who* or *that*. Model the activity with one of the S's examples. (e.g., *The dark-haired woman who / that is riding a bicycle is very athletic.*)
- Walk around and help as needed. Ask Ss to write their examples on the board. Correct as needed.

Lesson B Adjective clauses

Presentation

- Direct Ss' attention to the picture on page 87. Ask Ss: *Where does this scene take place?* Elicit an appropriate response, such as: *in a large electronics store.* Ask Ss: *What kind of merchandise is sold here?* (cameras, stereos, TVs, DVD players, video equipment, appliances, computers, etc.)

Practice

- Read the instructions aloud for Exercise **2B**.
- Ask a S to read the verbs in the word bank. Ask two other Ss to read the example conversation to the class.
- Ss complete the exercise in pairs. Walk around and help as needed.
- Direct Ss' attention to the second part of Exercise **2B** and read the instructions aloud.
- Model the exercise. Call on a S to read the example sentence. Tell Ss that their sentences must include an adjective clause with *who* or *that*.
- Ss work individually to complete the exercise. Help as needed.
- Have individual Ss write their sentences on the board. Make corrections on the board as needed.

Application

- Direct Ss' attention to Exercise **3A** and read the instructions and topics aloud.
- Model the task. Ask three Ss to read the example dialog to the class.
- Ss work in small groups to complete the exercise. Tell Ss that for the topic *your idea,* they should choose a place that they go to frequently, or enjoy going to, such as a park, or the beach. Walk around and help as needed.
- Direct Ss' attention to Exercise **3B** and read the instructions aloud.
- Ask groups to share the information they discussed.

Expansion activity (small groups)

- Tell Ss that this activity is a guessing game in which they have to identify stores, movie theaters, restaurants, and other places in their neighborhood. You can also adapt this activity – especially if Ss are not familiar with the neighborhood surrounding the school – so that Ss identify movies, songs, music groups, or celebrities.
- Ss in groups. Model the activity. Say: *I like a store that sells Caribbean foods.* Ask a S to guess which store it is and then make a sentence with an adjective clause about a location that the next S has to identify. For example:

I like a restaurant that is very big and has a red sign above the door. If a S doesn't know the answer, the next person in the group tries to answer.
- Make sure that Ss are using adjective clauses correctly and that each S has several chances to ask and answer. Walk around and help as needed.
- Ask a S from each group to come to the board to write an example sentence. Make corrections on the board as needed.

Expansion activity (individual work)

- Ask Ss to draw a map of their neighborhood, marking the places where they usually go. For each place, Ss should write a sentence with an adjective clause.
- Model the task. Write the following example sentences on the board:
This is the market that sells the best fruit.
This is the movie theater that's always crowded.
- Ss share their maps with a partner. Call on Ss to share several of the sentences they wrote.

Evaluation

- Books closed. Direct Ss' attention to the lesson focus on the board.
- Write these two sets of simple sentences on the board:
My friend told me about a market. It sells many kinds of Asian foods.
The clerk is very nice. She works at the first register.
- Ask a S to read the first set of sentences and to combine them, changing the second sentence into an adjective clause. Elicit: *My friend told me about a market that sells many kinds of Asian foods.*
- Ask another S to read aloud the second set of sentences and to combine them. Elicit: *The clerk who / that works at the first register is very nice.*
- Check off the lesson focus as Ss demonstrate an understanding of what they have learned in the lesson.

> **More Ventures** (whole group, pairs, individual)
> Assign appropriate exercises from the *Teacher's Toolkit Audio CD / CD-ROM, Add Ventures,* or the *Workbook.*

B **Talk** with a partner. Ask and answer questions to identify the following people in the picture: the cashier, the cleaning person, the customer, the greeter, the stock clerk, and the store manager. Use adjective clauses with *who* or *that*. Choose verbs from the box.

clean	have	listen	smile	sweep
give	hold	put	stand	wear

A Which one is the cashier?
B He's the man who's putting the video camera into the bag.

A You mean the one who's smiling?
B Right.

Write sentences about the people in the picture.

The cashier is the man who's putting the video camera into the bag.

3 Communicate

A **Work** in a small group. Ask and answer questions about the topics. Use adjective clauses.

- supermarkets
- restaurants
- salesclerks
- clothing stores
- malls
- (your idea)

A Nadia, what kind of supermarkets do you like?
B I like supermarkets that are open 24 hours a day. What about you, Phuong?
C I like supermarkets that have lots of fresh fish.

B **Share** information about your classmates.

1 Grammar focus: *that* as the object of a dependent clause

Simple sentences	**Sentences with an adjective clause**
I like the car. You bought it.	I like the car (that) you bought.
The mechanic has 20 years of experience. I use him.	The mechanic (that) I use has 20 years of experience.

For a grammar explanation, turn to page 150.

2 Practice

A Write. Combine the sentences. Change the second sentence into an adjective clause with *that*.

> **Useful language**
> You can omit the word *that* when it is the object of the dependent clause.

1. Suzy is a good friend. I've known her for several years.
   Suzy is a good friend that I've known for several years.

2. Last January, her old car stopped working. She was driving it.
   Last January, her old car that she was driving stopped working.

3. The mechanic couldn't fix it. Her friend recommended the mechanic.
   The mechanic that her friend recommended couldn't fix it.

4. Finally, she decided to buy a used car from a man. She knew the man at work.
   Finally, she decided to buy a used car from a man that she knew at work.

5. He's an honest person. She trusts him completely.
   He's an honest person that she trusts completely.

6. He gave her a good price. She couldn't refuse it.
   He gave her a good price that she couldn't refuse.

7. The used car is only three years old. He sold her the car.
   The used car that he sold her is only three years old.

8. It's a reliable car. She can drive it for a long time.
   It's a reliable car that she can drive for a long time.

 **Listen** and check your answers.

Lesson objective

- Introduce and practice *that* as an object of a dependent clause

Warm-up and review

- Before class. Write today's lesson focus on the board.
  Lesson C:
  Use that as the object of a dependent clause
- Begin class. Books closed. Write the following simple sentences on the board:
  The salesclerk helped a woman. She had a problem with her digital camera.
  The MP3 player costs $125. It is on sale.
- Ask a S to combine the first two sentences and change the second sentence into an adjective clause. Elicit: *The salesclerk helped a woman who / that had a problem with her digital camera.*
- Ask another S to combine the second set of sentences and change the second sentence into an adjective clause: *The MP3 player that is on sale costs $125.*

Presentation

- Direct Ss' attention to the grammar chart in Exercise **1**. Read aloud the first set of statements under the heading *Simple sentences*. Then read the combined sentence under *Sentences with an adjective clause*. Continue with the second set of sentences in each of the two columns.
- Say: *Which part of each sentence is the adjective clause?* Elicit: *(that) you bought and (that) I use.*
- Ask Ss what the adjective clause does in each sentence. Elicit an appropriate response, such as: *It adds information about the noun it is modifying, or it makes the meaning of the noun clearer.*

Useful language

Read the tip box aloud. Refer Ss to the statements under *Sentences with an adjective clause,* and have a S read them aloud omitting *that.* Tell Ss that in these sentences *that* is optional. These sentences, in which *that* is the object of the dependent clause, are grammatically correct even when *that* is not used. Lead Ss to see, however, that subject pronouns (such as *that* and *who* from the previous lesson) cannot be omitted.

- Write the following sentences on the board:
  Rosa bought a camera. She returned the camera.
  Rosa returned the camera that she bought.
- Say the third sentence twice, once with *that,* and once without.

- Ask Ss to work independently to make up similar sentences using *that* as the object of the dependent clause.
- Call on Ss to share their examples, and write them on the board. Have Ss read their sentences with and without *that.*

▼ **Teaching tip**
Refer Ss to the grammar explanation on page 150 in the Student's Book.

Practice

- Direct Ss' attention to Exercise **2A** and read the instructions aloud.
- Ask a S to read aloud the first sentence containing the sample answer.
- Ss complete the exercise individually. Walk around and help as needed.

Comprehension check

- Read aloud the second part of the instructions for Exercise **2A**.
- [Class Audio CD2 track 26] Play or read the audio program (see audio script, page T-163). Ss listen and check their answers.
- Write the numbers *1–8* on the board. Ask eight Ss to come to the board to write their answers. Work with the class to make corrections on the board as needed.

Expansion activity *(student pairs)*

- Invite partners to talk to each other about the places where they grew up. They should try to use as many adjective clauses as possible to describe their hometown. Have partners listen and ask questions.
- After pairs have finished their discussion, ask each S to write at least one sentence using an adjective clause about his or her partner's hometown.
- Model the activity. For example, write the following on the board:
  There's a park that everyone likes.
- Have Ss come to the board to write their sentences. Work with the class to make corrections on the board as needed.

Lesson C *Adjective clauses*

Presentation

- Direct Ss' attention to the picture in Exercise **2B**. Have Ss look carefully at the picture and describe what is happening. Elicit an appropriate response, such as: *The young couple is opening gifts, but there is a problem.*

Practice

- Read the instructions aloud. Call on three Ss in turn to read each of the columns in the chart (the item, where Ted and Lisa got it, and the problem).
- Explain vocabulary as needed and write any new words on the board. Ask a S to read the example sentence.
- Ss complete the exercise in pairs. Walk around and help as needed.
- Read the instructions aloud for the second part of Exercise **2B**. Ask a S to read the example sentence to the class.
- Ss complete the exercise individually. Walk around and help as needed.
- Ask several Ss to write their sentences on the board. Call on other Ss to read each of the sentences. For each sentence ask Ss: *Is this sentence correct?* Make corrections on the board as needed.

Application

- Direct Ss' attention to Exercise **3A** and read the instructions aloud. Ask a S to read the five questions.

> **Useful language**
> Read the tip box aloud. Explain any new adjectives as needed. Ask Ss if they know of any similar words or expressions (*ripped, wrong size, irregular*, etc.), and write them on the board.

- Model the task. Ask two Ss to read the example dialog.
- Ss complete the exercise in small groups. Walk around and help as needed.
- Direct Ss' attention to Exercise **3B** and read the instructions aloud.

- Ask a S from each group to tell what he or she learned about a classmate's shopping mistake. Ask the S to make a sentence about the information the S's partner shared, for example: *The book that (Marta) ordered online was damaged. It was raining really hard, and the box got wet. She called the company. They told her that they would send her another book as soon as she sent back the first one.*
- Continue the exercise by asking different Ss to share information they learned from their classmates. Encourage Ss to use adjective clauses.

Expansion activity *(individual work)*

- Have Ss use the situation they discussed in Exercise **3A** as the basis of a paragraph. Collect these paragraphs, or have Ss exchange papers with their partner and use this as an opportunity for peer-correction.
- You may wish to place these paragraphs in a class book called *Shopping Mistakes.*
- Any artists in the class may illustrate the book with amusing cartoons or illustrations.

Evaluation

- Direct Ss' attention to the lesson focus on the board. Ask Ss to look at the picture on page 89 and make sentences about Ted and Lisa's wedding presents using adjective clauses (e.g., *The rug that Lisa's aunt ordered from a catalog was the wrong color*). Ss should say their sentences aloud. Make corrections as needed.
- Check off the lesson focus as Ss demonstrate an understanding of what they have learned in the lesson.

> **More Ventures** *(whole group, pairs, individual)*
> Assign appropriate exercises from the *Teacher's Toolkit Audio CD / CD-ROM, Add Ventures,* or the *Workbook.*

B **Talk** with a partner. Ted and Lisa got married recently. Unfortunately, they have had some bad luck. Look at the chart and make sentences by choosing an item from each column.

The dishes that Ted and Lisa received from Aunt May were broken.

computer	found on the Internet	the wrong size
dishes	bought on sale	scratched
car	ordered from a catalog	broken
camera	got as a wedding present	damaged
rug	received from Aunt May	torn
lamps	picked up at a garage sale	the wrong color
coffee table	purchased from a friend	too slow

Write sentences about Ted and Lisa.

The dishes that they received from Aunt May were broken.

3 Communicate

A **Work** in a small group. Tell about a shopping "mistake." Include the information below.

- What was the item?
- When did you buy it?
- Where did you buy it?
- What was wrong with it?
- What did you do about it?

> **A** The chicken that I bought last week at Paglia's Meats was spoiled.
> **B** What did you do about it?
> **A** I took it back to the store and asked them to give me a fresh package.

B **Share** information about your classmates.

1 Before you read

Talk with your classmates. Answer the questions.

1. Have you ever tried to exchange an item or get a refund? Tell about your experience.
2. In your native country, is it easy or difficult for people to get a refund for something that they purchased?

2 Read

SELF-STUDY
AUDIO CD

Read the newspaper advice column. Listen and read again.

The Smart Shopper

Dear Smart Shopper,

I'm a jewelry lover, and I enjoy shopping online. Unfortunately, I just bought a pair of gold earrings that I don't like. When I tried to return them, I learned that the seller has a no-return policy. Don't I have the right to get a refund?

Mad Madelyn

Dear Mad Madelyn,

If the merchandise is defective, the seller must return your money or make an exchange. However, if the merchandise was in good condition when you received it, and if the retailer has a no-return policy, there is nothing you can do. This is true for store purchases as well as Internet purchases. In the future, here are some questions you should ask before you buy anything:

- Does the seller say "satisfaction guaranteed or your money back"?
- Is there a time limit on returns, such as two weeks?
- Who pays the shipping costs on items that are returned?
- Do you need to return the merchandise in its original package?
- Is the original receipt required?
- Does the retailer give a store credit instead of a cash refund?
- If the retailer has a store in your area, can you return the merchandise to the store instead of shipping it?

Next time, find the return policy on the merchant's Web site and print it, or ask the merchant for the return policy in writing. It's important to get all the facts that you need before you buy!

Smart Shopper

Sometimes an important word is replaced by a synonym. This makes the reading more interesting. For example, *seller* and *retailer* are two nouns that have the same meaning.

Lesson objectives

- Introduce and read "The Smart Shopper"
- Practice using new topic-related vocabulary
- Identify and use compound nouns

Warm-up and review

- Before class. Write today's lesson focus on the board.
  Lesson D:
  Read and understand "The Smart Shopper"
  Practice new vocabulary related to buying and
  returning merchandise
  Identify and use compound nouns

- Begin class. Books closed. Direct Ss' attention to the words *Smart Shopper* in the lesson focus. Write them on the board. Ask Ss: *What do you think a smart shopper is?* Elicit appropriate responses, such as: *Someone who knows where to buy things at a good price, someone who uses coupons and finds sales.*

- Tell Ss that they are going to read a newspaper advice column about shopping. Ask Ss if they are familiar with magazines or newspaper columns that offer shopping advice or tips. If possible, show Ss a few examples. (There are many examples online.)

- Point to *"The Smart Shopper"* on the board and ask Ss to predict what this newspaper advice column is about. Elicit responses, such as: *It's about how to make good shopping decisions.* Write some of the Ss' predictions on the board.

Presentation

- Books open. Direct Ss' attention to Exercise **1** and read the instructions aloud.

- Focus Ss' attention on the questions in Exercise **1** and ask two Ss to read them aloud.

- Ss in small groups discuss their answers to the questions. Walk around and help as needed.

- Call on individual Ss to share their answers with the class.

Practice

- Read the instructions aloud for Exercise **2**. Ask Ss to read the advice column silently before listening to the audio program.

- [Class Audio CD2 track 27] Play or read the audio program and ask Ss to read along (see audio script, page T-163). Repeat the audio program as needed.

- While Ss are listening and reading the advice column, ask them to underline any words or expressions they don't know. When the audio program is finished, write the new words on the board.

- Point to each word. Say it and have Ss repeat. Give a brief explanation of each word, or ask Ss who know the word to explain it. If Ss prefer to look up the new words in their dictionaries, allow them to do so.

Call on a S to read the tip aloud. Have Ss recall the definition of a synonym – a word that has the same meaning as that of another word. Explain that writers use synonyms to make an article or another piece of writing more lively and interesting. Also, remind Ss that when they read, they can use synonyms as context clues to figure out the meaning of unfamiliar words. Ask Ss if they know of synonyms for words used in this unit (e.g., *product = merchandise, purchase = buy, ripped = torn*). Write some of the synonyms on the board. Read each one aloud and have Ss repeat.

Learner persistence *(individual work)*

- [Self-Study Audio CD track 24] Exercise **2** is recorded on the Ss' self-study CD at the back of the Student's Book. Ss can listen to the CD at home for reinforcement and review. They can also listen to the CD for self-directed learning when class attendance is not possible.

Expansion activity *(small groups)*

- **Materials needed** Poster board and markers.

- Have Ss work in small groups to present a list of "Smart Shopping Tips" in the form of a poster.

- Tell Ss in each group to brainstorm ideas based on what they have read in the article, along with their personal experiences, and if possible, additional research. Encourage a group recorder to take notes and to read these notes after the brainstorming session.

- Have Ss discuss their tips with their group using the notes as a guide.

- Elicit some "smart shopping tips" from each group and write them on the board.

- Encourage groups to use the tips on the board as well as their own to create a poster of smart shopping tips.

- When groups have finished, have them display their posters around the room.

- Allow time for a representative from each group to read and explain the group's poster.

Lesson D *Reading*

Comprehension check

- Direct Ss' attention to Exercise **3A** and read the instructions aloud.
- Ask eight Ss to read the questions aloud, one at a time. Make sure that Ss understand all the questions.
- Ss complete the exercise individually. Walk around and help as needed.
- Check answers with the class. Ask where in the reading the answers are found.

Expansion activity (student pairs)

- Have Ss work together to imagine and role-play a sitaution between the Smart Shopper columnist and someone who has had a problem with a purchase or an exchange. Ss may refer to the reading on page 90 for some ideas.
- When pairs have finished writing their role play, encourage them to practice it.
- Then ask several pairs to perform their role play for the class.

Practice

- Direct Ss' attention to Exercise **3B**. Read the introductory information about compound nouns.
- Call on a S to read aloud the instructions in number 1.
- Have another S read the example and the adjective clause in the chart that explains the compound noun.
- Ask a S to read the other adjective clauses in the chart.
- Ss work individually to complete the chart. Walk around and help as needed.
- Focus Ss' attention on number 2 in Exercise **3B** and read the instructions aloud. Ss work individually to find two more compound nouns in the reading and fill in the corresponding adjective clauses.
- Direct Ss' attention to number 3 in Exercise **3B** and read the instructions aloud.
- Ss work in small groups to compile a list of compound nouns and explanations of each. Walk around and help as needed.
- Write the following headings on the board:
  Compound noun   *Explanation*
- Ask Ss to come to the board to write the nouns and corresponding adjective clauses they discussed with their group. Make corrections on the board as needed.

Learner persistence (individual work)

- Encourage Ss to use their notebook or index cards to write new vocabulary words. Suggest that Ss review new words daily and practice them as much as possible.

Application

- Focus Ss' attention on Exercise **3C** and read the instructions aloud.
- Ask three Ss to read the three questions, one at a time.
- Ss complete the exercise in pairs.
- Ask several pairs to share their answers with the class.

Evaluation

- Books closed. Direct Ss' attention to the lesson focus on the board.
- Ask individual Ss to retell the main points of the advice column, "The Smart Shopper."
- Books open. Focus Ss' attention on the words that they wrote in the chart for number 1 of Exercise **3B**. Ask Ss to write sentences with these words to show that they understand the meanings.
- Check off each part of the lesson focus as Ss demonstrate an understanding of what they have learned in the lesson.

Learner persistence (individual work, student pairs)

- You may wish to assign Extended reading worksheets from the *Teacher's Toolkit Audio CD / CD-ROM* for Ss to complete outside of class. The purpose of these worksheets is to encourage Ss to read for pleasure in English outside of the English class. The worksheets can also be assigned as extended reading in class.

> **More Ventures** (whole group, pairs, individual)
> Assign appropriate exercises from the *Teacher's Toolkit Audio CD / CD-ROM, Add Ventures,* or the *Workbook*.

3 After you read

A Check your understanding.

1. What is Madelyn's problem?
2. If an item is defective, does a purchaser have the right to return it?
3. Does Madelyn have the right to get a refund? Why or why not?
4. Is the Smart Shopper's advice for Internet purchases, store purchases, or both?
5. What should Madelyn have done before she bought the earrings?
6. What is the meaning of "satisfaction guaranteed or your money back"?
7. *Seller* and *retailer* are synonyms. What is another word in the reading with the same meaning?
8. Smart Shopper lists several questions that purchasers should ask before they buy. In your opinion, which question is the most important?

B Build your vocabulary.

Compound nouns are *noun + noun* combinations that have special meanings.
Sometimes you can explain compound nouns with adjective clauses.
For example, a *jewelry lover* is a person who loves jewelry.

1. Find compound nouns in the reading that match the explanations.
Write them in the chart.

Compound noun	Explanation
1. *jewelry lover*	a person who loves jewelry
2. *time limit*	a limit that is related to time
3. *shipping costs*	costs that are related to shipping
4. *store credit*	a credit that is given by a store
5. *cash refund*	a refund that is made in cash
6. *return policy*	a policy that is related to returns
7. *store purchases*	*things you buy in a store*
8. *Internet purchases*	*things you buy online*

2. Find two more compound nouns in the reading. Write them in the chart.
Use adjective clauses to explain what they mean.

3. Work in a small group. Make a list of other compound nouns you know.
Use adjective clauses to explain what they mean.

C Talk with a partner.

1. Are you a jewelry lover? What do you love to buy?
2. What things have a time limit?
3. Have you ever gotten a cash refund? What for?

1 Before you write

A Talk with a partner. List some reasons why people should or shouldn't shop online.

Why people should shop online	Why people shouldn't shop online
It's convenient.	It's hard to choose merchandise you can't touch.
(Answers will vary.)	

B Read the paragraph.

Why You Shouldn't Shop Online

There are some good reasons why you shouldn't shop online. First, it's hard to choose merchandise that you can't touch. For example, a piece of jewelry might look very good on the computer screen, but after you buy it and look at it closely, you may find that it's very ugly and poorly made. Furthermore, shopping online is slow. It may take several days to receive the merchandise. If you are not satisfied, it may take weeks to exchange the merchandise or get your money back. Finally, shopping online can be dangerous. People can steal your credit card number and use it to buy expensive items. An irresponsible seller can take your money and never send you the merchandise. I'm going to do my shopping in stores!

Use transition words such as *first, secon* *next, furthermore, moreover,* and *finally* t signal a list of reasons in a paragraph.

Warm-up and review

- Before class. Write today's lesson focus on the board.
  Lesson E:
  Write a persuasive paragraph about shopping online
  Use transition words to organize a paragraph
- Begin class. Books closed. Review vocabulary from the unit. Write the words *shopping online* on the board. Ask Ss: *How many of you have shopped online?* Ask Ss where they have shopped and what kind of purchases they have made (e.g., books, clothing, shoes).
- Remind Ss about the newspaper advice column they read on page 90. Ask the following questions:
  What was Mad Madelyn's complaint? (She wanted a refund for earrings she bought online from a store that has a no-return policy.)
  What did the Smart Shopper tell her? (Unless the merchandise is defective, there's nothing she can do.)
  What does Smart Shopper suggest in the article? (Smart Shopper suggests that before making any purchases, the buyer should check the store's return policy.)
  Where can you find a store's return policy? (You can find it online or at the store. If you look at a merchant's Web site, you should be able to find it there. Often a return policy is printed on a store's receipt. If not, you can ask the merchant in person to give you a written copy of the return policy.)

Presentation

- Books open. Direct Ss attention to Exercise **1A** and read the instructions aloud.
- Call on two Ss to read the two boldfaced headings: *Why people should shop online* and *Why people shouldn't shop online.*
- Ask two other Ss to read the example answers.
- Ss work in pairs to list their reasons in the appropriate column. Walk around and help as needed.
- Write the two headings on the board. Ask Ss to share with the class some of the information they talked about with their partner. Write Ss' reasons on the board.

Practice

- Direct Ss' attention to Exercise **1B** and read the instructions aloud.
- Ss read the paragraph silently. Tell them to underline any words they don't understand.
- Have Ss write the new words on the board. Point to each word. Say it and ask Ss to repeat.

> Read the tip aloud. Ask Ss to reread the paragraph and underline the transition words. Call on Ss to say and locate each of the transition words in the paragraph (e.g., *First* appears in the second sentence; *furthermore* appears in the fourth sentence). Point out that transition words help the writer to organize a paragraph and make it easier for the reader to follow the list of reasons in a persuasive paragraph. Tell Ss that there are many more transition words in English but that these are some of the most common.

Expansion activity *(small groups)*

- Tell Ss that they are going to work with a small group to share some online shopping tips.
- Direct Ss' attention to the advice column on page 90. Ask Ss: *How does the Smart Shopper share advice related to shopping?* (The Smart Shopper lists seven important questions for readers to consider prior to making a purchase.)
- Invite members in each group to brainstorm a list of similar advice questions about online shopping. If you have computers in class, you can also have Ss look up online shopping tips, since there are several sites that offer them.
- Model the activity. Write on the board: *Does the Web site have a security statement?*
- Open up the discussion to the entire class. Call on Ss to share their online shopping tips. Write several examples on the board.

Presentation

- Direct Ss' attention to Exercise **1C** and read the instructions aloud.
- Call on a S to read aloud the two boldfaced headings: *Transition words* and *Reasons and supporting details*.
- Call on another S to read the example answers.
- Ss work in pairs to complete the informal outline of the model paragraph on page 92.
- Write an outline on the board similar to the one in the Student's Book.
- Have Ss come to the board, one at a time, to fill in the outline with the information from the model paragraph. Make corrections on the board as needed.

Practice

- Direct Ss' attention to Exercise **1D** and read the instructions aloud. Explain that it will be easier for Ss to write a paragraph if they plan it carefully.
- Ss complete their outline individually. Walk around and help as needed.

▼ **Teaching tip**
Before Ss begin to write, have them talk about the topic in a prewriting activity. Talking with a partner or a small group will help Ss focus on the reasons they are going to use to support their argument in Exercise **2**.

Application

- Focus Ss' attention on Exercise **2** and read the instructions aloud.
- Ss complete the task individually. Walk around and help as needed.

Learner persistence (individual work)

- If you have any Ss who have difficulty writing, sit with them and help them as the other Ss are writing. Help Ss use their notes from their outline in Exercise **1D** to add strong reasons to support their opinion of why you *should* shop online.

Comprehension check

- Direct Ss' attention to Exercise **3A**.
- This exercise asks Ss to develop skills to review and edit their own writing.
- Ss check their own paragraph against the writing checklist. Walk around and help as needed. If any Ss check *No* for one or more of the checklist items, ask

them to revise and edit their paragraph to include the missing information.

Evaluation

- Focus Ss' attention on Exercise **3B**. Read the instructions aloud. This exercise enables Ss to work together to peer-correct their writing. Reading aloud enables the writer to review his or her own writing. Reading to a partner allows the writer to understand the need to write clearly for an audience.
- Ss complete the exercise in pairs. Tell Ss to take turns reading their paragraphs to each other. Walk around and help as needed.
- Listen to Ss as they ask their partner one question about the paragraph and tell their partner one thing they learned from it.
- Ask several Ss to read their paragraph aloud. Have other Ss ask questions and mention one thing they learned from the paragraph.
- Direct Ss' attention to the lesson focus on the board.
- Check off each part of the lesson focus as Ss demonstrate an understanding of what they have learned in the lesson.

Community building (small groups)

- Identify some people in the community who have stores nearby, and invite them to come to the class to talk about their business. Tell the storeowners that you have been talking about the advantages and disadvantages of online shopping and would like their views.
- Prepare Ss for the visits beforehand by having them work in small groups to brainstorm a list of five to seven questions to ask each guest speaker. Encourage Ss to incorporate as much new vocabulary as possible. Ss should write down their questions. Walk around and help as needed.
- Call on groups to say some of their questions aloud. Correct as needed.
- On the day of the event, have group members take turns asking the questions they discussed in their group.
- After the event, call on Ss to share ideas. Ask Ss questions, such as: *What was the most interesting thing you learned? Did anything surprise you? What was it?*

More Ventures (whole group, pairs, individual)
Assign appropriate exercises from the *Teacher's Toolkit Audio CD / CD-ROM*, *Add Ventures*, or the *Workbook*.

C Complete the outline with information from the model paragraph.

Transition words	Reasons and supporting details	
First	First reason:	*Hard to choose merchandise you can't touch.*
	Example:	*Merchandise might look better on the computer.*
Furthermore	Second reason:	*Shopping online is slow.*
	Fact:	*Takes several days to receive the merchandise.*
	Fact:	*Can take weeks to exchange merchandise or get money back.*
Finally	Third reason:	*Shopping online can be dangerous.*
	Fact:	*People can steal your credit card number.*
	Fact:	*An irresponsible seller can take your money and never send you the merchandise.*

D Plan a paragraph about why you *should* shop online. Think of two or more reasons and one or more supporting details (facts or examples) for each reason. Make notes on your ideas in an outline like the one in Exercise 1C. Use your own paper. *(Answers will vary.)*

2 Write

Write a paragraph about why you *should* shop online. Use the paragraph in Exercise 1B and the outlines in Exercises 1C and 1D to help you.

3 After you write

A Check your writing.

	Yes	No
1. I wrote two or more reasons to shop online.	☐	☐
2. I gave one or more supporting details (facts or examples) for each reason.	☐	☐
3. I used transition words like *first*, *furthermore*, and *finally* to signal my list of reasons.	☐	☐

B Share your writing with a partner.

1. Take turns. Read your paragraph to a partner.
2. Comment on your partner's paragraph. Ask your partner a question about the paragraph. Tell your partner one thing you learned.

1 Life-skills reading

JedsSports.com

RETURNED-MERCHANDISE FORM

Please complete this form and send it with the returned merchandise within 21 days to JedsSports.com, 887 13th Avenue, San Francisco, CA 94122. Include a copy of the invoice and the original packaging. Call us for a Returned-Merchandise Authorization number (M–F, 8 a.m.–5 p.m., PST) at 800-555-4143.

Name: *Rita Miller*   **RMA#:** *98704370*   Check one:

Address *271 Dade Drive* **City** *Largo* **State** *FL* **Zip** *33771* ☐ **Store Credit**

List items for return: ☑ **Exchange**

Item #	Description	Size	Color	Reason	Additional Comments:
P4103	*sweatshirt*	*medium*	*red*	*wrong size*	*I ordered a large.*

List items to receive in exchange:

Item #	Description	Size	Color		
P4128	*sweatshirt*	*large*	*red*		

A Read the questions. Look at the returned-merchandise form. Circle the answers.

1. Why is the buyer using this form?
   a. She wants her money back.
   b. She wants a store credit.
   c. She wants to exchange the merchandise.
   d. none of the above

2. What does the buyer need to include with this form?
   a. the invoice
   b. the item that she is returning
   c. the original packaging
   d. all of the above

3. Which statement is true?
   a. The buyer must return the items within 21 days.
   b. The buyer is satisfied with her purchase.
   c. The buyer needs a smaller sweatshirt.
   d. The buyer lives in California.

4. Which statement is *not* true?
   a. The buyer is returning one item.
   b. The buyer needs a different size.
   c. The merchandise was defective.
   d. The buyer wants the same color.

5. What does "RMA#" mean?
   a. returned-merchandise invoice number
   b. returned-merchandise authorization number
   c. credit card number
   d. none of the above

6. How did Rita get the RMA number?
   a. She e-mailed the store.
   b. She called an 800 number.
   c. She got it from the original invoice.
   d. It was written on the merchandise.

B Talk with your classmates. Do you think it is difficult to return or exchange merchandise at this store. Why or why not?

Warm-up and review

- Before class. Write today's lesson focus on the board. *Lesson F:*
  Read and understand a returned-merchandise form
  Review topic vocabulary and grammar from Unit 7
  Complete the project and the self-assessment
- Begin class. Books closed. Point to the words on the board: *returned-merchandise form*.
- Ask Ss: *What kind of information do you think this form would have?* Elicit appropriate answers, such as: *the item purchased*; *the store policy for returns*; *a description of the item, a reason for the return.*
- Ask Ss: *When would you use this form?* Elicit an appropriate response, such as: *You would use this form when you're unhappy with something you bought and want to exchange it or get a refund.*
- Tell Ss that in this lesson, they will practice reading and understanding a returned-merchandise form.

Presentation

- Books open. Call on individual Ss to read the form and the filled-in information in Exercise **1**. Explain vocabulary as needed.

▼**Teaching tip**

Tell Ss that learning to read these kinds of forms is a useful skill for everyday life. Ask Ss if they have used similar forms. If no one says *yes*, explain that they may be in situations in the future in which they will need to use a form like this.

Practice

- Read the instructions aloud for Exercise **1A**. This task helps prepare Ss for standardized-type tests they may have to take. Be sure that Ss understand the task. Have Ss individually scan for and circle the answers.

Comprehension check

- Check answers with the class. Make sure that Ss have followed the instructions and circled their answers.
- Have Ss read aloud the questions and answers they circled. Ask Ss: *Is this answer correct?* Correct Ss' answers as needed.

Application

- Direct Ss' attention to Exercise **1B** and read the instructions aloud.
- Ss in small groups. Have groups discuss whether it is difficult to return or exchange merchandise at JedsSports.com. Walk around and help as needed.
- Open up the discussion to the entire class.

Expansion activity (small groups)

- **Materials needed** Samples of returned-merchandise forms (they can be found online) – one form for each group.
- Bring in samples of returned-merchandise forms. Although most of them are basically the same, it will be more interesting for Ss if you can find forms for different kinds of merchandise.
- Distribute one form to each small group of Ss. Review vocabulary as needed. Have Ss in each group think of an appropriate product to "return" to the store. Encourage Ss to be creative. Walk around and help as needed.
- Call on groups to share their completed returned-merchandise forms with the class.
- Leave time for a question-and-answer session.

Presentation

- Books closed. Write on the board: *Idioms*. Say the word and have Ss repeat.
- Ask Ss if they know what an idiom is. You can ask a S to look up the word in a dictionary. Elicit appropriate responses, such as: *a group of words whose meaning as a unit is different from the meaning of each word separately.* Explain further as needed.
- Tell Ss that idioms and idiomatic expressions often make it difficult to understand native speakers, especially on the radio, on television, and in the movies. Learning idioms is very important for understanding and communicating in English.

Practice

- Books open. Direct Ss' attention to Exercise **2A** and read the instructions aloud.
- Call on individual Ss to read the six statements in the *Idiom* column. Call on another S to read all the items in the *Definition* column. Explain vocabulary as needed.
- Ss complete the exercise with a partner. Walk around and help as needed.
- Check answers with the class.

Application

- Direct Ss' attention to Exercise **2B** and read the instructions aloud.
- Ask three Ss to read the three situations, one at a time.
- Model the exercise. Have two Ss read the example conversation.
- Ss complete the exercise in pairs. Walk around and help as needed.
- Read the instructions aloud for the second part of Exercise **2B**. Ask pairs to perform their role play for the class.

Expansion activity *(student pairs)*

- Ss in pairs. Ask Ss to create similar shopping situations to the ones in Exercise **2B**, using vocabulary from this unit.
- Tell Ss to write their situation on a piece of paper. Walk around and help as needed.

- Have pairs exchange situations. Partners should write short conversations as they did for Exercise **2B**, only this time, they should try to incorporate as many of the idioms from Exercise **2A** as possible. Each pair should practice its role play before performing it for the class.

> **More Ventures** *(whole group, pairs, individual)*
> Assign appropriate exercises from the *Teacher's Toolkit Audio CD / CD-ROM, Add Ventures,* or the *Workbook.*

Application

Community building

- **Project** Ask Ss to turn to page 139 in their Student's Book and complete the project for Unit 7.

Evaluation

- Before asking Ss to turn to the self-assessment on page 144, do a quick review of the unit. Have Ss turn to Lesson A. Ask the class to talk about what they remember about this lesson. Prompt Ss, if necessary, with questions, for example: *What are the conversations about on this page? What vocabulary is in the pictures?* Continue in this manner to review each lesson quickly.
- **Self-assessment** Read the instructions for Exercise **3**. Ask Ss to turn to the self-assessment page to complete the unit self-assessment. The self-assessments are also on the *Teacher's Toolkit Audio CD / CD-ROM*. If you prefer to collect the assessments and save them as part of each S's portfolio assessment, print out the unit self-assessment from the Toolkit, ask Ss to complete it, and collect and save it.
- If Ss are ready, administer the unit test on pages T-190–T-192 of this *Teacher's Edition* (or on the *Teacher's Toolkit Audio CD / CD-ROM*). The audio and audio script for the tests are on the *Teacher's Toolkit Audio CD / CD-ROM*.

2 Fun with language

A **Work** with a partner. Match the idioms with the definitions. Then write new sentences using the idioms.

Idiom

1. This dress is **a steal**! Yesterday, I saw it for $30 more in another store. __e__

2. You paid $299 for a camera phone? What **a rip-off**! __c__

3. My shoes **cost a fortune**, but they look beautiful and fit perfectly. I love them! __f__

4. These CDs are **marked down** from their regular price. __a__

5. Stella is going to **shop around** for her husband's birthday present. __b__

6. Jack bought a used car, and it turned out to be a real **lemon**. __d__

Definition

a. reduced in price

b. look in more than one store

c. something that costs much more than it's worth

d. something that is poorly made

e. something that is a really good price

f. are very expensive

B **Work** with a partner. Role-play one of the following situations. Write a short conversation and act it out in front of the class.

1. You want to return a textbook to the school bookstore. You bought the book three weeks ago. Since you bought it, you have changed your class and you no longer need the book.

> *A* I'd like to return this textbook.
> *B* What's the problem?
> *A* I changed my class, and I don't need it any longer.
> *B* Do you have the receipt?
> *A* No. I lost it, but you can see that the book is new.
> *B* I'm sorry, but you'll need to show us the receipt.

2. You bought some milk at the supermarket. When you get home, you find that it is sour. The expiration date on the milk carton was two weeks ago. You are annoyed, and you take the milk back to the store.

3. For your birthday, you received a nice sweater that was purchased at an expensive shop in the mall. The sweater is too small, and it's a color that you don't like. You want to exchange the sweater for something else, but you don't have the receipt.

Perform your role play for the class.

3 Wrap up

Complete the **Self-assessment** on page 144.

Lesson **A** *Get ready*

1 Talk about the pictures

A What do you see?

B What is happening?

Lesson objectives
- Introduce students to the topic
- Find out what students know about the topic
- Preview the unit by talking about the pictures
- Practice key vocabulary
- Practice listening skills

Warm-up and review

- Before class. Write today's lesson focus on the board.
  Lesson A:
  Discuss work schedules
  Talk about workplace problems and their solutions
  Ask questions about work experience

- Begin class. Books closed. Direct Ss' attention to the lesson focus. Point to *work schedules*. Ask Ss: *What are some work schedules?* List Ss' responses on the board, for example: *part-time, full-time, seasonal, weekdays, weekends, 9 to 5.*

- Point to *workplace problems*. Ask Ss: *What are some examples of workplace problems?* List Ss' responses on the board, for example: *long hours, no days off, not enough sick days, not enough vacation time, difficult co-workers, demanding boss.*

- Point to *work experience*. Ask Ss: *What is work experience?* List Ss' responses on the board, for example: *previous jobs, past responsibilities, volunteer work.* Ask Ss: *When do you usually talk about this?* Elicit appropriate responses, such as: *in a job interview, when applying for a job.*

Presentation

- Books open. Set the scene. Direct Ss' attention to the first picture on page 96. Ask the question from Exercise **1A**: *What do you see?* Elicit and write on the board as much vocabulary about the picture as possible: *donut shop, workers, counter, apron, uniform,* etc. Explain any words Ss don't know. Continue eliciting words to describe the remaining pictures.

- Ask individual Ss to look at the three pictures and talk about the similarities (e.g., Yolanda is in all of them) and the differences (e.g., the first two pictures are in Daria's Donut Shop, and the last picture is in a different coffee shop).

- Direct Ss' attention to the question in Exercise **1B**: *What is happening?* Hold up the Student's Book. Point to Picture 1. Ask: *What's Yolanda doing here?* (She's talking to David, who looks as if he's leaving.)

- Point to Picture 2. Ask: *What's Yolanda doing here?* (She's leaving work after locking up.)

- Point to Picture 3. Ask: *What's Yolanda doing here?* (Yolanda is talking with her friends. She looks upset.)

Expansion activity (student pairs)

- Have Ss work with a partner. Ask pairs to create a role play between Yolanda and David or between Yolanda and her friends.

- Call on several pairs to perform their role play for the class.

▼ **Teaching tip**
Encourage Ss to be creative in their discussions of the opening pictures for the unit. At this point, there is no single correct answer.

Expansion activity (small groups)

- Ask Ss: *Have any of you ever worked in a restaurant? If you have, what is the most difficult part about restaurant work?*

- Write *Advantages* and *Disadvantages* on the board. Have Ss work in small groups to discuss and list on a sheet of paper the advantages and disadvantages of working in various places, such as a hospital, an office, a beauty shop, a school, a factory.

- After several minutes, ask each group to share its list with the class. On the board, write the name or type of job, and then write several examples under *Advantages* and *Disadvantages*. For example:

  Restaurant work

Advantages	*Disadvantages*
You can make tips.	*You have to be on your feet for long periods of time.*

- At the end of the activity, poll Ss to see which job they think is the hardest one.

Presentation

- Books open. Direct Ss' attention to Exercise **2A**. Read the instructions aloud. Tell Ss that they are going to hear two different conversations.
- [Class Audio CD3 track 2] Play or read the audio program (see audio script, page T-163).
- Ask Ss if they understand everything in the listening exercise. Write any unfamiliar words on the board and help Ss understand the meaning of each.
- Partners complete Exercise **2A**. Elicit answers to the questions in the exercise.
- Have Ss focus their attention on Exercise **2B**. Read the instructions aloud. Tell Ss to listen and complete the diagram based on the information they hear.
- [Class Audio CD3 track 3] Tell Ss to listen for details about Yolanda's conversation with David and her friends' suggested solutions. Model the exercise. Play or read the audio program again. Pause the program after Yolanda says in Part 2: *It's really frustrating.*
- Model the first answer in the diagram. Draw the diagram on the board as it appears on page 97. Point to the blank in the web that says *Yolanda's problem* underneath it. Ask Ss: *What is Yolanda's problem?* Elicit appropriate responses, such as: *David is not doing his share of the work.* Write the answer on the line in the diagram on the board. Play or read the rest of the audio program. Ss listen and complete the diagram.
- Read aloud the second part of the instructions for Exercise **2B**.
- [Class Audio CD3 track 3] Play or read the audio program again (see audio script, page T-163). Ss listen and check their answers. Repeat the audio program as needed.
- Ask Ss to come to the board to write the answers in the diagram. Make corrections on the board as needed.

Practice

- Direct Ss' attention to Exercise **2C**. Read the instructions aloud. Tell Ss that the story in this exercise is a summary of what happened in the pictures on the previous page.
- Focus Ss' attention on the words in the word bank. Say each word aloud. Ask Ss to repeat. Correct pronunciation as needed. Make sure that Ss understand the meaning of each word. Explain any words that are new to Ss.
- Model the exercise. Ask a S to read aloud the first two sentences in the story, including the example answer.
- Ss complete the exercise individually. Walk around and help as needed.

Comprehension check

- [Class Audio CD3 track 4] Play or read the audio program (see audio script, page T-164). Ss listen and check their answers. Repeat the audio program as needed.
- Write the numbers *1–8* on the board. Ask Ss to come to the board to write only the answers. Have other Ss read the sentences, filling in each blank with the answer on the board. Make corrections as needed.

Learner persistence (individual work)

- [Self-Study Audio CD tracks 25 and 26] Exercises **2A**, **2B**, and **2C** are recorded on the Ss' self-study CD at the back of the Student's Book. Ss can listen to the CD at home for reinforcement and review. They can also listen to the CD for self-directed learning when class attendance is not possible.

Application

- Focus Ss' attention on Exercise **2D** and read the instructions aloud.
- Ss complete the exercise with a partner. Walk around and help as needed.
- Ask several pairs to ask and answer the questions for the class. Discuss Ss' opinions about how to handle problems at work and at school.

Expansion activity (small groups)

- Ask Ss to work with a small group to imagine that David is their co-worker and that they are having the same problem with him that Yolanda is having. Have each group write a note, an e-mail, or a letter to David in which Ss talk about the situation that is bothering them and propose a possible solution. Ss can use the ideas that Yolanda's friends presented or their own ideas.
- Have each group share its writing with the class.

Evaluation

- Direct Ss' attention to the lesson focus on the board. Ask individual Ss to look at the pictures on page 96 and make sentences using the words from the word bank in Exercise **2C**.
- Check off each part of the lesson focus as Ss demonstrate an understanding of what they have learned in the lesson.

More Ventures (whole group, pairs, individual)
Assign appropriate exercises from the *Teacher's Toolkit Audio CD / CD-ROM*, *Add Ventures*, or the *Workbook*.

---

2 Listening

 **A** **Listen** and answer the questions.

1. Who are the speakers?
2. What are they talking about?

 B **Listen again.** Complete the diagram.

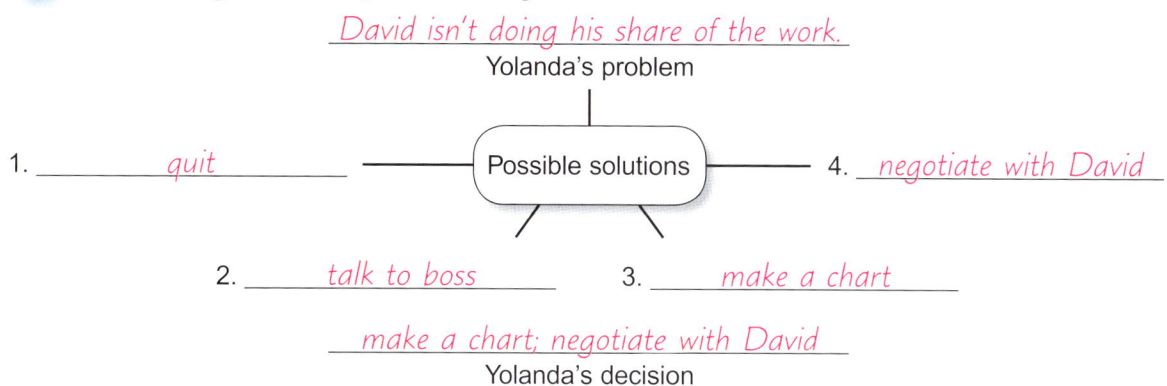

David isn't doing his share of the work.
Yolanda's problem

Possible solutions

1. *quit*
2. *talk to boss*
3. *make a chart*
4. *negotiate with David*

make a chart; negotiate with David
Yolanda's decision

Listen again. Check your answers.

 **C** **Read.** Complete the story. Listen and check your answers.

| chart | deal with | initials | share |
| close up | exhausted | negotiate | work (something) out |

Yolanda and David work at Daria's Donut Shop. Lately, David has been leaving work early, and Yolanda has to ___*close up*___ the shop by herself. Tonight, Yolanda
1

is having coffee with her friends. She is ___*exhausted*___ . Her friends give her
2

advice. Teresa thinks she should talk to her boss, but Yolanda wants to try to

___*work*___ things ___*out*___ with David first. Julie thinks Yolanda should
3

make a ___*chart*___ of their duties. Then she should ___*negotiate*___ with David and
4   5

decide who is going to do which tasks. When they finish a task, they should write

their ___*initials*___ on the chart. If David isn't doing his ___*share*___ of the work,
6   7

it will show in the chart. Then Yolanda can show the chart to their boss and let her

___*deal with*___ the situation.
8

D **Discuss.** Talk with your classmates. Have you ever had a problem at work or school? How did you solve it?

Lesson B *Tense contrast*

1 Grammar focus: present perfect and present perfect continuous

Present perfect (recently finished action)	Present perfect continuous (continuing action)
Yolanda has (just) mopped the floor. It's clean now.	Yolanda has been mopping the floor for 15 minutes.

For a grammar explanation, turn to page 151.
For a list of past participles, turn to page 154.

2 Practice

A Write. Complete the sentences. Use the present perfect or present perfect continuous forms of the verbs. Use *just* where possible.

1. Daria Thompson is the owner of Daria's Donut Shop.

   She _____*has been selling*_____ donuts at this location for
            (sell)
   more than 20 years.

2. It's 7:00 a.m. Daria _____*has been making*_____ donuts for
            (make)
   three hours.

3. It's 7:30 a.m. Daria _____*has just opened*_____ the shop
            (open)
   for customers.

4. It's 10:30 a.m. Daria's son _____*has been helping*_____ her
            (help)
   all morning.

5. He _____*has just finished*_____ cleaning the counters and
            (finish)
   shelves. Everything is spotless.

6. Daria needs more help in the shop. She _____*has been interviewing*_____
            (interview)
   candidates all week.

7. Yolanda's shift begins at 6:00 a.m. today. She _____*has been waiting*_____ for
            (wait)
   the bus for 30 minutes. She's worried that she's going to be late.

8. It's 6:05 a.m. Yolanda _____*has just called*_____ to say she will be late.
            (call)

💿 **Listen** and check your answers.

Lesson objective
- Contrast and practice the present perfect and present perfect continuous

Warm-up and review

- Before class. Write today's lesson focus on the board. *Lesson B:*
  Use the present perfect and present perfect continuous

- Begin class. Books closed. Write these two sentences on the board: *Yolanda has just spoken to her friends about David. Yolanda has been speaking to her friends about David.* Underline the present perfect and the present perfect continuous forms.

- Ask Ss if there is a difference in meaning between the two sentences. Elicit appropriate responses, such as: *The first sentence suggests that Yolanda recently finished talking to her friends. The second sentence suggests continued action – Yolanda started talking in the past and may still be talking.*

Presentation

- Direct Ss' attention to the grammar chart in Exercise **1**. Read aloud the two headings: *Present perfect* and *Present perfect continuous*. Then read the explanation and the example sentences under the headings.

- Write on the board: *Present perfect* and *Present perfect continuous*. Tell Ss that both the present perfect and the present perfect continuous express the idea of an action or a situation that began in the past and has continued to the present moment. However, the present perfect suggests recent completion of an action or situation, whereas the present continuous suggests that something continues, although it is unknown for how long.

- Remind Ss that the present perfect is formed with the verb *have* (*have* or *has*) + the past participle and that the present perfect continuous is formed by the verb *have* (*have* or *has*) + *been* + the present participle (ending in *-ing*).

- Point out that the present perfect often talks about something that has *just* finished; the *just* adds emphasis to the fact that a specific action has very recently finished. Point out to Ss that *just* is not used with the present perfect continuous.

Teaching tip
It might be helpful to refer Ss to the grammar explanation on page 151 and to the list of past participles on page 154 in the Student's Book.

Practice

- Direct Ss' attention to Exercise **2A** and read the instructions aloud.

- Have a S read the example aloud, and make sure that Ss understand the exercise.

- Ss complete the exercise individually. Walk around and help as needed.

Comprehension check

- [Class Audio CD3 track 5] Play or read the audio program (see audio script, page T-164). Ss listen and check their answers. Repeat the audio program as needed.

- Write the numbers *1–8* on the board. Ask several Ss to come to the board to write the complete sentences. Work with the class to make corrections on the board as needed.

Expansion activity *(student pairs)*

- Ss work in pairs to create dialogs using the present perfect and the present perfect continuous.

- Model the activity. Write the following on the board, and call on two Ss to read the dialog aloud.

  S1: I've just finished sending my son a text message!
  S2: Good for you! I've been trying to send a text message for weeks. It's very hard for me!
  S1: Well, I have been practicing for about a month because my kids always text me.

- Walk around and listen as Ss take turns speaking. Correct grammar and pronunciation as needed. Call on Ss to share their dialogs with the class.

Lesson B Tense contrast

Practice

- Books open. Direct Ss' attention to Yolanda's work schedule in Exercise **2B**. Tell Ss that they are going to read and talk about Yolanda's work schedule. Call on eight Ss to read each of the times and the corresponding activity.
- Read the instructions aloud for Exercise **2B**.
- Ask two Ss to read aloud the sample time and corresponding activities.
- Ss complete the exercise in pairs. Remind Ss that several of the past participles are irregular (*gone, taken, eaten*). Walk around and help as needed.
- Direct Ss' attention to the second part of Exercise **2B** and read the instructions aloud.
- Call on a S to read the example sentences.
- Ss work individually to complete the exercise. Walk around and help as needed.
- Ask individual Ss to come to the board to write their sentences. Make corrections on the board as needed.

Application

- Direct Ss' attention to Exercise **3A** and read the instructions aloud.
- Model the task. Ask two Ss to read the example dialog to the class.
- Ss work with a partner to complete the exercise. Walk around and help as needed.
- Direct Ss' attention to Exercise **3B** and read the instructions aloud.
- Have Ss take turns sharing with the class information they learned about their partner.

Expansion activity *(small groups)*

- Have Ss take out a piece of notebook paper. They should draw a schedule, using Yolanda's schedule on page 99 as a model.
- Tell Ss to title the schedule with their name and to fill it in with information based on what they typically do during their workday. (Ss who don't work can complete the schedule with the chores, errands, or school work they do.)

- Collect all the schedules. Then redistribute them, making sure that each S receives someone else's schedule.
- Ss in small groups. Write a time on the board and have Ss tell one another what their person has been doing and what he or she has just done.
- After a few minutes, change the time. Ss in each group continue to exchange information using the schedules and the grammar from this lesson.

Evaluation

- Books closed. Direct Ss' attention to the lesson focus on the board.
- Write the following on the board. (Note: Adjust the time to fit your class's schedule.)
  It's 3:00 p.m. We _____ English for three hours.
  (study)
  It's 3:05 p.m. We _____ our English lesson for the day.
  (finish)
- Ask Ss to tell you the correct form of each of the verb, and fill in the blanks. Elicit: *have been studying* and *have just finished*.
- Ask a S to tell you the difference between the perfect tenses in these two sentences. Elicit an appropriate response: *In the first sentence, the emphasis is on a continuing action of studying for three hours. In the second sentence, the emphasis is on talking about something that has recently finished.*
- Check off the lesson focus as Ss demonstrate an understanding of what they have learned in the lesson.

> **More Ventures** (whole group, pairs, individual)
> Assign appropriate exercises from the *Teacher's Toolkit Audio CD / CD-ROM*, *Add Ventures*, or the *Workbook*.

B **Talk** with a partner. Look at Yolanda's work schedule. Make sentences about the things she has just done and has been doing at the following times: 6:15, 6:30, 7:30, 11:00, 12:00, 2:00, and 4:00.

It's 6:15 a.m. Yolanda has just arrived.

It's 11:00 a.m. Yolanda has been serving customers for three and a half hours.

Yolanda's Schedule

6:15 a.m.	Arrive Turn off the security alarm
6:30 a.m.	Open the cash register Make coffee
7:30 a.m.	Open the shop for customers
7:30 a.m.–11:00 a.m.	Serve customers Take phone orders
11:00 a.m.–12:00 noon	Eat lunch Go to the bank
12:00 noon–4:00 p.m.	Serve customers Take phone orders
2:00 p.m.	Refill sugar containers Receive shipment of coffee
4:00 p.m.	Go home

Write sentences about Yolanda's schedule.

It's 6:15 a.m. Yolanda has just arrived.
It's 11:00 a.m. Yolanda has been serving customers for three and a half hours.

3 Communicate

A **Work** with a partner. Think about your own schedule. Your partner says a time. You say what you have been doing and what you have just done.

A Natalia, it's 10:30 a.m.
B I've been working for two hours.
I've just read my e-mail.

B **Share** information about your partner.

It's 10:30 a.m. Natalia has been working for two hours. She has just read her e-mail.

Participial adjectives

1 **Grammar focus:** adjectives ending in *-ed* and *-ing*

Adjective *-ed*

I'm tired of this job.
He's interested in this task.

Adjective *-ing*

This is a tiring job.
This is an interesting task.

This job is tiring.
This task is interesting.

For a grammar explanation, turn to page 151.

2 **Practice**

A **Write.** Circle the correct adjective.

1. **A** I heard that Juan and his friends went to a party after work. How was the party?
   B It was really **exciting** / **excited**.

2. **A** How did Juan feel the next day at work?
   B He was **exhausting** / **exhausted**.

3. **A** How long did he have to work?
   B He had to work from 9:30 to 6:30. It was a **tiring** / **tired** day.

4. **A** Does Juan usually start working at 9:30?
   B No, he overslept! He was **shocking** / **shocked** that he didn't hear the alarm clock.

5. **A** How did his boss react when he showed up late?
   B His boss was **irritating** / **irritated**.

6. **A** What did his boss say to him?
   B He told Juan that he was **disappointing** / **disappointed** in him.

7. **A** Juan didn't have a good day, I guess. What did he do later that night?
   B He stayed home and had a **relaxing** / **relaxed** night in front of the TV.

8. **A** So, is Juan going to go out again on a weeknight?
   B I don't think so. He said it was an **exhausting** / **exhausted** experience.

Listen and check your answers. Then practice with a partner.

Warm-up and review

- Before class. Write today's lesson focus on the board.
  Lesson C:
  Use participial adjectives ending in -ed and -ing
- Begin class. Books closed. Write *bored* and *boring* on the board.
- Write the sentences: *The movie was so slow and boring. It was a boring movie! Because the movie was so slow, I was bored.* Say the sentences and have Ss repeat.
- Tell Ss that verb forms ending in *-ed* or *-ing* are called participles, and that participles can be adjectives, too.

Presentation

- Books open. Direct Ss' attention to the grammar chart in Exercise **1**. Read aloud the two headings and corresponding sentences.
- Explain to Ss that the present participle, like other adjectives, can come before or after the noun it's modifying. For example:
  *The **frightening** movie made everyone nervous! That movie was **frightening**!*
- Explain that only things can be described with the *-ing* form because things can't have emotions. For example, you can say *The movie was boring,* but not *The movie was bored.* (The movie can't have feelings.)
- On the other hand, people can be described using either *-ing* or *-ed* forms because they can produce emotions in other people as well as experience emotions themselves. For example: *The man is bored* is correct, but so is *The man is boring!* Point out that the sentences have different meanings. For example, in the first sentence, the man is bored by whatever he is doing, but he may not be a boring person.
- Have Ss make up similar sentences using *tired, tiring, interested,* and *interesting.* Walk around and help as needed.
- Ask Ss to come to the board to write their sentences. Make corrections on the board as needed.

▼ **Teaching tip**
It might be helpful to refer Ss to the grammar explanation on page 151 in the Student's Book.

Practice

- Direct Ss' attention to Exercise **2A** and read the instructions aloud.
- Ask a S to read aloud the first example conversation, including the circled answer.
- Ss complete the exercise individually. Walk around and help as needed.

Comprehension check

- Read aloud the second part of the instructions for Exercise **2A**.
- 💿 [Class Audio CD3 track 6] Play or read the audio program (see audio script, page T-164). Ss listen and check their answers.
- Have Ss sit in pairs to practice the conversations with a partner. Walk around and correct pronunciation as needed.

Expansion activity *(small groups)*

- **Materials needed** A collection of tabloid-style newspapers or magazines. Try to find articles about celebrities that use a lot of adjectives. Ask Ss what some of the characteristics of these publications are. Elicit, for example: *They use a lot of exaggerated language; there are a lot of photographs of celebrities; they may not always tell the complete truth.*
- Write the following words on the board: *exciting, exhausting, tiring, shocking, irritating, disappointing, relaxing, excited, exhausted, tired, shocked, irritated, disappointed, relaxed.*
- Ss work in small groups to develop their own magazine articles – about a celebrity or another person of their choice – using as many of these participial adjectives as possible.
- Encourage Ss to have fun with this activity. Walk around and help as needed.
- Have Ss take turns presenting their articles to the class.

Participial adjectives

Practice

- Direct Ss' attention to the six pictures in Exercise **2B**. Ask Ss to describe what they see in each picture.
- Read the instructions aloud in Exercise **2B**.
- Call on a S to read the two headings: *Positive* and *Negative*. Ask another S to read each of the adjectives under *Positive*. Ask another S to read each of the adjectives under *Negative*.
- Explain vocabulary as needed, and ask Ss to repeat any words they don't know.
- Have two Ss read the example sentences above the two adjective charts.
- Ss complete the exercise with a partner. Walk around and help as needed.
- Read the instructions aloud for the second part of Exercise **2B**. Ask two Ss to read the two example sentence to the class.
- Ss complete the exercise individually. Walk around and help as needed.
- Ask several Ss to come to the board to write their sentences.
- Call on other Ss to read each of the sentences on the board. Ask: *Is this sentence correct?* Work with the class to make corrections on the board as needed.

Expansion activity *(student pairs)*

- Ask Ss to role-play a conversation between two of the people in the pictures. They can be on the phone or talking in person. Ss can ask and answer questions using the pictures and words in Exercise **2B** as a guide.
- Model the activity. Write this example on the board.

  S1: Did you see this award I got? I'm so excited.
  S2: Yeah, well, that's great. I just had the most boring meeting at work!

- Encourage Ss to have fun with this activity. Ask several pairs to act out their role play for the class.

Application

- Direct Ss' attention to Exercise **3A** and read the instructions aloud.
- Model the exercise. Ask two Ss to read the example dialog to the class.

- Ss complete the exercise in small groups. Walk around and help as needed.
- Direct Ss' attention to Exercise **3B** and read the instructions aloud.
- Model the task. Say: *I learned that Tan has an exciting job. He meets people from all over the world and practices his English every day.*
- Continue the exercise by asking several Ss to share information they learned about one another.

Expansion activity *(individual work)*

- Ask Ss to think about two experiences they have had, one positive, the other negative.
- Ss should choose one of their experiences and write a paragraph about it, using as many of the adjectives from Exercise **2B** as possible.
- Model the activity as needed. Write this (positive) example on the board:

  My bus trip to Niagara Falls was fascinating! Even though I thought the bus ride was going to be boring, it was very exciting. There was so much to see. My friends and I talked and told stories about what we did when we were younger. Some of our stories were amusing!

- Ask Ss to share their paragraphs with their partner. Call on several Ss to read their paragraphs aloud.

Evaluation

- Direct Ss' attention to the lesson focus on the board. Ask Ss to look at the six pictures on page 101 and use participial adjectives to make new sentences about each one. Students should say their sentences aloud.
- Check off the lesson focus as Ss demonstrate an understanding of what they have learned in the lesson.

More Ventures *(whole group, pairs, individual)*
Assign appropriate exercises from the *Teacher's Toolkit Audio CD / CD-ROM*, *Add Ventures*, or the *Workbook*.

B Talk with a partner. For each picture, describe the person and the activity. Choose participial adjectives from the boxes.

The man is excited.

Getting an award is exciting.

Positive		Negative	
amusing	amused	boring	bored
exciting	excited	frightening	frightened
interesting	interested	frustrating	frustrated

Write two sentences about each picture.

The man is excited.
Getting an award is exciting.

3 Communicate

A Work in a small group. Ask and answer questions about your experiences. Use the adjectives from Exercise 2B.

> **A** What's an amusing experience that you have had at work?
> **B** I was very amused when . . . . It was amusing because . . .

B Share information about your classmates.

1 Before you read

Talk with your classmates. Answer the questions.

1. What are some skills, such as following directions, that are necessary for most jobs?
2. What special skills do you have?

2 Read

SELF-STUDY AUDIO CD  **Read** the magazine article. Listen and read again.

Hard and Soft Job Skills

Som Sarawong has been working as an automotive technician at George's Auto Repair for over five years. Today was a special day for Som, a 35-year-old Thai immigrant, because he received the Employee of the Year award. According to Ed Overton, Som's boss, Som received the award "because he's a great 'people person' and he has superb technical skills. I even have him work on my own car!"

Som has the two kinds of skills that are necessary to be successful and move up in his career: soft skills and hard skills. Soft skills are personal and social skills. Som gets along with his co-workers. He has a strong work ethic; in five years, he has never been late or absent from work. Customers trust him. Hard skills, on the other hand, are the technical skills a person needs to do a job. Som can repair cars, trucks, and motorcycles. He learned from his father, who was also a mechanic. Then he took classes and got a certificate as an auto technician.

Soft and hard skills are equally important, but hard skills are easier to teach and assess than soft skills. People can learn how to use a machine and then take a test on their knowledge. However, it's harder to teach people how to be cooperative and have a good work ethic. George Griffith, the owner of George's Auto Repair, explains, "I've been working in this business for over 30 years, and most of the time when I've needed to fire someone, it was because of weak people skills, not because they didn't have technical abilities." Soft skills and good technical knowledge are a winning combination, and today, Som Sarawong was the winner.

> Quotations are used to explain or support a main idea. They also make a reading more interesting.

Lesson objectives

- Introduce and read "Hard and Soft Job Skills"
- Practice using new topic-related vocabulary
- Learn about prefixes and roots

Warm-up and review

- Before class. Write today's lesson focus on the board.
  Lesson D:
  Read and understand "Hard and Soft Job Skills"
  Practice new vocabulary related to job skills
  Learn and use different prefixes and roots

- Begin class. Books closed. Ask Ss: *What are job skills?* Elicit: *abilities you need for a specific job.* Then ask: *What are some examples of job skills?* Elicit appropriate responses, such as: *A chef needs to know how to cook.*

- Direct Ss' attention to the title of the reading on the board: "Hard and Soft Job Skills." Ask Ss what they think this reading is about. Elicit responses, such as: *The reading is about different kinds of job skills.* Write Ss' predictions on the board.

Presentation

- Books open. Direct Ss' attention to Exercise **1** and read the instructions aloud.

- Ask two Ss to read the questions in Exercise **1** to the class.

- Ss in small groups. Invite Ss to discuss their answers to the questions. Walk around and help as needed.

- Call on individual Ss to share their answers with the class.

Practice

- Read the instructions aloud for Exercise **2**. Ask Ss to read the magazine article silently before listening to the audio program.

- [Class Audio CD3 track 7] Play or read the audio program, and ask Ss to read along (see audio script, page T-164). Repeat the audio program as needed.

- While Ss are listening and reading the magazine article, ask them to underline any words they don't know. When the audio program is finished, have Ss write the new vocabulary words on the board.

- Point to each word on the board. Say it and have Ss repeat. Give a brief explanation of each word, or ask Ss who know the word to explain it.

Culture note

Ask Ss if they have ever heard of an Employee of the Year award. Explain that many companies – including banks, restaurants, hotels, and supermarkets – also choose an Employee of the Month. Often these employees' photos are posted on the walls of the establishments.

Read the tip aloud. Write *quotations* on the board. Ask Ss what the word means. Write on the board: *Quotations are words or sentences that people have spoken or written.* Ask: *How do we indicate that something is a quotation?* Elicit: *by using quotation marks.* Draw quotation marks on the board. Have Ss identify the two quotations in the text. Lead Ss to see that these quotations not only explain or support the main idea but also make the article come alive. Point out, too, that *soft* and *hard* are in quotation marks. Explain that sometimes we use quotation marks to highlight words or terms. In this case, the quotation marks show that "hard" and "soft" are the adjectives we use to describe certain job skills, even though they may seem like unusual adjectives to use in this way. Point out that the term "people person" is in single quotes. Tell Ss that when there is a quote within a quote, we use single, not double, quotation marks.

Learner persistence (individual work)

- [Self-Study Audio CD track 27] Exercise **2** is recorded on the Ss' self-study CD at the back of the Student's Book. Ss can listen to the CD at home for reinforcement and review. They can also listen to the CD for self-directed learning when class attendance is not possible.

Expansion activity (small groups)

- Write the following list on the board:
  Job   Skills required
  Librarian Good with people (S), knowledge of books (H),
  *   knowledge of how to look up information (H)*

- Ss in small groups. Ask Ss to brainstorm ideas to create a list of jobs and then decide which skills are important for that job. Ss should identify each skill with an *H* for hard skills and an *S* for soft skills.

- Model the activity. Call on a S to read the example on the board.

- Ss work together to complete the exercise. Walk around and help as needed.

- Have Ss share the information they discussed with the class.

Lesson D Reading

Comprehension check

- Direct Ss' attention to Exercise **3A** and read the instructions aloud.

> **Culture note**
> Call on a S to read the culture note aloud. Tell Ss that the word *ethic* means "a set of rules that someone lives by." A *work ethic* is something that many people in the United States believe in and follow. Ask Ss what the advantages and disadvantages might be of having a strong work ethic.

- Call on six Ss to read the six questions, one at a time.
- Ss complete the exercise individually. Walk around and help as needed.
- Check answers with the class. Whenever possible, have Ss indicate where they found the answers in the reading.

Practice

- **Materials needed** A dictionary for each S.
- Direct Ss' attention to number 1 of Exercise **3B**. Read the instructions aloud. Remind Ss that a prefix is a letter or group of letters added to the beginning of a word, base, or root; a root is the base of a word. Tell Ss that they should write each word with the prefix or root in the column under the heading: *Example from reading*.
- Call on a S to read the instructions aloud for number 2 of Exercise **3B**. Have Ss use a dictionary to write the meaning of the words in the column under the heading: *Meaning of word*.
- Ask a S to read aloud the instructions for number 3 of Exercise **3B**. Guide Ss to guess and then write the meaning of each prefix or root in the column under the heading: *Meaning of prefix or root*.
- Have another S read the first example in the chart.
- Ss work individually to find the words in the reading and then complete the chart. Walk around and help as needed.
- Read the instructions aloud for number 4 of Exercise **3B**. Ss work in small groups to make a list of other words they know with the same prefix or root. Walk around and help as needed.
- Review with the class. Write a chart on the board that is similar to the one on page 103. Call on six Ss to come to the board to fill in the chart. Make corrections on the board as needed. Ask Ss to share the additional words they discussed in their groups and their example sentences.

Application

- Direct Ss' attention to Exercise **3C**. Read the instructions aloud.
- Call on four Ss to read the questions in Exercise **3C**, one at a time. Ask Ss if they know what *superbly* means (extremely well). Explain additional vocabulary as needed.
- Ss ask and answer questions with a partner.
- Ask several pairs to share the answers they discussed.

Expansion activity (individual work)

- Ask partners to interview each other about their hard and soft job skills.
- Encourage Ss to take notes and to use their notes to write a brief article about their partner's job skills for an "Employee of the Week" newsletter. Ask Ss to include at least one quotation from their partner or from a co-worker, perhaps another S in the class.
- Have Ss share their articles with the class, calling on several Ss to read them aloud. If possible, have Ss take pictures of their partner and post the articles, along with the photos, on the bulletin board.

Evaluation

- Books closed. Direct Ss' attention to the lesson focus on the board.
- Ask individual Ss to retell the main points of the reading "Hard and Soft Job Skills."
- Books open. Focus Ss' attention on the words that they wrote in the chart in Exercise **3B**. Ask Ss to make sentences with these words to show that they understand the meanings.
- Check off each part of the lesson focus as Ss demonstrate an understanding of what they have learned in the lesson.

Learner persistence (individual work, student pairs)

- You may wish to assign Extended reading worksheets from the *Teacher's Toolkit Audio CD / CD-ROM* for Ss to complete outside of class. The purpose of these worksheets is to encourage Ss to read for pleasure in English outside of the English class. The worksheets can also be assigned as extended reading in class.

> ***More Ventures*** (whole group, pairs, individual)
> Assign appropriate exercises from the *Teacher's Toolkit Audio CD / CD-ROM*, *Add Ventures*, or the *Workbook*.

3 After you read

A Check your understanding.

1. According to Som Sarawong's boss, why did Som get the Employee of the Year award?
2. What's the difference between a soft skill and a hard skill? Give examples.
3. Which example shows that Som has a good work ethic?
4. Why is it easier to teach hard skills than soft skills?
5. According to what George Griffith says, do more workers lose their jobs because of weak soft skills or weak hard skills?
6. Do you agree with George Griffith? Why or why not?

Culture note
The expression "work ethic" is the belief that if you work hard in life you will get ahead and become successful.

B Build your vocabulary.

1. Find an example in the reading of each prefix and root. Write it in the chart.

2. Use a dictionary. Write the meaning of the words.

3. Guess the meaning of the prefixes and roots in the chart.

Prefixes and roots	Example from reading	Meaning of word	Meaning of prefix or root
1. re-	repair	to fix what is torn or broken	again
2. co-	cooperative	working or acting together willingly	together, with
3. auto	automotive	relating to cars	self
4. tech	technician; technical	a worker trained with special skills to operate machines or equipment	art, skill
5. super	superb	of the best quality; excellent	over, above
6. mot	motorcycles	motor vehicles similar to bicycles	move
7. equ	equally	in equal parts or amounts	equal

4. Work in a small group. Make a list of other words you know with the same prefixes and roots. Write a sentence for each new word.

C Talk with a partner.

1. What is something that you can do superbly?
2. What are some examples of technical skills?
3. What is a hobby or profession that requires good technical skills?
4. Are you good at repairing things? What can you repair?

1 Before you write

A Talk with a partner. Answer the questions.

1. What is a cover letter? What information does it include?
2. Have you ever written a cover letter? Tell about your experience.

B Read the cover letter.

Ester Yitbarek
4 South 8th Ave., Apt. 303
Chicago, IL 60601
September 30, 2008

Lynn Stevens
Director of Human Resources
Highland School District
625 S. 30th St.
Chicago, IL 60609

Dear Ms. Stevens:

I read your advertisement online for a position as a teacher's assistant. I am very interested in this position and have enclosed my resume.

I have been working as a teacher's assistant at Hilltop Elementary School for three years. In this job, I have taught reading and math to students in small groups. I have also tutored individual students who were having problems with the lessons. I'm very interested in child development, and I love working with children. I get along very well with my co-workers, and I'm also skilled at dealing with parents.

I am planning to move to a new home in your district. I hope you will call me to schedule an interview. I look forward to hearing from you.

Sincerely,

Ester Yitbarek

Ester Yitbarek

> **Culture note**
> Applicants are always expected to include a resume — a written statement of their educational and work experience — with their cover letter.

- Write a cover letter to apply for a job

Warm-up and review

- Before class. Write today's lesson focus on the board.
  Lesson E:
  Write a cover letter to apply for a job
- Begin class. Books closed. Focus Ss' attention on the words *cover letter* in the lesson focus on the board. Say it aloud and have Ss repeat. Ask Ss if they have ever written a cover letter. If any Ss say *yes*, ask them when they wrote it. Elicit appropriate responses.
- Tell Ss that today's lesson is about writing a cover letter in order to apply for a job.

Presentation

- Books open. Direct Ss' attention to Exercise **1A** and read the instructions aloud.
- Ask two Ss to read aloud the questions in Exercise **1A**.
- Ss work with a partner to ask and answer the questions. Walk around and help as needed.

Practice

- Direct Ss' attention to Exercise **1B** and read the instructions aloud.
- Ss read the cover letter silently. Ask Ss to underline any words in the letter with which they are unfamiliar.
- Have Ss tell you the words they underlined and write them on the board. Go over the meaning of each word.

▼ **Teaching tip**

Lead Ss to see that like a standard business letter, a cover letter is composed of five parts: the sender's address, the address of the person to whom you are writing, the greeting (or salutation), the body of the letter, and the closing. Ask Ss to look carefully at the sample cover letter as you go over each of these parts. You might want to bring in sample cover letters for Ss to examine and discuss.

Culture note

Read the culture note aloud. Say the word *resume* and have Ss repeat. Tell Ss that the word comes from the French, meaning "summary." Some Ss may be familiar with the Latin term *curriculum vitae* (CV), which, like a resume, is a short account of someone's career and qualifications. Most employers in the United States require a resume or CV when a person applies for a job, so if any Ss are unfamiliar with resumes, show them examples. Point out that in English, the word *resume* can also be written as it is in French, with two accent marks: *résumé*.

Expansion activity *(small groups)*

- **Materials needed** Sample resumes, one for each small group. (These resumes can be found online or in a public library.)
- Write on the board these essential elements of a resume:
  Contact information
  Employment goal or job objective
  Work experience and dates of jobs
  Education
  Any awards and organizations
  Special skills, interests, and abilities
- Have Ss work in small groups to discuss the elements of the resume they are examining. Explain vocabulary as needed.
- Remind Ss that there is not just one way to write a resume and that often the contents of a resume are tailored to the job Ss are applying for and to the experience they have.

Lesson E — Writing

Presentation

- Books open. Focus Ss' attention on Exercise **1C**. Read the instructions aloud.
- Ask six Ss to read the questions, one at a time.

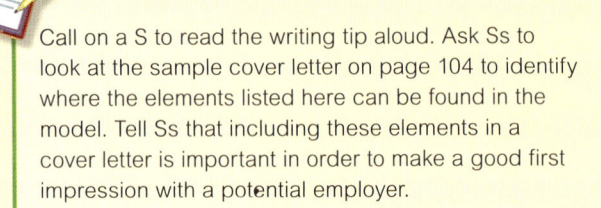

> Call on a S to read the writing tip aloud. Ask Ss to look at the sample cover letter on page 104 to identify where the elements listed here can be found in the model. Tell Ss that including these elements in a cover letter is important in order to make a good first impression with a potential employer.

- Ss answer the questions with a partner.
- Check answers with the class.

Practice

- Direct Ss' attention to Exercise **1D** and read the instructions aloud. Tell Ss that taking the time to plan their cover letter carefully will make it easier to write the letter.
- Ss should work individually to complete their plan for a cover letter. Walk around and help as needed.

Application

- Focus Ss' attention on Exercise **2**. Read the instructions aloud.
- Ss complete the task individually. Walk around and help as needed.

Learner persistence (individual work)

- If you have any Ss who have difficulty writing, sit with them and help them as the other Ss are writing. Encourage them to use their plan (or informal outline) from Exercise **1D** to help them.

Comprehension check

- Direct Ss' attention to Exercise **3A**. This exercise asks Ss to develop skills to review and edit their own writing.
- Ss check their own cover letters against the writing checklist. Walk around and help as needed. If any Ss check *No* for one or more of the checklist items, ask them to revise and edit their letters to include the missing information.

Evaluation

- Focus Ss' attention on Exercise **3B**. Read the instructions aloud. This exercise enables Ss to work together to peer-correct their writing. Reading aloud enables the writer to review his or her own writing. Reading to a partner allows the writer to understand the need to write clearly for an audience.
- Ss complete the exercise in pairs. Tell Ss to take turns reading their letters to each other. Walk around and help as needed.
- Listen to Ss as they ask their partner a question about the letter and tell their partner one thing they learned from it.
- Ask several Ss to read their letters aloud. Have other Ss ask questions and mention something they learned from the letter.
- Direct Ss' attention to the lesson focus on the board.
- Check off the lesson focus as Ss demonstrate an understanding of what they have learned in the lesson.

Expansion activity (student pairs)

- **Materials needed** Help-wanted ads from a local newspaper or an online Web site – one ad for each pair of Ss.
- Ss in pairs. Distribute a help-wanted ad to each pair and have partners review the ad together to find a job for which they would consider applying in a role play.
- Ss in each pair should take turns being the potential employer and employee. Using the information from their cover letters as a basis for discussion, partners should conduct simple interviews. Interviewers should ask about the potential employee's work experience and qualifications.
- Call on several Ss to perform their role play for the class.

> **More Ventures** (whole group, pairs, individual)
> Assign appropriate exercises from the *Teacher's Toolkit Audio CD / CD-ROM, Add Ventures,* or the *Workbook.*

C **Work** with a partner. Answer the questions.

1. Who wrote the letter?
2. Who did she write it to?
3. What position is she applying for?
4. Where did she hear about the job?
5. How much experience does she have?
6. What are some of her skills?

> In the body of a cover letter, include:
> - the title of the job you are applying for
> - how you found out about the job
> - information about your skills and experience

D **Plan** a cover letter for a real or an imaginary job. Complete the information.

1. Date: _(Answers will vary.)_ _____

2. Inside address

   Name and title of addressee: _____

   Address: _____

3. Position you are applying for

   Job title: _____

   How you found out about it: _____

4. Your skills and experience: _____

   _____

   _____

   _____

2 Write

Write a cover letter for a real or an imaginary job that you are interested in.
Use the cover letter in Exercise 1B and your outline in Exercise 1D to help you.

3 After you write

A **Check** your writing.

	Yes	No
1. My first sentence says the title of the job I am applying for.	☐	☐
2. I included how I heard about the job.	☐	☐
3. I gave two or more examples of my skills and experience.	☐	☐

B **Share** your writing with a partner.

1. Take turns. Read your letter to a partner.
2. Comment on your partner's letter. Ask your partner a question about the letter. Tell your partner one thing you learned.

1 Life-skills reading

Skills Required in the Fastest-growing Service Occupations

Skills	Janitor	Waiter	Food-service worker	Home health aide	Nursing aide
Listening well / Understanding instructions	●	●	●	●	●
Managing time	●	●			●
Monitoring one's own performance and that of others				●	●
Reading comprehension related to work documents	●	●		●	●
Talking to others to convey information effectively	●	●	●	●	●
Teaching job duties to others	●	●	●	●	●

Source: www7.nationalacademies.org/CFE/future_Skill_Demands_Mary_Gatta_Paper.pdf

A Read the questions. Look at the chart. Circle the answers.

1. Which occupation requires listening?
   a. food-service worker
   b. janitor
   c. nursing aide
   d. all of the above

2. Which skill is required by all of the occupations?
   a. reading comprehension
   b. monitoring performance
   c. teaching others
   d. none of the above

3. Which skill is required for a food-service worker?
   a. monitoring performance
   b. listening well
   c. reading
   d. managing time

4. Which skills are required for a waiter?
   a. listening well
   b. managing time
   c. reading
   d. all of the above

5. Which skill is required by the fewest occupations?
   a. managing time
   b. reading comprehension
   c. monitoring performance
   d. teaching others

6. Which occupation requires managing time?
   a. nursing aide
   b. home health aide
   c. food-service worker
   d. all of the above

B Talk with your classmates. Which skills from the chart do you have? Which skills have you used at a previous or current job?

Lesson objectives

- Practice reading and understanding a chart about required job skills
- Review vocabulary and grammar from the unit
- Introduce the project
- Complete the self-assessment

Warm-up and review

- Before class. Write today's lesson focus on the board.
  Lesson F:
  Read and understand a chart that lists job skills required in the fastest-growing service occupations
  Review topic vocabulary
  Complete the project and the self-assessment

- Begin class. Books closed. Write on the board: *skills required in service occupations.*

- Ask Ss: *What do you think the service occupations are?* Elicit appropriate answers, such as: *jobs that provide a service to people, such as cleaning, nursing, working in restaurants.*

- Ask Ss: *What do you think the skills needed for service occupations are?* Elicit appropriate responses, such as: *getting along well with customers, listening well.* Write the examples on the board.

- Say: *The chart that you're going to look at in this lesson lists the fastest-growing service occupations. What do you think are the fastest-growing service jobs?* Elicit appropriate answers, such as: *waiters, food-service workers, home health aides.*

Presentation

- Books open. Read the title of the chart to the class.
- Call on a S to read the jobs listed at the top of the chart.
- Call on six Ss in turn to read the skills listed. Explain vocabulary as needed.

▼ **Teaching tip**
Tell Ss that learning to read these kinds of charts is a useful skill for everyday life. Ask Ss if they have seen similar types of charts. If no one says *yes,* explain that this is the kind of chart they may find in a newspaper or magazine article.

Practice

- Direct Ss' attention to **1A** and read the instructions aloud. This task helps prepare Ss for standardized-type tests they may have to take. Be sure that Ss understand the task. Have Ss individually scan for and circle the answers.

Comprehension check

- Check answers to Exercise **1A** with the class. Make sure that Ss have followed the instructions and circled their answers.
- Have Ss read aloud the questions and answers they circled. Ask: *Is that answer correct?* Make corrections as needed.

Application

- Direct Ss' attention to Exercise **1B** and read the instructions aloud. Make sure that Ss understand the questions.
- Model the task. Ask a S: *What skills from the chart do you have?* Elicit an appropriate response, such as: *I can manage my time well.* Ask the S if he or she uses this skill in his or her current job.
- Ss work in small groups to ask and answer the questions. Walk around and help as needed.

Expansion activity (small groups)

- **Materials needed** Large pieces of paper, one for each group.
- Draw a chart on the board similar to the one in Exercise **1** and write these headings: *Skills, Janitor, Waiter, Food-service worker, Home health aide, Nursing aide.* Leave all the other spaces blank.
- Ss in small groups. As a way of expanding the skills listed in the chart on page 106, invite one S from each group to copy the chart on the board onto a large piece of paper.
- Have Ss begin by reviewing the skills listed in the chart on page 106. Tell Ss that they are going to add additional skills to their own group chart.
- Model the task. Write *Being patient with elderly people* in the first space under the *Skills* column on the board. Ask Ss which jobs this skill applies to (waiter, home health aide, nursing aide). Place a check mark under each appropriate occupation.
- Tell groups to brainstorm skills needed for the service occupations listed on the board and to write these skills in their group chart. Ss should place check marks under the occupations where the skill applies. Walk around and help as needed.
- Ask a representative from each group to come to the board to write one of the additional skills his or her group placed on its chart. Discuss the skills with the class, and make corrections as needed.

Presentation

- Books closed. Write on the board: *important skills for a manager*. Read the phrase aloud and have Ss repeat.
- Ask Ss what they think are the most important skills for a manager. Elicit appropriate responses, such as: *cares about his or her co-workers, listens carefully to employees, gives clear directions*. Write Ss' responses on the board.

Practice

- Books open. Focus Ss' attention on the photos in Exercise **2A**. Ask Ss what the people are doing in each photo.
- Read the instructions aloud for Exercise **2A**.
- Call on four Ss to read the description of each of the candidates for the job.
- Ss work in small groups to decide which candidate to hire as a manager. Walk around and help as needed.

Application

- Direct Ss' attention to Exercise **2B**. Read the instructions aloud.
- Call on a spokesperson from each group to share the group's hiring decision and the reasons for the choice. Make sure that Ss mention hard and soft job skills.

Expansion activity (student pairs)

- Ss in pairs. Tell Ss to imagine that one S in each pair is going to interview for the job of manager of the Custom Cleaning Company, as described on page 107. The other S will be the interviewer.
- The person applying for the job should pretend to be one of the job candidates (Richard, Jackie, Pearl, or Hassan).
- Have Ss work together to role-play an interview using the information from this lesson.
- After several minutes, the interviewer and the person applying for the job should switch roles.
- Ask pairs to perform their role-play for the class.

Expansion activity (individual work)

- Have Ss imagine that they are applying for the job of manager of the Custom Cleaning Company, as described on page 107. Ask Ss to write a cover letter explaining their qualifications. Tell Ss to refer to pages 104–105 in the Student's Book to help them write their letter. Walk around and help as needed.

- Ask Ss to take turns reading their letters to their partners. After pairs have finished reading, invite Ss to share their letters with the class.
- Discuss the cover letters with the class and offer suggestions for revisions.

> **More Ventures** (whole group, pairs, individual)
> Assign appropriate exercises from the *Teacher's Toolkit Audio CD / CD-ROM, Add Ventures*, or the *Workbook*.

Application

Community building

- **Project** Ask Ss to turn to page 139 in their Student's Book to complete the project for Unit 8.

Evaluation

- Before asking Ss to turn to the self-assessment on page 144, do a quick review of the unit. Have Ss turn to Lesson A. Ask the class to talk about what they remember about this lesson. Prompt Ss, if necessary, with questions, for example: *What are the conversations about on this page? What vocabulary is in the pictures?* Continue in this manner to review each lesson quickly.
- **Self-assessment** Read the instructions for Exercise **3**. Ask Ss to turn to the self-assessment page to complete the unit self-assessment. The self-assessments are also on the *Teacher's Toolkit Audio CD / CD-ROM*. If you prefer to collect the assessments and save them as part of each S's portfolio assessment, print out the unit self-assessment from the Toolkit, ask Ss to complete it, and collect and save it.
- If Ss are ready, administer the unit test on pages T-193–T-195 of this Teacher's Edition (or on the *Teacher's Toolkit Audio CD / CD-ROM*). The audio and audio script for the tests are on the *Teacher's Toolkit Audio CD / CD-ROM*.

2 Fun with language

A **Work** in a small group. Read about the four people who are applying for a manager position at the Custom Cleaning Company. Discuss each person. Then make a group decision about who to hire as manager. Consider their hard and soft skills in making your decision.

Richard
- Always looks for ways to help people
- Good at teaching job duties to others
- Knows how to use the equipment
- Sometimes leaves early or arrives late for work
- Goes to night school to get a business degree

Jackie
- Manages her time well
- Good listener and communicator
- Bilingual English / Spanish
- Sometimes forgets safety rules
- Was assistant manager for five years at her previous job

Pearl
- Works well with the team
- Good listener and communicator
- Often absent from work on Fridays
- Solves problems as they happen
- 15 years' experience with the company

Hassan
- Has a positive attitude – polite and friendly
- Reads and follows instructions well
- Sometimes talks too much and doesn't finish work
- Writes reports effectively
- Bilingual English / Persian

B **Share** your decision with your classmates. Give reasons for your group's choice.

3 Wrap up

Complete the **Self-assessment** on page 144.

Review

1 Listening

Listen. Take notes on a class lecture.

Job skills for an electronics store	Job skills for a restaurant
1. *good communication skills*	4. *effective time management*
2. *good listening skills*	5. *good communication skills*
3. *good problem-solving skills*	6. *ability to train others*

Talk with a partner. Check your answers.

2 Grammar

A Write. Complete the story.

Joanie's Problem

Joanie is at the electronics store. She wants to return a scanner. She

___*has been talking*___ with a clerk in customer service for the past

1. has talked / has been talking

15 minutes. He told her she could exchange the scanner. However, Joanie

___*has been looking*___ at scanners for several months, and she still

2. has looked / has been looking

___*hasn't found*___ another one she likes. She wants a refund. The

3. hasn't found / hasn't been finding

clerk ___*has just called*___ his manager this minute to see if Joanie

4. has just called / has been calling

can get a refund, but the manager is not in his office. This situation is very

___*frustrating*___ for Joanie. She's ___*tired*___ and wants

5. frustrating / frustrated   6. tiring / tired

to go home.

B Write. Look at the words that are underlined in the answers. Write
the questions.

1. **A** *What does Joanie want to return?*

   B Joanie wants to return <u>her scanner</u>.

2. **A** *How long has Joanie been talking to the clerk?*

   B Joanie has been talking to the clerk <u>for 15 minutes</u>.

3. **A** *Who said that she could exchange the scanner?*

   B <u>The customer-service clerk</u> says that she can exchange the scanner.

Talk with a partner. Ask and answer the questions.

Warm-up and review

- Before class. Write today's lesson focus on the board. *Review unit:*
  Review vocabulary and grammar from Units 7 and 8
  Practice pronouncing stressed function words

- Begin class. Books closed. Review vocabulary and grammar from Units 7 and 8. Ask Ss: *What are some of the qualities you look for if you want to make an important purchase, such as a camera, a computer, or a car?* Encourage Ss to answer using adjective clauses, for example: *I want a camera that . . .*

- Review the present perfect and the present perfect continuous. Write these sentences on the board, and ask Ss to fill in the blanks with the appropriate form of the present perfect or the present perfect continuous. Then ask Ss to make up similar sentences.
  It's 3:00 p.m. We _____ English for three hours. (study)
  It's 3:05 p.m. We _____ our English lesson for the day. (finish)

- Review adjectives ending in *-ed* and *-ing*. Write the following words on the board: *excited, relaxing, exhausting, shocked, boring.* Ask Ss to make up sentences using these adjectives.

Presentation

- Books open. Direct Ss' attention to Exercise **1** and read the instructions aloud. Tell Ss that they will hear a class lecture to which two business owners have been invited to speak.

- [Class Audio CD3 track 8] Model the task. Play or read only the first part of the lecture on the audio program (see audio script, page T-164). Pause after Mr. Sullivan says, *So, talking about job skills, I would say that first and most importantly, my employees need to have good communications skills.*

- Direct Ss' attention to number 1 in the chart under *Job skills for an electronics store,* and ask: *What does Mr. Sullivan say is one of the most important job skills for his employees in his electronics store?* (good communication skills)

- Ask a S to read aloud the other chart heading (*Job skills for a restaurant*). Say: *Now listen and complete the chart.*

- [Class Audio CD3 track 8] Play or read the complete audio program (see audio script, page T-164). Ss listen and complete the chart. Repeat the audio program as needed.

Comprehension check

- Read aloud the second part of the instructions for Exercise **1**.

- Ss check their answers in pairs. Help as needed.

Practice

- Direct Ss' attention to Exercise **2A**. Ask Ss: *What is the title of this story?* ("Joanie's Problem")

- Read the instructions aloud for Exercise **2A**.

- Ask a S to read aloud the first three sentences in the story, including the sample answer. Tell Ss to continue reading the story and filling in the blanks.

- If Ss are unfamiliar with scanners, explain that a scanner is a device that *optically scans* (similar to photographing) images, printed text, handwriting, or an object, and changes it to a digital image.

- Ss complete the exercise individually. Walk around and help as needed.

- Write the numbers *1–6* on the board. Ask Ss to come to the board to write the answers only.

- Call on several Ss to read the complete story using the answers on the board. Correct as needed.

▼**Teaching tip**
Encourage the Ss who are comfortable with this grammar review to help those who are less comfortable with these key grammar points.

Comprehension check

- Direct Ss' attention to Exercise **2B**. This exercise reviews question formation related to the reading, "Joanie's Problem."

- Read the instructions aloud. Model the task. Focus Ss' attention on the answer to number 1. Ask: *What question can you ask to get this answer?*

- Ss complete the exercise individually. Walk around and help as needed.

- Check answers with the class. Call on Ss to read their questions to the class. Correct as needed.

- Read aloud the second part of the instructions for Exercise **2B**.

- Ss work in pairs to ask and answer the questions. Help as needed.

Review

Presentation

- Books closed. Write on the board: *stressing function words*. Ask Ss if they can recall from the review for Units 5 and 6 which words are usually stressed and which are unstressed. Elicit the response: *Content words are usually stressed, and function words are usually unstressed.*
- Ask Ss to tell you which words are the function words (pronouns, prepositions, conjunctions, articles, and auxiliary verbs).
- Say the following sentence, stressing the underlined words: *Bob <u>buys</u> a <u>new cell phone</u> as soon as a <u>new one comes out</u>.*
- Ask Ss which words are stressed and which ones are unstressed. Write the sentence on the board. Indicate the stressed words by underlining them.
- Erase the underlining from the sentence on the board. Tell Ss that you are going to say the sentence in a different way. Say the sentence again, stressing the underlined words: *Bob buys a new cell phone <u>as soon as</u> a new one comes out.*
- Ask Ss: *Which words were stressed?* (as soon as) Underline *as soon as* on the board. Ask Ss: *Why would you stress these particular words?* Elicit an appropriate answer, such as: *Because this time, you want to emphasize <u>when</u> something happened.*
- Tell Ss that although we typically stress content words, we sometimes stress function words, depending on the situation and how we feel about it.

> ▼ **Teaching tip**
> Some Ss may find it difficult to differentiate between stressed and unstressed words. Take extra time to review the sounds. Exaggerate the stress in usually unstressed words so that Ss can hear the differences.

- Books open. Direct Ss to page 109, and call on a S to read the information at the top of the page.
- Focus Ss' attention on Exercise **3A** and read the instructions aloud.
- 💿 [Class Audio CD3 track 9] Play or read the complete audio program (see audio script, page T-165).
- Read the second part of the instructions for Exercise **3A**.
- 💿 [Class Audio CD3 track 10] Repeat the audio program. Pause after each phrase to give Ss time to repeat. Play the audio program as many times as needed.

Practice

- Direct Ss' attention to Exercise **3B** and read the instructions aloud.
- 💿 [Class Audio CD3 track 11] Model the activity. Play or read the first sentence on the audio program (see audio script, page T-165). Ask Ss to tell you which words are stressed.
- Have Ss pay attention to the stressed words in each sentence as they listen and repeat. Play or read the audio program, stopping as needed for Ss to repeat.
- Play or read the complete audio program again. Ss identify the stressed words by underlining them.
- Read aloud the second part of the instructions for Exercise **3B**.
- Ss complete the task in pairs. Walk around and help Ss to pronounce the stressed words correctly.

Comprehension check

- Direct Ss' attention to Exercise **3C** and read the instructions aloud.
- Ss practice the conversations with a partner. Listen to Ss' pronunciation of the stressed function words.

Application

- Focus Ss' attention on Exercise **3D** and read the instructions aloud.
- Ss work with a partner to write new conversations.
- Call on Ss to share the conversations they wrote. Correct as needed.

Evaluation

- Direct Ss' attention to the lesson focus on the board.
- Write these sentences on the board: *The DVD player was defective. I bought the DVD player at an electronics store last year.* Ask Ss to combine the sentences, using an adjective clause with *that*. (The DVD player that I bought at the electronics store last year was defective.)
- Write on the board:
  We _____ all afternoon. (have been cooking)
  (cook)
  It's 8:00 p.m. We _____ dessert. (have just eaten)
  (eat)
  Have Ss complete them with the correct form of the verb in parentheses. Tell Ss to use *just* where possible.
- Check off each part of the lesson focus as Ss demonstrate an understanding of what they have learned in the lesson.

3 Pronunciation: stressing function words

Normally, function words such as pronouns, prepositions, conjunctions, articles, *to be* verbs, and auxiliary verbs are *not* stressed. However, when strong feelings or disagreements are expressed, function words can receive strong stress.

A 💿 **Listen** to the stressed function words in each conversation.

1. **A** Is the camera defective?
   B It's defective <u>and</u> too small!

2. **A** Don't you usually finish at 5:00?
   B I <u>do</u> usually finish at 5:00, but not today.

3. **A** Why aren't you applying for that job?
   B I <u>am</u>. I'll go there tomorrow.

4. **A** I don't trust the man who sold you this car.
   B Well, <u>I</u> <u>do</u>! It's <u>my</u> decision, not <u>yours</u>.

5. **A** Is he excited about his new job?
   B No, but his wife <u>is</u>.

6. **A** Did you put the returned merchandise on my desk?
   B No, I put it <u>in</u> your desk.

💿 **Listen again and repeat.** Stress the underlined function words.

B 💿 **Listen and repeat.** Then underline the stressed function words.

1. **A** I'd like to exchange this sweater.
   B Why?
   A It's too big, <u>and</u> it has a hole.

2. **A** You <u>can't</u> leave early again!
   B Yes, I <u>can</u> and I <u>will</u>.

3. **A** Why don't you clean the counters?
   B Why don't <u>you</u>?

4. **A** Let's talk about a raise after you've worked here for six months.
   B Can we talk <u>before</u> six months?

Talk with a partner. Compare your answers.

C **Talk** with a partner. Practice the conversations. Pay attention to the stressed function words.

1. **A** We don't give refunds or exchanges on watches.
   B My warranty says you <u>can</u> if the merchandise is defective.
   A So, <u>is</u> it defective?
   B Yes, it <u>is</u>.
   A Then I <u>can</u> give you a refund.

2. **A** Who just mopped the floors, <u>you</u> or <u>Kevin</u>?
   B <u>I</u> did. <u>And</u> I cleaned the tables.
   A Good work. I <u>do</u> enjoy seeing a clean bakery.
   B And <u>I</u> love working here.

D **Write** two new conversations using stressed function words. Practice with a partner.

A Does Karen need more help?
B No, but <u>I</u> do.

Lesson **A** *Get ready*

1 Talk about the pictures

A What do you see?
B What is happening?

Mr. Conway
The Living Green Council

Mei

Lesson objectives
- Introduce students to the topic
- Find out what students know about the topic
- Preview the unit by talking about the pictures
- Practice key vocabulary
- Practice listening skills

Warm-up and review

- Before class. Write today's lesson focus on the board.
  Lesson A:
  Ask questions about "living green"
  Discuss causes and effects of environmental problems
  Discuss human actions that could help the environment

- Begin class. Books closed. Direct Ss' attention to the words *environmental problems* in the lesson focus. Ask Ss: *What are some examples of environmental problems?* List Ss' responses on the board, for example: *pollution, global warming, rain-forest destruction (deforestation), endangered species, overpopulation.*

- Point to *human actions that could help the environment.* Ask Ss: *What are some actions we could take to help save the environment?* List Ss' responses on the board, for example: *cleaning up litter, recycling, saving energy, driving less, carpooling, using alternative forms of energy.*

- Ask Ss: *What do you think "living green" means?* Answers will vary, but may include: *trying to be more environmentally aware, changing personal habits to help the environment.* Write Ss' responses on the board.

Presentation

- Books open. Set the scene. Direct Ss' attention to the first picture on page 110. Ask the question from Exercise **1A**: *What do you see?* Elicit and write on the board as much vocabulary about the picture as possible, for example: *classroom, fluorescent lightbulb, regular lightbulb, charts about the body, biology textbook.* Continue eliciting words to describe the second picture and write them on the board. Explain any unfamiliar words.

- Ask individual Ss to look at the two pictures and talk about the similarities and differences. Elicit appropriate responses, such as: *Mei is in both of them. In the first one, she is at school; in the second one, she is at home with her parents.*

- Direct Ss' attention to the question in Exercise **1B**: *What is happening?* Read it aloud. Hold up the Student's Book. Point to the first picture. Ask: *What's Mei doing here?* (She's listening to the speaker.) Say: *What do you think the speaker is talking about?*

- Point to the second picture. Ask: *What's Mei doing here?* (She's looking at something on her computer.)

▼ Teaching tip
Encourage Ss to be creative. At this point, there is no single correct answer.

Expansion activity (small groups)

- Ss in small groups. Assign each group one of the pictures in the Student's Book, and have Ss create a conversation between the people in the picture (either between Mei and the speaker, or Mei and her parents).

- Listen as two or three Ss practice their conversation. Walk around and help as needed.

- Ask several Ss to perform their role play for the class.

Expansion activity (small groups)

- Write the following on the board: *Your community's environmental activities.*

- Ask Ss: *Do you know of any activities in your community that are environmentally friendly?* Then say: *Talk with your classmates and make a list of these activities. If your community doesn't do anything right now, make a list of what it could do, such as saving water, cleaning up a park, or promoting a recycling program.*

- Ss work in small groups to discuss the question and make a list. Walk around and help as needed.

- After several minutes, invite Ss to share information they discussed with their groups.

- Write several examples on the board, for example: *reducing waste, reusing bottles, recycling newspapers and cans, cleaning up a lake or beach, protecting wildlife.*

Presentation

- Books open. Direct Ss' attention to Exercise **2A**. Have Ss listen for the main idea. Read the instructions aloud.
- [Class Audio CD3 track 12] Play or read the audio program (see audio script, page T-165).
- Ask Ss if they have understood everything in the listening exercise. Write any unfamiliar words on the board and help Ss understand the meaning of each word.
- Elicit answers to the questions.
- Focus Ss' attention on Exercise **2B**. Read the instructions aloud.
- [Class Audio CD3 track 13] Tell Ss to listen for details about Mei's conversation with her parents and her suggestions for what they could try to do at home to conserve energy and protect the environment. Play or read the audio program again. Pause the program after Mei says: *OK, well, first of all, he said we need to cut down on driving, so we should walk, ride a bicycle, carpool, or take public transportation.*
- Point to where *walk, bike, carpool, take public transportation* is written in the chart. Tell Ss to listen and complete the chart with the ideas for "living green." Play or read the rest of the audio program.
- Direct Ss' attention to the second part of the instructions for Exercise **2B**.
- [Class Audio CD3 track 13] Play or read the audio program again (see audio script, page T-165). Ss listen and check their answers.
- Copy the chart from Exercise **2B** on the board. Ask several Ss to come to the board and write their answers. Make corrections on the board as needed.

Practice

- Focus Ss' attention on Exercise **2C**. Read the instructions aloud. Tell Ss that the story in this exercise is a summary of what happened in the pictures on the previous page.
- Direct Ss' attention to the words in the word bank. Say each word aloud. Ask Ss to repeat. Explain any unfamiliar words.
- Model the exercise. Ask a S to read aloud the first two sentences in the story, including the sample answer for number 2. Point out that Ss need to fill in the remaining blanks with the words from the word bank.
- Ss complete the exercise individually. Walk around and help as needed.

Comprehension check

- [Class Audio CD3 track 14] Play or read the audio program (see audio script, page T-165). Ss listen and check their answers. Repeat the audio program as needed.
- Write the numbers *1–8* on the board. Ask eight Ss to come to the board to write their answers.

Learner persistence (individual work)

- [Self-Study Audio CD tracks 28 and 29] Exercises **2A**, **2B**, and **2C** are recorded on the Ss' self-study CD at the back of the Student's Book. Ss can listen to the CD at home for reinforcement and review. They can also listen for self-directed learning when class attendance is not possible.

Application

- Focus Ss' attention on Exercise **2D** and read the instructions aloud.
- Ss work in a small group to answer the questions. Walk around and help as needed.
- Open up the discussion to the class. Ask Ss to share the suggestions that are difficult for them, and have them tell why.

Expansion activity (student pairs)

- Have Ss imagine that they are having a conversation with their family similar to the one that Mei is having with her parents. What would they say? What would their parents (or children) say? Have Ss take turns in their group talking about their "living green" conversation with a relative.
- Have Ss in each group form pairs. Ask pairs to write a dialog based on their conversation. Ss can use the ideas that Mei presented or their own.
- Ss practice their dialog with a partner. Walk around and help as needed.
- Ask several pairs to perform their dialogs for the class.

Evaluation

- Direct Ss' attention to the lesson focus on the board. Ask individual Ss to look at the pictures on page 110 to make sentences using the words in Exercise **2C**.
- Check off each part of the lesson focus as Ss demonstrate an understanding of what they have learned in the lesson.

> **More Ventures** (whole group, pairs, individual)
> Assign appropriate exercises from the *Teacher's Toolkit Audio CD / CD-ROM, Add Ventures,* or the *Workbook*.

2 Listening

 **A** 🔊 **Listen** and answer the questions.

1. Who are the speakers?
2. What are they talking about?

 **B** 🔊 **Listen again.** Complete the chart.

Ideas for living green	Will the family try?
1. *walk, bike, carpool, take public transportation*	*No*
2. *recycle*	*Yes*
3. *turn off unnecessary lights*	*Yes*
4. *wash clothes in cold water*	*Yes*
5. *buy energy-efficient appliances*	*No*
6. *switch to energy-efficient lightbulbs*	*Yes*

Listen again. Check your answers.

 **C** 🔊 **Read.** Complete the story. Listen and check your answers.

appliances	cut down on	environment	recycle
carpool	energy-efficient	global warming	responsibility

Mei was late to dinner because she was looking at the Web site of the Living Green Council. "Living green" means taking ___*responsibility*___ for saving the
1
earth from ___*global warming*___ . Mei tells her parents about the guest speaker
2
who came to her class. The speaker suggested simple things people could do to reduce their energy use and protect the ___*environment*___ . For example, they could
3
___*carpool*___ instead of driving alone, ___*recycle*___ their bottles
4   5
and cans, and use ___*energy-efficient*___ lightbulbs. Mei's parents agree that it is
6
important to ___*cut down on*___ energy use since it would also help them save
7
money. However, they can't afford to buy new ___*appliances*___ right now.
8

D **Discuss.** Talk with your classmates. Which of the speaker's suggestions can you try? Which are difficult for you? Why?

Conditional sentences

1 Grammar focus: present unreal conditional

If everybody drove smaller cars, we would use less gasoline.
We would use less gasoline if everybody drove smaller cars.

For a grammar explanation, turn to page 152.

> **Useful language**
> Use *would* when you are 100 percent s
> Use *could* if you are less certain.

2 Practice

A Write. Complete the sentences. Use the present unreal conditional.

1. Many people put their newspapers in the trash can.

   If everybody _____ *recycled* _____ newspapers,
   (recycle)

   we _____ *would save* _____ millions of trees.
   (save)

2. Noah never takes his car in for a tune-up.

   Noah's car _____ *would use* _____ less gas if he
   (use)

   _____ *tuned up* _____ his car regularly.
   (tune up)

3. Mr. Brown drives his own car to his job downtown.

   Mr. Brown _____ *would save* _____ money on gas if he
   (save)

   _____ *carpooled* _____ to work.
   (carpool)

4. Many items in the supermarket are packaged in plastic.

   If you _____ *bought* _____ products that are packaged with recycled
   (buy)

   paper, you _____ *would help* _____ to reduce global warming.
   (help)

5. Jessica always stays in the shower for a very long time.

   If Jessica _____ *took* _____ shorter showers, she
   (take)

   _____ *would save* _____ water.
   (save)

6. Some kinds of fish contain large amounts of lead, a poisonous metal.

   You _____ *would be* _____ healthier if you _____ *stopped* _____
   (be)   (stop)

   eating fish that contains lead.

   Listen and check your answers.

Warm-up and review

- Before class. Write today's lesson focus on the board. *Lesson B:*
  Use the present unreal conditional
- Begin class. Books closed. Review key vocabulary from the unit by asking Ss what it means to "live green" and how they can protect the environment. Elicit appropriate responses, such as: *Living green means taking responsibility for helping to save the earth. Instead of driving, walk, ride a bicycle, carpool, or take public transportation. Recycle bottles, cans, glass, plastic, aluminum products, and paper. Wash clothes in cold water. Buy energy-efficient appliances and lightbulbs.* Write Ss' responses on the board.

Presentation

- Books open. Direct Ss' attention to the grammar chart in Exercise **1**. Read the two sentences aloud.

> **Useful language**
>
> Read the tip box aloud. Write the two sentences from the grammar focus on the board: *If everybody drove smaller cars, we would use less gasoline. We would use less gasoline if everybody drove smaller cars.* Say each of the sentences aloud. Tell Ss that because we are positive that the result of driving smaller cars would save gasoline, we use *would,* instead of *could.* If we want to talk about something that is possible but not definite, we often use *could.* For example: *If we changed our living habits, we could make a difference.*

- Tell Ss that the present unreal conditional is used to talk about what people would generally do in imaginary, or unreal, situations. Direct Ss' attention to the sentences on the board. Say: *It's not possible that everyone would drive a smaller car, so the situation is considered unreal.*
- Point out that the present unreal conditional is formed with *if* + subject + past tense form of the verb in the dependent clause, and subject + *would* + base form of the verb in the main clause. However, the form of the verb *be* is always *were,* not *was.* For example, Ss should use: *If I were you,* not *If I was you,* when giving advice.

- Direct Ss' attention to the first sentence on the board. Circle the comma. Tell Ss that they should use a comma only if the *if* clause (the dependent clause) is at the beginning of a sentence. Show Ss that there is no comma in the second sentence on the board because the *if* clause is not at the beginning of the sentence.
- Explain to Ss that changing the order of the clauses in a present unreal conditional statement does not affect the meaning.

> ▼ **Teaching tip**
> It might be helpful to refer Ss to the grammar explanation on page 152 in the Student's Book.

Practice

- Focus Ss' attention on Exercise **2A** and read the instructions aloud.
- Call on a S to read the first example. Make sure that Ss understand the exercise.
- Ss complete the exercise individually. Walk around and help as needed.

Comprehension check

- Direct Ss' attention to the second part of the instructions for Exercise **2A**.
- [Class Audio CD3 track 15] Play or read the audio program (see audio script, page T-165). Ss listen and check their answers. Repeat the audio program as needed.
- Write the numbers *1–6* on the board. Ask several Ss to come to the board to write their answers in complete sentences. Make corrections on the board as needed.

Conditional sentences

Practice

- Books open. Tell Ss that they are going to read and talk about the causes and effects of different activities related to living green. Read the instructions aloud for Exercise **2B**.
- Direct Ss' attention to the phrases under the two headings, *Actions* and *Results*. Call on one S to read the actions and another S to read the results.
- Model the task. Call on a S to read the example sentence.
- Ss complete the exercise in pairs, matching each action with an environmentally friendly result. Walk around and help as needed.
- Direct Ss' attention to the second part of Exercise **2B** and read the instructions aloud.
- Ask a S to read the example sentence to the class.
- Ss work individually to complete the exercise. Walk around and help as needed.
- Have individual Ss come to the board to write their sentences. Work with the class to make corrections on the board as needed.

Application

- Direct Ss' attention to Exercise **3A** and read the instructions aloud. Point out that *could* is used in this exercise because the sentences are about the possibility of something occurring.
- Model the task. Ask a S to read the example sentence.
- Ss work in a small group to complete the exercise. Walk around and help as needed.
- Direct Ss' attention to Exercise **3B** and read the instructions aloud.
- Have Ss take turns sharing information they discussed with their groups.

Expansion activity (student pairs)

- Ask partners to prepare a dialog in which they suggest that someone change his or her habits in order to protect the environment. Ss take turns being the one who convinces and the one who needs convincing. Instruct Ss to use the vocabulary from the unit as well as the grammar just discussed. Tell Ss that they are not required to write the dialog for their role play.

- Model the task. Write the following on the board:
  - *S1: We can all take more responsibility for saving the earth.*
  - *S2: I'm only one person! What can I do?*
  - *S1: Well, if you recycled your garbage, you could reduce the amount of trash in landfills.*
  - *S2: How can I do that? I'm so busy!*
  - *S1: All you need to do is separate your cans, glass, plastic, newspapers, cardboard, and other paper products.*
- Call on two Ss to read the sample dialog. Ss complete the exercise in pairs.
- After a few minutes, call on several pairs to perform their role play for the class.

Evaluation

- Books closed. Direct Ss' attention to the lesson focus on the board.
- Write the following on the board:
  If everybody _____ cans, bottles, and glass, we _____
       (recycle)   (have)
  a lot less garbage.
  We _____ millions of trees if everybody _____ paper.
       (save)   (recycle)
- Ask Ss to tell you the correct form of the verbs and to fill in the blanks. Elicit: *recycled, would have; would save* or *could save, recycled.*
- Check off the lesson focus as Ss demonstrate an understanding of what they have learned in the lesson.

More Ventures (whole group, pairs, individual)
Assign appropriate exercises from the *Teacher's Toolkit Audio CD / CD-ROM, Add Ventures,* or the *Workbook.*

B **Talk** with a partner. Match each action with a result. Some items have more than one correct answer. Use the present unreal conditional.

> If everybody bought energy-efficient appliances, we would save electricity.

Actions	Results
buy energy-efficient appliances	save gas
fix water leaks	cut down on energy use
replace lightbulbs with energy-efficient ones	save water
recycle cans, bottles, glass, and paper	reduce air-conditioning and heating use
put enough air in their tires	reduce the amount of trash in landfills
close off unused rooms	save electricity

Write sentences about the actions and results.

If everybody bought energy-efficient appliances, we would save electricity.

3 Communicate

A **Work** in a small group. Look at the picture. Talk about actions people could take to help the environment at the beach.

> If people picked up the trash on the beach, everyone could enjoy a clean beach.

B **Share** ideas with your classmates.

Lesson C Connectors

1 Grammar focus: *since, due to, consequently, as a result*

Connectors of cause

Since the earth is getting warmer, the polar ice caps are melting.
Due to the warmer temperatures, the polar ice caps are melting.

Connectors of effect

The earth is getting warmer. Consequently, the polar ice caps are melting.
The earth is getting warmer. As a result, the polar ice caps are melting.

For a grammar explanation, turn to page 152.

Useful langua;

Because can replace
Because of can repla
due to.

Therefore can replac
consequently or
as a result.

2 Practice

A Write. Combine the sentences. Use the connectors in parentheses.

1. There is a buildup of harmful gases in the atmosphere. Global warming is increasing.

   (Due to) *Due to a buildup of harmful gases in the atmosphere, global warming is increasing.*

2. Warm water is expanding in the oceans. The sea level is rising.

   (As a result) *Warm water is expanding in the oceans. As a result, the sea level is rising.*

3. The sea level is rising. Towns near oceans are in danger of flooding.

   (Since) *Since the sea level is rising, towns near oceans are in danger of flooding.*

4. Global warming changes weather patterns. Many places will have less rainfall.

   (Since) *Since global warming changes weather patterns, many places will have less rainfall.*

5. Mosquitoes will increase. There will be an increase in diseases like malaria.

   (Consequently) *Mosquitoes will increase. Consequently, there will be an increase in diseases like malaria.*

6. Ocean water is getting warmer. Typhoons and hurricanes are becoming more frequent.

   (Due to) *Due to ocean water getting warmer, typhoons and hurricanes are becoming more frequent.*

7. Cities are growing. Many plants and animals may lose their natural habitats.

   (As a result) *Cities are growing. As a result, many plants and animals may lose their natural habitats.*

   Listen and check your answers.

Lesson objective
- Introduce the connectors *since, due to, consequently, as a result*

Warm-up and review

- Before class. Write today's lesson focus on the board.
  Lesson C:
  Use since, due to, consequently, and as a result
- Begin class. Books open. Direct Ss' attention to the phrases on page 113 under *Actions* and *Results*. Call on a S to make a sentence using these phrases with *if* and *would* in the present unreal conditional. Elicit an appropriate response, such as: *If everybody fixed water leaks, we would save water.*
- Write the following on the board:
  Since there are many water leaks, a lot of water is wasted.
  Due to many water leaks, a lot of water is wasted.
  There are a lot of water leaks. Consequently, a lot of water is wasted.
  There are a lot of water leaks. As a result, a lot of water is wasted.
- Call on four Ss in turn to read the four example sentences on the board.
- Ask Ss what the underlined words have in common. Elicit an appropriate response, such as: *The underlined words are connectors. They show causes and effects. They can be used to combine sentences.*

Presentation

- Books open. Direct Ss' attention to the grammar chart in Exercise **1**. Read aloud the two headings and the corresponding statements.
- Focus Ss' attention on the sentence beginning with *Due to*. Explain that *Due to* and *Because of* must be followed by a noun or noun phrase (e.g., *the warmer temperatures*), rather than a main clause consisting of a subject and a verb.
- Point out the positioning of the connectors of effect. Ss should notice that although *consequently* and *as a result* can begin a sentence, related information has to be included in the previous sentence to connect the ideas.

Useful language

Read the tip box aloud. Point to the sentences you wrote on the board in the Warm-up. On the board, write *Because* (next to *Since*), *Because of* (next to *Due to*), and *Therefore* (above *Consequently* and *As a result*). Read aloud the sentences with the substituted words. Ask Ss: *If these connectors mean the same thing, why do we use them?* Elicit an appropriate answer, for example: *It helps writers make their writing more interesting and less repetitive.*

- Tell Ss that when using *since, due to, because,* or *because of,* they should use a comma when the dependent clause occurs at the beginning of the sentence. For example, a comma follows *Since the earth is getting warmer* and *Due to the warmer temperatures* in the example sentences. *Therefore, as a result,* and *consequently* are immediately followed by a comma.

▼ Teaching tip

It might be helpful to refer Ss to the grammar explanation on page 152 in the Student's Book.

Practice

- Direct Ss' attention to Exercise **2A** and read the instructions aloud.
- Ask a S to read aloud the first two sentences in number 1 and the example combined sentence. Point out to Ss that in the combined sentence, *There is* is omitted. *Due to* is immediately followed by the noun phrase: *a buildup of harmful gases in the atmosphere*.
- Call on another S to read number 2 and the example answer.
- Ss complete the exercise individually. Walk around and help as needed.

▼ Teaching tip

You might wish to mention that when combining two sentences, Ss can use a semicolon instead of a period, before a connector of effect, such as *consequently, as a result,* and *therefore.* Tell Ss that a comma always follows the connector.

Comprehension check

- Read aloud the second part of the instructions for Exercise **2A**.
- 🔘 [Class Audio CD3 track 16] Play or read the audio program (see audio script, page T-165). Ss listen and check their answers.
- Write the numbers *1–7* on the board. Ask seven Ss to come to the board to write their answers. Make corrections on the board as needed.

Practice

- Read the instructions aloud for Exercise **2B**.
- Focus Ss' attention on the cause-and-effect chart. Call on a S to read the two headings: *Causes* and *Effects*. Ask six Ss to read each of the causes and corresponding effects.
- Explain vocabulary as needed. Write any words on the board that are unfamiliar to Ss.
- Have two Ss read the example dialog above the chart. Ask Ss to identify the connectors in each sentence. (Since, As a result)
- Ss complete the exercise with a partner. Walk around and help as needed.
- Read the instructions aloud for the second part of Exercise **2B**. Call on a S to read aloud the example sentence.
- Ss complete the exercise individually. Walk around and help as needed.
- Ask several Ss to write their sentences on the board. Ask other Ss to read aloud each of the sentences. Ask: *Is this sentence correct?* Make corrections on the board as needed.

Expansion activity (small groups)

- Ask Ss to talk about the causes and effects of air, land, or water pollution. Have them discuss the causes and effects using connectors.
- Ss work in groups to write several sentences on the topic of pollution using the connectors *since, because, because of, due to, consequently, therefore,* and *as a result.*
- Walk around and help as needed.
- Call on Ss from each group to write sentences on the board. Work with the class to make corrections on the board as needed.

Application

- Direct Ss' attention to Exercise **3A** and read the instructions aloud.
- Focus Ss' attention on the pictures in Exercise **3A**. Ask three Ss to read the headlines. Make sure that Ss understand what has happened in each picture.
- Call on another S to read the example sentence.

- Ss work in a small group to complete the exercise. Walk around and help as needed.
- Direct Ss' attention to Exercise **3B** and read the instructions aloud.
- Continue the exercise by asking each group to share information they discussed with another group of classmates.

Expansion activity (small groups)

- **Materials needed** Enough copies of one or more newspaper or magazine articles about habitat loss for each small group of Ss.
- Distribute to each small group a copy of the same (or a different) newspaper or magazine article about habitat loss and how it is endangering species and frightening people in communities.
- If possible, before reading, elicit from Ss the causes of habitat loss, including the suburbanization of rural areas, which is causing animals, such as alligators, coyotes, deer, and the Florida panther, to lose their homes and invade populated areas.
- Encourage each group to make a cause-and-effect chart to organize the article as they take turns reading and to share their chart with the class, using connectors of cause and effect in their discussion.

Evaluation

- Direct Ss' attention to the lesson focus on the board. Ask Ss to look at the pictures on page 115 and write sentences about each picture. Call on Ss to read their sentences aloud.
- Check off the lesson focus as Ss demonstrate an understanding of what they have learned in the lesson.

> ***More Ventures*** (whole group, pairs, individual)
> Assign appropriate exercises from the *Teacher's Toolkit Audio CD / CD-ROM, Add Ventures,* or the *Workbook.*

B Talk with a partner. Combine sentences in different ways using the connectors *since*, *because*, *because of*, *due to*, *consequently*, *therefore*, and *as a result*.

> **A** Since people are building homes in forests, animals are losing their natural habitats.
> **B** People are building homes in forests. As a result, animals are losing their natural habitats.

Causes	Effects
1. People are building homes in forests.	Animals are losing their natural habitats.
2. There is habitat loss.	Animals are moving into towns and cities.
3. Animals are moving into towns and cities.	The animals are frightened.
4. The animals are frightened.	Sometimes they attack people.
5. Wild animals sometimes attack people.	People are afraid of them.
6. People are afraid of wild animals.	They kill the animals.

Write sentences about the causes and effects.

Since people are building homes in forests, animals are losing their natural habitats.

3 Communicate

A Work in a small group. Read the newspaper headlines. Discuss the possible causes and effects of each event. Think of other possible headlines to discuss.

> Coyotes are losing their natural habitats. As a result, they're moving into towns.

THE MESSENGER
Another Coyote Moves into Town

THE NEWS
WHALE WASHES UP ON SHORE

THE DAILY
POLAR BEARS DROWNING AS ICE CAPS MELT

B Share information with your classmates.

1 Before you read

Talk with your classmates. Answer the questions.

1. What is a *fable*?
2. Do you know any fables or folktales from your native country? Which ones?

2 Read

SELF-STUDY
AUDIO CD  **Read** the fable. Listen and read again.

~ All Things Are Connected ~

Long ago, there was a village chief who never allowed anyone to disagree with him. Whenever he wanted to do something, he asked the members of his court for their advice. But whether the chief's idea was wise or foolish, his advisors always said the same thing: "Indeed, it is wise." Only one old woman dared to give a different answer. Whenever the chief asked for her advice, she always replied, "All things are connected."

One night, the chief was awakened by the sound of frogs croaking in the swamp. It happened again the next night and the next and the next. The chief decided to kill all the frogs in the swamp. When he consulted the members of his court, they replied as usual: "Indeed, it is wise." But the old woman kept silent. "And you, old woman, what do you think?" the chief demanded. "All things are connected," she replied. The chief concluded that the old woman was a fool, and he ordered his servants to kill all the frogs. As a result, the chief slept peacefully.

But soon the mosquitoes in the swamp began to multiply since there were no frogs to eat them. They came into the village and made everyone miserable. The chief ordered his servants to go into the swamp and kill the mosquitoes, but it was impossible. Furious, the chief summoned the members of his court and blamed them, saying, "Why didn't you tell me that killing the frogs would make the mosquitoes multiply and everyone would be miserable? I should have listened to the old woman."

Due to the mosquitoes, all the people of the village were forced to go away. Finally, the chief and his family left, too. Until he died, the chief never forgot the old woman's words: "All things are connected."

Warm-up and review

- Before class. Write today's lesson focus on the board.
  Lesson D:
  Read and understand "All Things Are Connected"
  Practice new vocabulary related to the environment
  Use synonyms
- Begin class. Books closed. Focus Ss' attention on the title of the reading, "All Things Are Connected." Ask Ss these questions: *What do you think the title means? How do you think the reading will relate to the environment?* Elicit appropriate responses, for example: *The title means that everything we do has an effect on everything else on earth. If we cut down on pollution, we will help save the earth.*

Presentation

- Books open. Direct Ss' attention to Exercise **1** and read the instructions aloud.
- Have Ss focus on the two questions in Exercise **1**. Ask two Ss to read them aloud.
- Ss answer the questions with a partner, citing fables or folktales they know from their home country.
- Call on pairs to share their answers with the class. Elicit a lively discussion of world folktales, guiding Ss to see that similarities exist among many folktales of different cultures or countries.

Practice

- Read the instructions aloud for Exercise **2**. Ask Ss to read the fable silently before listening to the audio program.
- [Class Audio CD3 track 17] Play or read the audio program and ask Ss to read along (see audio script, page T-166). Repeat the audio program as needed.
- While Ss are listening and reading the fable, ask them to underline any words they don't know. When the audio program is finished, have Ss write the new vocabulary words on the board.

- Point to each word on the board, say it, and have Ss repeat. Give a brief explanation of each word, or ask Ss to guess the meaning of each word from context clues in the fable. Allow Ss to look up new words in their dictionaries.

Learner persistence *(individual work)*

- [Self-Study Audio CD track 30] Exercise **2** is recorded on the Ss' self-study CD at the back of the Student's Book. Ss can listen to the CD at home for reinforcement and review. They can also listen to the CD for self-directed learning when class attendance is not possible.

Expansion activity *(small groups)*

- **Materials needed** A dictionary for each group of three to four Ss and a different Aesop's fable for each group. (Review the fables before class to familiarize yourself with the content and to preview any vocabulary that you may need to preteach to Ss.)
- Explain to Ss that all fables, such as the one they have just read, teach a lesson, or *moral*. Ask Ss: *What is the moral of "All Things Are Connected"?* Write Ss' answers on the board, such as: *All things in nature are connected. Everything in nature depends on everything else for its survival.*
- Ss in groups of three or four. Distribute a different fable to each group. Preteach vocabulary as needed. Have Ss in each group take turns reading the fable aloud and looking up any new words in the dictionary. Walk around and help as needed.
- Ss should prepare a summary of their group's fable and talk about the moral it teaches.
- Encourage a S from each group to summarize the group's fable for the class without telling the moral. Then invite Ss from other groups to guess the moral of the fable.

Lesson D Reading

Comprehension check

- Direct Ss' attention to Exercise **3A** and read the instructions aloud.
- Ask nine Ss to read the questions. Make sure that all Ss understand the questions.
- Ss complete the exercise individually. Walk around and help as needed.
- Discuss the answers to the questions with the class. Have Ss indicate where they found the answers in the reading.

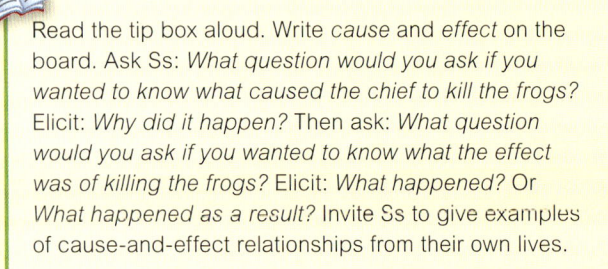

Read the tip box aloud. Write *cause* and *effect* on the board. Ask Ss: *What question would you ask if you wanted to know what caused the chief to kill the frogs?* Elicit: *Why did it happen?* Then ask: *What question would you ask if you wanted to know what the effect was of killing the frogs?* Elicit: *What happened?* Or *What happened as a result?* Invite Ss to give examples of cause-and-effect relationships from their own lives.

Expansion activity *(student pairs)*

- Draw a cause-and-effect chart on the board similar to the one on page 115.
- Tell Ss that they should refer to the fable in Exercise **2** on page 116 to complete the chart.
- Model the task. Write *Frogs were croaking in the swamp.* on the board and ask Ss: *What was the effect?* Elicit an appropriate response, such as: *The chief couldn't sleep.* Write the examples in the chart on the board.

Causes	Effects
Frogs were croaking in the swamp.	*The chief couldn't sleep.*

- Ss work in pairs to find three cause-and-effect relationships in the story. Call on pairs to share what they wrote. Write their answers in the chart on the board.

Practice

- **Materials needed** A dictionary for each S.
- Direct Ss' attention to Exercise **3B**. Read the instructions aloud for number 1. Call on Ss to read each of the seven words in the chart in number 3.
- Ss work individually to underline the words from the chart in the reading, "All Things Are Connected."
- Call on a S to read the instructions for number 2 of Exercise **3B**.
- Say the word *synonym* and have Ss repeat. Tell Ss that we use synonyms to make our writing or speech more lively or interesting and less repetitive.

- Focus Ss' attention on the headings in the chart. Read aloud the three headings. Call on a S to read the first example in the chart.
- Ss work individually to write the part of speech and a synonym for each word in the chart. Help as needed.
- Ss in pairs. Have Ss show their partner where they underlined the words in the reading and the synonym they chose for each of the words.
- Review with the class. Write the chart on the board from page 117. Call on seven Ss to come to the board to fill in the chart. Work with the class to make corrections on the board as needed.
- Call on a S to read the instructions for number 3 of Exercise **3B**.
- Ss work in small groups to write sentences with the synonyms in the chart. Walk around and help as needed.

Application

- Direct Ss' attention to Exercise **3C** and read the instructions aloud.
- Call on five Ss to read the questions in Exercise **3C**.
- Ss ask and answer questions with a partner.
- Ask several pairs to share their answers with the class.

Evaluation

- Direct Ss' attention to the lesson focus on the board.
- Books closed. Ask individual Ss to retell the main points of the reading, "All Things Are Connected."
- Focus Ss' attention on the words from the reading passage in the first column of the chart in Exercise **3B**. Ask Ss to write a sentence for each word to show that they understand the meaning of each word.
- Check off each part of the lesson focus as Ss demonstrate an understanding of what they have learned in the lesson.

Learner persistence *(individual work, student pairs)*

- You may wish to assign Extended reading worksheets from the *Teacher's Toolkit Audio CD / CD-ROM* for Ss to complete outside of class. The purpose of these worksheets is to encourage Ss to read for pleasure in English outside of the English class. The worksheets can also be assigned as extended reading in class.

More Ventures *(whole group, pairs, individual)*
Assign appropriate exercises from the *Teacher's Toolkit Audio CD / CD-ROM, Add Ventures,* or the *Workbook.*

3 After you read

A Check your understanding.

1. Why couldn't the chief sleep?
2. What did he decide to do?
3. What did the members of his court say?
4. What did the old woman say?
5. What did the servants do?
6. What happened as a result?
7. Why was the chief furious?
8. Why did the people leave the village?
9. After reading the story, what does the title mean to you?

Ask yourself questions when you read to identify a cause-and-effect relationship.

- To find an effect, ask, "What happened?"
- To find a cause, ask, "Why did it happen?"

B Build your vocabulary.

1. Underline the words from the chart in the reading passage.

2. Use a dictionary or a thesaurus. Write the part of speech. Write a synonym for each word. A synonym is a word that has the same or similar meaning.

3. Work in a small group. Write sentences with the synonyms.

Word	Part of speech	Synonym
wise	adjective	sensible (Answers may vary.)
replied	verb	responded; answered
connected	adjective	joined
peacefully	adverb	calmly; undisturbed
multiply	verb	increase
miserable	adjective	unhappy
furious	adjective	angry

C Talk with a partner.

1. Do you think it is wise to follow other people's advice? Why or why not?
2. Give examples to show how plants and animals are connected.
3. How can people solve their conflicts peacefully?
4. What kind of weather makes you miserable?
5. What makes you furious?

1 Before you write

A **Talk** with a partner. Look at the picture. Answer the questions.

1. What is the environmental problem in this photo?
2. Why is it a problem? (causes)
3. How does this problem hurt people and the environment? (effects)

B **Read** the paragraph.

The Causes and Effects of Smog

Smog is a serious environmental problem in my city. One cause is that there are too many cars on the roads and highways. Most of the cars have only one person – the driver. People seem to take a lot of unnecessary trips. They drive to the drugstore instead of walking two blocks. Another cause of smog in my city is that we use too much electricity. Since many homes are not energy-efficient, our city's power plant has to produce more electricity. The burning coal from the power plant produces more air pollution. Due to the smog, the air is hard to breathe. Consequently, on many days it is unsafe for children and senior citizens to be outside. Smog also kills many trees and plants that produce oxygen and clean the air. If people drove less and used less electricity, I am sure our air quality would improve.

> One way to organize a paragraph is to discuss the causes and effects of a problem.

C **Work** with a partner. Complete the outline of the model paragraph.

Problem: Smog

Causes	Effects
1. *too many cars*	
(detail) a. *most cars have only one driver*	
(detail) b. *people take unnecessary trips*	1. *air hard to breathe*
2. *use too much electricity*	2. *unsafe for children and senior citizens to be outside*
(detail) a. *many homes not energy-efficient*	3. *smog kills trees and plants that produce oxygen and clean the air*
(detail) b. *burning coal from power plant produces air pollution*	

- Write a paragraph about an environmental problem

Warm-up and review

- Before class. Write today's lesson focus on the board.
  Lesson E:
  Write a paragraph about an environmental problem
- Begin class. Books closed. Review cause and effect by asking Ss questions about the fable in Lesson D:
  What was the fable "All Things Are Connected" about? (It was about what happens when you don't think carefully about how your actions will affect the environment.)
  What was the cause of the chief's problem? (He couldn't sleep because of the sound of the frogs croaking in the middle of the night.)
  What advice did the chief receive but decide not to follow? (He didn't listen to the wise old woman, who warned him not to kill all the frogs because in nature, "all things are connected.")
  What was the effect of the chief's not listening to the old woman's advice? (The mosquitoes multiplied, and all the people in the village were forced to leave.)

Presentation

- Books open. Direct Ss' attention to Exercise **1A** and read the instructions aloud.
- Ask three Ss to read the questions in Exercise **1A**.
- Ss work with a partner to answer the questions. Partners may wish to list the causes and effects of the environmental problem shown in the picture. Walk around and help as needed.

Practice

- Direct Ss' attention to Exercise **1B** and read the instructions aloud.
- Ss read the paragraph silently. Ask Ss to underline any words with which they are unfamiliar.
- Have Ss tell you the words they underlined, and write them on the board. Go over the meaning of each word.

▼**Teaching tip**
Tell Ss that this paragraph is an example of cause-and-effect writing. Point out the use of the connector *since* to signal a cause of smog. *Consequently* signals one of the effects of smog on people.

Read the tip aloud. Tell Ss that by organizing a paragraph or an essay by causes and effects, the writer makes the information clearer and easier for the reader to follow. Tell Ss that this method of cause-and-effect organization is often used in writing informational paragraphs or essays.

- Focus Ss' attention on Exercise **1C** and read the instructions aloud.
- Model the task. Direct Ss' attention to the second sentence in the model paragraph that states that one cause of smog is that there are too many cars on the roads and highways. Call on a S to read the first example cause in the outline: *too many cars.*
- Ss work with a partner to complete the outline of the model paragraph, filling in the causes and effects of smog.
- Write the skeleton of the outline on the board.
- Call on individual Ss to fill in the information they discussed with their partners. Make corrections to the chart on the board as needed.

Expansion activity (whole class)

- Prepare Ss for the writing they will do in the next part of this lesson by having the class brainstorm a list of environmental problems in their city or community.
- Write Ss' responses on the board, or call on a S to come to the board to write Ss' responses.
- Tell Ss that they will be using one of the environmental problems listed on the board to plan, organize, and write their own paragraphs.

Practice

- Books open. Direct Ss' attention to Exercise **1D** and read the instructions aloud.
- Ask Ss to choose an environmental problem in their city or community as the topic of their paragraph.
- Tell Ss that the information they use here in planning will be helpful for them as they write their paragraph.
- Ss work individually to complete the outline for their paragraph. Walk around and help as needed.

Application

- Focus Ss' attention on Exercise **2** and read the instructions aloud.
- Ss complete the task individually. Walk around and help as needed.

Learner persistence *(individual work)*

- If you have any Ss who have difficulty writing, sit with them and help them while other Ss are writing. Encourage them to look at their outline of the model paragraph in Exercise **1C** on page 118. Ss should also use their outline from Exercise **1D** to help them write.

Comprehension check

- Direct Ss' attention to Exercise **3A**. This exercise asks Ss to develop skills to review and edit their own writing.
- Ss check their own paragraphs against the writing checklist. Walk around and help as needed. If any Ss checked *No* for one or more of the checklist items, ask them to revise and edit their paragraphs to include the missing information.

Evaluation

- Focus Ss' attention on Exercise **3B** and read the instructions aloud. This exercise enables Ss to work together to peer-correct their writing. Reading aloud enables the writer to review his or her own writing. Reading to a partner allows the writer to understand the need to write clearly for an audience.
- Ss complete the exercise in pairs. Tell Ss to take turns reading their paragraphs to each other. Walk around and help as needed.

- Listen to Ss as they ask their partner a question about his or her paragraph and tell their partner one thing they learned from it.
- Ask several Ss to read their paragraphs aloud. Have other Ss ask questions and mention something they learned from the paragraph.
- Direct Ss' attention to the lesson focus on the board.
- Check off the lesson focus as Ss demonstrate an understanding of what they have learned in the lesson.

Expansion activity *(individual work, whole class)*

- **Materials needed** An example of a letter to the editor – ideally, one with an environmental theme.
- Ask Ss if they have ever read a letter to the editor in a newspaper or magazine. Ask Ss why they think people write these letters. Elicit an appropriate response, such as: *to complain about a problem, to show people another way to look at a situation, to express their opinion, to try to persuade others to agree with their point of view, to try to persuade others to take a certain course of action.*
- Distribute copies of an example letter to the editor to each S. Ss read the letter independently.
- Review the letter with the class, and call on Ss to read it aloud. Write new vocabulary on the board.
- Call on Ss to explain how the writer defends his or her opinion (through the use of persuasive words and phrases, such as *should, must, I feel, in my opinion*).
- Tell Ss to work individually to write their own letter to the editor about an environmental problem in the community that is different from the one they wrote about in Exercise **2**. Encourage Ss to use the vocabulary, grammar, and connectors learned in this unit. Walk around and help as needed.
- Call on individual Ss to read their letter to the editor to the class.

More Ventures *(whole group, pairs, individual)*
Assign appropriate exercises from the *Teacher's Toolkit Audio CD / CD-ROM, Add Ventures,* or the *Workbook*.

D Plan a paragraph about an environmental problem in your city or community. Include the cause(s) and effect(s) of the problem. Use the outline to make notes on your ideas.

Problem: _(Answers will vary.)_ _____

Causes	Effects
1. _____	
(detail) a. _____	
_____	1. _____
(detail) b. _____	_____
_____	2. _____
2. _____	_____
(detail) a. _____	3. _____
_____	_____
(detail) b. _____	
_____	

2 Write

Write a paragraph about an environmental problem in your city or community. Use the paragraph in Exercise 1B and the outlines in Exercises 1C and 1D to help you.

3 After you write

A Check your writing.

	Yes	No
1. My topic sentence identified an environmental problem.	☐	☐
2. I clearly explained the causes and effects.	☐	☐
3. I used connectors of cause and effect correctly.	☐	☐

B Share your writing with a partner.

1. Take turns. Read your paragraph to a partner.
2. Comment on your partner's paragraph. Ask your partner a question about the paragraph. Tell your partner one thing you learned.

Another view

1 Life-skills reading

A Number of Reasons to Live Green

150	**400**	**1,000**
percent more energy is used by regular lightbulbs than energy-efficient (compact fluorescent) bulbs.	gallons of water are wasted every month when you have a leaky faucet.	years is how long plastic bottles take to decompose in landfills.
1,200	**95,000**	**14,000,000**
pounds of organic garbage are thrown out by the average American in a year.	pounds of pollution are produced by driving a car for one year.	trees are cut down to produce the 10,000,000,000 paper bags that Americans use every year.

A Read the questions. Look at the chart. Circle the answers.

1. How long do plastic bottles remain in landfills?
   a. 34 years
   b. 1,000 years
   c. 1,200 months
   d. none of the above

2. What does the number 95,000 represent?
   a. pounds of organic garbage thrown out
   b. pounds of smog from factories
   c. pounds of pollution from a car in one year
   d. none of the above

3. The number 400 represents _____ .
   a. dollars
   b. gallons
   c. months
   d. days

4. How much organic garbage is thrown out each year by the average American?
   a. 21 pounds
   b. 200 pounds
   c. 1,200 pounds
   d. 95,000 pounds

5. How many paper bags do Americans use every year?
   a. 10,000,000
   b. 14,000,000
   c. 10,000,000,000
   d. 14,000,000,000

6. What can you do to help the environment?
   a. Recycle plastic bottles.
   b. Fix faucets that leak.
   c. Replace regular lightbulbs with energy-efficient ones.
   d. all of the above

B Talk with your classmates. What do you do in your home to "live green"?

Lesson objectives

- Practice reading and understanding a chart about reasons to live green
- Review vocabulary and grammar from the unit
- Introduce the project
- Complete the self-assessment

Warm-up and review

- Before class. Write today's lesson focus on the board.
  Lesson F:
  Read and understand a chart about reasons to live green
  Review topic vocabulary
  Complete the project and the self-assessment
- Begin class. Books closed. Write on the board: *What would happen if people didn't try to live green?* Read the question aloud. Elicit appropriate responses, for example: *The air, land, and water would become more polluted. The air would be so polluted that it would be hard for us to breathe.*
- Say: *Today we will practice reading and understanding a chart about the importance of living green.*

Presentation

- Books open. Read the title of the chart aloud.
- Call on six Ss to read each of the six reasons in the chart.
- Explain vocabulary as needed.

Practice

- Direct Ss' attention to Exercise **1A** and read the instructions aloud. This task helps prepare Ss for standardized-type tests they may have to take. Make sure that Ss understand the task. Have Ss individually scan for and circle the answers.

Comprehension check

- Check answers to Exercise **1A** with the class. Make sure that Ss have followed the instructions and circled their answers.
- Have Ss read aloud the questions and answers they circled. Ask: *Is that answer correct?* Make corrections as needed.

Application

- Direct Ss' attention to Exercise **1B** and read the instructions aloud.
- Ss work in small groups to draw on their own experiences to answer the question. Walk around and help as needed.

Expansion activity *(small groups)*

- **Materials needed** Poster board and colored markers. If possible, bring in a collection of magazines that have pictures related to the environment and nature.
- Provide each group with poster board, markers, and magazines, if available.
- Ss should work in a small group to choose from the chart one of the reasons to live green and make a poster or ad designed to convince people that they should do something related to that point.
- Encourage Ss to use pictures from the magazines or draw their own to make their poster visually appealing.
- Model the task. Write the following on the board:
  It's time to make a change!
  Problem: Due to the lack of recycling, there are too many plastic bottles in our landfills.
  Fact: It takes 450 to 1,000 years for plastic bottles to decompose in landfills.
  What we can do:
  If we saved our bottles and reused them, we wouldn't need to buy new ones.
  If we recycled our plastic bottles, we would create less trash.
  We would help the environment if we used less plastic.
- Tell Ss to work together to write three conditional sentences in their poster about what people can do related to the environmental point they chose. Walk around and help as needed.
- Call on groups to present and explain their poster to the class. Display the posters in the classroom if possible.
- Leave time for a question-and-answer session.

Practice

- Books open. Focus Ss' attention on Exercise **2A** and read the instructions aloud.
- Call on eight Ss to read the eight questions in the quiz, one at a time. Explain content vocabulary as needed.
- Ss complete the quiz individually. Walk around and help as needed.
- Direct Ss' attention to the second part of Exercise **2A**.
- Ss work in small groups to review their answers.
- Review the answers to the quiz with the class. Ask Ss if any of the answers surprised them.
- (The answers to Exercise **2A** are as follows: 1. false – New water-saving, energy-efficient dishwashers use less water. 2. false – The earth's temperature has risen about two degrees Farenheit. 3. true 4. false – Alternative-fuel cars perform equal to or better than conventional cars. 5. true 6. true 7. false – The causes of global warming are primarily due to what humans are doing to harm the environment. 8. true)

Application

- Read the instructions aloud for Exercise **2B**. Write *e-n-v-i-r-o-n-m-e-n-t* on the board. Tell Ss to use the letters in as many combinations as they can to make new words (*never, one, time, meet,* etc.).
- Ss work with a partner to complete the exercise. Walk around and help as needed.
- Ask partners to come to the board to write their words.
- **Option** You may wish to make this activity into a game so that the pairs with the most words wins.

Expansion activity *(small groups)*

- **Materials needed** Three or four sayings or poems about nature or the environment from different cultures, at least three different ones per group. Make enough copies so that each S has one of the sayings or poems.
- This is an example of material that would be appropriate for this activity:
  Only after the last tree has been cut down;
  Only after the last river has been poisoned;
  Only after the last fish has been caught;
  Only then will you find that money cannot be eaten.
  – Cree Indian Prophecy
- Tell Ss that this prophecy, or prediction, comes from the Cree Indians. The Cree are a vast group of Native Americans living in various parts of North America (mostly in Canada).

- Give Ss a number depending on how many sayings or poems you were able to find. For example, if you found three sayings, have Ss count off: *1, 2, 3, 1, 2, 3,* etc. Give all the ones the same saying, all the twos the same saying, and all the threes the same saying.
- Ss read their saying or poem silently. Guide Ss to think about the meaning.
- After several minutes, Ss should form groups consisting of a one, a two, and a three.
- Ss read their saying or poem to the other Ss in their group.
- Invite the group to discuss how the saying or poem relates to the class discussion about the environment.

> **More Ventures** *(whole group, pairs, individual)*
> Assign appropriate exercises from the *Teacher's Toolkit Audio CD / CD-ROM, Add Ventures,* or the *Workbook.*

Application

Community building

- **Project** Ask Ss to turn to page 140 in their Student's Book to complete the project for Unit 9.

Evaluation

- Before asking Ss to turn to the self-assessment on page 145, do a quick review of the unit. Have Ss turn to Lesson A. Ask the class to talk about what they remember about this lesson. Prompt Ss, if necessary, with questions, for example: *What are the conversations about on this page? What vocabulary is in the pictures?* Continue in this manner to review each lesson quickly.
- **Self-assessment** Read the instructions for Exercise **3**. Ask Ss to turn to the self-assessment page to complete the unit self-assessment. The self-assessments are also on the *Teacher's Toolkit Audio CD / CD-ROM.* If you prefer to collect the assessments and save them as part of each S's portfolio assessment, print out the unit self-assessment from the Toolkit, ask Ss to complete it, and collect and save it.
- If Ss are ready, administer the unit test on pages T-196–T-198 of this *Teacher's Edition* (or on the *Teacher's Toolkit Audio CD / CD-ROM*). The audio and audio script for the tests are on the *Teacher's Toolkit Audio CD / CD-ROM.*

2 Fun with language

A **Talk** with a partner. Take the Living Green Quiz. Circle *true* or *false*. Then compare answers with your partner.

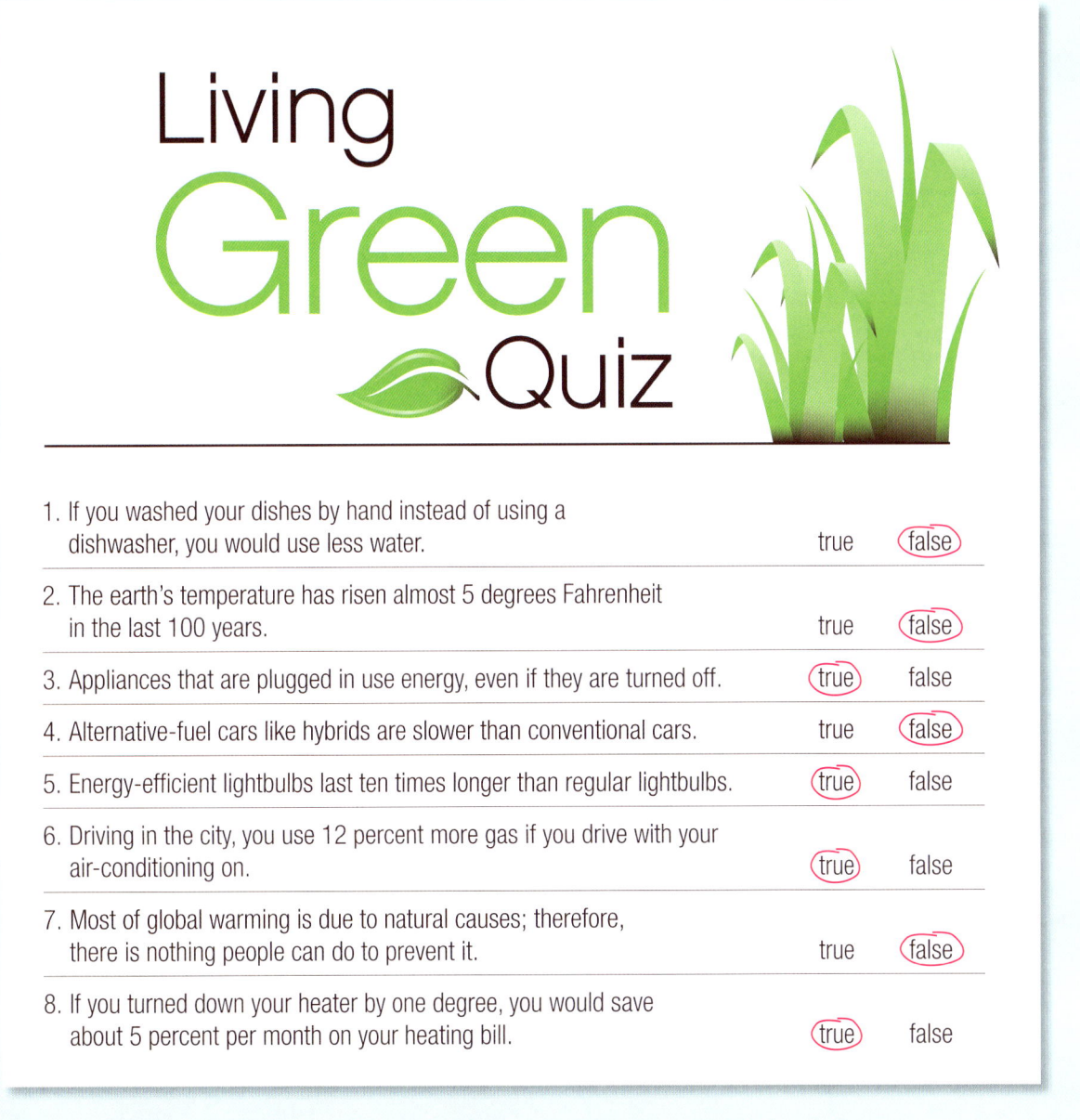

Living Green Quiz

1. If you washed your dishes by hand instead of using a dishwasher, you would use less water.	true	*(false)*
2. The earth's temperature has risen almost 5 degrees Fahrenheit in the last 100 years.	true	*(false)*
3. Appliances that are plugged in use energy, even if they are turned off.	*(true)*	false
4. Alternative-fuel cars like hybrids are slower than conventional cars.	true	*(false)*
5. Energy-efficient lightbulbs last ten times longer than regular lightbulbs.	*(true)*	false
6. Driving in the city, you use 12 percent more gas if you drive with your air-conditioning on.	*(true)*	false
7. Most of global warming is due to natural causes; therefore, there is nothing people can do to prevent it.	true	*(false)*
8. If you turned down your heater by one degree, you would save about 5 percent per month on your heating bill.	*(true)*	false

Share answers with your classmates. Check with your teacher for the correct answers.

B **Work** with a partner. How many new words can you make with the letters from the word *environment*?

e-n-v-i-r-o-n-m-e-n-t

3 Wrap up

Complete the **Self-assessment** on page 145.

Lesson A *Get ready*

1 Talk about the pictures

A What do you see?

B What is happening?

Lesson objectives
- Introduce students to the topic
- Find out what students know about the topic
- Preview the unit by talking about the pictures
- Practice key vocabulary
- Practice listening skills

Warm-up and review

- Before class. Write today's lesson focus on the board.
  Lesson A:
  Ask about and compare wedding customs
- Begin class. Books closed. Direct Ss' attention to the lesson focus. Point to *wedding customs*. Ask Ss: *What are some examples of wedding customs in the United States?* List Ss' responses on the board, for example: *The bride wears a white gown. The groom wears a tuxedo. The couple cuts the wedding cake. Usually, the groom's parents host a dinner the night before the wedding.*

▼ **Culture tip**
Tell Ss that another wedding custom in the United States, although less popular today, is the bride's wearing of "something old, something new, something borrowed, something blue." To fulfill this tradition, the bride may borrow an older family member's wedding dress and wear a new blue garter or ribbon.

Presentation

- Books open. Set the scene. Direct Ss' attention to the first picture on page 122. Ask the question from Exercise **1A**: *What do you see?* Elicit and write on the board as much vocabulary about the picture as possible: *bride and groom, wedding reception, wedding dress, special dinner, envelopes,* etc. Explain any unfamiliar words. Continue eliciting words to describe the second picture.
- Tell Ss that whereas in the United States it is traditional to throw rice at a bride and groom, many couples choose not to do so because birds can get sick from eating rice left on the ground. Today, it is not unusual for guests to throw birdseed (which is safe for birds to eat) or flower petals at the bride and groom after the wedding ceremony.
- Ask individual Ss to look at the two pictures and talk about the similarities (e.g., both pictures show wedding customs) and differences (e.g., in the first picture, the bride and groom are greeting their guests, and in the second, they are leaving the reception).

- Direct Ss' attention to the question in Exercise **1B**: *What is happening?* Hold up the Student's Book. Point to the first picture. Ask: *What are the bride and groom doing here?* (They're receiving a gift, probably money, in an envelope. They're talking to and thanking their guests.)
- Point to the second picture. Ask: *What are the bride and groom doing here?* (They're trying to run through the confetti that is being thrown at them as they leave the ceremony.)

Practice

- Invite Ss to work with a partner to create a story from one of the pictures on page 122. One S writes the story as pairs work together.
- Call on several pairs to share their story with the class.

▼ **Teaching tip**
Encourage Ss to be creative. At this point, there is no single correct story.

Expansion activity (small groups)

- Write the following questions on the board: *What is your idea of the perfect wedding? What is the ceremony like? What is the reception like? Where would you go on your honeymoon?*
- Ask Ss if they understand the meaning of the word *honeymoon*. Explain that it is a vacation that a newly married couple (newlyweds) takes after the wedding.
- Tell Ss that even if they are already married, they can imagine a different wedding from the one they had. Encourage Ss to use their imagination to come up with an idea for their "dream wedding." Tell them that they have unlimited money to spend.
- Ss work in small groups to discuss their dream wedding.
- Call on each group to share information from their group discussion.
- If any Ss in the class are married, ask them what they liked most about their own wedding. Ss may wish to bring their wedding album to class to share pictures with their group.

Lesson A Get ready

Presentation

- Books open. Direct Ss' attention to Exercise **2A**. Have Ss listen for the main idea. Read the instructions aloud.
- 💿 [Class Audio CD3 track 18] Play or read the audio program (see audio script, page T-166).
- Ask Ss if they understand everything in the listening exercise. Write any unfamiliar words on the board and help Ss understand the meaning of each.
- Elicit answers to the questions, for example: *The speakers are Cathy and Thanh. They're talking about wedding customs. Cathy says she doesn't know what to get Bao and An for their wedding gift. Thanh tells her about Vietnamese wedding customs. Thanh explains that according to Vietnamese customs, the ceremony is usually a private one just for the family, but the reception is a huge party with a lot of people and food.*
- Focus Ss' attention on Exercise **2B** and read the instructions aloud. Have Ss listen and complete the chart based on the information they hear.
- 💿 [Class Audio CD3 track 19] Tell Ss to listen for details about Cathy's conversation with Thanh. Model the task. Play or read the audio program again. Pause the program after Cathy says: *They make a list of what they want, and then people can go to the store or the store's Web site and buy something on the couple's list.*
- Model the first answer in the chart. Draw the chart on the board as it appears on page 123. Point to the heading that says *American wedding customs*. Call on a S to read the sample answer (*register in a store*). Write it on the board. Play or read the rest of the audio program. Ss listen and complete the chart.
- Read aloud the second part of the instructions for Exercise **2B**.
- 💿 [Class Audio CD3 track 19] Play or read the audio program again (see audio script, page T-166). Ss listen and check their answers. Repeat the audio program as needed.
- Ask Ss to come to the board to write the answers in the chart. Make corrections on the board as needed.

Practice

- Direct Ss' attention to Exercise **2C** and read the instructions aloud. Tell Ss that the story in this exercise is a summary of what happened in the pictures on the previous page.
- Focus Ss' attention to the words in the word bank. Say each word and ask Ss to repeat. Correct pronunciation as needed. Make sure that Ss understand the meaning of each word.

- Model the task. Ask a S to read aloud the first two sentences in the story, including the example answer.
- Ss complete the exercise individually. Help as needed.

Comprehension check

- 💿 [Class Audio CD3 track 20] Play or read the audio program (see audio script, page T-166). Ss listen and check their answers. Repeat the audio program as needed.
- Write the numbers *1–8* on the board. Ask Ss to come to the board to write only the answers. Have other Ss read the sentences, filling in each blank with the answer on the board. Make corrections as needed.

Learner persistence (individual work)

- 💿 [Self-Study Audio CD tracks 31 and 32] Exercises **2A**, **2B**, and **2C** are recorded on the Ss' self-study CD at the back of the Student's Book. Ss can listen to the CD at home for reinforcement and review. They can also listen for self-directed learning when class attendance is not possible.

Application

- Focus Ss' attention on Exercise **2D** and read the instructions aloud.
- Call on two Ss to read the questions.
- Ss complete the exercise in small groups. Walk around and help as needed.
- Ask Ss to share information they learned with the class.

Expansion activity (individual work)

- Have Ss choose a wedding custom from their culture to write about in a paragraph. Tell Ss that their paragraph should contain a topic sentence that introduces the main idea of the paragraph.
- Ss in pairs. Have Ss read their paragraph to a partner.
- You may also choose to assign the writing task as homework.

Evaluation

- Direct Ss' attention to the lesson focus on the board. Ask individual Ss to look at the pictures on page 122 and make sentences using the words in Exercise **2C**.
- Check off the lesson focus as Ss demonstrate an understanding of what they have learned in the lesson.

> **More Ventures** (whole group, pairs, individual)
> Assign appropriate exercises from the *Teacher's Toolkit Audio CD / CD-ROM, Add Ventures,* or the *Workbook.*

T-123   Unit 10

2 Listening

F-STUDY
UDIO CD  **A** 🔊 **Listen** and answer the questions.

1. Who are the speakers?
2. What are they talking about?

F-STUDY
UDIO CD  **B** 🔊 **Listen again.** Complete the chart.

	American wedding customs	Vietnamese wedding customs
1. Gifts	*register in a store*	*cash in an envelope*
2. Use of rice	*throw it at bride and groom*	*eat red sticky rice*
3. Dress color	*white*	*red*

Listen again. Check your answers.

F-STUDY
UDIO CD  **C** 🔊 **Read.** Complete the story. Listen and check your answers.

acquaintances	fortune	reception	symbolizes
courses	looking forward	registered	tradition

Cathy and Thanh are talking about wedding customs. Cathy is invited to a Vietnamese wedding, and she is surprised that the bride and groom are not _____*registered*_____ for gifts at any stores. In contrast, Thanh is surprised by the American _____*tradition*_____ of throwing rice at the bride and groom. Next, they talk about clothes. Thanh says a Vietnamese bride wears a red dress because the color red _____*symbolizes*_____ good _____*fortune*_____ . Then Cathy asks why she was invited only to the wedding _____*reception*_____ , not the ceremony. Thanh explains that traditionally the ceremony is only for the family. The couple's friends and _____*acquaintances*_____ are invited to the evening reception. In fact, Thanh says the evening party will include seven or eight _____*courses*_____ of food. Cathy says she is _____*looking forward*_____ to the wedding.

D Discuss. Talk with your classmates.

1. Share some special wedding customs from your culture.
2. Have you ever attended an American wedding? What did you think about it?

1 Grammar focus: future real conditional and unreal conditional

Future real conditional (possible)

If I go to the wedding, I will wear my new shoes.

If Jane doesn't have to work that day, she will go to the wedding.

For a grammar explanation, turn to page 152.

Unreal conditional (not possible)

If I went to the wedding, I would wear my new shoes. (But I'm not going.)

If Jane didn't work that day, she would go to the wedding. (But Jane has to work.)

Useful language

The unreal conditional form of the verb *be* is **were**.

If I were you, I would give them cash for their wedding.

If it were warmer, we could have the wedding outdoor

2 Practice

A Write. Complete the sentences. Use the future real or unreal conditional forms of the verbs.

1. The Patels are from India, but they live in the United States now. They are planning a wedding for their daughter, Parveen. If they _____*lived*_____ in India, (live) the groom's family ___*would pay*___ for the wedding. (pay)

2. The wedding will be in the United States. If the Patels _____*had*_____ the wedding in India, the (have) wedding celebration ___*would last*___ three days. Here (last) it will last for one day.

3. The Patels don't have a lot of money. If they _____*were*_____ rich, they ___*would invite*___ 300 people; instead, they will invite about 150. (be) (invite)

4. The Patels are planning to have music for the reception. If a band *doesn't charge* (not / charge) too much, they ___*will have*___ live music. (have)

5. It's possible that the weather will be nice on the day of the wedding. If the weather _____*is*_____ nice, they ___*will have*___ the ceremony outside. (be) (have)

6. Parveen and her new husband will live in their own apartment. If they _____*were*_____ (be) in India, they ___*would live*___ with the groom's parents. (live)

 Listen and check your answers.

Warm-up and review

- Before class. Write today's lesson focus on the board. *Lesson B:*
  Use the future real conditional and unreal conditional

- Begin class. Books closed. Review key vocabulary from the unit by asking Ss questions about different wedding customs.
  What is one American wedding custom? (Guests sometimes throw rice at the bride and groom just after they are married.)
  What is one Vietnamese wedding custom? (A Vietnamese bride traditionally wears a red dress.)
  What does it mean to be registered at a store? (For many American weddings, the bride and groom make a list of the gifts they would like from a particular store, and then people can go to the store or the store's Web site to buy something on the couple's list.)

Presentation

- Books open. Direct Ss' attention to the grammar chart in Exercise **1**. Read aloud the two headings: *Future real conditional (possible)* and *Unreal conditional (not possible)*. Call on two Ss to read the sentences under each heading, including the words in parentheses.

- Write the following on the board:
  Future real conditional (possible)
  If + subject + present verb . . . subject + future verb
  Unreal conditional (not possible)
  If + subject + past verb . . . subject + <u>would</u> + base form of verb

- Tell Ss that the future real conditional is used to talk about events that you think will happen or expect to happen in the future. Point to the first example sentence under *Future real conditional,* and say that Jane might go to the wedding. Explain that the unreal conditional is used to talk about situations that you know will not happen in the future. Point out that the words in parentheses under *Unreal conditional* are there to emphasize that the situations are not possible. However, the information in parentheses isn't usually stated because it is understood.

Practice

- Focus Ss' attention on Exercise **2A** and read the instructions aloud.

- Have a S read number 1 aloud, including the two example answers. Make sure that Ss understand the exercise.

- Ss complete the exercise individually. Walk around and help as needed.

Comprehension check

- 💿 [Class Audio CD3 track 21] Play or read the audio program (see audio script, page T-166). Ss listen and check their answers. Repeat the audio program as needed.

- Write the numbers *1–6* on the board. Ask several Ss to come to the board to write the complete sentences. Work with the class to make corrections as needed.

Expansion activity (student pairs)

- Ask Ss: *What would you do if you won the lottery?* Then say: *Name five activities that you couldn't do before that you would now be able to do. Share your ideas with a partner.*

- Model the activity. Write the following on the board and ask a S to read it aloud: *If I won the lottery, I would take a long trip to Egypt.*

- Ss discuss the question with a partner. Walk around and help as needed.

- Invite pairs to share their "wish list" of activities with the class.

Practice

- Books open. Direct Ss' attention to Exercise **2B** and read the instructions aloud.
- Direct Ss' attention to the chart of real and imaginary plans for New Year's Eve. Call on two Ss to read aloud Victor's real and imaginary plans.
- Call on two Ss to read the sample dialog aloud.
- Ss use the real and imaginary situations from the chart to complete the exercise with a partner. Walk around and help as needed.
- Direct Ss' attention to the second part of Exercise **2B** and read the instructions aloud.
- Ask a S to read aloud the example sentences.
- Ss work individually to complete the exercise. Walk around and help as needed.
- Ask individual Ss to come to the board to write their sentences. Work with the class to make corrections on the board as needed.

Application

- Direct Ss' attention to Exercise **3A** and read the instructions aloud. Explain any unfamiliar vocabulary.
- Call on a S to read the three headings and the words under *Holiday or event*.
- Model the task. Ask two Ss to read the examples in the chart.
- Ss talk with a partner and then individually complete the chart. Tell Ss that in the chart where it says *your idea*, they should add their own choices or reasons for celebration. Tell Ss they could be holidays from their own culture or country or important occasions (job promotion, engagement, etc.). Walk around and help as needed.
- Direct Ss' attention to Exercise **3B** and read the instructions aloud.
- Call on two Ss to read aloud the example dialog about real and imaginary plans.
- Ss in small groups. Ss ask and answer questions about each other's plans.
- Read aloud the instructions in Exercise **3C**.
- Invite Ss to take turns sharing with the class information they learned about their partner. Have Ss use the future real conditional and the unreal conditional in their discussions.

Expansion activity (individual work)

- Tell Ss to write about the plans they discussed in Exercise **3B**. They should write one paragraph either about a real plan or an imaginary plan for New Year's Eve.
- Walk around and help as needed.
- Ss exchange paragraphs with a partner. Ss discuss the paragraphs they wrote.
- Call on Ss to share with another pair the information they discussed with their partner.

Evaluation

- Books closed. Direct Ss' attention to the lesson focus on the board.
- Write the following on the board:
  1. If I go to the party, I _____ .
  2. If he doesn't go to his friend's house on Friday night, he _____ .
  3. If I went to the movies, I _____ .
  4. If he didn't go to a restaurant for dinner, he _____ .
  5. If she were free that evening, she _____ .
  6. If I were rich, I _____ .
- Ask Ss to write the numbers *1–6* in their notebooks and to complete the sentences using the future real conditional or the unreal conditional.
- Ss work individually to complete the sentences. Walk around and help as needed.
- Ask Ss which sentences express the future real conditional (the first two) and which express the unreal conditional (the last four).
- Call on six Ss to write their sentences on the board and read them aloud. Make corrections on the board as needed.
- Check off the lesson focus as Ss demonstrate an understanding of what they have learned in the lesson.

More Ventures (whole group, pairs, individual)
Assign appropriate exercises from the *Teacher's Toolkit Audio CD / CD-ROM*, *Add Ventures*, or the *Workbook*.

B Talk with a partner. Take turns making sentences about Victor's real and imaginary plans for New Year's Eve.

> **A** If Victor stays home on New Year's Eve, he will have a party with his friends.
> **B** But if he traveled to Florida, he would spend New Year's Eve near the beach.

Real	Imaginary
stay home / have a party with his friends	travel to Florida / spend New Year's Eve near the beach
go to his parents' house / have a quiet celebration with family	be in Mexico / eat 12 grapes at midnight
travel to New York / celebrate New Year's Eve in Times Square	travel to Brazil / watch fireworks on the beach at midnight
go to a club / dance all night	be in France / have a special dinner

Write sentences about Victor's real and imaginary plans.

If Victor stays home on New Year's Eve, he will have a party with his friends.

If he traveled to Florida, he would spend New Year's Eve near the beach.

3 Communicate

A Talk with a partner. Complete the chart with your real and imaginary plans for some future holidays or special events.

Holiday or event	Real	Imaginary
New Year's Eve	*stay home*	*be in my native country*
birthday		
(your idea)		
(your idea)		

B Work in a small group. Share your charts. Ask and answer questions about each other's plans.

> **A** If you stay home on New Year's Eve, how will you celebrate?
> **B** If I stay home, I'll invite my friends to come over and celebrate with me.

> **A** If you were in your native country on New Year's Eve, how would you celebrate?
> **B** If I were in my native country, I would watch fireworks at midnight.

C Share information about your classmates.

Expressing hopes and wishes

1 Grammar focus: *hope* and *wish*

Possible situations

Samira hopes her cousin will come to her wedding.
Samira hopes her cousin comes to her wedding.
Nick hopes he can go to the party.

Situations that are not possible

Samira wishes her cousin would come to her wedding.
Nick wishes he could go to the party.

For a grammar explanation, turn to page 153.

Useful language

In expressing hopes, using the modal *will* or the simple present tense are both correct.

I hope you will attend.
I hope you attend.

2 Practice

A Write. Complete the sentences. Use *hopes* or *wishes* and the correct form of the verb or modal.

1. Paul's high school graduation is tomorrow.

   His friend Luis has to work. Luis _____*wishes*_____ he

   _____*could go*_____ to Paul's graduation.
   (can go)

2. Paul's father has asked for the day off so that

   he can attend his son's graduation. He _____*hopes*_____

   he _____*gets*_____ the day off.
   (get)

3. Paul's grandfather has been sick. He's not sure if he will attend the graduation.

   Paul _____*hopes*_____ his grandfather _____*will attend*_____ the ceremony.
   (will attend)

4. The graduation ceremony will be outside. Paul _____*hopes*_____ it _____*will not rain*_____ .
   (will not / rain)

5. Paul's mother would like to buy him a new car, but she can't afford it.

   She _____*wishes*_____ she _____*could buy*_____ him a new car.
   (can buy)

6. Paul wasn't accepted to the university, so he will go to a community college.

   Paul _____*wishes*_____ he _____*could go*_____ to the university.
   (can go)

7. It's possible that Paul will be able to transfer to the university in two years.

   He _____*hopes*_____ he _____*can transfer*_____ in two years.
   (can transfer)

Listen and check your answers.

Lesson objective

- Express hopes and wishes

Warm-up and review

- Before class. Write today's lesson focus on the board.
  Lesson C:
  Use hope and wish to talk about different situations
- Begin class. Books closed. Write *hope* and *wish* on the board.
- Write these two sentences: *I hope I can visit my uncle in California next month. I wish I could visit my uncle in California next month.*
- Underline the verbs *can* and *could* in the sentences. Ask Ss if they can figure out the rule for verb usage with *hope* and *wish*. Tell Ss that *hope* is used with a present or future verb or modal. *Wish,* on the other hand, is used with *could* (or *would*) and the base form of the verb.

Presentation

- Books open. Direct Ss' attention to the grammar chart in Exercise **1**. Read the two headings and corresponding statements to the class.
- Ask Ss if they can guess the difference in meaning between *hope* and *wish*. Elicit appropriate answers, for example: *Hope* is used to talk about something you want in the future that is possible, and *wish* is used to talk about something that is not possible at this time.
- Have Ss make up similar sentences using *hope* and *wish*. Walk around and help as needed.
- Ask Ss to come to the board to write their sentences. Make corrections on the board as needed.

▼ **Teaching tip**

It might be helpful to refer Ss to the grammar explanation on page 153 in the Student's Book.

Useful language

Read the tip box aloud. Tell Ss that although the meaning of the two sentences is similar, the use of *will* softens the statement; it becomes more polite.

Practice

- Direct Ss' attention to Exercise **2A** and read the instructions aloud.
- Ask a S to read aloud the sentences in number 1, including the example answers.
- Ss complete the exercise individually. Walk around and help as needed.

Comprehension check

- Read aloud the second part of the instructions for Exercise **2A**.
- [Class Audio CD3 track 22] Play or read the audio program (see audio script, page T-167). Ss listen and check their answers.
- Write the numbers *1–7* on the board. Ask several Ss to come to the board to write their answers. Make corrections on the board as needed.

Expansion activity *(small groups)*

- Write *wish* and *hope* on the board.
- Have small groups of Ss sit in a circle and take turns saying something they want to do. The first S makes a statement, and the second S decides whether it is a hope or a wish. The second S makes a sentence about the first S and then says a new sentence beginning with *I want* for the next S in the circle.
- Model the activity. Write the following on the board:

  S1: I want to visit Rome some day.
  S2: (Maria) hopes to visit Rome someday. I want to live on the moon for a month.
  S3: (Ben) wishes he could live on the moon for a month. I want to have a conversation with the president.

- Encourage Ss to have fun with this activity. Walk around and help as needed.

Lesson C Expressing hopes and wishes

Practice

- Direct Ss' attention to Exercise **2B** and read the instructions aloud.
- Call on seven Ss to read each of the statements to the class.
- Have a S read aloud the example situation and the example statement.
- Ss complete the exercise with a partner. Walk around and help as needed.
- Read aloud the instructions for the second part of Exercise **2B**. Call on a S to read the example sentence.
- Ss complete the exercise individually. Walk around and help as needed.
- Ask several Ss to write their sentences on the board.
- Call on other Ss to read each of the sentences. Ask: *Is this sentence correct?* Work with the class to make corrections on the board as needed.

Application

- Direct Ss' attention to Exercise **3A** and read the instructions aloud.
- Model the exercise. Ask a S to read the example answer.
- Ss work individually to complete the exercise. Walk around and help as needed.
- Direct Ss' attention to Exercise **3B** and read the instructions aloud.
- Call on three Ss to read the example conversation to the class.

Useful language
Read the tip box aloud. Call on two Ss to read the example sentences. Ask Ss if they can think of other expressions using *hope* that are used to end conversations. Elicit appropriate responses, such as: *I hope to see you soon. I hope to talk to you soon.* Tell Ss that they should use *hope* when they respond to what their partners say in this exercise, as in the example.

- Ss work in a small group to complete the exercise. Walk around and help as needed.
- Read the instructions aloud for Exercise **3C**. Model the task. Say: *I learned that Juan wishes he could visit his parents in Mexico on his birthday.*
- Continue the exercise by asking Ss to share information they learned about one another with the class.

Expansion activity *(individual work)*

- Write the following on the board: *I wish I could _____ .*
- Tell Ss that they should complete this sentence and then use it as the topic sentence for a written paragraph. Have them use conditional sentences and sentences with *hope* or *wish*.
- Model the activity. Write this example on the board: *I wish I could fly! If I were able to fly, I would spend a lot of my time traveling. I would visit my family in Brazil. Then I would travel to Argentina to eat a delicious steak. After that, I would fly to . . .*
- Ask Ss to share their paragraph with a partner.
- After Ss have had time to share their writing with a partner, call on several Ss to read their paragraph to the class.

Evaluation

- Direct Ss' attention to the lesson focus on the board.
- Encourage Ss to look at the photo on page 126 and make sentences about the photo using *hope* and *wish*. Elicit appropriate responses, such as: *Paul wishes he could go to the university this fall. Paul hopes he can transfer to the university in the future.*
- Check off the lesson focus as Ss demonstrate an understanding of what they have learned in the lesson.

More Ventures *(whole group, pairs, individual)*
Assign appropriate exercises from the *Teacher's Toolkit Audio CD / CD-ROM, Add Ventures*, or the *Workbook*.

B Talk with a partner. Read the situations. Make statements with *hope* or *wish*.

> Ryan wants to get a new cell phone as a birthday gift.

> Ryan hopes he will get a new cell phone as a birthday gift.

1. Ryan wants to get a new cell phone as a birthday gift.
2. Soraya can't go home for Thanksgiving because she has to work.
3. Marla wants to have a big graduation party, but her apartment is too small.
4. Avi is trying to get a plane reservation so that he can attend his cousin's wedding in Las Vegas.
5. Karl plans to ask Marta to marry him next weekend. He doesn't know if she will say yes.
6. Maria wants to marry Jeffrey, but she knows that he doesn't love her.
7. Anton and Ilsa are expecting a baby. They want the baby to be healthy.

Write a sentence for each situation.

Ryan hopes he will get a new cell phone as a birthday gift.

3 Communicate

A Write three holidays or celebrations that you observe. Think about something you wish you could change about each one.

Mother's Day: *I wish I could have the day off to be with my children.*

1. _____: _____

_____

2. _____: _____

_____

3. _____: _____

_____

B Work in a small group. Talk about your wishes. Listen to your classmates' hopes for you.

> *A* I don't have Mother's Day off. I wish I could have the day off to be with my children.
> *B* I hope you get the day off next year.
> *C* I hope your children will do something special for you.

Useful language

Expressing hope is a common way of ending a conversation.

I hope you feel better soon.
I hope you have a good time.

C Share information about your classmates.

Lesson D Reading

1 Before you read

Talk with your classmates. Answer the questions.

1. How are birthdays usually celebrated in your culture?
2. Are some birthdays more special than others? Which ones?

2 Read

SELF-STUDY AUDIO CD  **Read** the magazine article. Listen and read again.

Special Birthdays Around the World

In most cultures, there are certain birthdays that are especially important in a young person's life. If you were an American teenager, for example, you would eagerly look forward to your 16th birthday because in most states that is the age to get a driver's license. Other cultures also have birthdays with special meanings:

Mexico For Mexican girls, the 15th birthday – the "Quinceañera" – symbolizes a girl's transition into adulthood. To celebrate, the girl's family throws a huge party. The girl wears a ball gown similar to a wedding dress. The girl performs a waltz, a formal dance, with her father.

A girl's quinceañera

China On a child's first birthday, parents place their baby in the center of a group of objects, such as a shiny coin, a book, and a doll. Then they watch to see which object the baby picks up first. Most parents hope their child will pick up the coin because, according to tradition, it means the child will be rich.

Nigeria The 1st, 5th, 10th, and 15th birthdays are considered extremely important. Parties are held with up to 100 people. The guests enjoy a feast of a roasted cow or goat.

Japan A girl's 3rd and 7th birthdays and a boy's 5th birthday are considered special. In a ceremony known as "7, 5, 3," children wear their best kimonos (ceremonial gowns) and receive bags of sweets with "sweets for 1,000 years of life" written on them.

Israel A boy's 13th and a girl's 12th birthdays are serious as well as happy occasions. On these birthdays, children become responsible for their own religious and moral behavior.

Adult birthdays also have special significance in many cultures. In the United States, for example, birthdays ending in "0" – 30, 40, 50, etc. – are especially meaningful.

Lesson objectives

- Introduce and read "Special Birthdays Around the World"
- Practice using new topic-related vocabulary
- Learn about multiple-meaning words

Warm-up and review

- Before class. Write today's lesson focus on the board.
  Lesson D:
  Read and understand "Special Birthdays Around the World"
  Practice vocabulary related to birthday celebrations
  Learn and use words with more than one meaning

- Begin class. Books closed. Write *birthday celebrations* on the board. Ask Ss: *What do you think of when you think about birthday celebrations?* Elicit appropriate responses, such as: *candles, birthday cake, birthday cards, birthday gifts, balloons, streamers, party.* Write Ss' responses on the board.

- Direct Ss' attention to the title on the board: "Special Birthdays Around the World." Ask Ss to predict what they think this reading is about. Elicit appropriate responses, such as: *I think it's about different birthday celebrations in different cultures.* Write some of the Ss' predictions on the board.

Presentation

- Books open. Direct Ss' attention to Exercise **1** and read the instructions aloud.
- Have Ss focus on the questions, and ask two Ss to read them to the class.
- Ss in small groups. Ss discuss their answers to the questions. Walk around and help as needed.
- Call on individual Ss to share their answers with the class.

Practice

- Read the instructions aloud for Exercise **2**. Ask Ss to read the magazine article silently before listening to the audio program.
- [Class Audio CD3 track 23] Play or read the audio program and ask Ss to read along (see audio script, page T-167). Repeat the audio program as needed.
- While Ss are listening and reading the magazine article, ask them to underline any words they don't know. When the audio program is finished, have Ss write the new vocabulary words on the board.

- Point to each new vocabulary word on the board. Say it aloud and have Ss repeat. Give a brief explanation of each word, or ask Ss who know the word to explain it. If Ss prefer to look up the new words in their dictionaries, allow them to do so.

Learner persistence *(individual work)*

- [Self-Study Audio CD track 33] Exercise **2** is recorded on the Ss' self-study CD at the back of the Student's Book. Ss can listen to the CD at home for reinforcement and review. They can also listen to the CD for self-directed learning when class attendance is not possible.

Expansion activity *(whole group, small groups)*

- Tell Ss that they're going to develop a "birthday questionnaire" with the class.
- Write some example questions on the board, such as: *What was your favorite birthday celebration? How do you choose birthday gifts for your friends and family members?*
- Ask the class to brainstorm a list of approximately 12 to 15 birthday-related questions, and write them on the board. Have the class choose ten of the questions for the class questionnaire.
- Ss in small groups. Ss discuss their answers to the questions. Have one S take notes. Walk around and help as needed.
- Once all the groups have finished answering the questions, they should share the results with the class.
- Ask Ss: *Was there anything you learned about your classmates that surprised you? Explain. What did the majority of Ss say was their favorite way to spend their birthday?*
- You can follow up this activity by having a class birthday celebration. Choose a day to celebrate everyone's birthday at once, and decide as a class how you will celebrate.

Comprehension check

- Books open. Direct Ss' attention to Exercise **3A** and read the instructions aloud.

> Read the tip box aloud. Write *punctuation* on the board. Ask Ss to refer to the reading on page 128 to find examples of the different punctuation marks mentioned in the tip and circle them. Call on Ss to share their findings. For each set of dashes and parentheses, ask Ss if the punctuation mark is being used to signal definitions, examples, or explanations.

- Call on six Ss to read the six questions, one at a time.
- Ss complete the exercise individually. Walk around and help as needed.
- Check answers with the class. Whenever possible, have Ss indicate where they found the answers in the reading.

Practice

- **Materials needed** A dictionary for each S.
- Direct Ss' attention to number 1 of Exercise **3B** and read the instructions aloud.
- Focus Ss' attention on the headings in the chart below number 3. Read the three headings aloud. Call on a S to read the words in the left-hand column.
- Ask another S to read the first example definition in the chart, under *Meaning in story*.
- Ss work individually to underline the words in the reading and then write in the second column of the chart the meaning of the word as it is used in the story. Walk around and help as needed.
- Call on a S to read the instructions for number 2 of Exercise **3B**. Tell Ss that they should look in the dictionary to write a different meaning of the word, under *Other meaning* in the chart.
- Have a S read the instructions aloud for number 3 of Exercise **3B**. Ss should write sentences using the other meaning of each of the seven words in the chart.
- Review with the class. Write the chart on the board from page 129. Call on seven Ss to come to the board to fill in the chart. Work with the class to make corrections on the board as needed.

Learner persistence *(individual work)*

- Encourage Ss to use their notebook or index cards to write new vocabulary words. Suggest that Ss review new words and practice them as much as possible.

Application

- Focus Ss' attention on Exercise **3C** and read the instructions aloud.
- Ask five Ss to read aloud the questions in Exercise **3C**, one at a time.
- Ss ask and answer the questions with a partner.
- Ask several pairs to share the answers they discussed.

Expansion activity *(student pairs)*

- Ss in pairs. Have Ss work together to write a conversation using as many of the words from the chart in Exercise **3B** as possible. They can choose the meaning of the words that best fits their conversation.
- Ask Ss to practice their conversation with their partner until they know it well.
- Call on several pairs to perform their conversations for the class.

Evaluation

- Books closed. Direct Ss' attention to the lesson focus on the board.
- Ask individual Ss to retell the main points of the reading "Special Birthdays Around the World."
- Books open. Focus Ss' attention on the words in the first column of the chart in Exercise **3B**, under *Word in story*. Ask Ss to make sentences with these words to show that they understand the meaning of each word as it is used in the story.
- Check off each part of the lesson focus as Ss demonstrate an understanding of what they have learned in the lesson.

Learner persistence *(individual work, student pairs)*

- You may wish to assign Extended reading worksheets from the *Teacher's Toolkit Audio CD / CD-ROM* for Ss to complete outside of class. The purpose of these worksheets is to encourage Ss to read for pleasure in English outside of the English class. The worksheets can also be assigned as extended reading in class.

> **More Ventures** *(whole group, pairs, individual)*
> Assign appropriate exercises from the *Teacher's Toolkit Audio CD / CD-ROM*, *Add Ventures*, or the *Workbook*.

3 After you read

A Check your understanding.

1. Why do American teenagers look forward to their 16th birthdays?
2. What is the Spanish name for a girl's 15th birthday?
3. What is a waltz?
4. What is a kimono?
5. Which birthdays are especially meaningful in the United States?
6. Are any of the special birthdays described in the reading similar to traditions in your culture?

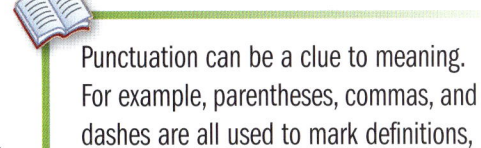

Punctuation can be a clue to meaning. For example, parentheses, commas, and dashes are all used to mark definitions, examples, or explanations.

B Build your vocabulary.

1. Underline the words from the chart in the reading passage. Write the meaning from the story.

2. Use a dictionary and write a different meaning of each word.

3. Write sentences using the other meaning of each word.

Word in story	Meaning in story	Other meaning
1. states	*areas that are part of a country*	*conditions of the mind*
2. object	*a thing that can be seen, held, or touched*	*the purpose or goal of an activity or game*
3. rich	*have a lot of money*	*food containing a lot of oil, butter, eggs, or cream*
4. transition	*move from one stage of life to another*	*words, phrases, or sentences that connect a topic to one that follows*
5. throw	*give*	*to send something through the air*
6. party	*a social gathering*	*a political group with the same beliefs*
7. ball	*a formal dance*	*a round object used in games that is thrown, hit, or kicked*

C Talk with a partner.

1. How many states are there in your native country?
2. Do you have a favorite object? What is it? Why do you like it?
3. What transitions have you made in your life?
4. Have you ever thrown a large party? What was the occasion?
5. Have you ever attended a ball? If so, what did you wear?

1 Before you write

A Talk with a partner.

1. Look at the pictures. Can you guess where the people are from and what holiday they are celebrating?

2. What is your favorite holiday or celebration? Why?

B Read the paragraph.

My Favorite Celebration

My favorite celebration is the Iranian New Year, *Norouz* ("new day"). This holiday begins on the first day of spring and lasts 13 days. On the Wednesday before Norouz, people build bonfires and jump over them. Iranian people believe that if they do this, they will get rid of their illnesses and misfortunes. On Norouz Eve, the family gathers around a table with seven items that begin with the letter "s" in Persian: an apple, wheat pudding, dried berries, vinegar, a coin, a beautiful flower, and garlic. A bowl of goldfish, a Koran, colored eggs, and a mirror are also on the table. These items symbolize beauty, health, prosperity, and fertility. On Norouz Day, people kiss each other and say, "I hope you will live for one hundred years." We spend the next 13 days visiting each other and eating sweets. Finally, on the last day of the celebration, everyone goes to a park for a big picnic. I wish my whole family lived with me here so that we could celebrate Norouz together.

> The conclusion is an important part of a paragraph. One way to conclude a paragraph is to relate the topic to your personal life.

Lesson objective
- Write a paragraph about a favorite holiday or celebration

Warm-up and review

- Before class. Write today's lesson focus on the board.
  Lesson E:
  Write a paragraph about a favorite holiday or celebration
- Begin class. Books closed. Review vocabulary from the unit. Write *holidays* and *celebrations* on the board. Ask Ss for several examples. Elicit appropriate responses, such as: *New Year's Eve, birthdays, weddings.*
- Ask Ss: *What are some examples of significant birthdays around the world?* (In Nigeria, the 1st, 5th, 10th, and 15th birthdays are very important. In Mexico, a girl's 15th birthday – Quinceañera – is very important. In Japan, a girl's 3rd and 7th birthdays and a boy's 5th birthday are considered special. In Israel, a boy's 13th and a girl's 12th birthday are considered important.)
- Ask Ss: *What's an important birthday for American teenagers?* (The 16th birthday is important because in most states it marks a teenager's ability to get a driver's license.)

Presentation

- Books open. Direct Ss' attention to Exercise **1A** and read the instructions aloud.
- Ask two Ss to read the questions in Exercise **1A** to the class.
- Ss work with a partner to ask and answer the questions. Walk around and help as needed.

Practice

- Direct Ss' attention to Exercise **1B** and read the instructions aloud.
- Ss read the paragraph silently. Ask Ss to underline any words in the paragraph with which they are unfamiliar.
- Have Ss tell you the words they underlined, and write them on the board. Go over the meaning of each word.

> Ask a S to read the tip box aloud. Call on another S to read the last sentence of "My Favorite Celebration." Tell Ss that just as the topic sentence introduces the topic, the concluding sentence wraps up the topic and often summarizes the key points. Explain that there are many ways to conclude a paragraph and that ending on a personal note is one option, especially for a paragraph that expresses the writer's opinion or tells an event from the writer's own life.

Expansion activity *(student pairs)*

- Have Ss compare the celebration in the model paragraph with a celebration from their home culture or country, or with a celebration they have attended in the United States. Write the following on the board: *How does this celebration compare with another celebration you have attended? How are they the same? How are they different?*
- Ss discuss the questions with a partner.
- Write a list of words and phrases on the board that Ss could use to compare and contrast celebrations.
- Words and phrases used to compare could include: *similar, both, like, alike, in the same way.* Words or phrases used to contrast, or show differences, could include: *unlike, difference, but, while, on the other hand, in a different way.*
- Ask Ss to use words of comparison and contrast to share with the class information they discussed with their partner.
- As a follow-up activity, have Ss bring in photos of celebrations they have attended either in the United States or in their home countries.

Expansion activity *(small groups)*

- **Materials needed** Photographs or magazine clippings of different kinds of celebrations.
- Ss in small groups. Distribute one photograph to each group.
- Have Ss in each group look carefully at the photograph and describe what they see.
- Encourage Ss to describe the details of the celebration, such as the food, clothing, and decorations. Ss should also compare the celebration they see in the photograph with a similar one they have celebrated.
- Call on groups to share the information they learned with the class.
- To conclude the activity and help Ss develop their visual literacy skills, ask: *Why do you think the photographer took the picture in the way he (or she) did? Would you have focused on the same people and details? Why or why not?*

Lesson E Writing

Presentation

- Books open. Focus Ss' attention on Exercise **1C** and read the instructions aloud.
- Ask a S to read aloud the headings in the outline.
- Call on another S to read the sample topic.
- Ss work with a partner to complete the outline of the model paragraph on page 130.
- Check answers with the class.

Practice

- Direct Ss' attention to Exercise **1D** and read the instructions aloud. Tell Ss that the information that they use here in writing their outline will help them plan, organize, and write their paragraphs.
- Ss should work individually to complete their outlines. Walk around and help as needed.

> ▼ **Teaching tip**
> Before Ss begin to write, invite them to talk with a partner about the topic. Talking about the topic will help Ss narrow the topic and focus on the details, facts, and examples that they are going to use to support their ideas and opinion in Exercise **2**.

Application

- Focus Ss' attention on Exercise **2** and read the instructions aloud.
- Ss complete the task individually. Walk around and help as needed.

Learner persistence *(individual work)*

- If you have any Ss who have difficulty in writing, sit with them and help them as the other Ss are writing. Work with Ss to use the model paragraph in Exercise **1B** on page 130 and the outlines in Exercises **1C** and **1D** on page 131 to help them plan, organize, and write their paragraphs. Also help Ss write a conclusion that relates the topic to their personal life and experiences (as illustrated in the model).

Comprehension check

- Direct Ss' attention to Exercise **3A**. This exercise asks Ss to develop skills to review and edit their own writing.
- Ss check their own paragraphs against the writing checklist. Walk around and help as needed. If any Ss check *No* for one or more of the checklist items, ask them to edit their paragraphs to include the missing information.

Evaluation

- Focus Ss' attention on Exercise **3B** and read the instructions aloud. This exercise enables Ss to work together to peer-correct their writing. Reading aloud enables the writer to review his or her own writing. Reading to a partner allows the writer to understand the need to write clearly for an audience.
- Ss complete the exercise in pairs. Guide Ss to take turns reading their paragraphs to each other. Walk around and help as needed.
- Listen to Ss as they ask their partner one question about the paragraph and tell their partner one thing they learned from it.
- Ask several Ss to read their paragraphs aloud. Have other Ss ask questions and mention something they learned from the paragraph.
- Direct Ss' attention to the lesson focus on the board.
- Check off the lesson focus as Ss demonstrate an understanding of what they have learned in the lesson.

Expansion activity *(small groups)*

- First, have the class work together to brainstorm a list of questions for a survey on favorite holidays or celebrations in the United States. Then have small groups of Ss ask several people outside the class, in English, about their favorite holiday or celebration in the United States.
- Model the activity. Write the following questions on the board: *What's your favorite American holiday? Why?*
- Encourage each group to look at the headings in the outline in Exercise **1C** to come up with additional questions to ask, for example: *What is the meaning of this holiday or celebration? When is it? How long does it last? What customs are related to the celebration? Who participates?* Have Ss take notes.
- Ask each group to share the results of its findings with the class.

> **More Ventures** *(whole group, pairs, individual)*
> Assign appropriate exercises from the *Teacher's Toolkit Audio CD / CD-ROM*, *Add Ventures*, or the *Workbook*.

C **Work** with a partner. Complete the outline of the model paragraph.

    I. Topic: _My Favorite Celebration – Norouz_

   II. Meaning or symbolism: _Iranian New Year ("new day")_

  III. When celebrated: _begins on the first day of spring; lasts 13 days_

  IV. Customs:

        A. _People build bonfires and jump over them to get rid of illnesses and misfortunes._

        B. _Family gathers around a table with 7 items that begin with "s" in Persian._

        C. _People kiss and say, "I hope you will live for one hundred years."_

        D. _People spend the next 13 days visiting each other and eating sweets._

        E. _Everyone goes to a park for a big picnic._

   V. Conclusion: _I wish my whole family lived with me here so that we could celebrate Norouz together._

D **Plan** a paragraph about your favorite holiday or celebration. Make an outline like the one in Exercise 1C. Include at least three customs. Use your own paper.
(Answers will vary.)

2 Write

Write a paragraph about your favorite holiday or celebration. Use the paragraph in Exercise 1B and the outlines in Exercises 1C and 1D to help you.

3 After you write

A **Check** your writing.

	Yes	No
1. I described at least three customs for my favorite holiday or celebration.	☐	☐
2. I wrote a conclusion relating the celebration to my personal life.	☐	☐
3. I used _hope_ and _wish_ correctly.	☐	☐

B **Share** your writing with a partner.

1. Take turns. Read your paragraph to a partner.
2. Comment on your partner's paragraph. Ask your partner a question about the paragraph. Tell your partner one thing you learned.

1 Life-skills reading

Pumpkin Pie

Preparation time: 15 minutes
Cooking time: 50 minutes

Ingredients

1 pre-made pie crust
1 (8-ounce) package cream
  cheese, softened
2 cups canned pumpkin,
  mashed

¼ teaspoon salt
1 cup sugar
1 egg plus 2 egg yolks,
  lightly beaten
1 cup heavy cream

¼ cup (½ stick) melted butter
1 teaspoon vanilla extract
½ teaspoon ground cinnamon
¼ teaspoon ground ginger,
  optional

1. Preheat the oven to 350 degrees Fahrenheit.
2. Beat the softened cream cheese.
3. Add the pumpkin and beat until blended.
4. Then add the salt and sugar, and beat until blended.
5. Then add the egg mixed with the yolks, cream, and melted butter, and beat until blended.
6. Finally, mix in the vanilla, cinnamon, and ginger.

7. Pour the filling into the pre-made pie crust, and bake for 50 minutes, or until the center is firm.
8. Set the pie on a wire rack, and cool until it is room temperature. Cut into slices and serve with whipped cream or ice cream.
Serves 6–8 people.

A Read the questions. Look at the recipe. Circle the answers.

1. How much sugar do you need to make the pie?
   a. ¼ cup
   b. ½ cup
   c. 1 cup
   d. 2 cups

2. What is the total cooking time for the pie?
   a. 10 minutes
   b. 15 minutes
   c. 30 minutes
   d. 50 minutes

3. Which of the following statements is true?
   a. Soften the butter.
   b. Use 1 cup of milk.
   c. Use 1 stick of butter.
   d. Beat the eggs.

4. What should you do after you blend the cream cheese and pumpkin?
   a. Add the salt and sugar.
   b. Bake the pie.
   c. Add the eggs.
   d. Pour the filling into the pie crust.

5. How many people does this recipe serve?
   a. 1–2
   b. 3–4
   c. 5–6
   d. 6–8

6. Which ingredient is not required?
   a. vanilla
   b. ginger
   c. cinnamon
   d. cream cheese

B Talk with a partner. What is a traditional meal or recipe for a celebration in your native country? Describe the meal or recipe to your partner.

Warm-up and review

- Before class. Write today's lesson focus on the board.
  Lesson F:
  Read and understand a recipe
  Review topic vocabulary
  Complete the project and the self-assessment
- *Begin class.* Books closed. Write the word *recipe* on the board. Make sure that Ss understand the meaning of the word.
- Ask Ss: *How many of you like to cook? What do you like to make? Do you like to follow a recipe or cook without following directions?*
- Ask Ss: *What information do you find in a recipe?* Elicit appropriate responses, such as: *ingredients, measurements, cooking time, how-to directions or steps, how many people the recipe is for.* Write the examples on the board.
- Tell Ss that they will be reading a recipe for pumpkin pie. Ask Ss if they know when this pie is typically prepared and eaten in the United States (on Thanksgiving). Ask if anyone in the class has ever tasted pumpkin pie.

Presentation

- Books open. Read the title of the recipe aloud, as well as the preparation and cooking time.
- Call on Ss to read each of the recipe ingredients aloud. Explain any new words.
- Ask eight Ss to read the eight steps, one at a time. Explain vocabulary as needed.

▼ **Teaching tip**
Tell Ss that learning to read a recipe is a useful skill for everyday life. Ask Ss if they have ever followed recipes, either in their native language or in English. Explain to Ss that they may read recipes at home in the future, or they may have jobs in which they will need to read, understand, and follow recipes or how-to directions, such as those used in a recipe.

Practice

- Read the instructions aloud for Exercise **1A**. This exercise helps prepare Ss for standardized-type tests they may have to take. Be sure that Ss understand the task. Have Ss individually scan for and circle the answers.

Comprehension check

- Check answers to Exercise **1A** with the class. Make sure that Ss have followed the instructions and circled their answers.
- Have Ss read aloud the questions and answers they circled. Make corrections as needed.

Application

- Direct Ss' attention to Exercise **1B** and read the instructions aloud. Make sure that Ss understand the questions.
- Ss work in pairs to ask and answer the question. Walk around and help as needed.

Expansion activity (small groups)

- Tell Ss that they are going to write a recipe for a holiday dish from their native culture or country. Write this chart on the board:

Typical dish	Holiday
pumpkin pie	Thanksgiving (U.S.)

- Call on a S to read the two headings. Ask another S to read the example.
- Invite Ss in small groups to talk about a specific dish from their culture or country and the holiday for which it is usually prepared.
- Have Ss come to the board to add their examples to the chart.
- Tell groups that they should choose a dish that they have just discussed, or one that they especially enjoy, and write it in recipe format as in the model on page 132.
- Ask each group to share its recipe with the class. Walk around and help as needed.
- Collect the recipes and put them together in a class cookbook that all Ss can consult.
- If possible, have Ss prepare the recipe at home and then bring it to class to celebrate the completion of *Ventures Student's Book 4.*

  Option You can give Ss the option of preparing the pumpkin pie recipe presented in Exercise 1.

Presentation

- Books open. Focus Ss' attention on the picture in Exercise **2**. Have Ss look at the picture and describe what they see. Ask Ss: *What is being celebrated? How is it being celebrated? Do you think that this is a real holiday?* Explain vocabulary as needed.

Practice

- Direct Ss' attention to Exercise **2A** and read the instructions aloud.
- Call on three Ss to read each of the three parts of the outline: *Origin, Location, Traditions*.
- Ss work in small groups and use the outline to complete the exercise. Walk around and help as needed.
- Direct Ss' attention to the second part of Exercise **2A** and read the instructions aloud.
- Call on Ss from each group to share information about the holiday or celebration they designed.

Expansion activity *(small groups)*

- **Materials needed** Poster board and colored markers, colored pencils, or crayons.
- Provide each group with poster board and colored markers, colored pencils, or crayons.
- Ss work with their group from Exercise **2A** to draw a picture of people celebrating the holiday they designed. All Ss in the group should help determine the details and composition of the picture, as well as a title for the holiday to write on the poster.
- Have each group choose one or two designated artists. Ss who do not feel comfortable drawing can present the group's picture to the class. Walk around and help as needed.
- Call on the presenters from each group to display and explain their poster to the class.
- Leave time for a question-and-answer session.

Expansion activity *(individual work)*

- Tell each S to write a paragraph about the holiday his or her group designed. Refer Ss to the model paragraph on page 130. Ss should begin their paragraphs with a topic sentence, followed by supporting details, and a strong concluding sentence. Walk around and help as needed.
- Ask Ss to join their group from Exercise **2A** to take turns reading their paragraphs to the group.
- Invite Ss to share their paragraphs and ideas about their group poster with the class.

Application

- Direct Ss' attention to Exercise **2B** and read the instructions aloud.
- Ask a S to read aloud the example greeting.
- Have Ss work with a partner to share greetings for important holidays. Walk around and help as needed.
- Direct Ss' attention to the second part of the instructions in Exercise **2B**.
- Call on individual Ss to share their holiday greetings with the class.

> ***More Ventures*** *(whole group, pairs, individual)*
> Assign appropriate exercises from the *Teacher's Toolkit Audio CD / CD-ROM, Add Ventures*, or the *Workbook*.

Community building

- **Project** Ask Ss to turn to page 140 in their Student's Book to complete the project for Unit 10.

Evaluation

- Before asking Ss to turn to the self-assessment on page 145, do a quick review of the unit. Have Ss turn to Lesson A. Ask the class to talk about what they remember about this lesson. Prompt Ss, if necessary, with questions, for example: *What are the conversations about on this page? What vocabulary is in the pictures?* Continue in this manner to review each lesson quickly.
- **Self-assessment** Read the instructions for Exercise **3**. Ask Ss to turn to the self-assessment page to complete the unit self-assessment. The self-assessments are also on the *Teacher's Toolkit Audio CD / CD-ROM*. If you prefer to collect the assessments and save them as part of each S's portfolio assessment, print out the unit self-assessment from the Toolkit, ask Ss to complete it, and collect and save it.
- If Ss are ready, administer the unit test on pages T-199–T-201 of this *Teacher's Edition* (or on the *Teacher's Toolkit Audio CD / CD-ROM*). The audio and audio script for the tests are on the *Teacher's Toolkit Audio CD / CD-ROM*.

2 Fun with language

A **Work** in a small group. Design a new holiday or celebration. Use the outline as a guide to organize your group's ideas.

   I. Origin
    A. What is the name of the holiday or celebration?
    B. When is it? What month and day(s)? How long does it last?
    C. Describe the holiday or celebration. Is there some history behind it? Why is it celebrated? What does it symbolize?
    D. Who celebrates the holiday – everyone? only children?

  II. Location
    A. Where is it celebrated – outside? inside?
    B. Are there special places to visit or go to?

 III. Traditions
    A. What are three customs related to the holiday?
    B. Are any special clothes worn or foods eaten?

Share your holiday or celebration with your classmates.

B **Work** with a partner. Share greetings for important holidays.

> In the United States, people say "Happy New Year" on January 1.

1. Holiday: _____   Greeting: _____
2. Holiday: _____   Greeting: _____

Share information with your classmates.

3 Wrap up

Complete the **Self-assessment** on page 145.

Review

1 Listening

Listen. Take notes on a street interview.

Things that bring good luck	Things that bring bad luck
1. *wear bright colors like red*	4. *don't sweep the house*
2. *open all the doors and windows of your house at midnight*	5. *don't buy new shoes*
3. *eat a lot of candy*	6. *don't use knives or scissors*

Talk with a partner. Check your answers.

2 Grammar

A Write. Complete the story.

A New Year's Eve Celebration

Sergei _____*wishes*_____ his friend Olga could visit him in New York
1. hopes / wishes

over the holidays, but she can't get the time off. _____*Consequently*_____ , they
2. Consequently / Since

won't be together on New Year's Eve. If she _____*were*_____ in New York,
3. is / were

he would take her to Times Square _____*because of*_____ the big celebration
4. since / because of

there. Every year at one minute before midnight, a large crystal ball starts to

drop slowly from high above the street. When it reaches the bottom, everybody

goes crazy _____*since*_____ it's the beginning of the New Year. Sergei
5. since / due to

really _____*hopes*_____ that Olga can come next year. If she comes, she
6. hopes / wishes

_____*will*_____ have a great time.
7. will / would

B Write. Look at the words that are underlined in the answers. Write the questions.

1. **A** *Where would Sergei take Olga if she were in New York?*

   B Sergei would take Olga to <u>Times Square</u> if she were in New York.

2. **A** *What starts to drop at one minute before midnight?*

   B <u>The crystal ball</u> starts to drop at one minute before midnight.

3. **A** *When does Sergei hope that Olga can come?*

   B Sergei hopes that Olga can come <u>next year</u>.

Talk with a partner. Ask and answer the questions.

Lesson objectives
- Review vocabulary and grammar from Units 9 and 10
- Practice identifying thought groups

Warm-up and review

- Before class. Write today's lesson focus on the board.
  Review unit:
  Review vocabulary and grammar from Units 9 and 10
  Practice identifying thought groups in sentences

- Begin class. Books closed. Review vocabulary and grammar from Units 9 and 10. Write these sentences on the board. Have Ss complete the sentences using the present unreal conditional and the words in parentheses.
  If you _____ energy-efficient appliances, you _____ on energy use. (buy, cut down)
  We _____ millions of trees if everyone _____ their newspapers. (save, recycle)

- Say this sentence to Ss: *Due to global warming, the sea levels are rising.* Ask: *What are some other consequences of global warming?* If your Ss don't know the answer, lead them to see that many scientists think that global warming is causing climate changes as well as extreme weather, such as hurricanes and other storms. Encourage Ss to use the connectors of cause (*since, due to, because,* and *because of*) and the connectors of effect (*consequently, as a result,* and *therefore*).

- Review the future real conditional and the unreal conditional. Write these sentences on the board.
  Future real conditional: If you don't stay home on New Year's Eve, what will you do?
  Unreal conditional: What would you do if you won a lot of money?

- Encourage Ss to answer each question using *if* + the future real or the unreal conditional form of the verb.

- Review *hope* and *wish*. Write these sentences on the board. Have Ss read the situations and make statements with *hope* and *wish*.
  Jenny can't go home for Thanksgiving because she doesn't have enough money. (Jenny wishes she could go home for Thanksgiving.)
  Gustavo wants to get a new TV as a birthday gift. (Gustavo hopes he will get a new TV as a birthday gift.)

Presentation

- Books open. Direct Ss' attention to Exercise **1** and read the instructions aloud. Tell Ss that they will hear an interview between an interviewer and two different people.

- 💿 [Class Audio CD3 track 24] Model the task. Play or read only the first part of the interview on the audio program (see audio script, page T-167). Pause after Angela says, *Well, it's traditional to wear bright colors, such as red.*

- Direct Ss' attention to number 1 in the chart (*Things that bring good luck*) and ask: *What does Angela say is*

one of the things that people can do to bring good luck? (wear bright colors like red)

- Ask a S to read aloud the other chart heading (*Things that bring bad luck*). Say: *Now listen and complete the chart.*

- 💿 [Class Audio CD3 track 24] Play or read the complete audio program (see audio script, page T-167). Ss listen and complete the chart. Repeat the audio program as needed.

Comprehension check

- Read aloud the second part of the instructions for Exercise **1**.

- Ss complete the exercise in pairs. Walk around and help as needed.

- Ask several Ss to make sentences about things that bring good luck and bad luck, using the information in the chart.

Practice

- Direct Ss' attention to Exercise **2A**. Ask: *What is the title of this story?* ("A New Year's Eve Celebration")

- Read the instructions aloud in Exercise **2A**. Point out that in this exercise, Ss choose the correct word(s) to complete each sentence.

- Ask a S to read aloud the first sentence in the story, including the sample answer. Have Ss continue reading the story and filling in the blanks. Explain any unfamiliar vocabulary as needed.

- Ss complete the exercise individually. Help as needed.

- Write the numbers *1–7* on the board. Ask Ss to come to the board to write the answers only.

- Call on several Ss to read the complete story using the answers on the board. Make corrections as needed.

Comprehension check

- Direct Ss' attention to Exercise **2B**. This exercise reviews question formation related to the reading, "A New Year's Eve Celebration."

- Read the instructions aloud. Model the exercise. Focus Ss' attention on the answer to number 1. Ask: *What question can you ask to get this answer?*

- Ss complete the exercise individually. Help as needed.

- Check answers with the class. Call on three Ss to read their questions. Make corrections as needed.

- Read aloud the second part of the instructions for Exercise **2B**.

- Ss work in pairs to ask and answer the questions. Help as needed.

Review

Presentation

- Books closed. Write on the board: *Thought groups.* Tell Ss that learning about *thought groups,* which are small chunks of sentences, will help them with their pronunciation in English. Ask Ss: *What kinds of words are usually stressed – content words or function words?* Elicit: *Content words are usually stressed.* Explain that thought groups are phrases that usually have one strongly stressed content word.

- Write on the board: *It's time that we stop wasting* / *and start recycling.* Read the sentence aloud, stressing the underlined words.

- Ask Ss which words are stressed. (*wasting* and *recycling*) Indicate the stressed words by underlining them. Show Ss how the two words fall into two different parts of the sentence. Point out the slash that separates the two thought groups and signals a short pause between them.

- Lead Ss to see that by dividing sentences into *thought groups,* long sentences are broken into shorter pieces with pauses between them. Chunking makes it easier for listeners to understand the meaning of a sentence.

> ▼ **Teaching tip**
> Some Ss may find it difficult to detect thought groups. If necessary, exaggerate the pause between thought groups, as well as the emphasis on the strongly stressed word in each group so that Ss can hear the differences.

- Books open. Direct Ss to page 135, and call on a S to read the information at the top of the page.
- Focus Ss' attention on Exercise **3A** and read the instructions aloud.
- [Class Audio CD3 track 25] Play or read the complete audio program (see audio script, page T-167).
- Read aloud the second part of the instructions for Exercise **3A**.
- [Class Audio CD3 track 26] Repeat the audio program. Pause after each phrase to give Ss time to repeat. Play the audio program as many times as needed. Focus Ss' attention on the thought groups and pauses.

Practice

- Direct Ss' attention to Exercise **3B** and read the instructions aloud.
- [Class Audio CD3 track 27] Model the exercise. Play or read the first sentence on the audio program (see audio script, page T-167). Ask Ss to tell you where they put the slash marks.

- Tell Ss to pay attention to the thought groups in each sentence as they listen. Play or read the audio program, stopping as needed for Ss to repeat the sentences.
- Play or read the complete audio program again. Repeat the audio program as needed.
- Read aloud the second part of the instructions in Exercise **3B**.
- Ss complete the task in pairs. Help as needed.

Comprehension check

- Direct Ss' attention to Exercise **3C** and read the instructions aloud.
- Ss work in pairs to practice the conversations and divide each sentence into thought groups. Walk around and listen to Ss' pronunciation of the stressed words in the thought groups. Help as needed.
- Ask several partners to read the conversations aloud. Call on other Ss to identify the thought groups. Write any sentence on the board with which Ss had trouble identifying the thought groups. Say the sentence and show Ss where the pauses are between the thought groups. Have Ss repeat.

Application

- Read the instructions aloud in Exercise **3D**.
- Ss work individually to complete the exercise.
- Ss work with their partner to ask and answer the questions.

Evaluation

- Direct Ss' attention to the lesson focus on the board.
- Write this sentence on the board, and ask Ss to complete it using the correct form of the present unreal conditional and the words in parentheses.
  If you _____ eating fish that contains lead, you _____ healthier. (stop, be)
- Ask Ss to give examples of sentences using these connectors: *since, due to, consequently,* and *as a result.*
- Write these sentences on the board: *If I go to Mexico this summer, I will visit my family. If she traveled to Brazil, she would spend time at the beach.* Ask Ss to make up similar sentences using the future real conditional or the unreal conditional.
- Write these sentences on the board: *Ana really wants to go out to dinner with her husband on Valentine's Day. Ana doesn't have the night off.* Ask Ss to read the two sentences and make a statement with *hope* or *wish.* (Ana wishes she could go out to dinner with her husband on Valentine's Day.)
- Check off each part of the lesson focus as Ss demonstrate an understanding of what they have learned in the lesson.

3 Pronunciation: identifying thought groups

Thought groups are phrases that usually have one strongly stressed word. A sentence can have several thought groups that are separated by short pauses.

A 💿 **Listen** to the following sentences.

> **One thought group**
>
> 1. We need to save <u>energy</u>.
> 2. I always take the <u>bus</u> to work.
>
> **Two thought groups**
>
> 3. We need to <u>reduce</u> our energy use / and <u>protect</u> the environment.
> 4. When I lived in <u>Vietnam</u>, / I always <u>walked</u> to work.
>
> **Three or more thought groups**
>
> 5. There are <u>several</u> things you can do / to <u>reduce</u> your energy use / and <u>protect</u> the environment.
> 6. You can <u>walk</u>, / ride a <u>bicycle</u>, / <u>carpool</u>, / or take the <u>bus</u>.

💿 **Listen again and repeat.** Pay attention to the thought groups and pauses.

B 💿 **Listen and repeat.** Then put slash marks (/) between the thought groups.

1. People are very concerned/about the environment.
2. We need to take responsibility/for saving the earth.
3. There are many ways/that we can save energy.
4. One thing people can do/is to cut down/on their driving.
5. And also,/we need to be careful/not to waste electricity.
6. We can get a lot of information/about global warming/on the Internet.

Talk with a partner. Compare your answers.

C **Talk** with a partner. Practice the questions and answers. Divide each sentence into thought groups.

1. *A* Have you read about global warming?
   B Yes, I've read a lot about it.

2. *A* What uses more energy, your stove or your refrigerator?
   B I'm not sure, but I think my refrigerator uses more energy because it's 15 years old.

3. *A* What do guests bring to a Vietnamese wedding?
   B At a Vietnamese wedding, the guests just bring cash.

4. *A* What do people do on the last day of the celebration?
   B On the last day, everyone goes to a park for a big picnic.

D **Write** four questions about saving energy. Ask your partner.

Projects

Overview

The projects on pages 136–140 in the *Ventures* Student's Book are optional material to be used at the completion of a unit. There is one project per unit, and most of the projects can be completed in one class period.

Projects are valuable activities because they extend students' learning into a real-world context. They work within the unit topic, but they also go beyond the Student's Book.

These projects are designed to be fun and practical, with the goal of helping students become more independent while learning to live in a new culture and speak a new language.

Project set-up and materials

Projects may be done in class as a group activity or outside of class, individually.

There is a reference at the end of each unit in this Teacher's Edition to remind teachers about the projects. Some projects will need the teacher to gather simple materials to be used in class. For example, some require large poster paper, index cards, or authentic materials such as course catalogs, store ads, and sales receipts. In order to complete other projects, students will need access to a computer that is linked to the Internet.

Skills learned through the projects

Students learn different skills through these projects. For example, half the projects involve use of the Internet. Students search for information using key words. This is an essential skill that most students will need to use in English. In addition, the projects encourage students to practice other essential life skills, such as working collaboratively to make a class book, looking up information about holidays or celebrations, and learning about time-saving devices.

Community building and learner persistence

Ventures projects help build community inside and outside the classroom as students work together, using materials such as local newspapers and inviting guest speakers to class to get information. Building community, in turn, helps to promote learner persistence. As students apply essential life skills, they will become more confident in their English skills and will be more motivated to come to class to learn additional skills that will help them in daily life.

Projects

A job for your intelligence

A Use the Internet.

Find careers that match your primary intelligence.

Keywords (your primary intelligence), intelligence, careers

B Make a chart.

Make a list of careers that match your primary intelligence. Are you interested in any of them? Check your opinion.

Careers for bodily / kinesthetic intelligence	Interested	Not interested
carpenter		✓
actor	✓	
dancer		✓
landscaper	✓	

C Share your information.

Talk about your chart. Explain why you are or are not interested in the careers that match your primary intelligence.
Listen as your classmates present their charts. Suggest other careers for them.

Continuing education

A Find information about a class.

Look at a course catalog or class schedule from an adult school or community college. Find two classes you would like to take. Copy or print out the course description.

B Take notes. Answer these questions.

1. What are the class names?
2. When are the classes scheduled?
3. Where are they located?
4. What are the requirements, if any?
5. How much do the classes cost?

Class	Dates	Time	Location	Requirements	Cost
Culinary Arts 1	Jan. 15–Mar. 2	M–F: 8:30–2:30	ECC, Room 129	placement test	$95

C Share your information.

Tell your classmates about the classes you chose. Why did you choose them? Are you going to take them? Why or why not?

Projects

Household rules

A Make a list.

Write some rules that children should follow at home.

> Do homework.
> Take off shoes in the house.
> Help with chores around the house.

B Interview a partner.

Find more rules that children should follow. Add them to your list.

C Share your information.

Make a class wall chart.
Talk about the rules. Which ones are for young children (5 to 12 years old)?
Which ones are for teenagers? Are some rules too strict? Which ones?

Coping with test anxiety

A Use the Internet.

Find information about ways to cope with anxiety before or during tests.

Keywords   anxiety before tests   test anxiety

B Make a list.

Write ways to cope with anxiety
before or during tests.

C Share your information.

Talk to your classmates about ways to cope
with test anxiety.
Make a class poster.
What are the best ideas? Take a class vote.

> 1. Get a good night's sleep before the test.
> 2. Come to class early on the day of the test,
>   so you have time to relax.
> 3. Get comfortable in your chair.

Helping others

A Think about helping.

What are some things that people have done to help you? Share your experiences with a partner.

B Make a list.

Write the names of the people you have helped. What did you do to help them?

Person	What did you do to help?
My grandmother	took her to her doctor's appointment
My neighbor	cut his grass
My friend Donna	helped her with her homework

C Share your information.

Talk to your classmates about helping others.
Make a class wall chart of ways to help.

Time-saving devices

A Use the Internet.

Find information about a time-saving device you have or would like to have.

Keywords (name of time-saving device)   time-saving devices

B Take notes. Answer these questions.

1. Who invented it?
2. When was it invented?
3. What are some interesting things about this device?

Device	Who invented it?	When was it invented?	Interesting things
washing machine	Hamilton Smith	1858	There is a Washing Machine Museum in Colorado.

C Share your information.

Talk about the device.
Make a class wall chart.
Take a class survey. Which time-saving device do most of your classmates have?
Which one would most of them like to have?

Projects

What's the return policy?

A Find three ads or store receipts that show a store's return policy.

Underline the important information.

B Make a chart.

Write the name of the store and the return policy for that store.

Store	Return policy
Alta's Dress Shop	Receipt required for refund.
Jack's Secondhand Bookstore	Store credit or exchanges only.
Dickenson's Electronics	No returns after 30 days.

C Share your information.

Show your chart to your classmates.
Which store has the best return policy?
Which store has the worst return policy?

Tips for cover letters

A Use the Internet.

Find information about how to write a good cover letter.

Keywords | how to write a cover letter | | cover letter writing tips |

B Take notes.

1. Write three tips.
2. Print out a sample cover letter.

Tips for good cover letters

1. Research the company where you'd like to work.
2. Keep the letter short.
3. Check your spelling and your grammar carefully.

C Share your information.

Show the cover letter to your classmates.
Tell them why you think it's a good cover letter.
Make a class book of good cover letters.

"Green" tips for school

A Make a list.

What are some ways your school could be "green"? Write your ideas.

Use recycled paper napkins in the cafeteria.
Put recycle bins in the classrooms.
Turn off the lights in empty rooms.

B Interview a partner.

Find two more ideas for "living green" at school. Add them to your list.

C Share your information.

Make a class poster.
Invite a school administrator to your classroom.
Share your class poster with the administrator.

Celebrations around the world

A Use the Internet.

Choose a holiday or celebration. Find information about the way it is celebrated in another country.

Keywords | (holiday or celebration), customs around the world

B Take notes. Answer these questions.

1. What is the name of the celebration?
2. What is the country you researched?
3. What is the background or reason for the celebration?
4. What are some customs related to this holiday or celebration?

Celebration	Country	Background	Customs
Independence Day	Peru	Peru declared its independence from Spain on July 28, 1821.	People have two days off. The president gives a speech. There are parades. Families spend time together.

C Share your information.

Tell your class about the holiday or celebration you researched.
Make a class book.

Self-assessments

Overview

Each unit of *Ventures 4* Student's Book ends with a self-assessment. Self-assessments allow students to reflect on what they have learned and to decide whether they need more review of the material.

How self-assessments help students

- It is not possible for English language teachers to teach students all the English they need to know. Therefore, it is important that teachers help students develop strategies for learning and for measuring their learning. One important strategy is self-assessment. With self-assessment, students become aware of their own learning and focus on their own performance. Being able to self-assess is important for developing learner autonomy. It is that autonomy that will equip students for lifelong learning.

- Self-assessment allows students to participate in the assessment process. Responsibility for learning shifts from the teacher to the students as self-assessment makes the students more aware of their role in learning and monitoring their own performance.

- Self-assessment can also contribute to learner persistence. Learners will continue to attend classes when they have verification that learning has taken place. They can measure this learning when they complete the self-assessment checklists.

How self-assessments help teachers

- Teachers can use the results of the self-assessments to identify areas that need further instruction or review. Teachers can use the results of this assessment to meet with students and discuss items that have been mastered as well as those that need further study.

- The information on the self-assessment forms can also be used at the beginning of the unit to identify and discuss the learning objectives of the unit. In this way, students will have a clear understanding of the learning goals. If they know what the learning objectives are, they can better focus on their learning. This results in greater learner gains, which is gratifying to both students and teachers.

Self-assessment in *Ventures*

- Each self-assessment asks students to write eight new words they have learned and to rate the skills and functions they feel they have mastered or have not mastered. Students then decide if they are ready to take the unit test to confirm this acquisition of unit language. The self-assessments are in an easy-to-use form, making it easier for students to check how they feel they are progressing.

- If students feel they need additional study for a particular unit, the *Ventures* series provides additional practice in the Workbook and *Add Ventures*.

- The *Teacher's Toolkit Audio CD / CD-ROM* contains the same self-assessments that are found in the Student's Book. However, on the CD-ROM, each unit's self-assessment is on its own page and can be printed, distributed to, and completed by the student after each unit and placed in his or her learner portfolio. It can also be given to students to keep as a personal record of their progress.

Self-assessments

Unit 1 Personal information

A Vocabulary Write eight new words you have learned.

_____ _____ _____ _____

_____ _____ _____ _____

B Skills and functions Read the sentences. Rate yourself. Circle 3 (*I agree.*) OR
2 (*I'm not sure.*) OR 1 (*I can't do this.*).

I can use noun clauses to talk about what I think: *I believe **that every person is unique**.*	3 2 1
I can use adjectives and adverbs: *She's a **good** writer. She writes **well**.*	3 2 1
I can skim an article to get a general idea of what it is about.	3 2 1
I can write a paragraph with a general topic sentence and supporting details.	3 2 1
I can read and understand a diagram.	3 2 1

C What's next? Choose one.

☐ I am ready for the unit test.   ☐ I need more practice with _____ .

Unit 2 At school

A Vocabulary Write eight new words you have learned.

_____ _____ _____ _____

_____ _____ _____ _____

B Skills and functions Read the sentences. Rate yourself. Circle 3 (*I agree.*) OR
2 (*I'm not sure.*) OR 1 (*I can't do this.*).

I can ask and answer questions with the present passive: ***Are** internships **offered** for this program? Yes, internships **are offered**.*	3 2 1
I can use the present passive with infinitives: *The student **is required to take** a placement test.*	3 2 1
I can scan an article to find specific information.	3 2 1
I can write a paragraph using specific details such as facts, examples, and reasons to support my topic sentence.	3 2 1
I can read and understand a chart.	3 2 1

C What's next? Choose one.

☐ I am ready for the unit test.   ☐ I need more practice with _____ .

Unit 3 Friends and family

A Vocabulary Write eight new words you have learned.

_____ _____ _____ _____

_____ _____ _____ _____

B Skills and functions Read the sentences. Rate yourself. Circle 3 (*I agree.*) OR
2 (*I'm not sure.*) OR 1 (*I can't do this.*).

I can ask indirect *Wh-* questions: *I'd like to know **why Maria is** so strict. Can you tell me **why Maria is** so strict?*	3 2 1
I can ask indirect *Yes / No* questions: *I'd like to know **if you finished** your homework. Can you tell me **whether you finished** your homework?*	3 2 1
I can recognize words that are repeated to get an idea of what a reading is about.	3 2 1
I can write a paragraph using transition words to show the relationship between sentences or ideas in a paragraph.	3 2 1
I can read and understand a survey.	3 2 1

C What's next? Choose one.

☐ I am ready for the unit test.   ☐ I need more practice with _____ .

Unit 4 Health

A Vocabulary Write eight new words you have learned.

_____ _____ _____ _____

_____ _____ _____ _____

B Skills and functions Read the sentences. Rate yourself. Circle 3 (*I agree.*) OR
2 (*I'm not sure.*) OR 1 (*I can't do this.*).

I can make sentences with *ought to*, *shouldn't*, *have to*, and *don't have to* to express advice, necessity, or lack of necessity.	3 2 1
I can use *should have* and *shouldn't have* to talk about regrets and advice in the past.	3 2 1
I can relate what I read to my own experience.	3 2 1
I can write a paragraph organized by actions and results.	3 2 1
I can read and understand a bar graph.	3 2 1

C What's next? Choose one.

☐ I am ready for the unit test.   ☐ I need more practice with _____ .

Unit 5 Around town

A Vocabulary Write eight new words you have learned.

_____   _____   _____   _____

_____   _____   _____   _____

B Skills and functions Read the sentences. Rate yourself. Circle 3 (*I agree.*) OR
2 (*I'm not sure.*) OR 1 (*I can't do this.*).

I can make sentences with the time clauses *until* and *as soon as*: *She stayed* **until** *he finished lunch. She left* **as soon as** *he finished lunch.*	3 2 1
I can make sentences with repeated actions in the present and past: *She* **volunteers** *three times a month. She* **has volunteered** *several times this month.*	3 2 1
I can guess if a word is positive or negative by reading the words around it.	3 2 1
I can write a paragraph with details answering *Wh-* questions.	3 2 1
I can read and understand advertisements for volunteer positions.	3 2 1

C What's next? Choose one.

☐ I am ready for the unit test.   ☐ I need more practice with _____ .

Unit 6 Time

A Vocabulary Write eight new words you have learned.

_____   _____   _____   _____

_____   _____   _____   _____

B Skills and functions Read the sentences. Rate yourself. Circle 3 (*I agree.*) OR
2 (*I'm not sure.*) OR 1 (*I can't do this.*).

I can make sentences with *although* and *even though*: *I drive* **although** *the subway is cheaper. I drive* **even though** *the subway is cheaper.*	3 2 1
I can distinguish between *because* and *although*: *I drive* **because** *it is convenient. I drive* **although** *gas is expensive.*	3 2 1
I can distinguish between fact and opinion.	3 2 1
I can write a paragraph describing advantages and disadvantages.	3 2 1
I can read and understand a table.	3 2 1

C What's next? Choose one.

☐ I am ready for the unit test.   ☐ I need more practice with _____ .

Unit 7 Shopping

A **Vocabulary** Write eight new words you have learned.

_____   _____   _____   _____

_____   _____   _____   _____

B **Skills and functions** Read the sentences. Rate yourself. Circle 3 (*I agree.*) OR
2 (*I'm not sure.*) OR 1 (*I can't do this.*).

I can use adjective clauses as the subject of a dependent clause: *I want to get a camera **that's not too expensive**.*	3 2 1
I can use adjective clauses as the object of a dependent clause: *I like the car **that you bought**.*	3 2 1
I can recognize synonyms in a reading.	3 2 1
I can write a paragraph using transition words to signal a list of reasons.	3 2 1
I can read and understand a returned-merchandise form.	3 2 1

C **What's next?** Choose one.

☐ I am ready for the unit test.   ☐ I need more practice with _____ .

Unit 8 Work

A **Vocabulary** Write eight new words you have learned.

_____   _____   _____   _____

_____   _____   _____   _____

B **Skills and functions** Read the sentences. Rate yourself. Circle 3 (*I agree.*) OR
2 (*I'm not sure.*) OR 1 (*I can't do this.*).

I can use the present perfect and the present perfect continuous: *He **has just talked** to the manager.* *He **has been talking** to the manager for several minutes.*	3 2 1
I can use adjectives ending in *-ed* and *-ing* to describe feelings or characteristics: *She's **excited**. The job is **exciting**.*	3 2 1
I can recognize how quotations are used to support the main idea.	3 2 1
I can write a cover letter that includes all the important information.	3 2 1
I can read and understand a chart.	3 2 1

C **What's next?** Choose one.

☐ I am ready for the unit test.   ☐ I need more practice with _____ .

Unit 9 Daily living

A **Vocabulary** Write eight new words you have learned.

_____ _____ _____ _____

_____ _____ _____ _____

B **Skills and functions** Read the sentences. Rate yourself. Circle 3 (*I agree.*) OR
2 (*I'm not sure.*) OR 1 (*I can't do this.*).

I can make sentences using the present unreal conditional: *If everybody **drove** smaller cars, we **would use** less gasoline.*	3 2 1
I can use *since, due to, consequently,* and *as a result* to show cause and effect: ***Since** the earth is getting warmer, the polar ice caps are melting.* *The earth is getting warmer. **Consequently**, the polar ice caps are melting.*	3 2 1
I can ask myself questions when I read to identify a cause-and-effect relationship.	3 2 1
I can write a paragraph describing the causes and effects of a problem.	3 2 1
I can read and understand a chart.	3 2 1

C **What's next?** Choose one.

☐ I am ready for the unit test.   ☐ I need more practice with _____ .

Unit 10 Leisure

A **Vocabulary** Write eight new words you have learned.

_____ _____ _____ _____

_____ _____ _____ _____

B **Skills and functions** Read the sentences. Rate yourself. Circle 3 (*I agree.*) OR
2 (*I'm not sure.*) OR 1 (*I can't do this.*).

I can make statements using the future real conditional and unreal conditional: *If I **have** time, I **will call** you. If I **had** time, I **would call** you.*	3 2 1
I can make statements using *hope* and *wish*: *I **hope** I **can come** to the party. I **wish** I **could come** to the party.*	3 2 1
I can recognize punctuation in a reading that gives a clue to meaning.	3 2 1
I can write a conclusion that relates the topic to my personal life.	3 2 1
I can read and understand a recipe.	3 2 1

C **What's next?** Choose one.

☐ I am ready for the unit test.   ☐ I need more practice with _____ .

Reference

Clauses

A *clause* is a part of a sentence that has a subject and a verb.
A *main clause* is a complete sentence.
A *dependent clause* is not a complete sentence; it is connected to a main clause.
A sentence with the structure main clause + dependent clause or
dependent clause + main clause is called a *complex sentence*.

Noun clauses with *that*

Some complex sentences have the form main clause + noun clause (see Clauses above).
A noun clause is a type of dependent clause. Some noun clauses consist of *that* + subject + verb.
However, it is also correct to omit *that*. The main clause can be a statement or a question.

	Main clause	Noun clause
Statement	People think	(that) she is smart.
Question	Do you think	(that) she is smart?

Adjectives and adverbs

Adjectives give information about nouns.
Adverbs give information about verbs. Most adverbs end in *-ly*.
A few adverbs are irregular, such as *fast*, *well*, and *hard*.

Adjective	Regular adverb	Irregular adverb
Carol is an *intelligent* girl.	Carol speaks *intelligently*.	Carol speaks *well*.

Sometimes the same word can be an adjective or an adverb.

Adjective	Adverb
It's a *hard* test. John is a *fast* worker.	John works *hard* and *fast*.

Present passive

Active sentences have the form subject + verb + object. Passive sentences have the form subject + *be* + past participle. The object of an active sentence becomes the subject of a passive sentence. An active verb is used to say what the subject does. A passive verb is used to say what happens to the subject. A phrase consisting of *by* + noun comes after the passive verb if it is important to know who performs an action. More often, the passive is used without the *by* phrase.

See page 154 for a list of irregular past participles.

Affirmative statements

Active

| The college gives an English placement test twice a year. |
| The college offers online classes every semester. |

Passive

| Singular | An English placement test is given (by the college) twice a year. |
| Plural | Online classes are offered every semester. |

Yes / No questions

Active

| Does the college offer financial aid? |
| Does the college give online courses every semester? |

Passive

| Singular | Is financial aid offered (by the college)? |
| Plural | Are online courses given every semester (by the college)? |

Wh- questions

Active

| When does the college give the placement test? |
| Where does the college hold English classes? |

Passive

| Singular | When is the placement test given (by the college)? |
| Plural | Where are English classes held (by the college)? |

Infinitives after passive verbs

Some passive verbs can have an infinitive after them.

Active

| The teacher tells the students to bring a dictionary to class. |

Passive

| The students are told (by the teacher) to bring a dictionary to class. |

Verbs often followed by infinitives

advise	intend	require
allow	mean	tell
encourage	plan	use
expect	prepare	

Direct and indirect questions

A *direct* question is a complete sentence. An *indirect* question is a dependent clause (see Clauses on page 146). It comes after a main clause. The main clause can be a statement or a question. If it is a question, a question mark is used at the end of the sentence. Indirect *wh-* questions begin with question words (*who, what, where, when, why, how*). Indirect *yes / no* questions begin with *if* or *whether. Whether* is more formal.

Wh- questions

	Direct	Indirect
Present	When does the bus come?	Do you know when the bus comes?
Past	Where did she go?	Please tell me where she went.

Yes / No questions

	Direct	Indirect
Present	Do they have a test today?	Do you know if they have a test today? Do you know whether they have a test today?
Past	Did he finish his homework?	I wonder if he finished his homework. I'd like to know whether he finished his homework.

Common introductory clauses that are used with indirect questions

I'd like to know . . .	I wonder . . .	Do you have any idea . . . ?
I don't know . . .	Please explain . . .	Can you tell me . . . ?
I want to know . . .	Tell me . . .	Do you know . . . ?
I need to know . . .		

Present modals: *ought to, shouldn't, have to, don't have to*

Ought to is the same as *should*. It is used to give advice. *Shouldn't* is the opposite of both *ought to* and *should. Have to / Has to* mean that it is necessary to do something. The subject has no choice about it. *Don't have to / Doesn't have to* mean that it is not necessary to do something. The subject can choose to do it or not.

Affirmative statements

I You We They	ought to have to	relax.
He She	ought to has to	relax.

Negative statements

I You We They	shouldn't don't have to	work so hard.
He She	shouldn't doesn't have to	work so hard.

Past modals: *should have, shouldn't have*

Should have / Shouldn't have + past participle mean that the speaker is sorry about (regrets) something he or she did or did not do in the past. These modals can also be used to give advice about something in the past.

Affirmative statements

I You He She We You They	should have	left earlier.

Negative statements

I You He She We You They	shouldn't have	eaten so much.

Time clauses with *until* and *as soon as*

Dependent time clauses with *until* and *as soon as* can come at the beginning or end of a sentence. Use a comma (,) after a time clause that comes at the beginning of a sentence.

until	Use *until* in the dependent clause to say how long an action continues. *Until* the patient finished his lunch, the nurse stayed with him. The nurse stayed with the patient *until* he finished his lunch.
as soon as	Use *as soon as* in the dependent clause to mean "right after." *As soon as* the patient finished his lunch, the nurse left. The nurse left *as soon as* the patient finished his lunch.

Time words and expressions to describe repeated actions

In sentences that talk about repeated actions, the correct word order is subject + verb + number of times + time expression.

Past	In 2007, Sana volunteered at the homeless shelter *once a week*.
Present	This year, Sana is volunteering *twice a month*. This year, Sana volunteers *twice a month*.
Present perfect	Sana has volunteered *five times so far*.

Concession clauses with *although* and *even though*

Although and *even though* introduce dependent clauses of concession. Concession clauses give information that is surprising or unexpected compared to the information in the main clause. Concession clauses can come at the beginning or end of a sentence. Use a comma (,) after a concession clause at the beginning of a sentence. Usually you can use *but* or *however* to rephrase a sentence with *although* or *even though*, but the grammar is different.

although / *even though*	*Although / Even though* e-mail is convenient, Mr. Chung doesn't like to use it. Mr. Chung doesn't like to use e-mail *although / even though* it is convenient.
but	E-mail is convenient, *but* Mr. Chung doesn't like to use it.
however	E-mail is convenient. *However*, Mr. Chung doesn't like to use it.

Clauses of reason

Because introduces a dependent clause of reason, which gives reasons or uses for information in the main clause.

Because wireless technology is fast, many people use it.
Many people use wireless technology *because* it is fast.

Adjective clauses with *who* and *that*

An adjective clause comes after a noun. The noun can be in the middle or at the end of the sentence. It can be a person or a thing. *Who* and *that* are used to describe people. Only *that* is used to describe things. There are two kinds of adjective clauses, "subject pattern" and "object pattern."

Subject-pattern clauses

The adjective clause consists of *who* or *that* + verb.
Who or *that* is the subject of the adjective clause.

A camera *that is on sale* costs $99.
I want to buy a camera *that costs less than $100*.

The salesman *who helped me* gave me good advice.
The salesman *that helped me* gave me good advice.

Object-pattern clauses

The adjective clause consists of *that* + noun or pronoun + verb.
That is the object of the adjective clause. In object-pattern clauses you can omit *that*.

I like the car *that you bought*.
I like the car *you bought*.

The mechanic *that I use* has a lot of experience.
The mechanic *I use* has a lot of experience.

Present perfect

The present perfect is formed by *have* or *has* + past participle. One of the uses of the present perfect is to talk about recently finished actions (with or without *just*).
See page 154 for a list of irregular past participles.

Affirmative statements

I You We They	have (just)	cleaned the windows.
He She	has (just)	
It	has (just)	stopped raining.

Present perfect continuous

The present perfect continuous is formed by *have* or *has* + *been* + verb *-ing*. Use the present perfect continuous to talk about actions that started in the past, continue to now, and may continue in the future. Use *for* + length of time to give the meaning of *how long*.

Affirmative statements

I You We They	have been working	for a month.
He She It	has been working	

With verbs that are not actions (e.g., *have*, *be*, *know*), use the present perfect with *for*:
I have known him for two years.
With some action verbs, you can use either the present perfect or the present perfect continuous with *for*: *I have studied / been studying here for six months.*

Participial adjectives

Verb forms that end in *-ed* or *-ing* are called *participles*. Participles can be adjectives. There is a difference in meaning between the *-ed* and *-ing* forms. Often, the *-ing* form describes a thing or person, and the *-ed* form describes the way someone feels.

John's job is very *tiring*. At the end of the day, he is always *tired*.
Mary is at the movies. She is *bored* because the movie is very *boring*.

Connectors of cause and effect

English has many words and phrases to signal cause (reason) and effect (result). Although the meanings of these words and phrases are similar, their grammar is different.

because and *since*	Use these words in dependent clauses to signal the cause. Use a comma (,) when the dependent clause is at the beginning of a sentence. *Because / Since* the earth is getting warmer, the sea level is rising. The sea level is rising *because / since* the earth is getting warmer.
because of and *due to*	These words signal a cause. A noun or noun phrase comes after the prepositions. Use a comma (,) when the phrase is at the beginning of a sentence. *Because of / Due to* air pollution, the children could not play outside. The children could not play outside *because of / due to* air pollution.
therefore, as a result, and *consequently*	These words signal an effect. They come at the beginning of a main clause. They are followed by a comma. The earth is getting warmer. *As a result / Therefore / Consequently,* the sea level is rising.

Conditional sentences

Conditional sentences consist of a dependent clause and a main clause. The dependent clause begins with *if*. Use a comma (,) after an *if* clause at the beginning of a sentence. Conditional sentences can be real or unreal. "Real" means the situation in the sentence is possible. "Unreal" means the situation isn't possible; it is imaginary. In unreal conditional sentences, the form of the *be* verb in the dependent clause is *were* for all persons. The clause *if I were you* is used for giving advice.

Future real conditional

Dependent clause	Main clause	Example
if + subject + present verb	subject + future verb	If I *have* time, I *will bake* a cake. I *will bake* a cake if I *have* time.

Unreal conditional

Dependent clause	Main clause	Example
if + subject + past verb	subject + *would / could / might* + base form of verb	If I *had* time, I *would bake* a cake. I *would bake* a cake if I *had* time.
if + subject + *were*	subject + *would / could / might* + base form of verb	If I *were* you, I *would give* her a gift card for her birthday. I *would give* her a gift card for her birthday if I *were* you.

hope and *wish*

Use *hope* to talk about something you want in the future that is possible. Use *wish* to talk about situations that are not possible (imaginary). Both *hope* and *wish* occur in main clauses and are followed by dependent *that* clauses (see Noun clauses with *that* on page 146).

hope	The dependent clause has a present or future verb or modal. I *hope* (that) you *can come* to my wedding. Sandor *hopes* (that) his son *will fly* home for Thanksgiving.
wish	The dependent clause has a past verb or *would / could* + base form of the verb. I *wish* (that) you *could come* to my wedding. Sandor *wishes* (that) his son *would fly* home for Thanksgiving.

Spelling rules

Spelling rules for gerunds

- Verbs ending in a vowel-consonant pair repeat the consonant before adding -*ing*:

  stop → *stopping*   *get* → *getting*

- Verbs ending in silent -*e* drop the *e* before -*ing*:

  dance → *dancing*   *exercise* → *exercising*

  but:

  be → *being*   *see* → *seeing*

Spelling rules for regular past participles

- To form the past participle of regular verbs, add -*ed* to the base form:

  listen → *listened*

- For regular verbs ending in a consonant + -*y*, change *y* to *i* and add -*ed*:

  study → *studied*

- For regular verbs ending in a vowel + -*y*, add -*ed*:

  play → *played*

- For regular verbs ending in -*e*, add -*d*:

  live → *lived*

Irregular verbs

Base form	Simple past	Past participle	Base form	Simple past	Past participle
be	was / were	been	lose	lost	lost
become	became	become	make	made	made
begin	began	begun	meet	met	met
break	broke	broken	oversleep	overslept	overslept
bring	brought	brought	pay	paid	paid
build	built	built	put	put	put
buy	bought	bought	read	read	read
catch	caught	caught	ride	rode	ridden
choose	chose	chosen	run	ran	run
come	came	come	say	said	said
cost	cost	cost	see	saw	seen
cut	cut	cut	sell	sold	sold
do	did	done	send	sent	sent
drink	drank	drunk	set	set	set
drive	drove	driven	show	showed	shown
eat	ate	eaten	sing	sang	sung
fall	fell	fallen	sit	sat	sat
feel	felt	felt	sleep	slept	slept
fight	fought	fought	speak	spoke	spoken
find	found	found	spend	spent	spent
fly	flew	flown	stand	stood	stood
forget	forgot	forgotten	steal	stole	stolen
get	got	gotten / got	swim	swam	swum
give	gave	given	take	took	taken
go	went	gone	teach	taught	taught
have	had	had	tell	told	told
hear	heard	heard	think	thought	thought
hide	hid	hidden	throw	threw	thrown
hit	hit	hit	understand	understood	understood
hold	held	held	wake	woke	woken
hurt	hurt	hurt	wear	wore	worn
keep	kept	kept	win	won	won
know	knew	known	write	wrote	written
leave	left	left			

Class audio script

Welcome

Page 4, Exercise 3A – CD1, Tracks 2 and 3

1. Katrina usually cleans her house on Saturday.
2. How long has Samuel lived in Canada?
3. Laura talked to her school counselor yesterday.
4. Mr. Mansour is going to look for a new job.
5. Right now, Andrea is making food for a party.
6. Tony has been working part-time for six months.
7. Last night at 8:00 p.m., the Park family was watching television.
8. We have been waiting for two hours.

Page 4, Exercise 3B – CD1, Track 4

Last Monday evening, I was driving home from work when I had a car accident. It was dark, and it was raining. About five blocks from my house, I stopped for a red light. While I was waiting for the light to change, another car hit my car. I guess the driver didn't see me because of the rain. The accident damaged my car badly.

Since the accident, I have been going to work by bus. It's really inconvenient because I work more than 20 miles from my home. The bus is slow, and I have been late several times already. It will take at least two more weeks to fix my car. Until then, I need to find a better way to get to work. I don't want to be late anymore.

Unit 1: Personal information

Lesson A: Get ready
Page 7, Exercises 2A and 2B – CD1, Tracks 5 and 6

A Come on in. The door's open!
B Hi, Nina!
A Emily! Come on in. Have you been jogging?
B Yeah, I was just coming back from my run, and I thought I'd see what you're – whoa! Look at this kitchen!
A Yeah, it's a mess, isn't it? We're having 14 people for dinner tonight, and I'm going to be in the kitchen all afternoon!
B It smells great already! Hey, I just heard that Brenda got first place in the high school math contest. Is it true?
A Yes, it's true! She's really good at math. She just loves it.
B Brenda's such a "brain." I'm sure you're really proud of her!
A Yeah, she's very intelligent. But I have to say that Gerry and Danny are bright, too – they're just smart in different ways.
B What do you mean?
A Well, take Gerry. He's not mathematical like Brenda, but he's really musical. He plays four different instruments, he sings really well – he's even writing some of his own songs.
B I guess that's Gerry!
A Yeah.
B So Brenda's gifted in math, and Gerry's good at music. What about Danny? What's he good at?
A Well, he's good at fixing cars. He's the mechanical one in the family.
B Oh, I remember he bought that old, old car when he was 16. How's that coming? Is he still working on it?
A Emily, you should see that car now! It's gorgeous! He fixed everything, and it runs perfectly!
B Amazing! You know, it's really interesting how your kids are all smart in different ways. And, Nina, you're pretty smart, too!
A Me?
B Well, look at you! Maybe it's easy for you to cook for 14 people, but I could never do it. I have absolutely no aptitude for cooking!
A Gee, Emily. No one ever told me that I'm smart!
B Well, Nina, you are smart! And the smart thing for me to do is to go home and let you do your work. I'll talk to you tomorrow.
A Bye, Emily. Thanks for stopping by!

Page 7, Exercise 2C – CD1, Track 7

Emily stops by Nina's house on her way home from jogging. They talk about Nina's three children. Brenda is very mathematical. She's just won a math contest at school. When Emily calls Brenda a brain, Nina says that all her children are bright, but in different ways. Gerry isn't gifted in math, but he's very musical. He plays and sings very well and even writes music. Danny is the mechanical one in the family. He's good at fixing up old cars. Emily thinks that Nina is also smart because she is such a good cook. Emily has no aptitude for cooking.

Lesson B: Noun clauses
Page 8, Exercise 2A – CD1, Track 8

1. Do you believe that there are many kinds of intelligence?
2. Do you think that Nina has an interesting family?
3. Brenda's teacher agrees that she is very gifted in math.
4. Everyone believes that Gerry will be a famous musician someday.
5. I didn't realize that Danny has an aptitude for fixing up cars.
6. Do you feel that mechanical skills are very important?
7. Do you think that Nina is good at cooking?

Lesson C: Parts of speech
Page 10, Exercise 2A – CD1, Track 9

1. Carol speaks very intelligently. She's a bright girl.
2. That isn't a bad guitar, but he's playing it badly.
3. Benny is an excellent cook. His dinner last night was fantastic.
4. The mechanic did a good job on my car. Now it runs perfectly.
5. You danced very skillfully in the dance contest. You were wonderful!
6. I don't type very fast. I can't move my fingers very quickly.
7. That writing test was really hard. Writing is not an easy subject for me.
8. You sang that song beautifully! I didn't know you could sing so well!
9. Your report is great. You wrote it very clearly.
10. I work slowly. I have to be very careful.

Lesson D: Reading
Page 12, Exercise 2 – CD1, Track 10

Many Ways to Be Smart
Josh is a star on the school baseball team. He gets Ds and Fs on all his math tests. His brother, Frank, can't catch, throw, or hit a baseball, but he easily gets As in math. Which boy do you think is more intelligent? Howard Gardner, a professor of education at Harvard University, would say that Josh and Frank are both smart, but in different ways. His theory of multiple

intelligences identifies eight different "intelligences" to explain the way people understand, experience, and learn about the world around them.

Verbal / Linguistic Some people are good with words. They prefer to learn by reading, listening, and speaking.

Logical / Mathematical These people have an aptitude for math. They like solving logic problems and puzzles.

Musical / Rhythmical These people are sensitive to sound, melodies, and rhythms. They are gifted in singing, playing instruments, or composing music.

Visual / Spatial These "picture people" are often good at drawing or painting. They are sensitive to colors and designs.

Bodily / Kinesthetic Some people are "body smart." They are often athletic. Kinesthetic learners learn best when they are moving.

Interpersonal Certain people are "group smart." They easily understand other people. They are good at communicating and interacting with others.

Intrapersonal Some people are "self smart." They can understand their own feelings and emotions. They often enjoy spending time alone.

Naturalist These people are skilled in working with plants and animals in the natural world.

According to Gardner, many people have several or even all of these intelligences, but most of us have one or two intelligences that are primary, or strongest.

Unit 2: At school

Lesson A: Get ready
Page 19, Exercises 2A and 2B – CD1, Tracks 11 and 12

Part 1

Do you like to work with people? Do you enjoy traveling? Are you bilingual?

Then La Costa Community College's Hospitality and Tourism certificate program is for you. Our graduates find high-paying jobs with hotels, restaurants, airlines, travel agencies, and more! This growing industry needs leaders – it needs you! For more information about La Costa's certificate program in Hospitality and Tourism, call 866-555-6868 today!

Part 2

A Mrs. Ochoa?
B Oh, hi, Vasili. How's it going?
A Pretty well. Um, I was in my car this morning, and I heard an advertisement about a certificate program in hospitality and tourism.
B Yes, it's a great program. Are you interested?
A Yeah, but I have some questions.
B Well, I'll try to answer them for you.
A OK. So first, what are the requirements for the certificate? How many courses are required?
B There are six required courses, plus an internship.
A An internship? What's that?
B You work at a local tourism business for three months. There's no pay, but it's a great way to learn about the industry – you know, see if you like it.
A I see. Are the classes in the daytime or at night? Because you know, I can't quit my job, and . . .
B No problem, Vasili. Classes are scheduled at different times, and some of them are even offered online.
A Oh, yeah? That's great. Um, how long does it take to complete the program?
B Well, it depends. I'd say – with the internship – between one and two years. Some people just take one class at a time, so it takes them longer.
A OK, that's good. How much does the program cost?
B Well, let's see. There are six classes, and they're three units each. It's $20 a unit, so that's $360 for the certificate. Books are another $100 per class, and then there's parking and health fees. So the total is about $1,000.
A A thousand? Wow! That's a lot of money.
B Don't worry. There's financial aid for students who qualify.
A OK. You know, I think I'd like to apply. When's the registration deadline?
B Let's see. Looks like it's December fifteenth for the winter semester. You have time.
A But my English, is it good enough?
B Well, you're required to take an English placement test, but I'm sure you'll do fine, Vasili. You're bilingual, you're very motivated, and you have good interpersonal skills. Hospitality and tourism could be a really good career for you.

Page 19, Exercise 2C – CD1, Track 13

Vasili hears a radio ad about the Hospitality and Tourism certificate program at La Costa Community College. The ad says graduates can find high-paying jobs in the tourism industry. Vasili goes to see his ESL counselor, Mrs. Ochoa. She tells him about the program requirements, which include an internship in a local tourism business. She also tells him about the deadline for registration, and she says there is financial aid for students who qualify. Vasili is concerned about his English, but Mrs. Ochoa tells him not to worry. Vasili is bilingual, he's very motivated, and he has good interpersonal skills.

Lesson B: The passive voice
Page 20, Exercise 2A – CD1, Track 14

1. A When is the English placement test given to new students?
   B The English placement test is administered a week before the first day of class.
2. A Is a math placement test also required?
   B No, a math placement test is not needed.
3. A Where is the financial aid office located?
   B It is located next to the admissions office.
4. A Where are the classes held?
   B Most of the classes are held in the business building.
5. A Are classes offered at different times?
   B Yes. Both day and evening classes are offered.
6. A Are job placement services provided to graduates?
   B Yes. Job help is offered to students who qualify.

Lesson C: The passive voice
Page 22, Exercise 2A – CD1, Track 15

1. Applicants are expected to meet all application deadlines.
2. New students are told to come early for registration.
3. Are all new students required to take a writing test?
4. Some students are advised to enroll in an English composition class.
5. Are students expected to attend every class?
6. Students are encouraged to meet with a counselor regularly.
7. When are participants expected to complete their internships?
8. Students are required to earn a grade of C or better in each course.
9. Students are told to study with a partner and to go to tutoring often.

Lesson D: Reading
Page 24, Exercise 2 – CD1, Track 16

An Immigrant Family's Success Story
Choi and Lili Wei left China with their baby boy in the late 1980s. They were poor field workers in their native country, and they wanted their child to have the opportunities they lacked. They arrived in New York and found a one-bedroom apartment in a poor, unstable area. They could only afford a bicycle for transportation, yet they felt fortunate to have the chance to begin a new life in the United States.

Choi and Lili faced many obstacles because they couldn't speak English and had no skills. They found night work cleaning businesses and restaurants. They saved every penny, and after six years, they were able to buy a small restaurant of their own.

They were determined to learn English, get an education, and make a good life for their son. The couple sacrificed a great deal. They never went to a movie, never ate out, and hardly ever bought anything extra. In their free time, they attended English and citizenship classes. Both of them eventually earned their GED certificates. Choi then enrolled in college while Lili worked in the restaurant.

This past spring, Choi fulfilled a lifelong dream of graduating from college. Now he is registered in a master's degree program in business beginning this fall. And what about their "baby" boy? Their son, Peter, now 21, received a scholarship to a private university, where he is working on his own dream to become an architect.

Choi and Lili are proud to be models of the "American dream." Choi has this advice for other new immigrants: "Find your passion, make a plan to succeed, and don't ever give up."

Review: Units 1 and 2

Page 30, Exercise 1 – CD1, Track 17

A Hey, Faisal! I haven't seen you in a while. What's new?
B Hi, Angela. Um, I just talked to Mr. Ortiz, my career counselor. He gave me some information about a certificate program in automotive technology.
A Is that like car repair?
B Well, yeah, but these days, you know, cars are a lot more complicated than they used to be. Everything is computerized now. I've always liked fixing up cars, but . . .
A I remember back in high school when you fixed the transmission on my dad's truck. He said you had a real aptitude for mechanical things.
B Yeah, I guess so. But I need more education if I want to get a high-paying job in the auto industry.
A So what did Mr. Ortiz tell you?
B Well, there are eight required courses, plus two more courses that you're allowed to choose.
A That's a lot of classes. How long will it take to complete them all?
B Four semesters. It's pretty fast. And the classes are scheduled at all different times, you know – daytime and evening, and even on weekends.
A How much will it cost?
B Each course is sixty dollars. And I need ten courses. So the total is six hundred dollars, not including books and tools. Plus financial aid is offered to students who qualify.
A You sound really motivated.
B I am. I think this is the right program for me.

Page 31, Exercise 3A – CD1, Tracks 18 and 19

1. He has always liked playing number games.
2. She has worked as an accountant for ten years.
3. Emily has realized that Brenda has a good brain.
4. Naturalists are skilled in working with plants.
5. The little boy started counting when he was two.
6. She is gifted in singing and dancing.

Page 31, Exercise 3B – CD1, Track 20

1. Classes are located at various elementary schools.
2. All students are advised of the school rules.
3. An application is required for admission.
4. A math test is needed as well.
5. The test is administered once a week.
6. The students are expected to pay their fees soon.
7. Lucas hasn't talked with a counselor yet.
8. But he is finished with all his tests.

Unit 3: Friends and family

Lesson A: Get ready
Page 33, Exercises 2A and 2B – CD1, Tracks 21 and 22

Part 1
A You have one new message.
B This call is for Mrs. Wen Lee. This is the attendance office from Central High School calling on Tuesday, March 10th, at 2:00 p.m. We're calling to report an unexcused absence for your daughter, Lan, from her 7th period class today. Please call the office at 619-555-2300 to explain why your daughter missed class. Thank you.

Part 2
C I can't believe we're at the mall on a school day!
D Yeah. Do you think anyone at school is going to miss us?
C No way. There's a substitute teacher in my last period class.
D Mine, too! So, how's everything at home?
C It's the same old thing. I'm so frustrated. My mother won't let me do anything! She is so strict.
D Strict? Like how?
C Well, I'm not permitted to go anywhere without my parents or my brother. And my mom says I can't go out on a date without a chaperone until I'm 18!
D That's so unfair! I wonder why your mother's so strict.
C I don't know. I think she's trying to bring me up like she was raised in China. She just doesn't understand the customs here in the United States.

Part 3
C Hi, Mom.
E Hi, Lan. How was school today?
C Um, fine. Is something wrong?
E The school called and said you were absent from your 7th period class. Where did you go?
C Come on, Mom. Don't get excited.
E Tell me where you went!
C Mary and I just went to the mall right across the street from school, OK?
E But what about your last class?
C There was a substitute teacher, OK? I didn't miss anything!
E I don't understand how you could do this!
C Well, it's your fault! You're so strict that I had no choice. Everybody's allowed to go to the mall except for me. Why can't you trust me?
E This is not about trust. You broke the school rules. You're grounded for the next two weekends.

C Grounded?! What about Celia's birthday party next Saturday?

E I'm afraid you'll have to miss it. Next time, maybe you'll think before you act.

Page 33, Exercise 2C – CD1, Track 23

Mrs. Lee received a phone message from her daughter's school saying Lan missed her 7th period class. Lan left school early to go to the mall with her friend Mary. At the mall, Lan tells Mary that her mother is too strict. Lan thinks it's because her mother wants to bring her up the same way she was raised in China. That's why Lan needs a chaperone to go out on a date. At home, Lan and her mother have an argument. Lan is angry because she's not permitted to go to the mall alone. She thinks her mother doesn't trust her. Mrs. Lee is upset because Lan broke the rules. As a punishment, she says Lan is grounded for two weeks.

Lesson B: Indirect questions
Page 34, Exercise 2A – CD1, Track 24

1. *A* Do you know what the student's name is?
   B Her name is Lan.
2. *A* Can you please tell me what class she missed?
   B Mr. Latham's 7th period English class.
3. *A* I would like to know why she broke the rules.
   B I don't know why. Perhaps she was bored in class.
4. *A* I wonder when she and her friend left the school.
   B They left after 6th period.
5. *A* I want to know what they did at the mall.
   B They talked and went window-shopping.
6. *A* Can you please tell me what Lan's punishment was?
   B Her mother grounded her for two weeks.

Lesson C: Indirect questions
Page 36, Exercise 2A – CD1, Track 25

A Can I go to a party at Joe's house?
B Maybe. First I need to know if you finished your homework.
A Yes, I finished it an hour ago.
B OK. Can you tell me if his parents will be home?
A Yes, his parents will be there.
B That's good. I wonder if you need to take a birthday gift.
A No, I don't. It's not a birthday party.

B I wonder if they're going to serve dinner.
A Yes. They're going to barbecue chicken for us.
B What about your friend John? Do you know if he's invited to the party?
A Yes, I think so.
B Do you know if John's parents can bring you home?
A I'll ask them.

Lesson D: Reading
Page 38, Exercise 2 – CD1, Track 26

Barriers Between Generations

In immigrant families, language differences and work schedules often create barriers to communication between the generations. Dolores Suarez, 42, and her son, Diego, 16, face both kinds of barriers every day. Dolores is an immigrant from Mexico who works seven days a week as a housekeeper in a big hotel. She doesn't use much English in her job, and she has never had time to study it. Consequently, her English is limited. Her son, on the other hand, was raised in the United States. He understands Spanish, but he prefers to speak English. When his friends come over to visit, they speak only English. "They talk so fast, I can't understand what they are saying," says Dolores. To make the situation more complicated, Diego and Dolores live with Dolores's father, who speaks Nahuatl, a native language spoken in Mexico. Diego can't understand anything his grandfather says.

Dolores's work schedule is the second barrier to communication with Diego. Because she rarely has a day off, Dolores isn't able to spend much time with him. She doesn't have time to help him with his homework or attend parent-teacher conferences at his school. In 1995, when Dolores immigrated to the United States, her goal was to bring up her son with enough money to avoid the hardships her family suffered in Mexico. Her hard work has permitted Diego to have a comfortable life and a good education. But she has paid a price for this success. "Sometimes I feel like I don't know my own son," she says.

Unit 4: Health
Lesson A: Get ready
Page 45, Exercises 2A and 2B – CD1, Tracks 27 and 28
Part 1

A Cindy, have you seen Sara?
B No. I don't think she's here yet.
A She should have been here 25 minutes ago. Did she call to say she'd be late?
B No, she didn't.
C Oh! Uh, good morning, Mr. Stanley.
A Good morning, Sara.
C I'm sorry, I know I'm late, but the buses are so unreliable.
A I don't know about the buses, Sara, but I do know that if you're late one more time, I'm going to have to fire you.

Part 2

C Thanks for picking me up, Mike.
D No problem.
C We have to hurry – my driving test is in half an hour.
D We have plenty of time. The DMV is just ten minutes from here.
C All right.
D Are you OK? You seem tense.
C Yeah, I'm pretty stressed out.
D How come?
C I was late to work again this morning . . .
D Oh, no!
C And the boss said that if it happens again, he's going to fire me.
D No wonder you're stressed out.
C I'm so worried about losing my job, I can't sleep, I can't eat, I can't concentrate …
D You know, Sara, if you're not feeling well, you don't have to take the driving test today.
C Yes, I do, Mike. I have to pass this driving test so I can get my license and buy a car and stop depending on buses.
D OK, OK, I understand. But if you want to pass the test, then you have to calm down. Try to relax. Take a few deep breaths.
C OK.
D Now think positive thoughts. Tell yourself, "I'm a good driver. I'm going to pass my driving test."
C "I'm a good driver, I'm going to pass my driving test."
D Seriously, Sara. You ought to learn some techniques for coping with anxiety.
C Like what?
D Simple stuff. Like I said, deep breathing is good, um, thinking positive thoughts. And I find that it helps me to meditate every day.

C Meditation. Let's talk about it later. Here's the DMV.

D Good luck, and don't forget: You're a good driver!

C Thanks, Mike. You're a good friend.

Page 45, Exercise 2C – CD1, Track 29

Mike is driving Sara to the Department of Motor Vehicles (DMV) to take her driving test. He notices that she's very tense. Sara says she's stressed out because she was late to work again. She's worried that her boss will fire her if she's late one more time. She's so afraid of losing her job that she can't eat, she can't sleep, and she can't concentrate. Mike says that she has to calm down if she wants to pass her driving test. He suggests three techniques to help her cope with her anxiety. One is deep breathing. The second one is thinking positive thoughts, and the third one is meditation.

Lesson B: Modals
Page 46, Exercise 2A – CD1, Track 30

Ana and Bill just got engaged, and they are planning to get married in four weeks. Because the wedding is so soon, they are feeling a lot of pressure. Ana's mother wants a big wedding, but Ana and Bill don't. Because they are paying for the wedding themselves, they believe they ought to do what they want. Another pressure is all the things Ana and Bill have to do before the wedding. For example, Ana has to buy a dress, choose her bridesmaids, and send out the invitations. Bill has to plan the reception and order the food. Most importantly, they have to decide where the wedding will be. Ana wants to get married outdoors, but Bill thinks they shouldn't plan an outdoor wedding because it might rain. Now Bill has a different idea. He realizes that they shouldn't get married so soon. Maybe they ought to postpone the wedding until the spring. That way, they don't have to feel so much pressure.

Lesson C: Modals
Page 48, Exercise 2A – CD1, Track 31

1. She should have talked to someone about her problems.
2. She should have gone out.
3. She shouldn't have stayed home alone all the time.
4. She should have made new friends.
5. She should have exercised.

6. She should have eaten regular, balanced meals.
7. She shouldn't have eaten lots of junk food.
8. She shouldn't have slept a lot.
9. She should have called her family.

Lesson D: Reading
Page 50, Exercise 2 – CD1, Track 32

Stress: What You Ought to Know
What is stress?

Stress is our reaction to changing events in our lives. The reactions can be mental – what we *think* or *feel* about the changes – and physical – how our body *reacts* to the changes.

What causes stress?

Stress often comes when there are too many changes in our lives. The changes can be positive, like having a baby or getting a better job, or they can be negative, such as an illness or a divorce. Some stress is healthy. It motivates us to push forward. But too much stress over time can make us sick.

What are the signs of stress?

There are both physical and emotional signs of stress. Physical signs may include tight muscles, elevated blood pressure, grinding your teeth, trouble sleeping, an upset stomach, and back pain. Common emotional symptoms are anxiety, nervousness, depression, trouble concentrating, and nightmares.

How can you manage stress?

To prevent stress, you should eat right and exercise regularly. When you know there will be a stressful event in your day – such as a test, a business meeting, or an encounter with someone you don't get along with – it is really important to eat a healthy breakfast and to limit coffee and sugar.

When you find yourself in a stressful situation, stay calm. Take a few deep breaths to help you relax. Roll your shoulders or stretch to loosen any tight muscles. And take time to think before you speak. You don't want to say something you will regret later!

Review: Units 3 and 4

Page 56, Exercise 1 – CD2, Track 2

A Hi, Sue. This is Blanca.

B Hi! How are you?

A Well, to be honest, not so good.

B Why? What's wrong?

A I'm really worried about Yesenia. Lately she's been different. She seems tense and too quiet. It's

hard for her to concentrate on her schoolwork.

B She's 13 now, isn't she?

A Yeah. She just had a birthday last week.

B That's a hard age.

A You know, we raised her to always talk to us about her problems, but last night, I got angry at her. I shouldn't have shouted at her, but she wouldn't answer my questions.

B Do you know if she's having any problems at school?

A That's what I was asking her about. I don't know what's going on with her.

B You know, Blanca, when my daughter was 13, I took a parenting class at the middle school. It really helped me learn how to cope with teenagers.

A A parenting class? I don't know. I'll have to think about that.

B I also think you ought to call Yesenia's counselor at school. The counselor can talk to Yesenia and to her teachers and find out how she's doing.

A OK.

B And one more thing. You sound pretty stressed out, too. Why don't you and Yesenia take an exercise class together? It will help both of you to calm down and relax.

A That's a great suggestion, Sue. I'll ask her tonight. Thanks a lot.

Page 57, Exercise 3A – CD2, Tracks 3 and 4

A Where did he go?

B Can you tell me where he went?

Page 57, Exercise 3B – CD2, Track 5

1. *A* What does Ann do to reduce stress?
   B She listens to music.
2. *A* Why are you so tense?
   B I have my driver's test today.
3. *A* Do you know what Rodolfo does to calm down?
   B He walks or jogs.
4. *A* When did Ivan miss his class?
   B He missed his class on Tuesday.
5. *A* Can you tell me where Andy lives?
   B He lives on East Fifth Street.
6. *A* Do you know why they're always late?
   B No, I don't know.

Unit 5: Around town

Lesson A: Get ready
Page 59, Exercises 2A and 2B – CD2, Tracks 6 and 7

A Hi! Are you the volunteer coordinator?

B Yup, Steve Jones. And you're Almaz? Did I say it right?

A Yes, exactly, Almaz Bekele. Nice to meet you.

B You, too. Please have a seat. I was just looking over your application to volunteer here at Quiet Palms, and it looks really good. Is it OK if I ask you some questions?

A Of course. Go ahead.

B OK, let's see. You wrote that you've been a volunteer before. Can you tell me about that?

A Sure. I volunteered last summer at the public library downtown.

B What did you do there?

A I worked with adults who wanted to learn how to read. I also taught a little writing, and on Saturdays, I read stories to the kids.

B Did you enjoy that?

A Yeah, but what I really liked was working with the older people. It felt like I was doing something really worthwhile.

B Uh-huh. So now tell me why you want to volunteer in a nursing home.

A Well, I think I might want to work in the health-care field someday, but I won't know for sure until I get some experience.

B I see. Well, we'd love to have you volunteer here.

A Great! When can I start?

B I like your enthusiasm, but we have some health requirements. First, you need to take a blood test and a TB test. You can start as soon as we get the results. It usually takes two or three days.

A OK. I'll take care of that right away. Also, um, I was wondering – can you tell me what my responsibilities will be?

B Sure. One thing volunteers do is, uh, they help residents with their meals. You might encourage them to eat, or just keep them company during mealtime.

A Yeah, my grandmother always eats more when I'm with her. She likes having people around.

B Then I'm sure you understand that you need to be patient and compassionate with the residents.

A I know.

B Volunteers also deliver mail and flowers, and they take residents for walks. You'll get more responsibilities as soon as you feel more confident.

A Sounds good.

B There's an orientation next Monday at 8:30.

A I'll be there!

B One more thing. You'll need to make a commitment to volunteer at least three hours per week.

A No problem! I can't wait to start.

Page 59, Exercise 2C – CD2, Track 8

Last summer, Almaz volunteered at the public library downtown. She liked working with the older people because she felt that she was doing something worthwhile. Today, she is meeting with Steve, the volunteer coordinator at Quiet Palms, a nursing home. She wants to volunteer there to find out if she likes working in the health-care field. Steve tells her about some of her responsibilities at Quiet Palms. He says it's very important for volunteers to be compassionate and patient when they are working with the residents. He asks Almaz to make a commitment to volunteer at least three hours per week. Almaz agrees to attend an orientation. She says she can't wait to start volunteering.

Lesson B: Time clauses
Page 60, Exercise 2A – CD2, Track 9

1. *A* Mr. Shamash is in pain. When will he start to feel better?
   B He'll feel better as soon as he takes his medication.

2. *A* How long will Mr. Shamash stay at Quiet Palms?
   B He'll stay until his broken hip heals.

3. *A* When can Mr. Shamash begin exercising again?
   B As soon as Mr. Shamash feels stronger, he can start doing moderate exercise.

4. *A* When does Mr. Shamash get ready for his walk?
   B He gets ready as soon as Almaz arrives.

5. *A* How long will Mr. Shamash and Almaz play cards?
   B They'll play cards until it is time for lunch.

6. *A* How long will Almaz stay with Mr. Shamash?
   B She'll stay until his family arrives to visit him.

7. *A* When is Mr. Shamash going to go to sleep?
   B As soon as his visitors leave, he'll take his medicine and go to sleep.

Lesson C: Verb tense contrast
Page 62, Exercise 2A – CD2, Track 10

Sharing with Sally

Sally Sutherland created "Sharing with Sally," a volunteer organization that helps seniors stay connected with the outside world. The organization has delivered over 5,000 dinners to seniors so far. Sharing with Sally began six years ago. Every week, Sally and her volunteers deliver meals, talk to seniors on the phone, and visit the ones who can't leave their homes. Over 200 people volunteer at Sharing with Sally. Jake, a college student, volunteered all last year. He called elderly people on the phone once a week and talked to each person. He said it was a very valuable experience. Betsy, a 35-year-old mother of two, has volunteered for two years so far and loves it.

Lesson D: Reading
Page 64, Exercise 2 – CD2, Track 11

A Worthwhile Commitment

Imagine running with your eyes closed. How do you feel? Insecure? Afraid? Justin Andrews knows these feelings very well. Justin is a former long-distance runner who lost his vision because of a grave illness. For the past six months, he has been running twice a week with the help of volunteer runners at Running with Ropes, an organization that assists blind and visually impaired runners. "Running with Ropes has changed my life," Justin says. "Until I heard about it, I thought I'd never run outside again."

Volunteers at Running with Ropes make a commitment to volunteer two to four hours a week. Scott Liponi, one of the running volunteers, explains what they do. "We use ropes to join ourselves to the blind runners and guide them around and over obstacles, such as holes in the road and other runners." Scott has learned how to keep the rope loose so the blind runner has more freedom. He deeply respects the blind runners' tenacity. "They are incredibly determined," he says. "It doesn't matter if it's hot, raining, or snowing – they are going to run." Scott says it is gratifying to share in the joy of the runners and to feel that they trust him. "The four hours I spend at Running with Ropes are the most rewarding part of my week," he says. "It's really a worthwhile commitment."

Unit 6: Time

Lesson A: Get ready
Page 71, Exercises 2A and 2B – CD2, Tracks 12 and 13

Conversation 1
A Excuse me, ma'am.
B Yes?
A I'm a reporter for KESL Radio, and today we're asking people for their opinions about technology and time-saving devices. Do you have a minute to answer some questions for me?
B Sure.
A May I have your name?
B Jean Rosen. Mrs. Rosen.
A Do you have a favorite time-saving device?
B Let me see. . . . I guess it's this – my address stamper.
A Oh. I expected something electronic, not manual! Does it really save you time?
B Absolutely. It takes about a minute to handwrite a return address. The address stamper just takes seconds, even though it's not electronic.
A Thank you for your time, Mrs. Rosen.

Conversation 2
A Excuse me, sir. Do you have a minute?
C Well, I'm in a bit of a hurry.
A I'm a reporter for KESL Radio. I'm asking people for their opinions about how technology helps them save time.
C Technology – a time-saver? I'm afraid you're talking to the wrong man. I'm not a fan of technology.
A Why is that?
C Well, take e-mail, for example. Half the time it's spam. And it's distracting, too. It interrupts my work.
A But isn't it convenient?
C Not that I can see. If you ask me, most of this electronic stuff wastes more time than it saves. I still write letters by hand although I have a perfectly good computer at home.
A I see. Could I get your name before you go?
C Ronald Chung.
A Thank you for your time, Mr. Chung.

Conversation 3
A Good morning, ma'am. I'm a reporter for KESL Radio.
D Yes?
A I'm asking people their opinions about technology and time-saving devices.
D Oh, that sounds interesting.

A Do you have a favorite time-saving device?
D Oh, yes. I just love my cell phone.
A I guess it saves you lots of time because you can use it anywhere.
D That's right. You see, I go to lots of sales to buy clothes for my daughter. I take pictures with my camera phone of clothes I think she might like.
A Really?
D Yeah. Then I send her the pictures while I'm still in the store. She sends me a text message back. It says "Buy" or "Don't buy."
A Now that's innovative.
D Yeah. Not a bad idea, huh?
A I'm sure our listeners will enjoy hearing about such an unusual use.
D Happy to share. It really is a time-saver. But not a money-saver.
A I see what you mean! Oh, I didn't get your name.
D Patricia Morales.
A Well, thank you, Ms. Morales, for sharing your favorite time-saving device.

Page 71, Exercise 2C – CD2, Track 14

Today, a reporter from KESL Radio asked three people about technology and their favorite time-saving devices. Mrs. Rosen's favorite device is manual. She says it saves time, even though it isn't electronic. Mr. Chung isn't a fan of technology. In fact, he says technology *wastes* more time than it saves. For example, he says he doesn't like e-mail because he gets lots of spam. He also finds e-mail distracting. He doesn't think it is convenient. Ms. Morales *loves* technology. She uses the camera on her cell phone in a very innovative way – to send her daughter pictures of clothes that are on sale. Her daughter sends a text message back: "Buy" or "Don't buy."

Lesson B: Clauses of concession
Page 72, Exercise 2A – CD2, Track 15

1. Mr. Gormet doesn't want a microwave even though he knows they save time.
2. Even though Ms. Honig's car has a GPS system, she gets lost all the time.
3. Mr. Wang doesn't have a laptop computer even though he travels constantly.
4. Mrs. Sanchez can't operate her digital camera even though she read the instructions three times.

5. Mrs. Belcanto doesn't want a dishwasher even though she has six children.
6. Even though Ms. Kaye had urgent business in another state, she refused to travel by plane.
7. Even though my house has central air-conditioning, I prefer to use a fan when it's hot.
8. My grandmother doesn't use e-mail even though she has an e-mail address.
9. Even though DVD movies are very popular, I still watch movies on videocassettes.

Lesson C: Clauses of reason and concession
Page 74, Exercise 2A – CD2, Track 16

Although Pam and Beth are sisters, they are very different. Pam is very modern. She loves electrical appliances because they are fast and convenient. For example, she loves her microwave because she can use it to thaw meat quickly. She enjoys shopping for the latest kitchen devices, although some of them are very expensive.

Beth has a different attitude about modern technology. She prefers not to use electrical appliances. For instance, she never uses a microwave because she thinks the radiation is bad. She dries her clothes outside on a line because she likes their smell after they've been in the fresh air. She washes her dishes by hand because she says dishwashers waste energy. Pam doesn't understand why Beth is so old-fashioned. But although the sisters have different lifestyles, they appreciate and enjoy one another very much.

Lesson D: Reading
Page 76, Exercise 2 – CD2, Track 17

Hernando's Blog
Sunday, January 20th
Today, I went with my buddy Rich to a videoconferencing center here in Chicago. It was his birthday, and by using videoconferencing, he was able to have a virtual "party" with his relatives in Guatemala. It was amazing! Rich sat in front of a wide-screen TV here. Meanwhile, his whole family was in front of a screen thousands of miles away, and he could talk to everybody together. I think videoconferencing is an innovative way to keep in touch, even though it's not very convenient. I'm going to find out more about it.

Monday, January 21st

Today, I looked online for videoconferencing centers. Most are for business, so I imagine the costs are outrageous. The center Rich used last night specializes in "reunions" between immigrants and their families in Latin America. First, you have to decide on a date and time. Then, the center here makes the arrangement with a center in the other country. It seems to be pretty popular!

Wednesday, January 23rd

I found out about the costs. The center here charges $40 for a half hour. I think that's reasonable. Luckily, the fee at this center covers the expenses in both countries, so the person in the other country doesn't have to pay anything.

Thursday, January 24th

Well, I picked a date and time for a videoconference with my parents. I want them to meet my fiancée. This is going to be great – I'll be able to see the look on their faces when they "meet" her. Can't do that with a phone or e-mail!

Review: Units 5 and 6

Page 82, Exercise 1 – CD2, Track 18

A Good afternoon, listeners. Today we're talking with Rebecca Ford, Coordinator of Adult Literacy Services at our downtown library. Thank you for joining us, Ms. Ford.

B It's a pleasure to be here.

A To start off, could you describe your job for us?

B Sure. I'm responsible for training and supervising all the volunteer literacy tutors at the library.

A How many tutors are there?

B We have between 20 and 30 volunteer tutors at a time.

A And who are the students that they work with?

B The students are adults who don't have good reading and writing skills. Some of them are immigrants who can't read and write very well, even though they've been in this country for many years. But in one

A I see. Could you tell us more about your tutors? What kind of people are they?

B Well, our tutors are all different ages, and they have different backgrounds. Some of them are volunteering for the first time, and some have volunteered many times in their lives. But in one

way, they're all the same: they're very compassionate. They really care about helping other people. Also, they're very generous with their time.

A I suppose they also have to be very patient if they're teaching adults to read.

B Yes, that's right.

A What are the requirements for becoming a literacy tutor?

B OK. First, they're required to have 12 hours of training in tutoring techniques. Then, as soon as they complete their training, we match each tutor with a student. They're required to meet their student for at least one and a half hours per week, and the library requires a minimum commitment of six months.

A That's good to know. Ms. Ford, if any of our listeners are interested in volunteering, who should they contact?

B They can call my office. The number is 914-555-6700.

A OK, listeners, that number again is 914-555-6700 if you want to volunteer. We appreciate your taking the time to talk with us today, Ms. Ford.

B I enjoyed it. Thank you for having me.

Page 83, Exercise 3A – CD2, Tracks 19 and 20

1. Pam loves electrical appliances because they save her time.
2. She wants to volunteer in the health-care field.
3. Even though computers are time-savers, some people don't use them.
4. Will he go to sleep as soon as his visitors leave?

Page 83, Exercise 3B – CD2, Track 21

1. She delivers meals to seniors.
2. Volunteers should be patient and compassionate.
3. Do you walk to work or drive?
4. Mr. Chung isn't a fan of e-mail.

Unit 7: Shopping

Lesson A: Get ready
Page 85, Exercises 2A and 2B – CD2, Tracks 22 and 23

Part 1

A Excuse me. Do you work here?

B Yes. Do you need some help?

A Where do I take this thing?

B What have you got there?

A It's a camera, a digital camera. I'd like to get my money back, if possible.

B OK, if you want a refund, you need to talk to somebody in Customer Service. See that guy who's wearing a red tie over there? He'll help you.

A Thank you.

Part 2

C Who's next?

A Hi. I want to return this camera that I bought. I'd like to get my money back.

C You bought it here? Do you have the receipt?

A The receipt? Just a minute. Here it is.

C OK. That's good. Is the camera defective?

A What do you mean – "defective"?

C Well, is there something wrong with it? Doesn't it work?

A Oh, no – it's not broken or anything. I just don't like it.

C What's the problem?

A It's the screen.

C The screen?

A Yeah. The screen is too small. A few days ago, I was taking pictures. It was a sunny day, and I couldn't see the picture in the screen! Maybe it's my eyes.

C No, I don't think it's your eyes. That screen is kind of small. So, did you want to exchange it for another camera?

A I'm not sure. Is it possible to get my money back?

C Well, let me look at that receipt again. You got this on the 5th, and today is the 20th. So it's been 15 days. Our policy for a refund is that you have to bring it back within 10 days. So, sorry – no refund.

A Oh. I didn't know about the 10 days.

C Now, for an exchange: You have 30 days – if the merchandise is in perfect condition.

A Oh, it's just like new! I only used it a couple of times. Here, see for yourself.

C Yeah, you're right. Looks OK to me. Is everything in the box?

A I think so. Like I said, I hardly used the camera. Here's the case that came with it. And here's the instruction book, and the warranty card, and all the papers that –

C OK, great. Why don't I keep this camera here while you look around the store?

A You mean, I have to choose another camera today? I'm kind of in a hurry.

C Well, if you want, I could just give you a store credit instead. With a store credit, you can come back and shop anytime.

A Oh, that's a good idea. Maybe I can bring my nephew with me next time I come. He knows a lot about cameras.
C OK, let me get you a store credit.
A I really appreciate all your help.
C No problem.

Page 85, Exercise 2C – CD2, Track 24

Rosa wants to return the camera that she bought and get a refund. She is told that she needs to speak with someone in customer service. The clerk there asks Rosa if the camera is defective. Rosa says that it's not broken, but she doesn't like the screen. The clerk tells her about the store policy for returns and exchanges. It's too late for Rosa to return the camera, but she can exchange it if the merchandise is in perfect condition. Rosa still has the camera box with the instruction book and the warranty card. Since Rosa is in a hurry, she decides to get a store credit, and she will use it at a later time.

Lesson B: Adjective clauses
Page 86, Exercise 2A – CD2, Track 25

1. I want to buy a camera that's not too expensive.
2. I'd like to get a good camera that will last for many years.
3. Many people who are looking for cameras shop online. / Many people that are looking for cameras shop online.
4. My friend told me about a camera store that sells used merchandise.
5. Customers who appreciate good service like to shop at Super Camera. / Customers that appreciate good service like to shop at Super Camera.
6. The clerk who works in customer service is very helpful. / The clerk that works in customer service is very helpful.
7. These days, most people want a digital camera that holds a lot of pictures.
8. Digital cameras that have small screens are sometimes difficult to use.

Lesson C: Adjective clauses
Page 88, Exercise 2A – CD2, Track 26

1. Suzy is a good friend that I've known for several years.
2. Last January, her old car that she was driving stopped working.
3. The mechanic that her friend recommended couldn't fix it.

4. Finally, she decided to buy a used car from a man that she knew at work.
5. He's an honest person that she trusts completely.
6. He gave her a good price that she couldn't refuse.
7. The used car that he sold her is only three years old.
8. It's a reliable car that she can drive for a long time.

Lesson D: Reading
Page 90, Exercise 2 – CD2, Track 27

The Smart Shopper
A Dear Smart Shopper,
I'm a jewelry lover, and I enjoy shopping online. Unfortunately, I just bought a pair of gold earrings that I don't like. When I tried to return them, I learned that the seller has a no-return policy. Don't I have the right to get a refund?
– Mad Madelyn

B Dear Mad Madelyn,
If the merchandise is defective, the seller must return your money or make an exchange. However, if the merchandise was in good condition when you received it, and if the retailer has a no-return policy, there is nothing you can do. This is true for store purchases as well as Internet purchases. In the future, here are some questions you should ask before you buy anything:
• Does the seller say "satisfaction guaranteed or your money back"?
• Is there a time limit on returns, such as two weeks?
• Who pays the shipping costs on items that are returned?
• Do you need to return the merchandise in its original package?
• Is the original receipt required?
• Does the retailer give a store credit instead of a cash refund?
• If the retailer has a store in your area, can you return the merchandise to the store instead of shipping it?
Next time, find the return policy on the merchant's Web site and print it, or ask the merchant for the return policy in writing. It's important to get all the facts that you need before you buy!
– Smart Shopper

Unit 8: Work

Lesson A: Get ready
Page 97, Exercises 2A and 2B – CD3, Tracks 2 and 3
Part 1
A David. Can I talk to you for a second?
B Yeah, sure.
A Um, you know, you've been leaving early a lot lately, and when you do that, I have to stay later and close up the shop by myself.
B Oh, come on, Yolanda. That doesn't happen very often.
A Well, it happened twice last week, and it's happened once so far this week. I'd say that's pretty often. Plus, sometimes the shop is full of customers, and you're in the back room talking on your cell phone. So I feel like I've been doing my job and yours, too. It's not fair. Something's wrong here. We have to figure out a better system here so we divide the work more equally.
B OK, whatever – but I have to go now. See you!
Part 2
C Yolanda, over here!
A Hi, guys.
D Whoa, Yolanda – what's wrong?
A I'm exhausted. I've just finished work.
D Don't you usually finish at 4:00?
A Yeah, Teresa, but the other guy on my shift, David, he's going to night school, and lately he's been leaving early a lot. So then I have to clean up the shop and close up by myself. Sometimes I don't get out of there until 4:45 or 5:00. It's really frustrating.
D That's really unfair.
C I think you should quit that job!
D Quit? That's crazy, Julie. She can't quit – it's hard to find another job!
C Well, have you tried talking to David?
A Yeah, I talked to him, but it didn't help.
D What about your boss? Have you told her?
A No, not yet. I'd really like to try to work something out with David first.
C Listen, I have an idea. What about making a chart?
A A chart? How does that work?
C It's simple. You make a list of all the duties in your shift. You know – open up, make coffee, whatever. Then you negotiate with David and decide who's going to do which tasks.
A OK . . .

C And then, every day, as soon as you finish a task, you write your initials on the chart.

A I get it. So then if David isn't doing his share, it's easy to see.

C And if the problem continues, you can show the chart to your boss and let her deal with it.

A I like that idea, Julie. Especially the part about negotiating with David. I really hope we can work this out together.

Page 97, Exercise 2C – CD3, Track 4

Yolanda and David work at Daria's Donut Shop. Lately, David has been leaving work early, and Yolanda has to close up the shop by herself. Tonight, Yolanda is having coffee with her friends. She is exhausted. Her friends give her advice. Teresa thinks she should talk to her boss, but Yolanda wants to try to work things out with David first. Julie thinks Yolanda should make a chart of their duties. Then she should negotiate with David and decide who is going to do which tasks. When they finish a task, they should write their initials on the chart. If David isn't doing his share of the work, it will show in the chart. Then Yolanda can show the chart to their boss and let her deal with the situation.

Lesson B: Tense contrast
Page 98, Exercise 2A – CD3, Track 5

1. Daria Thompson is the owner of Daria's Donut Shop. She has been selling donuts at this location for more than 20 years.
2. It's 7:00 a.m. Daria has been making donuts for three hours.
3. It's 7:30 a.m. Daria has just opened the shop for customers.
4. It's 10:30 a.m. Daria's son has been helping her all morning.
5. He has just finished cleaning the counters and shelves. Everything is spotless.
6. Daria needs more help in the shop. She has been interviewing candidates all week.
7. Yolanda's shift begins at 6:00 a.m. today. She has been waiting for the bus for 30 minutes. She's worried that she's going to be late.
8. It's 6:05 a.m. Yolanda has just called to say she will be late.

Lesson C: Participial adjectives
Page 100, Exercise 2A – CD3, Track 6

1. *A* I heard that Juan and his friends went to a party after work. How was the party?
   B It was really exciting.
2. *A* How did Juan feel the next day at work?
   B He was exhausted.
3. *A* How long did he have to work?
   B He had to work from 9:30 to 6:30. It was a tiring day.
4. *A* Does Juan usually start working at 9:30?
   B No, he overslept! He was shocked that he didn't hear the alarm clock.
5. *A* How did his boss react when he showed up late?
   B His boss was irritated.
6. *A* What did his boss say to him?
   B He told Juan that he was disappointed in him.
7. *A* Juan didn't have a good day, I guess. What did he do later that night?
   B He stayed home and had a relaxing night in front of the TV.
8. *A* So, is Juan going to go out again on a weeknight?
   B I don't think so. He said it was an exhausting experience.

Lesson D: Reading
Page 102, Exercise 2 – CD3, Track 7

Hard and Soft Job Skills

Som Sarawong has been working as an automotive technician at George's Auto Repair for over five years. Today was a special day for Som, a 35-year-old Thai immigrant, because he received the Employee of the Year award. According to Ed Overton, Som's boss, Som received the award "because he's a great 'people person' and he has superb technical skills. I even have him work on my own car!"

Som has the two kinds of skills that are necessary to be successful and move up in his career: soft skills and hard skills. Soft skills are personal and social skills. Som gets along with his co-workers. He has a strong work ethic; in five years, he has never been late or absent from work. Customers trust him. Hard skills, on the other hand, are the technical skills a person needs to do a job. Som can repair cars, trucks, and motorcycles. He learned from his father, who was also a mechanic. Then he took classes and got a certificate as an auto technician.

Soft and hard skills are equally important, but hard skills are easier to teach and assess than soft skills. People can learn how to use a machine and then take a test on their knowledge. However, it's harder to teach people how to be cooperative and have a good work ethic. George Griffith, the owner of George's Auto Repair, explains, "I've been working in this business for over 30 years, and most of the time when I've needed to fire someone, it was because of weak people skills, not because they didn't have technical abilities." Soft skills and good technical knowledge are a winning combination, and today, Som Sarawong was the winner.

Review: Units 7 and 8
Page 108, Exercise 1 – CD3, Track 8

A Good evening, class. I've invited two business owners to our class to describe job skills that are important for their businesses. I'd like to introduce Len Sullivan, the owner of Sullivan's Electronics, and Cora Zimmer, the owner of Zimmer's Restaurant. First, let's hear from Mr. Sullivan.

B Thanks. It's a pleasure to be here. So, talking about job skills, I would say that first and most importantly, my employees need to have good communication skills. That's true for the salespeople on the floor as well as the ones working in customer service. And at the same time, I expect my people to be good listeners. I've been working in this business for 25 years, and I've hired a lot of people in that time. And I can tell you, my best employees are the ones who really know how to listen to customers and respond to their needs. And now the third important skill is that my employees need to be good problem solvers. They have to deal with all sorts of problems every day, and I expect them to work things out and find good solutions.

A Thank you, Mr. Sullivan. Now let's listen to Ms. Zimmer and find out what skills are important in the restaurant business.

C Thank you so much for inviting me. One important skill my employees need is to manage their time effectively. Restaurant work is very fast-paced and exhausting, so the waiters and also the cooks have to be good time managers. Another important job skill for my employees is good communication skills, just as Mr. Sullivan said. I want my employees to understand instructions and also be able to talk to our customers. Finally, I need employees who can train others in their job duties.

A Thank you both. I know the class is very interested in your comments. And now, I'd like to open this up for questions. Class, do you have questions that you would like to ask?

Page 109, Exercise 3A – CD3, Tracks 9 and 10

1. **A** Is the camera defective?
   B It's defective and too small!
2. **A** Don't you usually finish at 5:00?
   B I do usually finish at 5:00, but not today.
3. **A** Why aren't you applying for that job?
   B I am. I'll go there tomorrow.
4. **A** I don't trust the man who sold you this car.
   B Well, I do! It's my decision, not yours.
5. **A** Is he excited about his new job?
   B No, but his wife is.
6. **A** Did you put the returned merchandise on my desk?
   B No, I put it in your desk.

Page 109, Exercise 3B – CD3, Track 11

1. **A** I'd like to exchange this sweater.
   B Why?
   C It's too big, and it has a hole.
2. **A** You can't leave early again!
   B Yes, I can and I will.
3. **A** Why don't you clean the counters?
   B Why don't you?
4. **A** Let's talk about a raise after you've worked here for six months.
   B Can we talk before six months?

Unit 9: Daily living

Lesson A: Get ready
Page 111, Exercises 2A and 2B – CD3, Tracks 12 and 13

A Mei! Dinner!
B I'll be right there! Sorry I'm late. I was just checking something on the computer.
A OK. Sit down. We've been waiting for you.
B I know. I'm sorry, but I was looking at the Web site for this great organization called the Living Green Council.
C "Living green"? What does that mean? I don't even like that color.
B Dad, it means taking responsibility for saving the earth.

C Saving it from what?
B From global warming! We had a guest speaker today in biology class, and he mentioned a whole bunch of stuff – simple steps we can take to reduce our energy use and protect the environment.
A Like what?
B OK, well, first of all, he said we need to cut down on driving, so we should walk, ride a bicycle, carpool, or take public transportation.
C I'd do those things if I could. But my job is an hour away, and there's no bus service that goes there. And there's nobody for me to carpool with.
B I see your point, but how about recycling? I think we could do a better job of recycling bottles, cans, glass, paper . . .
A You're right. We could do that if we tried.
B Another idea was to turn off unnecessary lights. Look at this house: lights on in every room.
C I like that idea. It'll help cut down on the electric bill.
A What else did the speaker suggest?
B Let me think. Oh, he said that we should wash our clothes in cold water.
A Really? I'm not sure the clothes will get clean, but I suppose we can try.
C That'll save money on the electric bill, too.
B But isn't our washing machine really old? If we bought a new one that's more energy-efficient, it could help the environment *and* our electric bill!
A I don't think we can afford to buy new appliances right now.
B OK. But what about energy-efficient lightbulbs? We could switch to those, right?
A That sounds pretty simple, Mei.
B Cool!
C I have to say, I love your enthusiasm. I never realized how simple it can be to . . . what did you call it . . . "live green"?
B Yeah, the speaker said that if everyone did even one of these things every day, it would do a lot to reduce global warming.
C Speaking of warming, can we eat before the food gets cold?

Page 111, Exercise 2C – CD3, Track 14

Mei was late to dinner because she was looking at the Web site of the Living Green Council. "Living green" means taking responsibility for saving the earth from global warming. Mei tells her parents about the guest

speaker who came to her class. The speaker suggested simple things people could do to reduce their energy use and protect the environment. For example, they could carpool instead of driving alone, recycle their bottles and cans, and use energy-efficient lightbulbs. Mei's parents agree that it is important to cut down on energy use since it would also help them save money. However, they can't afford to buy new appliances right now.

Lesson B: Conditional sentences
Page 112, Exercise 2A – CD3, Track 15

1. Many people put their newspapers in the trash can. If everybody recycled newspapers, we would save millions of trees.
2. Noah never takes his car in for a tune-up. Noah's car would use less gas if he tuned up his car regularly.
3. Mr. Brown drives his own car to his job downtown. Mr. Brown would save money on gas if he carpooled to work.
4. Many items in the supermarket are packaged in plastic. If you bought products that are packaged with recycled paper, you would help to reduce global warming.
5. Jessica always stays in the shower for a very long time. If Jessica took shorter showers, she would save water.
6. Some kinds of fish contain large amounts of lead, a poisonous metal. You would be healthier if you stopped eating fish that contains lead.

Lesson C: Connectors
Page 114, Exercise 2A – CD3, Track 16

1. Due to a buildup of harmful gases in the atmosphere, global warming is increasing.
2. Warm water is expanding in the oceans. As a result, the sea level is rising.
3. Since the sea level is rising, towns near oceans are in danger of flooding.
4. Since global warming changes weather patterns, many places will have less rainfall.
5. Mosquitoes will increase. Consequently, there will be an increase in diseases like malaria.
6. Due to ocean water getting warmer, typhoons and hurricanes are becoming more frequent.

7. Cities are growing. As a result, many plants and animals may lose their natural habitats.

Lesson D: Reading
Page 116, Exercise 2 – CD3, Track 17

All Things Are Connected

Long ago, there was a village chief who never allowed anyone to disagree with him. Whenever he wanted to do something, he asked the members of his court for their advice. But whether the chief's idea was wise or foolish, his advisors always said the same thing: "Indeed, it is wise." Only one old woman dared to give a different answer. Whenever the chief asked for her advice, she always replied, "All things are connected."

One night, the chief was awakened by the sound of frogs croaking in the swamp. It happened again the next night and the next and the next. The chief decided to kill all the frogs in the swamp. When he consulted the members of his court, they replied as usual: "Indeed, it is wise." But the old woman kept silent. "And you, old woman, what do you think?" the chief demanded. "All things are connected," she replied. The chief concluded that the old woman was a fool, and he ordered his servants to kill all the frogs. As a result, the chief slept peacefully.

But soon the mosquitoes in the swamp began to multiply since there were no frogs to eat them. They came into the village and made everyone miserable. The chief ordered his servants to go into the swamp and kill the mosquitoes, but it was impossible. Furious, the chief summoned the members of his court and blamed them, saying, "Why didn't you tell me that killing the frogs would make the mosquitoes multiply and everyone would be miserable? I should have listened to the old woman."

Due to the mosquitoes, all the people of the village were forced to go away. Finally, the chief and his family left, too. Until he died, the chief never forgot the old woman's words: "All things are connected."

Unit 10: Leisure

Lesson A: Get ready
Page 123, Exercises 2A and 2B – CD3, Tracks 18 and 19

A Hi, Cathy. What are you doing this weekend?

B Oh, Thanh. I'm glad you asked. I was invited to Bao and An's wedding. It's Saturday night, and I haven't bought them a gift yet.

A So?

B Well, I don't know what to get them. They aren't registered at any stores.

A Registered? What's that?

B Well, for many American weddings, the bride and groom sign up with a gift registry service at a store. They make a list of what they want, and then people can go to the store or the store's Web site and buy something on the couple's list.

A I've never heard of that custom. At a Vietnamese wedding, guests just bring cash in an envelope.

B Really?

A Yeah, and during the reception, the bride and groom walk from table to table, greet the guests, and collect the envelopes. If I were you, I would just take an envelope.

B OK. Thanks for the advice. I guess customs are really different across cultures, aren't they?

A That's for sure. Do you know what really surprised me the first time I went to an American wedding?

B No, what?

A As the bride and groom were leaving the reception, the guests threw rice at them. What a waste of food! Where does that custom come from?

B Oh, that's a really old tradition. Rice is a symbol of fertility and longevity, so throwing rice represents the hope that the couple will have children and live a long life together.

A That's really interesting.

B Yeah. So, Thanh, what else happens at a Vietnamese wedding?

A Well, for one thing, it's traditional for a Vietnamese bride to wear a red dress.

B Red? Not white, like in this country?

A That's right. In our culture, red symbolizes good fortune. In fact, one of the traditional foods at a Vietnamese wedding is red sticky rice.

B Interesting. Let me ask you something else. My invitation was just for the wedding reception in the evening. What about the ceremony?

A Well, traditionally, the ceremony takes place at the bride's home, with just the family and close relatives. It's usually held in the morning. The reception in the evening is actually a huge party,

with all the couple's friends and acquaintances, lots of dancing, and lots of food. Be prepared for a seven- or eight-course dinner.

B Wow! I guess I won't eat anything beforehand. So, will I see you at Bao and An's wedding?

A I wish I could go, but I have to go to my nephew's graduation party. I hope you have a great time.

B I hope so, too. I'm really looking forward to it.

Page 123, Exercise 2C – CD3, Track 20

Cathy and Thanh are talking about wedding customs. Cathy is invited to a Vietnamese wedding, and she is surprised that the bride and groom are not registered for gifts at any stores. In contrast, Thanh is surprised by the American tradition of throwing rice at the bride and groom. Next, they talk about clothes. Thanh says a Vietnamese bride wears a red dress because the color red symbolizes good fortune. Then Cathy asks why she was invited only to the wedding reception, not the ceremony. Thanh explains that traditionally the ceremony is only for the family. The couple's friends and acquaintances are invited to the evening reception. In fact, Thanh says the evening party will include seven or eight courses of food. Cathy says she is looking forward to the wedding.

Lesson B: Conditional sentences
Page 124, Exercise 2A – CD3, Track 21

1. The Patels are from India, but they live in the United States now. They are planning a wedding for their daughter, Parveen. If they lived in India, the groom's family would pay for the wedding.

2. The wedding will be in the United States. If the Patels had the wedding in India, the wedding celebration would last three days. Here it will last for one day.

3. The Patels don't have a lot of money. If they were rich, they would invite 300 people; instead, they will invite about 150.

4. The Patels are planning to have music for the reception. If a band doesn't charge too much, they will have live music.

5. It's possible that the weather will be nice on the day of the wedding. If the weather is nice, they will have the ceremony outside.

6. Parveen and her new husband will live in their own apartment. If they

were in India, they would live with the groom's parents.

Lesson C: Expressing hopes and wishes
Page 126, Exercise 2A – CD3, Track 22

1. Paul's high school graduation is tomorrow. His friend Luis has to work. Luis wishes he could go to Paul's graduation.
2. Paul's father has asked for the day off so that he can attend his son's graduation. He hopes he gets the day off.
3. Paul's grandfather has been sick. He's not sure if he will attend the graduation. Paul hopes his grandfather will attend the ceremony.
4. The graduation ceremony will be outside. Paul hopes it will not rain.
5. Paul's mother would like to buy him a new car, but she can't afford it. She wishes she could buy him a new car.
6. Paul wasn't accepted to the university, so he will go to a community college. Paul wishes he could go to the university.
7. It's possible that Paul will be able to transfer to the university in two years. He hopes he can transfer in two years.

Lesson D: Reading
Page 128, Exercise 2 – CD3, Track 23

Special Birthdays Around the World
    In most cultures, there are certain birthdays that are especially important in a young person's life. If you were an American teenager, for example, you would eagerly look forward to your 16th birthday because in most states, that is the age to get a driver's license. Other cultures also have birthdays with special meanings:
Mexico: For Mexican girls, the 15th birthday – the "Quinceañera" – symbolizes a girl's transition into adulthood. To celebrate, the girl's family throws a huge party. The girl wears a ball gown similar to a wedding dress. The girl performs a waltz, a formal dance, with her father.
China: On a child's first birthday, parents place their baby in the center of a group of objects, such as a shiny coin, a book, and a doll. Then they watch to see which object the

baby picks up first. Most parents hope their child will pick up the coin because, according to tradition, it means the child will be rich.
Nigeria: The 1st, 5th , 10th, and 15th birthdays are considered extremely important. Parties are held with up to 100 people. The guests enjoy a feast of a roasted cow or goat.
Japan: A girl's 3rd and 7th birthdays and a boy's 5th birthday are considered special. In a ceremony known as "7, 5, 3," children wear their best kimonos (ceremonial gowns) and receive bags of sweets with "sweets for 1,000 years of life" written on them.
Israel: A boy's 13th and a girl's 12th birthdays are serious as well as happy occasions. On these birthdays, children become responsible for their own religious and moral behavior.

    Adult birthdays also have special significance in many cultures. In the United States, for example, birthdays ending in "0" – 30, 40, 50, etc. – are especially meaningful.

Review: Units 9 and 10
Page 134, Exercise 1 – CD3, Track 24

A This is Grace Leong, for KPFX News. I'm standing on the busy corner of Pacific Avenue and Grant Avenue in San Francisco's Chinatown. Tomorrow is the beginning of Chinese New Year, and with me I have two people who can give us some interesting information related to good luck in the coming year. Could you tell us your name, please?
B Angela Kwan.
A Angela, what are some things we can do to bring good luck?
B Well, it's traditional to wear bright colors, such as red. Red is a very bright and happy color, so it symbolizes a bright and happy future. Another thing is, at midnight on New Year's Eve, you should open all the doors and windows of your house. That's to let the old year out and make room for the new. And on New Year's Day, one good thing to do is to eat a lot of candy. If you do that, the new year will be very sweet.
A Very interesting, Angela. I think I'll go shopping for a new red dress, and I'm definitely looking forward

to eating all that candy! And what's your name, sir?
C Hi. My name's Martin Chan.
A Martin, Angela told us some things that bring good luck. What are some things that we should not do on New Year's?
C Well, you shouldn't sweep the house on New Year's Day because you might sweep away your family's good fortune. That's why people sweep the house very carefully before the start of the holiday. And it's bad luck to buy a pair of shoes, because . . .
A Not even red shoes?
C No. The word for "shoes" sounds like the word for "evil" in Mandarin, so you don't want to buy shoes. And you shouldn't use knives or scissors on New Year's Day because if you do, you might cut off your good fortune.
A Thank you, Martin and Angela, and I hope you both have a very happy new year.

Page 135, Exercise 3A – CD3, Tracks 25 and 26

One thought group
1. We need to save energy.
2. I always take the bus to work.
Two thought groups
3. We need to reduce our energy use and protect the environment.
4. When I lived in Vietnam, I always walked to work.
Three or more thought groups
5. There are several things you can do to reduce your energy use and protect the environment.
6. You can walk, ride a bicycle, carpool, or take the bus.

Page 135, Exercise 3B – CD3, Track 27

1. People are very concerned about the environment.
2. We need to take responsibility for saving the earth.
3. There are many ways that we can save energy.
4. One thing people can do is to cut down on their driving.
5. And also, we need to be careful not to waste electricity.
6. We can get a lot of information about global warming on the Internet.

Tests

Overview

The unit tests, midterm test, and final test help teachers assess students' mastery of the material in the *Ventures 4* Student's Book.

- Each of the ten unit tests covers one unit.
- The midterm test covers Units 1–5.
- The final test covers Units 6–10.
- Each test assesses listening, grammar, reading, and writing.

Students' performance on the tests helps to determine what has been successfully learned and what may need more attention. Successful completion of a test can also give students a sense of accomplishment.

Getting ready for a test

- Plan to give a unit test shortly after students have completed a unit and have had time for a review. The midterm should follow completion of Unit 5 and the review lesson for Units 5 and 6. The final test should follow completion of Unit 10 and the review lesson for Units 9 and 10. Tell students when the test will be given. Encourage students to study together and to ask you for help if needed.
- Explain the purpose of the test and how students' scores will be used.
- Prepare one test for each student. The tests may be photocopied from the Teacher's Edition, starting on page T-169, or printed from the *Teacher's Toolkit Audio CD / CD-ROM*.
- Schedule approximately 45 minutes to 1 hour for the tests. Allow more time if needed.
- Locate the audio program for each test's listening section on the *Teacher's Toolkit Audio CD / CD-ROM*. The CD is a hybrid. It will work in both a stereo and a computer CD-ROM drive.

Giving a test

- During the test, have students use a pencil and an eraser. Tell students to put away their Student's Books and dictionaries before the test.
- Hand out one copy of the test to each student.
- Encourage students to take a few minutes to look through the test without answering any of the items. Go through the instructions to make sure students understand them.

- Tell students that approximately 10 minutes of the tests will be used for the listening section.
- When playing the listening section of the test, you may choose to pause or repeat the audio program if you feel that students require more time to answer. The audio script appears in the Teacher's Edition on page T-205. The script can also be printed from the *Teacher's Toolkit Audio CD / CD-ROM* and read aloud in class.

Scoring

- You can collect the tests and grade them on your own. Alternatively, you can have students correct their own tests by going over the answers in class or by having students exchange tests with a partner and correcting each other's answers. The answer key is located in the Teacher's Edition on page T-209. It can also be printed from the *Teacher's Toolkit Audio CD / CD-ROM* Tests menu or the "View" button.
- Each test has a total score of 100 points. Each unit test has five sections worth 20 points each. The midterm and final tests have five sections worth 12.5 or 25 points each.

Track list for test audio program

Track 1: Introduction
Track 2: Unit 1 Test
Track 3: Unit 2 Test
Track 4: Unit 3 Test
Track 5: Unit 4 Test
Track 6: Unit 5 Test
Track 7: Midterm Test
Track 8: Unit 6 Test
Track 9: Unit 7 Test
Track 10: Unit 8 Test
Track 11: Unit 9 Test
Track 12: Unit 10 Test
Track 13: Final Test

TEST UNIT 1 *Personal information*

A 🔘 Listening

Listen. Complete the chart.

Classmate	Task at the party	Why was this classmate chosen?
Leonard		
Elena		
Jonathan		
George		
Carol		

B Grammar

Write sentences with *that* and a noun clause.

1. Girls are better at learning languages than boys. (Do you believe . . . ?)

   _____

2. He has an aptitude for art. (Samuel's parents realize)

   _____

3. Your son needs help in math class. (Do you feel . . . ?)

   _____

4. Naomi is gifted in dance. (Everyone agrees)

   _____

5. Karen has an aptitude for cooking. (Do you know . . . ?)

   _____

C Grammar

Complete the sentences with adjectives or adverbs.

1. Math is _____ for him. He has learned _____.
   (easy)   (quick)

2. That song was _____! Do you sing _____?
   (beautiful)   (professional)

3. I need a _____ mechanic. My car is running _____ now.
   (skillful)   (slow)

4. She used to be a _____ driver. Now she drives _____.
   (fast)   (careful)

5. He's a _____ communicator. He doesn't listen _____.
   (bad)   (good)

D Reading

Read the magazine article. Then read the sentences. Circle *T* (true) or *F* (false).

Multiple Intelligences in the Classroom

Harold Gardner's theory of multiple intelligences has impacted education across the United States. He has identified eight different "intelligences" to show that people understand, experience, and learn in different ways. Educators in the United States have carefully considered Gardner's theory. Many educators think that students gifted in the verbal / linguistic and logical / mathematical intelligences do better in traditional classrooms than those with other intelligences. This is because many traditional teachers teach by using textbooks, giving lectures, checking written homework, and giving written tests. Their methods of teaching are based on verbal / linguistic and logical / mathematical coursework.

Some teachers are changing the way they teach their students. These teachers think that if students think and learn in different ways, then teachers should think and teach in different ways. Their idea is to reach all students by using different intelligences in their classrooms. Teachers who are trained in multiple intelligences might use a visual / spatial activity to teach math. For example, they might ask students to take pictures of objects as they study geometry. Teachers may have students with interpersonal intelligence lead a discussion or teach new terms to other students. These teachers feel that teaching to each student's aptitude and getting each student to learn on his or her own is more important than teaching course subjects in the traditional way.

1. Educators have paid attention to Gardner's theory.   T   F

2. Traditional teachers in the United States often base their teaching
   methods on two intelligences.   T   F

3. It is impossible to teach multiple intelligences in one classroom.   T   F

4. A teacher might ask a student with visual / spatial intelligence to lead a
   group discussion.   T   F

5. Teachers who teach to multiple intelligences try to reach all students.   T   F

E Writing

1 Plan a paragraph about the primary intelligence of someone you know. Use the outline to make notes on your ideas.

Topic sentence: _____

Supporting details:

- _____
- _____
- _____
- _____

2 Write a paragraph about the primary intelligence of someone you know.

_____
_____
_____
_____
_____
_____
_____
_____
_____
_____
_____
_____
_____
_____
_____
_____
_____
_____
_____
_____
_____
_____
_____

TEST UNIT 2 *At school*

A 💿 Listening

Listen. Complete the chart.

1. Type of certificate	
2. Location of certificate program	
3. Reason for getting the certificate	
4. Number of required courses	
5. Estimated cost of the certificate	

B Grammar

Complete the sentences. Use the present passive voice.

1. **A** _____ bilingual skills _____ by many employers in this country?
   (expect)

   B Yes, bilingual skills _____ for many jobs in this country.
   (need)

2. **A** _____ an internship _____ to graduate from the program?
   (require)

   B Yes. Internships _____ by the school.
   (arranged)

3. **A** Where _____ the admissions office _____?
   (locate)

   B It _____ next to the business building.
   (locate)

4. **A** _____ most of the classes _____ in the morning?
   (hold)

   B Actually, many of the classes _____ in the evening.
   (offer)

5. **A** _____ scholarships _____ for students.
   (provide)

   B Yes, scholarships _____ to students by the financial aid office.
   (give)

C Grammar

Write complete statements or questions. Use the present passive with infinitives.

1. graduates / require / complete / their courses by May 4th.

   _____

2. all interns / expect / be on time for every meeting.

   _____

3. students / encourage / participate in work experience programs?

   _____

4. applicants / tell / meet with a counselor.

_____

5. students / allow / earn credit for work experience?

_____

D Reading

Read the story. Then read the sentences. Circle *T* (true) or *F* (false).

Kate Shelley

In 1865, when Kate Shelley was a baby, her family immigrated to the United States from Ireland. As a child, Kate faced many obstacles. When she was 12, her father and her brother died in separate accidents. These unfortunate events caused Kate's mother to become unhappy. Kate had to become the responsible member of the family. As a young girl, Kate was expected to take care of the household and the family farm.

Kate's life changed on March 25, 1881. A thunderstorm started to flood the farm and surrounding areas. At first, Kate went out to save the animals in the barn. On the way back to the house, she heard a loud crash. The bridge over Honey Creek fell. Kate knew a midnight train was scheduled to cross the bridge. She was determined to get to the station in time. She took a lantern and ran through the winds, rain, thunder, and lightning to warn the train station employees to stop the midnight train. Strong winds blew out Kate's lantern, so she had to find her way across a different bridge in the dark to reach the station. Kate arrived at the station in time. The midnight train stopped before its passengers crashed into the river. Everyone on the train was fortunate to have Kate's help that night.

For her courage, the railroad company gave Kate a free railroad pass for the rest of her life. Even now, people in Iowa remember the young girl when they use the Kate Shelley Bridge in Moingona, Iowa.

---

1. Kate grew up in Ireland.   T   F
2. Kate's father and brother died when she was a baby.   T   F
3. The bridge over Honey Creek fell after Kate's lantern blew out. T   F
4. Kate succeeded in stopping the midnight train.   T   F
5. Kate was rewarded for her courage and determination.   T   F

E Writing

1 Plan a paragraph about your obstacles and successes. Use the chart to make notes on your ideas.

My obstacles	My successes

2 Write a paragraph about your obstacles and successes.

_____

_____

_____

_____

_____

_____

_____

_____

_____

_____

_____

_____

_____

_____

_____

_____

_____

_____

_____

_____

_____

Name: _____

Date: _____

Score: _____

TEST UNIT 3 — *Friends and family*

A 💿 Listening

Listen. Circle *T* (true) or *F* (false).

1. Vanna doesn't like to dance.   T   F
2. She is not allowed to go to the dance with Mike.   T   F
3. Her parents are immigrants.   T   F
4. Her parents don't trust her.   T   F
5. Her parents will be at the dance.   T   F

B Grammar

Change the direct questions to indirect *Wh-* questions.

1. Why is he grounded?

   A I'd like to know _____ .
   B I think his grades were bad.

2. When did she start to trust him again?

   A I wonder _____ .
   B She started to trust him again after he apologized.

3. How can I get a better job?

   A Can you tell me _____ ?
   B First, you can continue to improve your English.

4. What time does the class start?

   A Do you know _____ ?
   B It starts at 5:30.

5. What grade did Lidia get in chemistry?

   A Can you tell me _____ ?
   B I think she got a B+.

C Grammar

Write indirect *Yes / No* questions with *whether*.

1. Do you know _____ ?
   (Did he break the school rules?)

2. Can you tell me _____ ?
   (Is there a bus stop nearby?)

3. I'd like to know _____ .
   (Is he grounded this weekend?)

4. Can you tell me _____?
(Did she leave school early?)

5. I wonder _____.
(Can she come to the party?)

D Reading

Read the article. Answer the questions.

Teenagers and Spending

Teenagers in the United States generally spend money on clothing, entertainment, food, computers, and even cars. Many teens get their spending money as an allowance from their parents or as paychecks for part-time jobs. Studies have shown that parents' attitudes toward their children and money may influence their spending habits. For example, some parents try to teach their children how to spend responsibly at a young age by giving their children weekly allowances. They may connect a weekly allowance to the child's age. In other words, a parent will give $15 a week to his or her 15-year-old. Other parents offer payment to children for chores they do around the house. For example, a teen may earn money for babysitting younger siblings or cleaning the house. Parents also encourage teenagers to get part-time jobs for their spending money. Recent studies have shown that 33 to 44 percent of teenagers have jobs while in school. They often work 15 to 20 hours per week. Teens like these, who have jobs or whose parents limit the amount of money they receive, may spend more responsibly.

However, problems with spending occur when teenagers have poor money-management skills. These teens will often choose to spend their money rather than save it. And they spend money on the latest fashions or the latest technology without thinking beyond the present. However, as these teens become more responsible adults, they will need to reconsider their spending habits.

1. What types of things do teens in the United States spend their money on?

   Name at least three. _____

   _____

2. What is one way teens in the United States get their spending money? _____

   _____

3. What is one way that parents in the United States try to teach their teenagers

   how to spend responsibly? _____

   _____

4. What do teens with poor money-management skills do? _____

   _____

5. What will teens who spend a lot of money need to do when they become adults? _____

   _____

E Writing

1 Plan a paragraph about the differences between you and your best friend. Use the outline to make notes on your ideas.

Topic sentence: _____

    A. Me:

        1. Example: _____

        2. Example: _____

        3. Example: _____

    Transition: *On the other hand*

    B. My best friend:

        1. Example: _____

        2. Example: _____

        3. Example: _____

2 Write a paragraph about the differences between you and your best friend.

_____

_____

_____

_____

_____

_____

_____

_____

_____

_____

_____

_____

_____

_____

_____

_____

_____

_____

_____

_____

_____

TEST UNIT 4 *Health*

A 💿 Listening

Listen. Circle *T* (true) or *F* (false).

1. Marcus and Sylvia have to buy their apartment.   T   F
2. They have 90 days before they have to move out.   T   F
3. Charlie had heard about the possible sale.   T   F
4. Sylvia and Marcus want to find an apartment in the same neighborhood because of their jobs.   T   F
5. Sylvia will start making a list of available apartments tomorrow.   T   F

B Grammar

Match the sentences with the advice.

1. She's often late for class. _____
2. She is worried that her boss will fire her. _____
3. She gets tense during tests. _____
4. She has no time for herself. _____
5. The rent is due today. _____

a. She has to learn to calm down and concentrate.
b. She has to pay today.
c. She doesn't have to do everything for her family!
d. She shouldn't lose her temper.
e. She ought to take an earlier bus.

C Grammar

Write sentences with *should have* and *shouldn't have*.

1. He couldn't concentrate during the test.

   _____
   (go to bed on time)

2. They spent too much money.

   _____
   (use a credit card every day)

3. She was late to work.

   _____
   (turn off her alarm clock)

4. He didn't understand the rules.

   _____
   (ask someone to explain them)

5. We lost our jobs.

   _____
   (be more responsible)

D Reading

Read the article. Answer the questions.

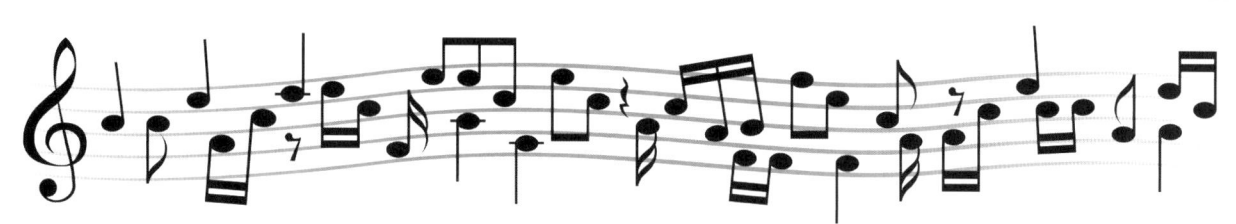

Stress and Music

Music can help you to calm down when you are stressed out. But it is important to find the best kind of music for you. You might assume that you should choose quiet music to help you to relieve stress. However, many doctors think that different types of music affect people differently. They say that each person's reaction to sounds and noises is unique and complicated. This means that the music that helps you to calm down may make another person anxious.

To discover the right music to help you relax, you ought to experiment. You should start by listening to music that you like. If you like loud music, you should start by seeing how loud music affects you. If you prefer quiet music, you should choose a calmer piece. To begin your experiment, feel for your pulse with your first and second fingers by pressing down on your wrist. Count the number of beats you feel in one minute. Write down the number. Next, pay attention to your muscles. Write down if they are tense or relaxed. A stressed-out person often has tense muscles and a fast pulse. Then, listen to the music for 20 minutes. React to the music in your own way. Relax, dance, sing along – do whatever your body wants to do. After 20 minutes, check your pulse and muscles again. Write down the changes that you have noticed. Is your pulse slower? Are your muscles less tense? If not, try the experiment again with another type of music.

1. How does music help someone who is stressed out? _____

_____

2. Do all people react to music in the same way? Why or why not? _____

_____

3. Why should you do an experiment with music? _____

_____

4. What are some of the physical signs that a person is stressed out? _____

_____

5. What are some of the physical signs that a person is relaxed? _____

_____

E Writing

1 Plan a paragraph about how you coped with a stressful situation in your past. Use the outline to make notes on your ideas.

Topic sentence: _____

_____

Actions you took	**Results of your actions**
_____	_____
_____	_____
_____	_____

2 Write a paragraph about how you coped with a stressful situation in your past.

_____

_____

_____

_____

_____

_____

_____

_____

_____

_____

_____

_____

_____

_____

_____

_____

_____

_____

_____

_____

_____

_____

TEST UNIT 5 — *Around town*

A 🔘 Listening

Listen. Answer the questions.

1. What is Jackie's job?

   _____

2. Who encouraged Yousef to volunteer at the library?

   _____

3. What experience does Yousef have in helping people with computers?

   _____

4. What languages does Yousef speak?

   _____

5. What time commitment does Yousef make?

   _____

B Grammar

Complete the sentences with *until* or *as soon as*.

1. **A** When will the party begin?

   B The party will begin _____ the first guests arrive.

2. **A** How long will Raul volunteer at the animal shelter?

   B He will volunteer there _____ he finds a full-time job.

3. **A** When will Samah eat lunch?

   B _____ she finishes her homework, she will eat lunch.

4. **A** How long will you and your wife live in the city?

   B We will live in the city _____ we have children.

5. **A** When will you take a vacation?

   B I will take a vacation _____ I have enough money!

C Grammar

Complete the sentences with the present, present perfect, or past forms of the verbs.

1. My husband _____ our neighbors several times last year.
   (help)

2. Jun-Ming _____ once last week.
   (oversleep)

3. My daughter _____ her grandmother twice a week.
   (visit)

4. I _____ with our new neighbors once so far.
   (speak)

5. Solange _____ her cousins many times in her life.
   (babysit)

D Reading

Read the article. Answer the questions.

Community Gardens

Members of communities in cities across the nation are changing the physical appearance and social setting of their neighborhoods. They are transforming unused, empty parking lots into community gardens. In these gardens, the residents of the neighborhoods grow their own vegetables, fruits, herbs, and flowers. The empty parking lots change into colorful, productive gardens, shared by different members of the community.

Community gardens don't just make neighborhoods more beautiful. They are worthwhile for residents in many ways. Some people use the gardens to save money on bills by growing their own fruits and vegetables. Others like the taste of their own fruits and vegetables. Immigrant families often grow fruits and vegetables from their native countries that they cannot find in supermarkets. Residents also go to the gardens for light exercise and fresh air.

When neighbors plant a garden together, they can create positive changes in a neighborhood. Community gardens bring neighbors closer together. In some neighborhoods, there has been less crime because neighbors work together to create, maintain, and harvest their community gardens. Community gardens offer safe, green space in city neighborhoods with few public parks. Finally, community gardens can help the environment. They help keep city air clean. No wonder there are about 100,000 community gardens in cities around the country! With all the great things gained from community gardens, we can expect to see many more in the near future!

1. Who is responsible for creating community gardens? _____

   _____

2. Where do people build community gardens? _____

   _____

3. Why are community gardens worthwhile for residents? Give two reasons. _____

   _____

4. How do community gardens result in less crime? _____

   _____

5. Why can we expect to see more community gardens in the future? _____

   _____

E Writing

1 Plan a paragraph about a famous person who has made a difference. Use the chart to make notes.

Who made a difference?	
What did he or she do?	
Why did this person do it?	
Where did it happen?	
When did it happen?	
How did this person make a difference?	

2 Write a paragraph about a famous person who has made a difference.

_____

_____

_____

_____

_____

_____

_____

_____

_____

_____

_____

_____

_____

_____

_____

_____

_____

_____

_____

_____

_____

_____

MIDTERM TEST | *Units 1–5*

A 💿 Listening

Listen. Answer the questions.

1. Why is Mrs. Brown worried? Why does she make an appointment with Mrs. Patterson?

   _____

   _____

2. According to Mrs. Patterson, what are some things that teenagers have to cope with in high school?

   _____

   _____

3. What kinds of things has Sam been doing lately?

   _____

   _____

4. What was Mr. and Mrs. Brown's solution to Sam's problems with school? Did it work?

   _____

   _____

5. What does Mrs. Patterson think might be Sam's problem? What is her suggestion?

   _____

   _____

B Grammar

Complete the sentences.

have to	shouldn't	that	until	whether

1. Molly can't have dessert _____ she turns off the television.

2. You _____ calm down before you lose your temper.

3. I wonder _____ John had a basketball game today.

4. My teachers realized _____ I was really good at math.

5. His parents _____ have let him go to the movies.

C Grammar

Complete the sentences.

1. We found the shopping mall _____.
   (easy / easily)

2. Students are encouraged _____ college credit for work experience.
   (earn / to earn)

3. He _____ learn how to manage his money.
   (ought to / shouldn't)

4. She will read to the children _____ they fall asleep.
   (as soon as / until)

5. We _____ at Running with Ropes three times last year.
   (volunteered / have volunteered)

D Reading

Read the article. Then read the sentences. Circle *T* (true) or *F* (false).

Resolving Conflict

In workplaces, school settings, and homes, conflict resolution techniques have been helping people to solve conflicts, or arguments, in better ways. In the workplace, co-workers may encourage teamwork and discussion, and in schools, children may be trained to become mediators, or peacekeepers, in order to help with conflicts among their fellow students.

People who help to resolve conflict learn about other people's interpersonal skills. They look at how people communicate with words and how people communicate with their bodies – their body language. When they look at how people communicate with words, they look at the words people choose to speak or write to others. For body language, they look at how people "say" things with their body's gestures, voice tone, and eye contact. From doing this, they understand how people communicate best.

Not being able to communicate clearly, or miscommunication, is one of the main reasons conflicts happen. So mediators often learn how to prevent miscommunication with good communication techniques. They do this by learning how to speak clearly and how to give feedback. They also learn how to listen carefully to understand another person's message. Once they've learned the best ways to communicate, they share them with their co-workers or classmates.

Conflict resolution techniques are not just used in offices and classrooms. They are used to solve arguments between parents and children and husbands and wives. They are also used for conflicts between companies, organizations, and countries. If conflict resolution techniques are used well, they can help change the outcome of many arguments and conflicts.

1. Conflicts occur in offices, schools, and homes.   T   F
2. Conflict resolution techniques are not usually successful.   T   F
3. Mediators help to resolve conflicts.   T   F
4. Children are too young to use conflict resolution techniques.   T   F
5. People who resolve conflicts learn about other people's intrapersonal skills.   T   F
6. Gestures, eye contact, and voice tone are examples of body language.   T   F
7. Miscommunication is a common reason conflicts occur.   T   F
8. People who help with conflicts don't know how to communicate well.   T   F
9. Conflict resolution techniques are not helpful between husbands and wives.   T   F
10. Conflict resolution techniques are also used for conflicts between countries.   T   F

E Writing

1 Plan a paragraph about a conflict you had with a family member or friend. How did you resolve the problem? Use the chart to make notes on your ideas.

Who did you have a conflict with?	
What happened?	
Why did the conflict happen?	
Where did it happen?	
When did it happen?	
How did you resolve the conflict?	

2 Write a paragraph about a conflict you had with a family member or friend. Use a separate piece of paper.

TEST UNIT 6 *Time*

A 💿 Listening

Listen. Answer the questions.

1. Why does Linda think cell phones are distracting?

_____

2. What happens during Chris's English class?

_____

3. Why does Linda think her family is different from other families?

_____

4. What is a "family plan"?

_____

5. Why do Chris and Linda need to talk to their children?

_____

B Grammar

Combine the sentences. Use *although*.

1. She doesn't understand the instructions. She read the manual many times.

_____

2. There are free computer classes at the community center. My parents still don't know how to use e-mail.

_____

3. I rarely use my microwave. Microwaves help me to make dinner quickly.

_____

4. He can take the subway to work. He prefers to walk for the exercise.

_____

5. She never used to write letters to her brother. She enjoys sending him e-mails now.

_____

C Grammar

Complete the sentences. Use *because* or *although*.

1. *A* Why is Julie always so busy?

   B _____ she has a full-time job, she volunteers at the senior center three times a week.

2. **A** Why doesn't David ever answer his phone?

   B Well, he rarely answers his cell phone _____ he forgets to turn it on.

3. **A** They don't often use their video camera _____ they have had it for years.

   B Maybe they'll let us borrow it!

4. **A** Why is Jason's mom concerned about his grades?

   B He has stopped reading books _____ he prefers to play video games.

5. **A** _____ Lana wants to try videoconferencing, she's worried about the cost.

   B Maybe she can look online for an affordable videoconferencing center.

D Reading

Read the article. Then read the sentences. Write *A* for advantage or *D* for disadvantage, based on the reading.

Saving Time with Microwaves

Do you look for ways to save time, especially in the kitchen? One of the most commonly used time-saving devices in homes today is the microwave. Because using a microwave can cut dinner preparation time from two or three hours to a half hour, they are used by many American families.

But microwaves aren't just used in the home. They're everywhere – in restaurants, trains, cafeterias, college dormitories, and lunch or break rooms in workplaces, for example. It's not surprising that microwaves are popular. Workers and students can put leftovers from last night's dinner in the microwave, heat them for a few minutes, and eat a delicious lunch. Supermarkets also add to the convenience of microwaves because they sell different types of "microwaveable" meals. These frozen dinners are packaged in microwave-safe containers.

Some people have health concerns about food cooked in a microwave. Others feel strongly that food cooked in a microwave does not taste as good as food cooked in a regular oven. They say that using a microwave takes away from the pleasure of cooking. Luckily for people who do not believe cooking is fun, microwaves can make their lives a lot easier.

_____ 1. Microwaves cut down on the time it takes to prepare meals.

_____ 2. Microwaves can be used in different places, such as homes, restaurants, and cafeterias.

_____ 3. Food cooked in microwaves may not taste as good as food cooked in regular ovens.

_____ 4. Microwaves make it easy for workers and students to bring leftovers for lunch.

_____ 5. Microwaves take away from the pleasure of cooking.

E Writing

1 Plan a paragraph that discusses the advantages and disadvantages of your favorite time-saving or technological device. Use the diagram to make notes on your ideas.

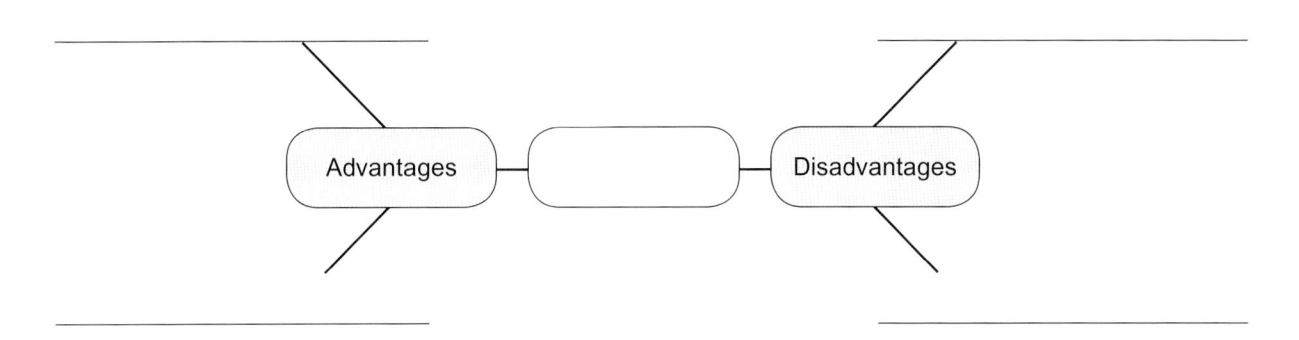

2 Write a paragraph that discusses the advantages and disadvantages of your favorite time-saving or technological device.

_____

_____

_____

_____

_____

_____

_____

_____

_____

_____

_____

_____

_____

_____

_____

_____

_____

_____

_____

_____

_____

_____

_____

TEST UNIT 7 | *Shopping*

A 🔘 Listening

Listen. Answer the questions.

1. What is the woman's problem?

   _____

2. What are the two choices Jack offers?

   _____

3. What does Jack mean by "upgrade"?

   _____

4. Which costs more, the upgrade or getting the same phone? How do you know?

   _____

5. What choice does the woman make?

   _____

B Grammar

Combine the sentences. Change the second sentence into an adjective clause with *that* or *who*.

1. Our merchandise comes with a warranty. It is good for two years.

   _____

2. Customers can order from our online store. They are looking for discounts.

   _____

3. Cellular phones are popular. They have Internet access.

   _____

4. The clerk is looking for the customer. She had a question about a product.

   _____

5. Store managers solve problems. They happen between clerks and customers.

   _____

C Grammar

Combine the sentences. Change the second sentence into an adjective clause with *that*.

1. He's a manager. I've worked with him for years.

   _____

2. The car is great! You recommended it to us.

   _____

3. The computer is defective. We bought it yesterday.

_____

4. The sweater was too small. I gave it to her.

_____

5. We bought it from a retailer. We trusted him.

_____

D Reading

Read the article. Answer the questions.

Thrift Stores

Shoppers who are looking for the lowest priced items don't usually go to the large shopping malls or the shopping centers in town. Instead, many bargain shoppers go to neighborhood thrift stores. At thrift stores, shoppers can buy used clothing, household items, books, jewelry, and furniture. The merchandise for sale is donated, or given, to the stores, and the salesclerks are volunteers. Because of this, thrift stores are able to offer used items that cost very little money.

However, thrift stores sell merchandise "as is," which means that the items for sale may or may not be defective. In most cases, if an item has small defects, such as small tears or stains, shoppers usually don't mind. But, in all cases, shoppers have to make sure the merchandise is in good condition because there are no refunds, exchanges, or warranties at thrift stores. Even so, shoppers usually consider shopping at thrift stores worthwhile because they often find valuable items that they can afford.

Finally, for many people, thrift stores are great places to give items that they no longer need. When people donate to thrift stores, they can be sure that their old clothes or furniture will be used again. Also, thrift stores are run by organizations that help people who need shelter, food, clothing, or money, like charities and churches. So those who donate know that the profits will help people in their communities as well.

---

1. Where do bargain shoppers go for the lowest prices? _____

_____

2. What kind of items can you buy at a thrift store? _____

_____

3. Why are prices so low at thrift stores? _____

_____

4. Do thrift stores sometimes sell defective items? Why? _____

_____

5. What benefits do thrift stores offer? _____

_____

E Writing

1 Plan a paragraph about your favorite place to shop. Use the chart to make notes on your ideas.

Transition words	Reasons and supporting details
	First reason:
	Example:
	Second reason:
	Fact:
	Fact:
	Third reason:
	Fact:
	Fact:

2 Write a paragraph about your favorite place to shop.

TEST UNIT 8 *Work*

A 🔊 Listening

Listen. Answer the questions.

1. How did Dan get the job?

_____

2. What is Tom uncomfortable about?

_____

3. How does Tom know that Dan hasn't been doing his duties?

_____

4. What reason does Dan give for not completing his duties?

_____

5. Why does Tom think the job is easy for Dan?

_____

B Grammar

Complete the sentences. Use the present perfect or present perfect continuous forms of the verbs. Use *just* where possible.

1. It's 7:00 a.m. Joe _____ making coffee.
   (finish)

2. Marie is exhausted. She _____ overtime all week.
   (work)

3. This book is so interesting! I _____ it all afternoon.
   (read)

4. I'm so excited. The clothes I ordered online _____.
   (arrive)

5. Mike's not home. He _____ to work.
   (go)

C Grammar

Circle the correct adjective.

1. I thought the movie was very **amusing** / **amused**.

2. My boss was **shocking** / **shocked** when I told him I was leaving.

3. After working so hard all day, Ricardo was **exhausting** / **exhausted**.

4. Everyone was in a bad mood because of the **disappointing** / **disappointed** results.

5. Jane's co-workers are **irritating** / **irritated** because she takes long lunches.

D Reading

Read the article. Answer the questions.

The "Hottest" Jobs in the Future

Every few years, the United States government issues a report on what the "hottest" jobs will be in the future. These reports suggest which jobs will have the largest growth and popularity in years to come. Based on information provided by the biggest job industries, they predict how quickly certain industries will need new employees. Students and workers who look at these reports can find out the most popular and fastest-growing jobs. They can use this information to help them decide which careers will be the most promising or which programs to study.

Recently, reports have said that some of the "hottest" jobs are service industry occupations. Jobs in the service industry include jobs in health care, hospitality, and food services, for example. There are many reasons why certain industries will have more jobs available in the future. One reason is a growing need for more people to do similar jobs.

Since people are living longer, more people are needed to take care of the elderly. Therefore, nurses, nursing aides, and home health aides are expected to be some of the "hottest" jobs in the near future. For jobs in health care, some hard skills are necessary, such as a certificate or a degree. However, the soft skills of having a good work ethic and patience are also just as important.

For all of the fastest-growing occupations, employers will look for hard and soft skills. Will you be ready for one of the "hottest" jobs in the future?

1. What does the article mean by the "hottest" jobs?

   _____

2. How can students and workers use job reports?

   _____

3. What are some service industry occupations?

   _____

4. What are some of the fastest growing health-care jobs?

   _____

5. What will employers look for?

   _____

E Writing

1 Plan a cover letter for a job in one of the service industries discussed in the article, such as health care, hospitality, or food services. Use the outline to make notes on your ideas.

1. Date: _____

2. Inside address: Mary Freeman
   Director of Human Services
   592 Highland Avenue
   Miami, FL 33136

3. Position you are applying for:

   Job title: _____

4. Your skills and experience: _____

   _____

   _____

2 Write a cover letter for a job in one of the service industries discussed in the article, such as health care, hospitality, or food services.

_____

_____

_____

_____

_____

_____

_____

_____

_____

_____

_____

_____

_____

_____

_____

_____

_____

_____

_____

_____

TEST UNIT 9 | *Daily living*

A 💿 Listening

Listen. Answer the questions.

1. What are George and Ed talking about?

   _____

2. What kind of car does George think Ed should buy?

   _____

3. What is a hybrid car?

   _____

4. How do hybrid cars cut down on the amount of gas you use?

   _____

5. What is one way Ed's old car causes pollution?

   _____

B Grammar

Complete the sentences. Use the present unreal conditional.

1. If more people _____ public transportation, we _____ on air pollution.

(take) (cut down)

2. We _____ energy if we _____ the air conditioning.

(save) (turn down)

3. If we _____ enough air in the tires, we _____ gas.

(put) (save)

4. There _____ less trash if everyone _____.

(be) (recycle)

5. If we _____ unused rooms, we _____ air conditioning and heating use.

(close off) (reduce)

C Grammar

Combine the sentences. Use the connectors in parentheses.

1. There has been a drought. There are fewer crops this season.

   (As a result) _____

2. Air pollution is trapping the sun's heat. The atmosphere is warming up.

   (Since) _____

3. Global warming changes weather. Hurricanes are stronger and more dangerous.

   (Consequently) _____

4. There are new laws. We may be forced to change our routines.

    (Due to) _____

5. I have learned more about the environment. I have become more responsible.

    (Since) _____

D Reading

Read the article. Answer the questions.

Carpool Slugs

Cities have been dealing with rush hour traffic problems for a long time. One way they have cut down on traffic jams has been to create High Occupancy Vehicle (HOV) lanes. In these lanes, also known as carpool lanes, drivers must have two or more people in their cars to enter. Neighbors and co-workers often carpool to gain access to these HOV lanes. With fewer cars and more people in each car, carpool lanes have helped rush hour traffic to run smoother and commuters to get to their destinations faster.

In recent years, commuters have started a new kind of carpooling. In this type of carpooling, a driver drives past bus stops or well-known parking lots and offers a free ride to people he doesn't know. This is so that the driver and the passenger can take the HOV lanes to work. The passengers are called carpool slugs, and they commute to work by *slugging*, or carpooling with strangers.

Both drivers and the carpool slugs are happy with slugging. Every day, slugs save up to $12 in transportation fares and parking fees. And drivers save up to $5,000 a year in gas. In addition, both drivers and slugs save from 30 to 60 minutes of travel time daily.

After many years of slugging, carpool slugs and drivers have become a community. Many of them know each other and have become friends. They look out for each other and may know each other by face, if not by name. Slugging has become an efficient way to commute in large cities and help the environment. Fewer cars on the road means less gas to pollute the air.

---

1. What is one way that many cities have dealt with rush hour traffic? _____

_____

2. What is an HOV lane? _____

_____

3. What is a carpool slug? _____

_____

4. What are two benefits of carpool slugging? _____

_____

5. What has started to happen between carpool slugs and drivers? _____

_____

E Writing

1 Plan a paragraph about one of these environmental problems: global warming, air pollution, or smog. Use the outline to make notes on your ideas.

Problem:	
Causes	**Effects**
1.	1.
(detail) a.	
(detail) b.	2.
2.	
(detail) a.	3.
(detail) b.	

2 Write a paragraph about one of these environmental problems: global warming, air pollution, or smog.

_____

_____

_____

_____

_____

_____

_____

_____

_____

_____

_____

_____

_____

_____

_____

_____

_____

_____

_____

_____

TEST UNIT 10 Leisure

A 💿 Listening

Listen. Answer the questions.

1. Where is Elena's cousin, Marie, getting married? Where is Marie's fiancé from?

_____

2. Why can't Elena go to the wedding?

_____

3. Who is invited to the reception? Where is the reception?

_____

4. Where will Marie's family have their meal? What type of meal is it?

_____

5. What do both Elena and Sara wish for?

_____

B Grammar

Complete the sentences. Use the future real or unreal conditional forms of the verbs.

1. **A** I'm looking forward to the party tonight!

   B I am, too. If everyone _____ , we _____ a lot of fun!
   (come)   (have)

2. **A** I heard that you're taking a trip to China! Do you speak Chinese?

   B No. If we _____ the language, we _____ more comfortable.
   (knew)   (feel)

3. **A** What will her family think about the wedding ceremony?

   B If she _____ the cultural traditions, she _____ her family.
   (not / follow)   (disappoint)

4. **A** What should I wear to the reception?

   B If I _____ you, I _____ a nice dress.
   (be)   (wear)

5. **A** Will Roberto be invited to the wedding ceremony?

   B If he _____ an acquaintance, the couple _____ him to the ceremony.
   (be)   (not / invite)

C Grammar

Complete the sentences. Use *hope* or *wish* and the correct form of the verb or modal.

1. He _____ he _____ , but he's too busy right now.
   (can visit)

2. They _____ the weather _____ nice for their picnic next Saturday.
   (will be)

3. She _____ her son _____ married. He doesn't seem interested in
   getting married. (get)

4. I _____ I _____ to Japan next summer. I'm saving money now for
   the trip. (can travel)

5. We _____ we _____ on vacation, but we don't have any free time.
   (can go)

D Reading

Read the article. Answer the questions.

New Year's in China

New Year's celebrations in China start with the New Moon, the first day of the New Year, and continue for 15 days. Celebrations involve family gatherings and visiting friends. During these days, many Chinese people put up special decorations, eat symbolic food, and participate in traditional activities.

During New Year's celebrations in China, many houses are decorated with vases of flowers, bowls of fruit, and a tray with dried fruit, candies, and sweets. Many Chinese people believe that flowers make the house beautiful and that they symbolize wealth and good luck. In addition, bowls of oranges and tangerines are placed around the home to represent happiness. The walls and doors are decorated with short poems written on red paper. In addition to decorating homes, many Chinese people visit friends and relatives. When they visit, they often bring gifts of fruit or red envelopes with money for children.

Traditional meals are prepared for the whole family, including those who cannot be there and ancestors – family members who have died. Ancestors are remembered and honored with respect during the celebrations. In addition, certain foods symbolize different things. Noodles represent a long life, and fish represent success. A chicken is served with all of its parts – the head, the legs, and the tail – to represent completeness.

Finally, everyone looks forward to the end of the celebration, the Lantern Festival. This is a fun night. Many people participate in parades with lanterns, while others watch as young men perform a dragon dance with dragons made of bamboo, silk, and paper. And everyone watches the fireworks and firecrackers.

---

1. When does the Chinese New Year begin? How long is it celebrated?

   _____

2. What do flowers symbolize?

   _____

3. What is done for ancestors during New Year's celebrations?

   _____

4. How is chicken served during Chinese New Year, and why?

   _____

5. What happens at the end of New Year's celebrations in China?

   _____

E Writing

1 Plan a paragraph about a ceremony you attended or a tradition you observed. Use the outline to help you make notes on your ideas.

I. Ceremony / tradition: _____

II. Reason for the ceremony / tradition: _____

_____

III. Where: _____

IV. When: _____

V. Special traditions / activities:

    A. _____

    B. _____

    C. _____

VI. Conclusion: _____

_____

2 Write a paragraph about a ceremony you attended or a tradition you observed.

_____

_____

_____

_____

_____

_____

_____

_____

_____

_____

_____

_____

_____

_____

_____

_____

_____

_____

_____

_____

FINAL TEST | *Units 6–10*

A 💿 Listening

Listen. Put a check (✓) under *Yes* or *No*.

	Yes	No
1. Jenny is interested in getting a job in telemarketing.	☐	☐
2. Telemarketers sell things to people who need them.	☐	☐
3. Michelle loves dealing with telemarketers.	☐	☐
4. Jenny doesn't want to receive phone calls from telemarketers.	☐	☐
5. If Jenny wants to stop the calls, she has to buy a new device.	☐	☐
6. Michelle didn't need to use special equipment to stop telemarketing calls.	☐	☐
7. The government started the National Do Not Call Registry.	☐	☐
8. To register her number, Michelle had to pay a fee.	☐	☐
9. There are two ways to register a phone number to stop the calls.	☐	☐
10. Jenny is excited about cutting down on unwanted phone calls.	☐	☐

B Grammar

Circle the correct word.

1. Salina **has** / **has been** negotiating with her co-worker for two days.

2. If I **was** / **were** you, I would take a vacation.

3. He **wishes** / **hopes** he could go to his cousin's quinceañera, but he didn't get the day off.

4. If we carpooled to work, we **will** / **would** save a lot of money on gas.

5. They were **amusing** / **amused** when they read Mike's blog.

C Grammar

Complete the sentences.

although	because	because of	just	that

1. _____ traditional customs, only family members will be invited to the wedding ceremony.

2. My friend has _____ learned how to send text messages.

3. The store manager refused to give the customer a refund _____ the customer didn't have a receipt.

4. Omar is interested in electronic devices _____ are innovative and energy-efficient.

5. _____ wireless technology is amazing, I cannot afford it.

D Reading

Read the article. Circle *T* (true) or *F* (false).

Habitat for Humanity

Habitat for Humanity is an international organization that brings volunteers together to help change the lives and living conditions of people around the world. The goal of the organization is to help homeless families worldwide. Because of donations of money and supplies and the help of volunteers, Habitat for Humanity houses are often built and repaired at very low cost.

To get started, poor and needy families apply to local programs to become "partner families" with Habitat for Humanity. Partner families may have to pay a down payment and monthly payments for their homes, but they also pay in "sweat equity." "Sweat equity" means that partner families have the responsibility of building and repairing their homes with the help of volunteers. So, partner families often spend many hours on the construction of their house and on houses for other families, too. In this way, partner families and volunteers from small businesses, large corporations, church groups, and individuals work together to build and repair many new homes.

Many of the building materials are donated by construction companies, and no one gets paid for their work. Professional construction workers offer their skills to build the foundation and the outside of the houses. Non-professional volunteers with no experience in housing construction learn skills from the professionals and work on the inside of the houses. In addition, all houses that are repaired and built are made to be more energy-efficient.

Even though the central office of Habitat for Humanity is in Atlanta, Georgia, the organization has been building homes in more than 90 countries around the world. In each country, people work together to strengthen communities, to unite cultures, and to give opportunities for affordable homes to more than one million people worldwide.

Source: http://www.habitat.org

1. Habitat for Humanity is a worldwide housing program.   T   F
2. Professional construction workers get paid for their work with Habitat for Humanity.   T   F
3. The organization succeeds because of donations of money and volunteers.   T   F
4. Families need to apply to get help from Habitat for Humanity.   T   F
5. Partner families have no financial responsibilities for their houses.   T   F
6. People who work on the exterior of the houses have hard skills.   T   F
7. Volunteers without construction skills can work on the inside of houses.   T   F
8. If you are unskilled, you may receive training from a professional.   T   F
9. It's too expensive for Habitat for Humanity to build energy-efficient houses. T   F
10. There are Habitat for Humanity houses in more than 90 countries.   T   F

E Writing

1 Plan a paragraph about a time you helped someone. Use the chart to make notes on your ideas.

Who did you help?	
What was the problem or situation?	
What did you do?	
When did this happen?	
How did you feel?	

2 Write a paragraph about a time you helped someone.

_____

_____

_____

_____

_____

_____

_____

_____

_____

_____

_____

_____

_____

_____

_____

_____

_____

_____

_____

_____

_____

_____

Tests audio script

This audio script contains the listening portions of the *Ventures 4* unit tests, midterm test, and final test. A printable copy is available on the *Teacher's Toolkit Audio CD / CD-ROM*. You can play the audio program using the *Teacher's Toolkit Audio CD / CD-ROM* in a computer or a stereo, or you can read the script aloud.

Unit 1: Personal information

Track 2

A Listening
Listen. Complete the chart.

A Well, Carol, having a class party is an excellent idea. But now we have to plan it. Where do we start?

B Why don't we start with the food and drinks? Any ideas, George?

A How about pizza and soda? Leonard works at Pizza Joe's. Maybe he can get a discount for us.

B Great. So let's ask Leonard to order the pizza and soda. Uh, how many pizzas should we order? How much will they cost with the discount?

A Sounds like a problem for Elena. She's really good at math. Let's ask her to figure out the total cost. Then she can tell us the cost for each classmate.

B OK. Now what about music?

A Did you know that Jonathan is a disk jockey? He's the DJ at the dance club downtown. I'm sure he has a lot of different kinds of music!

B You're right. He's got music from all around the world. He can choose the music. Oh, and we'll need some activities. George, you're a great organizer. Can you organize them?

A What do you mean? Like a dance contest? Something like that? Sure! I think I can organize a few things pretty easily. And what about decorations, Carol? You're creative and artistic – can you do those?

B Yeah, George, I'll decorate. Hey, this planning isn't very hard. Now, what are we missing? Who else can we ask to help?

Unit 2: At school

Track 3

A Listening
Listen. Complete the chart.

A Come in. Oh, hello, Joy! How are you doing?

B Good morning, Mrs. Almada. I need some advice.

A How can I help you?

B Well, I really need to start thinking about my future. I need a job where I can help my family.

A Do you have any ideas?

B Yes! I was talking to my teacher, Mrs. Ash. You know I'm taking that class in childcare, right?

A Yes, I know. Do you like it?

B I love it! I love working with young kids! And yesterday, Mrs. Ash told me that there's a certificate program in childcare at the community college. Do you know how I can learn more about the program?

A I have information about it. What would you like to know?

B Well, first of all – with a certificate, does it mean that I can open my own childcare business?

A Not exactly, Joy. It means that you are certified to work in childcare. There are other requirements for opening a childcare business, and you'll need to have a lot of work experience before you do that.

B But the certificate is the first step, right? Can you tell me about the program requirements? How many courses are required?

A There are seven required courses.

B And how much is each course?

A Well, let's see. There are seven courses, and each course is three units. That's 21 units, and it costs $35 a unit. So, the total cost of the courses is $735.

B $735? Whoa! That's more than I expected. How long does it take to complete the childcare program?

A It depends. Have a seat – let's look at the possibilities.

Unit 3: Friends and family

Track 4

A Listening
Listen. Circle *T* (true) or *F* (false).

A Hey! Vanna! How are you doing?

B I'm OK. Thanks.

A Listen, there's a dance Friday night. I was wondering if you plan to go.

B Well, I *might* go . . .

A What's the matter? Don't you like to dance?

B Yeah, sure. I like to dance.

A Well, then, would you like to go to the dance with me?

B Oh, Mike, I like to dance, and I'm planning to go to the dance – but I can't go with you.

A Yeah, that's cool. I understand.

B No, you don't understand, Mike. Listen, I have very strict parents. I'm not permitted to go anywhere alone with a boy.

A Well, can you tell them that we won't be alone? That we'll be at a dance?

B No, that won't work. My parents are from "the old country." Do you know what I mean? They are bringing me up the same way they were brought up in Cambodia.

A Wow. They don't trust you at all, huh?

B They do trust me. It's just that they only know one way to raise a daughter. Going out alone with a boy is against the rules!

A Well, you can still go to the dance, right?

B Yeah, I'm going with some other girls.

A And you're permitted to dance, right?

B Yes, I'm allowed to dance.

A So, will you save a dance for me?

B Yeah, of course, but . . . I guess I should tell you . . . my parents are going to be chaperones at the dance!

A Oh, no!

Unit 4: Health

Track 5

A Listening

Listen. Circle *T* (true) or *F* (false).

A Oh, no! This letter is bad news!

B Why? What's the matter, Marcus?

A It's from the landlord. He's sold the building. The new owner is going to make these apartments into condos!

B What does that mean?

A It means we have to make a decision, Sylvia: We have to buy this apartment, or we have to move out.

B But we don't want to buy this place! It's old, and it needs fixing up! We'll have to move out. How much time do we have?

A We have 60 days. We ought to start looking immediately. Oh, I should have listened to Charlie.

B Why? What did Charlie say?

A Well, a few months ago, Charlie mentioned that the landlord was trying to sell the place, but I didn't really pay attention.

B You should have told me! Now we have to start thinking and acting – fast! We have to find a place in this neighborhood. The kids shouldn't change schools.

A Let's calm down, honey. We don't have to panic yet. I'll take tomorrow off.

B No, Marcus, you shouldn't miss work. Let me think. . . . Tomorrow I'll look in the newspaper and start making a list of available apartments.

A OK. And we can start looking at apartments next weekend.

B That's right. But, listen, we have to stay in this area. I don't want the kids to be stressed out about changing schools. You should have told me.

A You're right. I'm sorry.

Unit 5: Around town

Track 6

A Listening

Listen. Answer the questions.

A Hi! I'm Jackie, the volunteer coordinator. Are you Yousef?

B Yes. Nice to meet you, Jackie.

A Well, I'm so happy you came by! I am glad that you are interested in volunteering here at the library. How would you like to help?

B Well, my English teacher told me that the library is looking for volunteers to help with the new computer lab.

A Oh, yes! Do you know a lot about computers?

B I know how to use a lot of software and how to do research on the Internet . . . that kind of stuff.

A Great. We have a lot of older people who come here. They know we have computers and want to learn how to use them, but they don't really know where to begin.

B Yes, I know. That's why my teacher encouraged me to come. She knows that I have been helping my parents and my aunts and uncles. I taught them how to use e-mail. They had no idea where to begin until I set up the computer and showed them how. As soon as I showed them, they sent a message to our family in Lebanon! It seems easy to me, but – as you said – they didn't know where to start. I had to be very patient with them.

A I understand. Sometimes it's harder to be patient with family members.

B That's true. Anyway, it was really worthwhile. They are so happy to be able to communicate so often and so cheaply!

A Exactly. And, Yousef, do you speak another language?

B Yes, I speak Arabic at home.

A Oh, that's great. We have a lot of people who could use your help. Now let's talk about your schedule. Can you make a commitment of three hours a week?

B Yes, if I can come on Saturday mornings.

A Terrific. We open at 10:00. Should we say, 10:00 to 1:00? Does that work?

B Yes, that works for me. Should I start this Saturday?

A Yes. I can't wait to get you started!

Midterm Test Units 1–5

Track 7

A Listening

Listen. Answer the questions.

A Hello, Mrs. Brown. Come into my office. I'm glad you made an appointment with me.

B Thank you, Mrs. Patterson. My husband and I are so worried about Sam. He is so bright and gifted in many areas. But we just don't know what his problem is. We really don't know why he's doing so poorly in high school. Do you think that you can help us figure out what's wrong with Sam?

A Well, Mrs. Brown, as a counselor with many years of experience working with teenagers, I can tell you – high school is difficult! Teenagers have to cope with a lot of things these days – new social situations, more difficult schoolwork, extracurricular activities, fitting in with others.

B Yes, I'm sure you're right. But I have no idea why his attendance is so bad. Or why he is missing so many classes. I'm really worried.

A Have you talked with Sam? What does he say?

B Actually, he doesn't say much. When he does talk, he says we're too strict. But recently his grades have been bad because he misses deadlines for homework assignments. He forgets a lot! He forgets his books, he forgets his keys, and he forgot his lunch twice last week!

A What solutions have you tried so far?

B Well, we grounded him a few times last month for not going to school and for bad grades. I think we were more stressed out than he was! He just stayed in his room and listened to music.

A Hmm. That doesn't seem to work. Does he have friends?

B Yes, he's very social. He has a large group of friends.

A Does he oversleep?

B No, that doesn't seem to be a problem.

A Does he seem to be stressed out about his grades at all?

B Yes, he does.

A Well, maybe he's just frustrated. He ought to get some help with his schoolwork. Maybe you should get a tutor for Sam. The school has professional tutors available. Do you think he would be interested in meeting with a tutor?

B I'll definitely ask him to go, and then we'll see what happens. Is there a fee?

A No, the school offers free tutoring three days a week after school.

B Well, that's a start! I'll talk to my husband and Sam about the tutor.

Unit 6: Time

Track 8

A Listening

Listen. Answer the questions.

A Linda, I've been thinking about getting cell phones for all of us.

B Oh? But, Chris, our family has been fine without cell phones so far!

A Yes, but I was thinking. . . . It would be nice for us to keep in contact during the day.

B Well, I think cell phones are so distracting. When I'm riding on the bus to work every day, I always hear people having conversations on their cell phones. I don't like listening to their private business!

A Yes, I know what you mean. In my English class, even though the teacher always reminds students to turn off their cell phones, someone always forgets.

B Well, then why do you want a cell phone all of a sudden?

A Well, they're very convenient, especially when we travel. We've been using pay phones, and sometimes it's hard to find one.

B That's true. Cell phones are more convenient than pay phones.

A Yeah, and also, I worry when you or the kids take the bus at night. I'd like to know that you can call me if you need me.

B Hmm. It's true that we are one of the few families that doesn't own a cell phone. Maybe we should look into it.

A I already have. We could get a family plan. All of us get a phone, and we pay one monthly bill for the whole family. It's less expensive that way.

B We have to talk to the kids about using cell phones

responsibly. I don't want them wasting time on the phone.

A I agree.

B So how much is this going to cost?

A Well, it's not going to be cheap, because cell phone plans always include a lot of taxes. But it will be good to know that we can reach each other if we need help.

B All right. I guess it's worth the money.

Unit 7: Shopping

Track 9

A Listening

Listen. Answer the questions.

A You have reached Swift Customer Service. My name is Jack. How can I help you?

B Well, I bought a cell phone for my daughter a few months ago. And I think the phone is defective. She can't make or receive calls. So, she needs a new phone.

A Well, let's see what we can do. Can you tell me the account number?

B Is the account number the same as the telephone number?

A No, it's the number that's at the top of your monthly bill.

B Oh, here it is: 6494 6603.

A OK, ma'am. I have the account here on the computer. Here's what we can do. You will need to mail the defective phone to us or bring it to one of our stores. If we see that it really is defective, you have two choices. We can exchange it for the same kind of phone, or we can offer you an upgrade.

B An upgrade? What do you mean?

A I mean you can get a better, newer phone that has more features. The newer phone has Internet access and a music player – I'm sure your daughter would love that. The monthly fee is only $15 more than the fee you are paying now.

B But my phone is still under warranty, right?

A Yes, that's right.

B So I can get another phone that is similar to the phone my daughter has for free, right?

A Well, the phone is free, but you will need to pay a small service charge for us to send it to you.

B Let's go with that. I don't want an upgrade at this time. Just send me a phone that works.

A OK. As soon as we receive the broken phone from you, we will send you a new one. Let me confirm your address.

Unit 8: Work

Track 10

A Listening

Listen. Answer the questions.

A Hey, Dan. How do you like the job so far?

B I like it a lot, Tom. Thanks for helping me get it. I'm excited about making some money, finally!

A Yeah. Well, that's what friends are for, right?

B Right! The job isn't that hard, and it's cool that we're working together.

A Yeah, it's great that we get to work together. But, actually, Dan, since I'm the manager here, there's something I need to tell you. It's sort of uncomfortable for me because we're buddies, but . . . well, I hate having to remind you about your responsibilities all the time.

B Well, I'm just learning. I've only been working here for two weeks, you know.

A Yeah, I know. But, you know about the chart, right? I just looked, and I didn't see your initials after any of the duties. What happened?

B Come on, Tom, I've been dealing with customers all morning, and I'm exhausted. And anyway, aren't we supposed to share the duties? I don't see your initials up there!

A Dan, I'm the manager. I don't have to write my initials on the chart, but you do! And another thing. You say this job "isn't that hard," but the reason it isn't hard is because you haven't been doing your share of the work. There's a chart up there for a reason.

B All right, all right! I'll initial the stupid chart! Then will you leave me alone?

A Dan. We're good friends, but I have to make sure things get done around here. You have to try to understand that.

B All right. I'll do the best I can.

A Good. I hope we can work this out somehow.

Unit 9: Daily living

Track 11

A Listening

Listen. Answer the questions.

A Hey, George! Do you have a minute?

B Sure, Ed, what's up?

A Well, Rita and I have been talking about getting a new car.

B That's great!

A And since you know so much about cars, I was wondering if you have any suggestions for a car that's more energy efficient.

B Yeah, I have a suggestion. You should get a hybrid.

A I've heard about hybrids, but I'm not sure how they work.

B Well, a hybrid is a mix between an electric and a standard car. In a hybrid, both electricity and gasoline power the car. The car runs with an electric motor and a gas engine, but the engine is smaller, and it uses a lot less gasoline than a standard car.

A I see, so, the hybrid runs with two different energy sources – that's really interesting.

B Yeah, and it's definitely more energy-efficient than a standard car. The batteries charge themselves with energy the car produces on its own. And since you're using batteries as well as gasoline, you can really cut down on the amount of gas you use. And that means less air pollution.

A Well, that's the main reason the kids want to get rid of our old car. They've learned that pollution from oil products like gasoline damages the environment and causes global warming. And we've started teaching them how to protect the environment and take responsibility. So the next thing you know, the kids are telling me that we have to replace our old car!

B Well, your kids are right, Ed! Since your car is so old, it uses a lot of gas, which is bad for the environment. Pollution from standard cars gets into the atmosphere and comes down as acid rain.

A So, driving a hybrid is better for the environment.

B Absolutely! Every little thing helps. And did you know the government gives you a tax credit for buying a hybrid?

A So, it's even good for our wallets!

Unit 10: Leisure

Track 12

A Listening

Listen. Answer the questions.

A Sara, did I tell you my cousin, Marie, is getting married next month . . . in France? Her fiancé is from France.

B Really? Are you going?

A No, I wish I could go, but the trip is too far and too expensive. But Marie told me all about it. Weddings in France are a big deal, and sometimes they last for two days! And her family is planning a very special celebration.

B It sounds exciting! What are they planning?

A Well, Marie said her wedding ceremony will start on a Saturday afternoon at a small church. Only family and close friends are invited. The ceremony will last about an hour. Then after the ceremony, all her fiancé's neighbors and acquaintances are invited to a reception in the courtyard of the church.

B Wow, Elena. How many people will there be?

A Lots of people! The reception will last about two hours, and they'll serve champagne and snacks.

B Oh, that sounds fun!

A But, Sara, that's not all! After the reception, the family and close friends are going to go to a castle for a five-course meal.

B A five-course meal of French food sounds delicious! I absolutely love French food.

A And after the meal, the dancing begins.

B Elena, if I ate a five-course meal, I'd never be able to dance!

A Well, it's not uncommon for the French to celebrate all day. The dancing will probably continue until very late. And afterward, the family will spend the night at the castle.

B Oh my gosh!

A Then finally, the next day, in the late morning or early afternoon, the friends will come back to the castle and join the family for another meal. Oh, I really wish I could go!

B I wish you could go, too! All of those activities sound exhausting, but so exciting. If I were you, I'd find a way to go.

Final Test Units 6–10

Track 13

A Listening

Listen. Put a check under *Yes* or *No*.

A Oh, Michelle, I am so frustrated!

B Why, Jenny? What's wrong?

A Oh, it's those annoying telephone calls that I get all the time! Last night, I was making dinner and I received three phone calls from people trying to sell me something again. They always call at the worst times.

B Oh, you mean telemarketers. They used to drive me crazy, too. I absolutely hated dealing with them.

A Michelle, what do you mean when you say "they used to drive you crazy"?

B Well, Jenny, we've just registered for the National Do Not Call Registry. Have you heard of it?

A No, but I'm very interested.

B It's a government program that you can use to stop telemarketers from calling you. If you register your telephone number with the system, the telemarketers are not allowed to call you! It's easy!

A Wow. Do you need to pay to do this? Do you have to buy any special devices?

B No, you don't have to pay anything or buy any special equipment.

A Well, that's good. So does the Do Not Call Registry really work?

B Absolutely. Since we registered our telephone number, we haven't had even one phone call from someone trying to sell us something or asking us to donate money.

A OK, I'm convinced. How do I register?

B You can register by phone or online – it doesn't take long.

A Michelle, thanks so much for the tip. I'm going to register my phone number right now. I'm really looking forward to ending those annoying phone calls!

Tests answer key

Each unit test item is 4 points. Unit test sections have five items; therefore, each section is worth 20 points, for a total of 100 points per unit test.

Unit 1: Personal information

A Listening
Leonard: order the pizza and soda; He works at Pizza Joe's.
Elena: figure out the total cost; She's good at math.
Jonathan: choose the music; He's a DJ and has a lot of different kinds of music.
George: organize the activities; He's a great organizer.
Carol: decorate; She's artistic and creative.

B Grammar
1. Do you believe that girls are better at learning languages than boys?
2. Samuel's parents realize that he has an aptitude for art.
3. Do you feel that your son needs help in math class?
4. Everyone agrees that Naomi is gifted in dance.
5. Do you know that Karen has an aptitude for cooking?

C Grammar
1. easy; quickly
2. beautiful; professionally
3. skillful; slowly
4. fast; carefully
5. bad; well

D Reading
1. T   2. T   3. F   4. F   5. T

E Writing
Answers will vary.
Sample answer:

   The primary intelligence of my brother, Daniel, is visual / spatial. All his life, he has drawn beautiful pictures. Everyone talks about his artistic aptitude. As a boy, he spent a lot of his free time drawing and painting. Now, as an adult, he uses his visual / spatial intelligence by painting and teaching art. He also has a fantastic sense of design. I wish I had his artistic aptitude.

Unit 2: At school

A Listening
1. childcare
2. the community college
3. Joy wants to work in childcare and then open her own business one day.
4. seven
5. $735

B Grammar
1. *A* Are bilingual skills expected by many employers in this country?
   B Yes, bilingual skills are needed for many jobs in this country.
2. *A* Is an internship required to graduate from the program?
   B Yes. Internships are arranged by the school.
3. *A* Where is the admissions office located?
   B It is located next to the business building.
4. *A* Are most of the classes held in the morning?
   B Actually, many of the classes are offered in the evening.
5. *A* Are scholarships provided for students?
   B Yes, scholarships are given to students by the financial aid office.

C Grammar
1. Graduates are required to complete their courses by May 4th.
2. All interns are expected to be on time for every meeting.
3. Are students encouraged to participate in work experience programs?
4. Applicants are told to meet with a counselor.
5. Are students allowed to earn credit for work experience?

D Reading
1. F   2. F   3. F   4. T   5. T

E Writing
Answers will vary.
Sample answer:

   My wife and I immigrated to the United States. We had many obstacles and successes. Our first obstacle was money. I was a teacher in my country, but I had to find a job cleaning buildings. I wanted my wife to stay home with the children, but we needed to make enough money to pay the rent and buy things for our house. I am happy to say that we have succeeded in earning and saving our money. The second obstacle was learning English. I study English so that I can teach one day in this country. I am not fluent, but I am making a lot of progress.

Unit 3: Friends and famiily

A Listening
1. F   2. T   3. T   4. F   5. T

B Grammar
1. I'd like to know why he is grounded.
2. I wonder when she started to trust him again.
3. Can you tell me how I can get a better job?
4. Do you know what time the class starts?
5. Can you tell me what grade Lidia got in chemistry?

C Grammar
1. Do you know whether he broke the school rules?
2. Can you tell me whether there is a bus stop nearby?
3. I'd like to know whether he is grounded this weekend?
4. Can you tell me whether she left school early?
5. I wonder whether she can come to the party.

D Reading
1. They spend their money on clothing, entertainment, food, computers, and cars.
2. They get their spending money from allowances from their parents, from part-time jobs, and from payment for chores.
3. Parents teach their teenagers how to spend responsibly by: giving their children weekly allowances connected to their age; giving their children weekly allowances connected to the chores they do around the

house; and encouraging them to get part-time jobs.
4. They spend their money rather than save it. They spend money on the latest fashions or technology.
5. They will need to reconsider their spending habits.

E Writing
Answers will vary.
Sample answer:

One difference between me and my best friend, Dan, is that we spend our evenings after work very differently. I prefer quiet nights at home. For example, when I get home, I cook a healthy dinner. Then, I like to watch a movie and go to bed early. On the other hand, Dan likes to go out after work. He loves fast food and enjoys eating in restaurants for dinner. He visits me and his other friends and then goes to bed very late. Dan and I are very different people, but he is still my best friend.

Unit 4: Health

A Listening
1. F   2. F   3. T   4. F   5. T

B Grammar
1. e   2. d   3. a   4. c   5. b

C Grammar
1. He should have gone to bed on time.
2. They shouldn't have used a credit card every day.
3. She shouldn't have turned off her alarm clock.
4. He should have asked someone to explain them.
5. We should have been more responsible.

D Reading
1. Music can help someone calm down or relax.
2. No. Many doctors think that a person's reaction to music is unique and complicated.
3. You should do an experiment with music to find out which kind of music helps you to relax.
4. A stressed-out person often has a fast pulse and tense muscles.
5. Some of the physical signs that a person is relaxed are a slower pulse and relaxed muscles.

E Writing
Answers will vary.
Sample answer:

I felt stressed out last summer when I spent too much on my credit card. I was anxious because I didn't have enough money to pay the bill. I stopped buying anything unnecessary, and I saved $40 each week. I worked for five more hours each week until I had enough money to pay the bill. I also decided to take a free yoga class at the community center. This class helped me to relax and to forget about all the stressful things in my life. I am going to take the yoga class again this summer!

Unit 5: Around town

A Listening
1. volunteer coordinator at the library
2. his English teacher
3. He taught his parents, aunts, and uncles how to use e-mail
4. Arabic and English
5. three hours every Saturday morning

B Grammar
1. as soon as   4. until
2. until   5. as soon as
3. As soon as

C Grammar
1. helped   4. have spoken
2. overslept   5. has babysat
3. visits

D Reading
1. Residents of a neighborhood, members of a community, and neighbors are responsible for creating community gardens.
2. People build community gardens in unused, empty parking lots.
3. Residents can save money by growing their own vegetables, fruits, herbs, and flowers. / Residents can grow food from their native countries. / Residents can get exercise and fresh air. / The gardens help keep the air clean. / There might be less crime in the neighborhood because neighbors know each other better.
4. Neighbors get to know each other. Neighbors work together in the gardens. / Community gardens are safe and clean parks.

5. Community gardens help keep the air clean and do good things for city neighborhoods.

E Writing
Answers will vary.
Sample answer:

Bill Gates is famous for starting the Microsoft Corporation in the 1970s. In recent years, he has also helped many people around the world with the Bill and Melinda Gates Foundation. This organization helps people who need health care in poor countries. It also donates money and materials to schools across the United States. The organization has the goal of giving people equal chances to get health care and education. Bill Gates has helped to improve many lives with his organization.

Midterm Test Units 1–5

A Listening
1. Sam is doing poorly in high school.
2. new social situations, more difficult schoolwork, extracurricular activities, and fitting in with others
3. missing school, getting bad grades, missing deadlines for homework assignments, and forgetting things
4. Mr. and Mrs. Brown grounded Sam a few times. / No, the solution didn't work.
5. Mrs. Patterson thinks that Sam is frustrated with his schoolwork. / She suggests a tutor.

B Grammar
1. until   4. that
2. have to   5. shouldn't
3. whether

C Grammar
1. easily   4. until
2. to earn   5. volunteered
3. ought to

D Reading
1. T   3. T   5. F   7. T   9. F
2. F   4. F   6. T   8. F   10. T

E Writing
Answers will vary.
Sample answer:

I had a conflict with my sister last year. While we were talking on the telephone, she told me about a problem she was having with her daughter. I gave her my opinion about the situation, and she got upset. She just wanted me to listen. She should have told me that! I was sad because my sister did not talk to me for the rest of the day. However, she called me back the next day and said she was sorry. We are now trying to communicate better with each other.

Unit 6: Time

A Listening
1. Linda hears people having conversations on their cell phones. She doesn't like listening to their private business.
2. Students in his class forget to turn off their cell phones.
3. Her family doesn't have a cell phone plan yet.
4. Everyone in the family gets a phone, and there is just one phone bill for the whole family.
5. They don't want their children to waste time on the cell phones.

B Grammar
1. She doesn't understand the instructions although she read the manual many times. / Although she read the manual many times, she doesn't understand the instructions.
2. Although there are free computer classes at the community center, my parents still don't know how to use e-mail. / My parents still don't know how to use e-mail although there are free computer classes at the community center.
3. I rarely use my microwave although microwaves help me to make dinner quickly. / Although microwaves help me to make dinner quickly, I rarely use my microwave.
4. Although he can take the subway to work, he prefers to walk for the exercise. / He prefers to walk for the exercise although he can take the subway to work.
5. Although she never used to write letters to her brother, she enjoys sending him e-mails now. / She enjoys sending her brother e-mails now although she never used to write letters to him.

C Grammar
1. Although
2. because
3. although
4. because
5. Although

D Reading
1. A   2. A   3. D   4. A   5. D

E Writing
Answers will vary.
Sample answer:

My computer is my favorite technological device. It has several advantages. When I want to look for jobs or find out information about something, it is easier to use my computer than to look through newspapers and books. Using a computer saves time because I don't have to go to the library for information. Another benefit of my computer is that it's very easy to communicate with my family. I can send my family an e-mail at any time of day, and it's free. But, of course, there are disadvantages. Information online is not always correct. I also get a lot of spam. So even though my computer makes things easier, it has drawbacks as well.

Unit 7: Shopping

A Listening
1. Her daughter's phone can't make or receive calls.
2. She can get the same kind of phone or an upgrade.
3. The upgrade is a newer phone with Internet access and a music player.
4. The upgrade costs more. She will have to pay $15 more every month.
5. She takes the same phone under the warranty, not the upgrade.

B Grammar
1. Our merchandise comes with a warranty that is good for two years.
2. Customers who / that are looking for discounts can order from our online store.
3. Cellular phones that have Internet access are popular.
4. The clerk is looking for the customer who / that had a question about a product.
5. Store managers solve problems that happen between clerks and customers.

C Grammar
1. He's a manager that I've worked with for years.
2. The car that you recommended to us is great!
3. The computer that we bought yesterday is defective.
4. The sweater that I gave her was too small.
5. We bought it from a retailer that we trusted.

D Reading
1. Bargain shoppers often go to neighborhood thrift stores for the lowest prices.
2. You can buy used items such as clothing, household items, books, jewelry, and furniture at a thrift store.
3. Prices are low at thrift stores because the merchandise is donated, and the salesclerks are volunteers.
4. Yes. Merchandise is sold "as is," so items may be defective. In most cases, if an item has small defects, shoppers usually don't mind.
5. Donors can be sure their donated items will be used, and the money from sales goes to people in need. / Thrift stores offer merchandise at low prices.

E Writing
Answers will vary.
Sample answer:

I like to shop at outlet malls. First, at outlet malls, there are many stores to choose from. There are discount clothing stores, shoe stores, drugstores, and music stores in one place. Furthermore, I like the convenience of outlet malls. I can park in the parking lot and spend a couple of hours getting my shopping done quickly. Finally, my husband and I like the discount prices! We were able to buy back-to-school clothing for our children for half the price of clothing at regular stores. There is also a big variety of clothing. Outlet malls are the best!

Unit 8: Work

A Listening
1. Dan's friend Tom helped him get the job.
2. Tom has to remind Dan about his responsibilities all the time.
3. Dan hasn't put his initials on the chart.
4. Dan says that he's been dealing with customers all morning.
5. Dan hasn't been doing his share of the work.

B Grammar

1. has just finished
2. has been working
3. have been reading
4. have just arrived
5. has just gone

C Grammar

1. amusing
2. shocked
3. exhausted
4. disappointing
5. irritated

D Reading

1. The hottest jobs are jobs that will have the largest growth and popularity in years to come.
2. Students and workers can use job reports to help them decide which careers will be the most promising or which programs to study.
3. Some service industry occupations are in health care, hospitality, and food services.
4. Some of the fastest growing health-care jobs are nurses, nursing aides, and home health aides.
5. Employers will look for hard and soft skills.

E Writing

Answers will vary.
Sample answer:

> [Student's Name]
> [Student's street address]
> [Student's city, state, zip]
> [Date]

Mary Freeman
Director of Human Services
592 Highland Avenue
Miami, FL 33136

Dear Ms. Freeman:

> *I read your advertisement online for the nursing aide position. I am very interested in this position and have enclosed my resume.*
> *I have just received nursing assistant's certification and have been volunteering at the hospital every Saturday. I also worked as a nursing assistant before I arrived in Florida two years ago. I am very interested in health care, and I am studying to be a nurse at the community college. I get along very well with my co-workers, and I am skilled in dealing with patients.*
> *I hope you will call me to schedule an interview. I look forward to hearing from you.*

> *Sincerely,*
> *[Student's name]*

Unit 9: Daily living

A Listening

1. George and Ed are talking about cars that are better for the environment.
2. George thinks Ed should buy a hybrid car.
3. A hybrid car runs with a combination of an electric motor and a gas engine.
4. Hybrid cars use gas and batteries for power.
5. Ed's old car causes air pollution by using a lot of gasoline.

B Grammar

1. If more people took public transportation, we would cut down on air pollution.
2. We would save energy if we turned down the air conditioning.
3. If we put enough air in the tires, we would save gas.
4. There would be less trash if everyone recycled.
5. If we closed off unused rooms, we would reduce air conditioning and heating use.

C Grammar

1. There has been a drought. As a result, there are fewer crops this season.
2. Since air pollution is trapping the sun's heat, the atmosphere is warming up.
3. Global warming changes weather. Consequently, hurricanes are stronger and more dangerous.
4. Due to new laws, we may be forced to change our routines.
5. Since I have learned more about the environment, I have become more responsible.

D Reading

1. Cities have dealt with rush hour traffic by creating HOV or carpool lanes.
2. An HOV lane is a High Occupancy Vehicle lane. Drivers must have two or more people in their cars in order to enter.
3. A carpool slug is a person who commutes to work in a car with strangers.
4. Slugs save on transportation fares and parking fees. / Drivers save on gasoline. / Both slugs and drivers save on travel time. / It's better for the environment if there are fewer cars on the road.
5. Carpool slugs and drivers have started to form a community. / Many of them have become friends.

E Writing

Answers will vary.
Sample answer:

> *Global warming is a serious environmental problem. One cause is air pollution. Burning gasoline and coal causes a lot of air pollution. People should drive less and use gas-efficient cars. Another cause of global warming is that people cut down trees to make paper and to build new homes. Trees produce oxygen and help clean the air. Since too many trees are cut down, there is a buildup of harmful gases in the atmosphere. Because of global warming, weather patterns change. Many places have less rainfall. Due to global warming, the sea level is rising. Towns near oceans are in danger of flooding. As a result of global warming, ocean water is also getting warmer. Typhoons and hurricanes are becoming more frequent. If we all took responsibility for saving the earth, we would help to reduce global warming.*

Unit 10: Leisure

A Listening

1. Marie is getting married in France. / Marie's fiancé is from France.
2. It is too far and too expensive.
3. neighbors and acquaintances / in the courtyard of the church
4. in a castle / a five-course meal
5. They wish Elena could go to the wedding.

B Grammar

1. comes, will have
2. knew, would feel
3. doesn't follow, will disappoint
4. were, would wear
5. were, wouldn't invite

C Grammar

1. wishes, could visit
2. hope, will be
3. wishes, would get
4. hope, can travel
5. wish, could go

D Reading

1. The Chinese New Year begins with the New Moon, the first day of the New Year. / It is celebrated for 15 days.

2. Flowers symbolize wealth and good luck.
3. They are remembered and honored during the celebrations.
4. A chicken is served with all its parts to represent completeness.
5. At the end of New Year's celebrations in China, people celebrate at the Lantern Festival. There are parades, dancers, fireworks, and firecrackers.

E Writing
Answers will vary.
Sample answer:

On January 1, I was invited to a traditional Greek celebration in New York. Everyone was there to celebrate the New Year. When we arrived, the family wished us "many more years" – a traditional greeting on the first day of the year. For dinner we had roast lamb, rice, green beans with tomatoes, and roasted potatoes. After dinner, some men played the bouzoukia (a musical instrument), and the guests sang songs. For dessert, we had the Vasilopita, a special cake. The cake is baked with a coin in it. The host slices a piece of cake for each member of the family and any guest. If you're the person who receives the coin in your slice, you will have good luck for the entire year. I didn't get the coin in my slice, but we all hoped for a year of good luck!

Final Test Units 6–10

A Listening
1. No	4. Yes	7. Yes	10. Yes
2. No	5. No	8. No	
3. No	6. Yes	9. Yes	

B Grammar
1. has been
2. were
3. wishes
4. would
5. amused

C Grammar
1. Because of
2. just
3. because
4. that
5. Although

D Reading
1. T	3. T	5. F	7. T	9. F
2. F	4. T	6. T	8. T	10. T

E Writing
Answers will vary.
Sample answer:

Last summer, there was a knock on my apartment door. It was about 10:00 p.m., so I was not sure if I should open the door. I opened the door a little and saw Mrs. Kim, my neighbor from across the hall. She was upset. Her husband, who is 90 years old, was hurt. He fell in the bathroom, and Mrs. Kim needed help. First, I called 911. Then, I went to the Kims' apartment. Although Mr. Kim wanted me to help him get up, I just sat with him and tried to make him calm down. I explained that I called 911 and that professional medical staff were coming. Finally, professional medical staff arrived and helped Mr. Kim get up. They checked him and said that he was fine and just needed some rest. I hope I'll be that strong when I'm 90 years old!

Teacher's Toolkit Audio CD/CD-ROM

Overview

The *Teacher's Toolkit Audio CD/CD-ROM* is an additional resource for teachers using the *Ventures 4* Student's Book. The *Teacher's Toolkit Audio CD/CD-ROM* provides reproducible, supplementary materials for use during in-class assessment, whole-class activities, and group work. It provides over 180 pages of additional material.

What's included in the *Teacher's Toolkit Audio CD/CD-ROM*:

- **Unit tests**, a **midterm test**, and a **final test** with corresponding **answer keys**, **audio scripts**, **audio program**, and instructions for administering and scoring the tests. When browsing the tests, a pop-up window can be opened that shows that test's audio script and answer key. The tests can be reproduced from the *Teacher's Toolkit Audio CD/CD-ROM* or from the printed test pages in the Teacher's Edition. Use a compact disc player or your computer's audio software to access the test audio program on the CD-ROM.

- The **self-assessments** from the *Ventures 4* Student's Book. Each unit self-assessment can be duplicated from the CD-ROM, completed by students, and saved as a portfolio assessment tool.

- **Collaborative Activity Worksheets**. For each lesson in the *Ventures 4* Student's Book, there is a reproducible activity worksheet to encourage collaborative pair and group work in class. On each worksheet screen, there is a pop-up window that can be opened to show the instructions for using the worksheet in class.

- **Extended Reading Worksheets**. For each unit in *Ventures 4* Student's Book, there is a reproducible reading worksheet. These worksheets encourage students to become independent learners by offering those students who have the time and interest an opportunity to read for pleasure at home. The readings are slightly longer, and slightly more difficult high-interest material related to the topics and themes of the Student's Book. The exercises that accompany each reading support the understanding of the text, reinforce skills introduced in the Student's Book, expand vocabulary-building strategies, and encourage critical thinking. The worksheets can also be used in class to practice and extend the reading skills and strategies in the Student's Book. On each worksheet screen, there is a pop-up window that can be opened by clicking the "View" button to show the worksheet answer key. The answer key can be printed from the pop-up window or from its own screen and distributed to students for self-correction or peer correction.

- A **vocabulary list**. All key vocabulary in *Ventures 4* Student's Book is listed alphabetically, with first occurrence page numbers included for easy reference.

- A **certificate of completion**. To recognize students for satisfactory completion of *Ventures 4,* a printable certificate is included.

Games

Overview

Games provide practice and reinforcement of skills, but in a fun and engaging manner. Students love to play games. Games raise motivation and enjoyment for learning. They can be used as a warm-up, practice, or review activity. The games described below can be adjusted and adapted to the skill level of the class.

1. Conversation Toss

Skills: speaking, listening
Objectives: to practice pronunciation, vocabulary, and grammar
Preparation: Prepare a dialog. Bring a soft ball to class

- Write a dialog on the board – for example, a pronunciation dialog from a review unit.
- Read the dialog and ask Ss to repeat, paying special attention to the key pronunciation point.
- Erase a key pronunciation word or two from each sentence so that Ss must fill in the missing word.
- Toss a ball to one S to start the dialog again, filling in the missing word or words. The S begins the dialog and then tosses the ball to a classmate. The classmate reads the next line of the dialog and then tosses the ball to a third S to continue.
- Continue until all lines of the dialog have been read.

2. Which Part Is It?

Skills: listening, writing
Objective: to increase vocabulary by identifying parts of speech and using words in sentences
Preparation: Prepare a list of vocabulary previously learned

- Write these parts of speech on the board:
    Noun   Verb   Adjective   Adverb
- Divide the class into teams of six Ss and assign a number from 1–6 to each team member.
- Call all number *1*s to the board and give each one a piece of chalk. Read the first word on the vocabulary list.
- The first S to write the word, label it with the correct part of speech (for example, *wise – adjective*), and use it correctly in a written sentence wins a point for his or her team.
- Call all number *2*s to the board and repeat with another word.
- Continue until all Ss have had a chance to come to the board and a winning team is identified.

3. Take One Away

Skills: listening, speaking, writing
Objective: to practice vocabulary and grammar
Preparation: Prepare a list of complex sentences Ss can understand from lessons taught

- Divide the class into teams of six Ss. Write a complex sentence that Ss will understand on the board. For example, *Because the earth is getting warmer, sea levels are rising.*
- Working in teams, Ss take turns changing one word or connector. For example:
    S1: *Because the earth is getting warmer, sea levels are rising.*
    S2: *Since the earth is getting warmer, sea levels are rising.*
    S3: *The earth is getting warmer. Consequently, sea levels are rising.*
- Team members must judge whether the sentence is correct. If it is not correct, they must offer a better suggestion.
- Teams continue making sentences until everyone has had a couple of turns or until Ss can make no more changes.
- Ask the member in each team who has made the last change to say his or her sentence to see the difference in the sentences the teams have made.

Adaptation: Assign a note-taker to record the changes. The note-takers from each team read all their team's changes to the class at the end of the game.

4. Variation on *Take One Away*

Skills: listening, speaking
Objective: to practice vocabulary and grammar
Preparation: Prepare a list of complex sentences Ss can understand from lessons taught

- Divide the class into two teams.
- Play as in *Take One Away*, but with two teams competing. Each team takes a turn changing a word or connector in the complex sentence. Each correct change earns one point.
- Teams continue taking turns making changes to the same sentence until one team makes a mistake or cannot change any more words.
- The team with the most points wins.

5. Pass the Paper, Please

Skills: speaking, writing
Objective: to review vocabulary from a unit
Preparation: none

- Ss form groups of four or five. Each group has a blank sheet of paper.
- Announce the topic, usually the unit topic just completed.

- The first S says a sentence related to the topic, writes the sentence on the paper, and passes the paper to the next S.
- That S says a new sentence related to the topic, writes the sentence on the paper, and passes the paper to the third S, who continues the process.
- Ss can ask for help from their teammates when they cannot think of a new sentence to add to the topic.
- The paper continues to pass around the table until no one can think of another related sentence.
- The team with the most creative sentences wins.

6. Bingo

Skills: listening, writing
Objective: to review vocabulary
Preparation: Bingo grids (3 x 3, 3 x 4, 4 x 4 . . .)

- Select enough words to fill a Bingo grid. Read and spell each new word and use it in a sentence.
- Ss write each word randomly on their bingo grids.
- When the grids are filled, play Bingo.
- The S who shouts "Bingo" first calls the next game.

Adaptation: Call the words by providing a definition or an example, or giving a synonym or an antonym.

7. Act It Out

Skill: speaking
Objective: to review vocabulary
Preparation: sets of vocabulary cards (one per team)

- Ss form teams of three or four. Give each team one set of vocabulary cards.
- One S chooses a card but does not tell the team members the word.
- This S acts out the word on the card.
- The other team members try to guess the word, using the clues.
- Ss take turns acting out words until all words have been used.
- The team that guesses the most words wins.

8. Make Bingo Predictions

Skills: reading or listening, writing, speaking
Objective: to develop the prereading or prelistening strategy of predicting
Preparation: Bingo grids (3 x 3, 3 x 4, 4 x 4 . . .)

- Provide Ss with the title or topic of a selection to be read or heard from an audio recording.
- In each square of the Bingo grid, Ss enter a word related to that topic that they think will appear in the reading or audio.
- Ss listen to the audio or read the text. When they hear or see a word that is on their Bingo grid, they circle it.

- Ss discuss in small groups how their word choices, both correct or incorrect, relate to the topic.

9. Going, Going, Gone

Skills: speaking, listening, reading, writing
Objective: to practice learning dialogs
Preparation: none

- Write a dialog on the board.
- Go over the dialog with the entire class, then have Ss practice the dialog in pairs.
- Erase one word from each line of the dialog each time pairs practice, until all words are gone.
- Have volunteers recite the dialog without support from words on the board.
- Then have Ss add words back on the board until all words are again in place.

10. Raise It!

Skills: listening or reading
Objective: to refine listening skills
Preparation: an audio clip or a reading text; an index card with a sentence from the clip on it (one sentence for each S)

- Select an audio clip or a reading segment.
- Provide each S with an index card containing a sentence that occurs in the clip or reading segment.
- Play or read the segment.
- Ss listen, paying particular attention for their sentence. They raise, then lower their index card when they hear the sentence.

Adaptation: Ss can listen for things other than sentences, such as clauses with *until* or *as soon as*, the passive voice, or verbs in the present perfect or present perfect continuous.

Alternatively, Ss can stand up or sit down when they hear their sentence, rather than raise their cards.

11. Treasure Hunt

Skills: reading, writing
Objective: to develop the reading skill of scanning
Preparation: Enlarge a reading selection from the Student's Book and cut it into paragraphs. Number each one. Create a handout with questions / items to be found in the reading.

- Post the pieces of the reading around the room.
- Ss, individually or in pairs, go around the room and locate specific information to enter into their handout. For example: *Write the compound nouns.*
- Ss check their answers by reading or reviewing the completed text in their books and sharing their answers as a class.

Multilevel classroom management

All classrooms are multilevel in some sense. No two students will ever be exactly the same. Learners vary in demographic factors such as culture and ethnicity, personal factors such as a willingness to take risks and differing learning styles, and experiential factors such as background knowledge and previous education. With all these differences, it will always be a challenge to provide useful learning activities for all members of the class. Yet there are some techniques that make working with a multilevel class more manageable.

1. Group work is one of the best ways of working with a multilevel class. Some tasks, such as watching a video, going on a field trip, or describing a picture, can be performed as a whole group. What will change in a multilevel class is the level of expectation of responses following the shared experience. Other tasks can be performed as a whole group, but the tasks are adapted for the students' levels. This could include interviews with varying difficulty of questions or a project such as a class newspaper, where students of differing levels contribute through activities appropriate to their abilities.

   Smaller, homogeneous groups allow students of the same level the opportunity to work together on activities such as a problem-solving task or a group writing activity. Smaller, heterogeneous groups are good for board games or jigsaw activities where the difficulty of the material can be controlled.

2. Varying the materials or activities is another help in addressing the issue of multiple levels in the classroom. *Add Ventures,* the multilevel component of *Ventures,* provides activities for learners at differing levels. These materials can be used in the classroom with heterogeneous or homogeneous groups because the answers are the same for all three levels of worksheets.

3. Self-access centers are another kind of classroom management technique. These centers would be located in corners of the classroom and would provide opportunities for learners to work at varying levels. By providing a variety of materials, which can be color-coded for levels of difficulty, students have the opportunity to make choices as to the level they feel comfortable working on. Students can self-correct with answer keys. In this way, students are working towards more learner autonomy, which is a valuable assistant in a multilevel classroom, and a good start towards promoting lifelong learning skills.

4. Computer-assisted learning, using computers located within the classroom, can provide self-directed learning through software programs geared to a student's individual ability. Most programs provide immediate feedback to students to correct errors and build in a level of difficulty as a student progresses. Like-ability groups of students can rotate their time on the computer, working in pairs, or students can work individually at their own level.

A multilevel classroom, while challenging to the teacher, should offer each learner appropriate levels of instruction according to the learner's abilities, interests, needs, and experiences, and it should be designed to maximize each learner's educational gains. Good management techniques call for the teacher to provide a mixture of whole class, small group, and individual activities, create a learner-centered class by establishing self-access materials, use computers, and incorporate variety in the difficulty of the tasks and materials given to each student.

Authors' acknowledgments

The authors would like to acknowledge and thank focus group participants and reviewers for their insightful comments, as well as CUP editorial, marketing, and production staffs, whose thorough research and attention to detail have resulted in a quality product.

The publishers would also like to extend their particular thanks to the following reviewers and consultants for their valuable insights and suggestions:

Francesca Armendaris, North Orange County Community College District, Anaheim, California; **Alex A. Baez**, The Texas Professional Development Group, Austin, Texas; **Kit Bell**, LAUSD Division of Adult and Career Education, Los Angeles, California; **Rose Anne Cleary**, Catholic Migration Office, Diocese of Brooklyn, Brooklyn, New York; **Inga Cristi**, Pima Community College Adult Education, Tucson, Arizona; **Kay De Gennaro**, West Valley Occupational Center, Woodland Hills, California; **Patricia DeHesus**, Illinois Community College Board, Springfield, Illinois; **Magali Apareaida Morais Duignan**, Augusta State University, Augusta, Georgia; **Gayle Fagan**, Harris County Department of Education, Houston, Texas; **Lisa A. Fears**, Inglewood Community Adult School, Inglewood, California; **Jas Gill**, English Language Institute at the University of British Columbia, Vancouver, British Columbia, Canada; **Elisabeth Goodwin**, Pima Community College Adult Education, Tucson, Arizona; **Carolyn Grimaldi**, Center for Immigrant Education and Training, LaGuardia Community College, Long Island City, New York; **Masha Gromyko**, Pima Community College Adult Education, Tucson, Arizona; **Jennifer M. Herrin**, Albuquerque TVI Community College, Albuquerque, New Mexico; **Giang T. Hoang**, Evans Community Adult School, Los Angeles, California; **Karen Hribar**, LAUSD West Valley Occupational Center, Los Angeles, California; **Patricia Ishill**, Union County College, Union County, New Jersey; **Dr. Stephen G. Karel**, McKinley Community School for Adults, Honolulu, Hawaii; **Aaron Kelly**, North Orange County Community College District, Anaheim, California; **Dan Kiernan**, Metro Skills Center, LAUSD, Los Angeles, California; **Kirsten Kilcup**, Green River Community College, Auburn, Washington; **Tom Knutson**, New York Association for New Americans, Inc., New York, New York; **Liz Koenig-Golombek**, LAUSD, Los Angeles, California; **Anita Lemonis**, West Valley Occupational Center, Los Angeles, California; **Lia Lerner**, Burbank Adult School, Burbank, California; **Susan Lundquist**, Pima Community College Adult Education, Tucson, Arizona; **Dr. Amal Mahmoud**, Highline Community College, Des Moines, Washington; **Fatiha Makloufi**, Hostos Community College, Bronx, New York; **Judith Martin-Hall**, Indian River Community College, Fort Pierce, Florida; **Gwen Mayer**, Van Nuys Community Adult School, Los Angeles, California; **Lois Miller**, Pima Community College, Tucson, Arizona; **Vicki Moore**, El Monte-Rosemead Adult School, El Monte, California; **Jeanne Petrus-Rivera**, Cuyahoga Community College, Cleveland, Ohio; **Pearl W. Pigott**, Houston Community College, Houston, Texas; **Catherine Porter**, Adult Learning Resource Center, Des Plaines, Illinois; **Planaria Price**, Evans Community Adult School, Los Angeles, California; **James P. Regan**, NYC Board of Education, New York, New York; **Catherine M. Rifkin**, Florida Community College at Jacksonville, Jacksonville, Florida; **Amy Schneider**, Pacoima Skills Center, Los Angeles, California; **Bonnie Sherman**, Green River Community College, Auburn, Washington; **Julie Singer**, Garfield Community Adult School, Los Angeles, California; **Yilin Sun**, Seattle Central Community College, Seattle, Washington; **André Sutton**, Belmont Community Adult School, Los Angeles, California; **Deborah Thompson**, El Camino Real Community Adult School, Los Angeles, California; **Evelyn Trottier**, Basic Studies Division, Seattle Central Community College, Seattle, Washington; **Debra Un**, New York University, American Language Institute, New York, New York; **Jodie Morgan Vargas**, Orange County Public Schools, Orlando, Florida; **Christopher Wahl**, Hudson County Community College, Jersey City, New Jersey; **Ethel S. Watson**, Evans Community Adult School, Los Angeles, California; **Barbara Williams**; **Mimi Yang**, Belmont Community Adult School, Los Angeles, California; **Adèle Youmans**, Pima Community College Adult Education, Tucson, Arizona.

Ventures Student's Book 4

Illustration credits

Ken Batelman: 73, 112
Adrian D'Alimonte: 12, 16
Nina Edwards: 9, 37, 46, 89, 133
Chuck Gonzales: 49, 66, 74, 75, 100, 116

Brad Hamann: 38, 64, 87
Ben Kirchner: 6, 18, 32, 44, 58, 60, 70, 84, 96, 98, 110, 122
Monika Roe: 24, 52, 61, 101, 113

Photography credits

1 (*clockwise from top left*) ©1Apix/Alamy; ©Inmagine; ©Jamie Squire/Getty Images; ©Kolvenbach/Alamy; ©Inmagine; ©Inmagine

17 (*clockwise from top left*) ©Hulton Archive/Getty Images; ©Kristian Dowling/Getty Images; ©James Knowler/Getty Images; ©AP Wide World Photo; ©Jennifer Graylock/AP Wide World Photo; ©Hulton Archive/Getty Images

26 ©Jupiter Images

29 (*clockwise from top left*) ©Eric Risberg/AP Wide World Photo; ©Dave Hogan/Getty Images; ©Interfoto/Pressebildagentur/Alamy; ©Charley Gallay/Getty Images; ©Dima Gavrysh/AP Wide World Photo; ©Frank Micelotta/Getty Images

36 ©Jupiter Images

40 (*both*) ©Shutterstock

47 (*left to right*) ©Alamy; ©Inmagine; ©Inmagine

50 ©Inmagine

62 ©Tina Manley/Alamy

69 (*clockwise from top left*) ©Inmagine; ©Inmagine; ©Reuters; ©Inmagine

78 ©Shutterstock

81 (*all*) ©Shutterstock

86 ©Inmagine

88 (*top to bottom*) ©Ryan Nelson/Alamy; ©Shutterstock

90 ©Inmagine

92 ©Shutterstock

102 ©Jupiter Images

107 (*clockwise from top left*) ©Jupiter Images; ©Inmagine; ©Michael Malyszko/Getty Images; ©Frank Pedrick/Jupiter Images

115 (*top*) ©Ron Yue/Alamy; (*bottom, left to right*) ©Daniel Avila/AP Wide World Photo; ©Inmagine; ©Hans Strand/Jupiter Images

118 ©Jupiter Images

124 ©Inmagine

126 ©Inmagine

128 ©Inmagine

130 (*left to right*) ©Newscom; ©Atta Kenare/Getty Images; ©Behrouz Mehri/Getty Images

132 ©Inmagine

Ventures Teacher's Edition 4

Collaborative Activities

Illustration credits

John Batten: 9, 10, 52, 53
Chuck Gonzales: 7, 8, 18, 19, 61, 62
Monika Roe: 15, 16, 43, 44, 80, 81
William Waitzman: 26, 27, 76, 77

Extended Reading Worksheets

Illustration credits

William Waitzman: 2.1, 3.1, 5.1, 6.1, 10.1

Ventures 4 Teacher's Toolkit Audio CD / CD-ROM

Minimum System Requirements

Windows 2000, XP, Vista
- Intel Pentium processor – minimum 400 MHz
- 128 MB RAM minimum
- Sound card. Speakers or headphones.

Macintosh
- PowerPC processor – minimum 300 MHz
- MacOS OSX
- 64 MB free RAM minimum
- Sound card. Speakers or headphones.

Browsers & Plug-ins
- Flash Player 8 or higher
- Mac: Microsoft Internet Explorer 5.2 or a comparable browser
- Windows: Microsoft Internet Explorer 6.0 or a comparable browser

Audio

To play the Audio CD portion of the *Teacher's Toolkit* on a computer, follow these instructions:

Insert the disc into the CD-ROM drive. Open a media player such as Windows Media Player or iTunes. Click "Play."

You can also play the Audio CD portion of the *Teacher's Toolkit* in a conventional Audio CD player.

Track Listing

1: Introduction
2: Unit 1 Test
3: Unit 2 Test
4: Unit 3 Test
5: Unit 4 Test
6: Unit 5 Test
7: Midterm Test
8: Unit 6 Test
9: Unit 7 Test
10: Unit 8 Test
11: Unit 9 Test
12: Unit 10 Test
13: Final Test

For information about the contents of the *Teacher's Toolkit*, please turn to page T-214.